Blue Flag

story and art by
KAITO

8

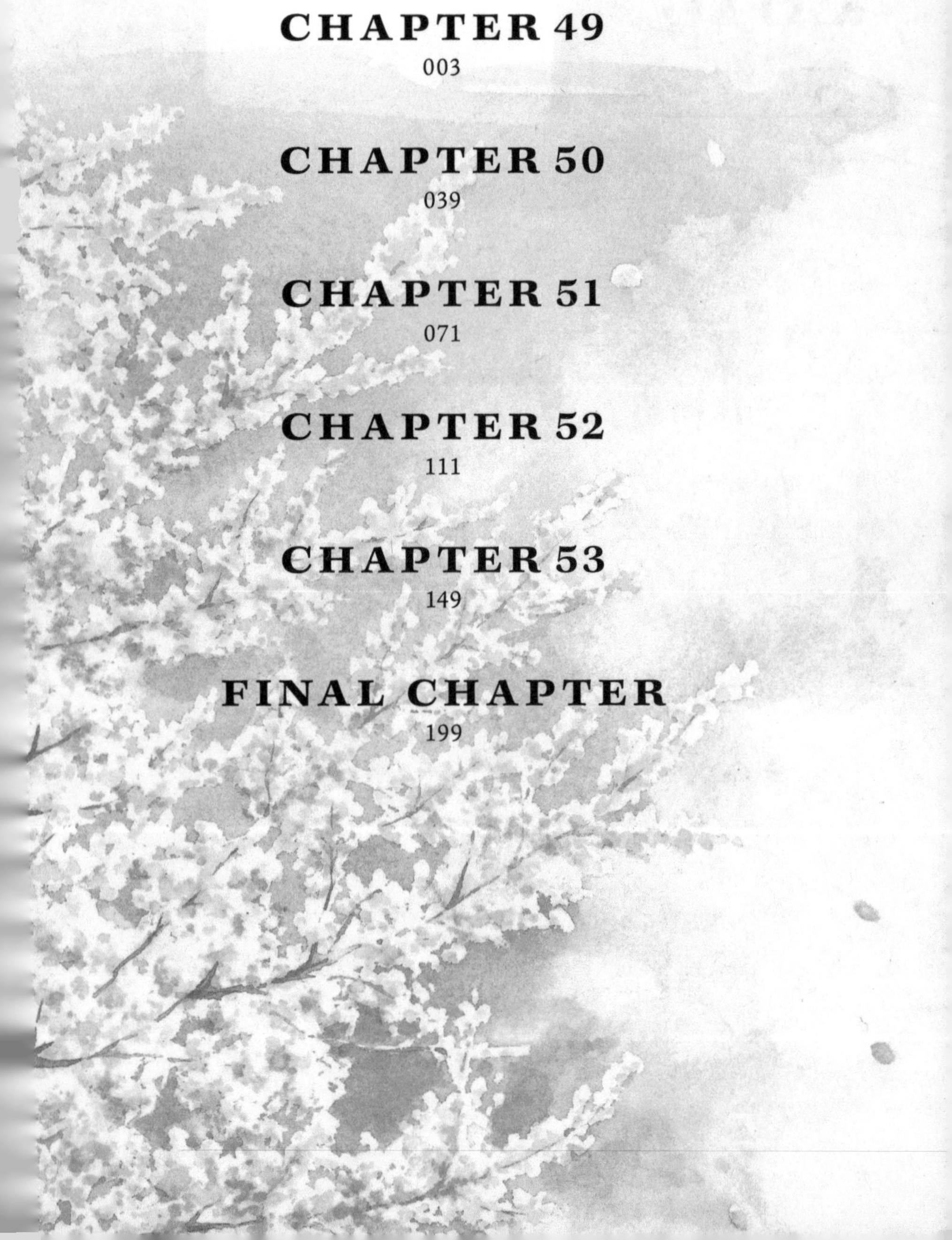

CHAPTER 49

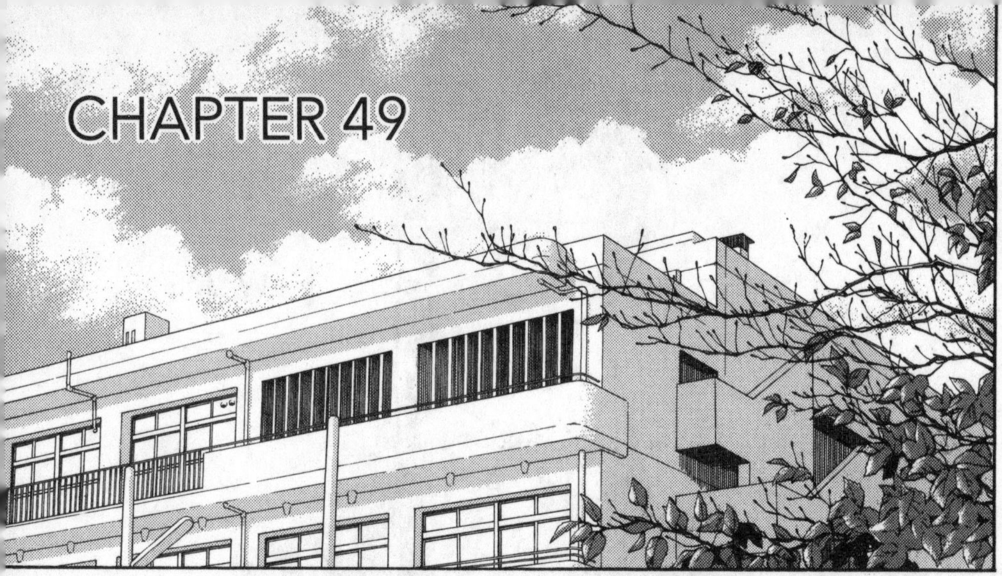

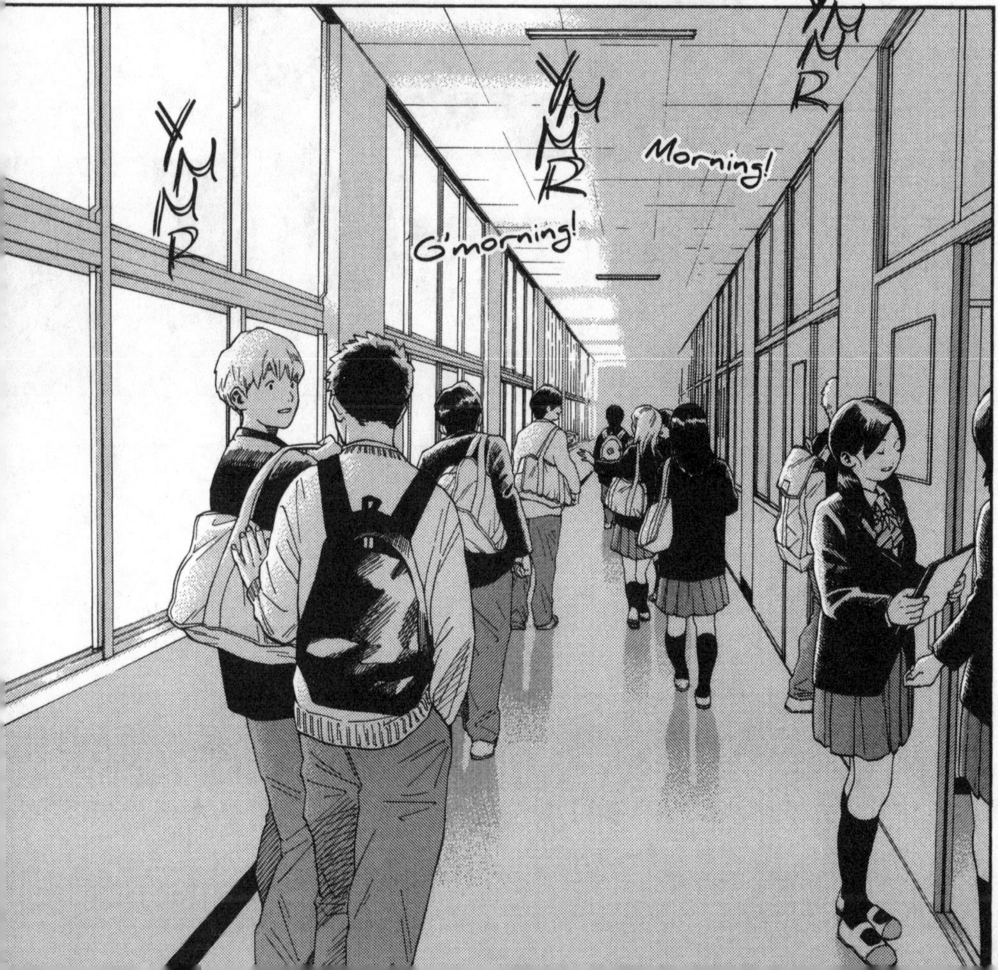
YMMR
Morning!
YMMR
G'morning!
YMMR

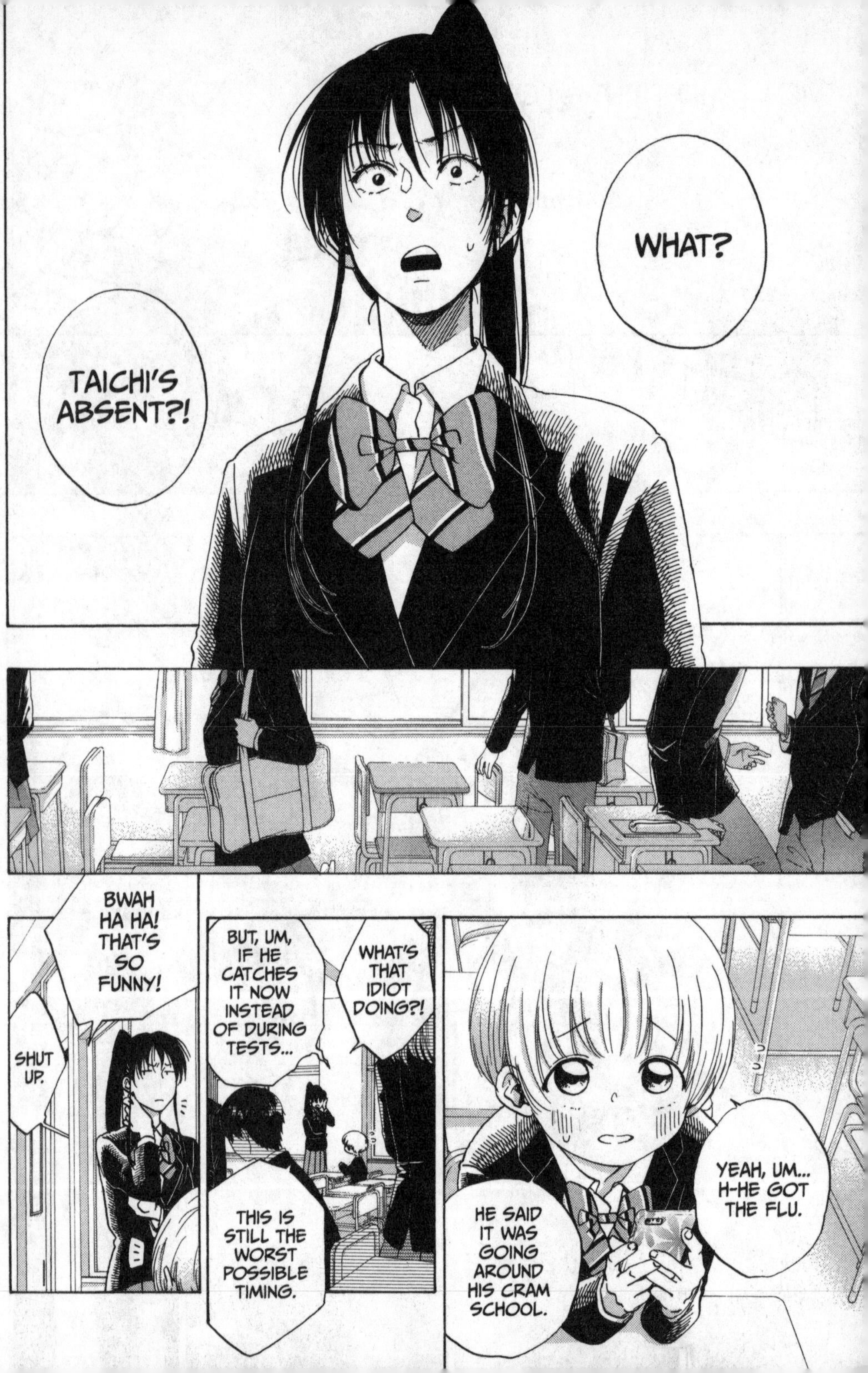
WHAT?
TAICHI'S ABSENT?!
YEAH, UM... H-HE GOT THE FLU.
HE SAID IT WAS GOING AROUND HIS CRAM SCHOOL.
WHAT'S THAT IDIOT DOING?!
BUT, UM, IF HE CATCHES IT NOW INSTEAD OF DURING TESTS...
THIS IS STILL THE WORST POSSIBLE TIMING.
BWAH HA HA! THAT'S SO FUNNY!
SHUT UP.

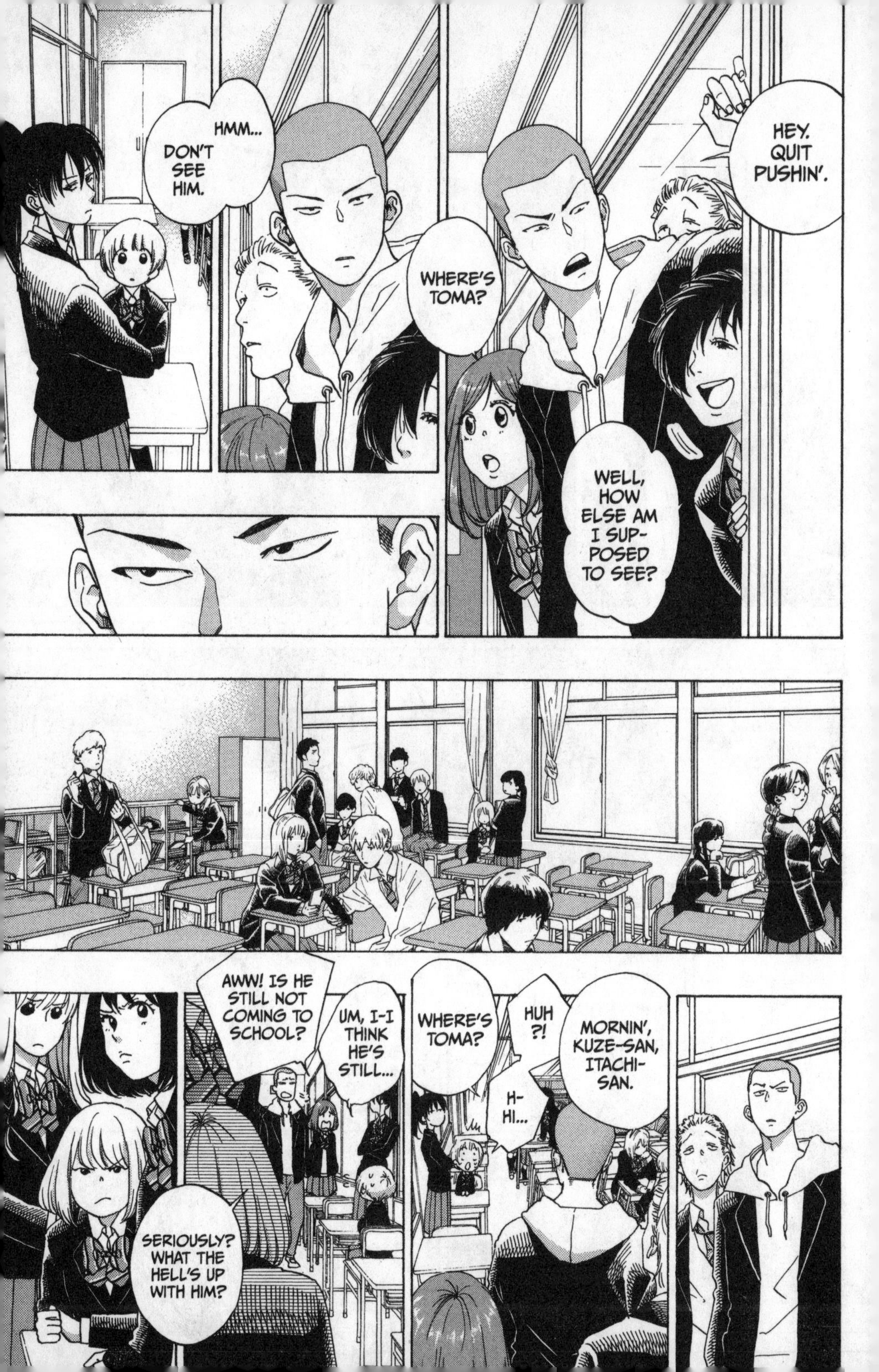
HEY. QUIT PUSHIN'.
WELL, HOW ELSE AM I SUP-POSED TO SEE?
WHERE'S TOMA?
HMM... DON'T SEE HIM.
MORNIN', KUZE-SAN, ITACHI-SAN.
HUH?!
H-HI...
WHERE'S TOMA?
UM, I-I THINK HE'S STILL...
AWW! IS HE STILL NOT COMING TO SCHOOL?
SERIOUSLY? WHAT THE HELL'S UP WITH HIM?

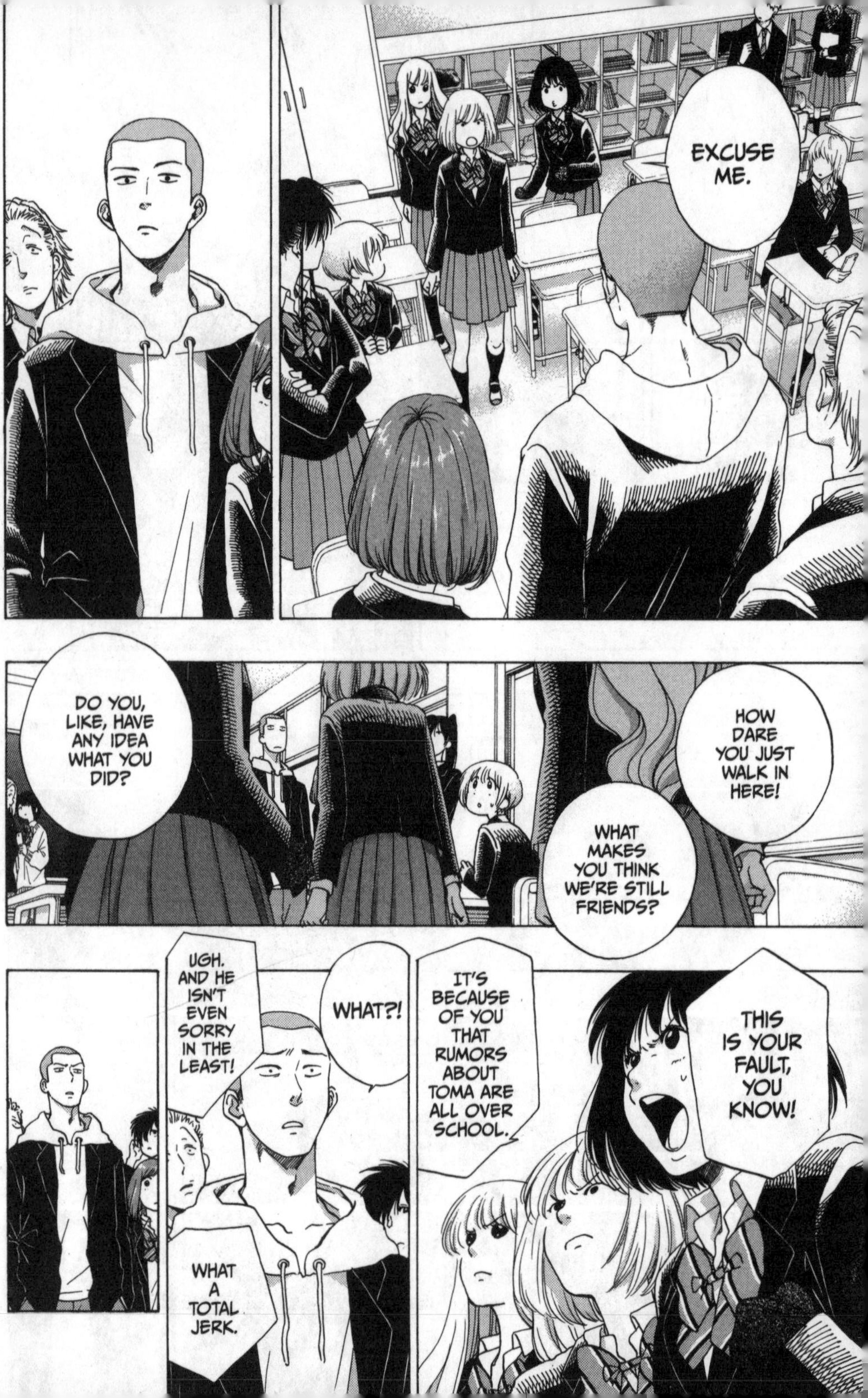
EXCUSE ME.
HOW DARE YOU JUST WALK IN HERE!
WHAT MAKES YOU THINK WE'RE STILL FRIENDS?
DO YOU, LIKE, HAVE ANY IDEA WHAT YOU DID?
THIS IS YOUR FAULT, YOU KNOW!
IT'S BECAUSE OF YOU THAT RUMORS ABOUT TOMA ARE ALL OVER SCHOOL.
WHAT?!
UGH. AND HE ISN'T EVEN SORRY IN THE LEAST!
WHAT A TOTAL JERK.

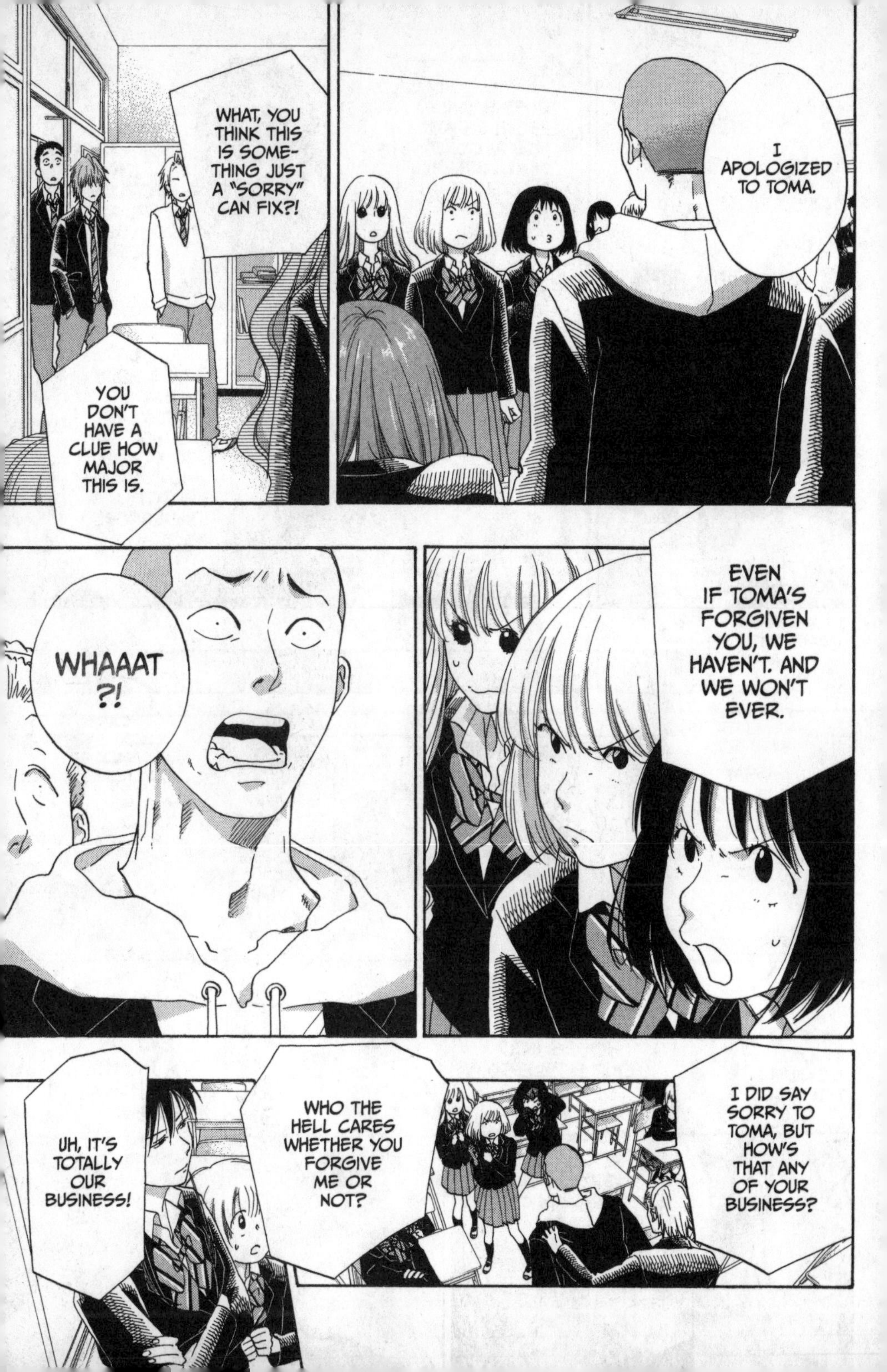
I APOLOGIZED TO TOMA.
WHAT, YOU THINK THIS IS SOME-THING JUST A "SORRY" CAN FIX?!
YOU DON'T HAVE A CLUE HOW MAJOR THIS IS.
EVEN IF TOMA'S FORGIVEN YOU, WE HAVEN'T. AND WE WON'T EVER.
WHAAAT?!
I DID SAY SORRY TO TOMA, BUT HOW'S THAT ANY OF YOUR BUSINESS?
WHO THE HELL CARES WHETHER YOU FORGIVE ME OR NOT?
UH, IT'S TOTALLY OUR BUSINESS!

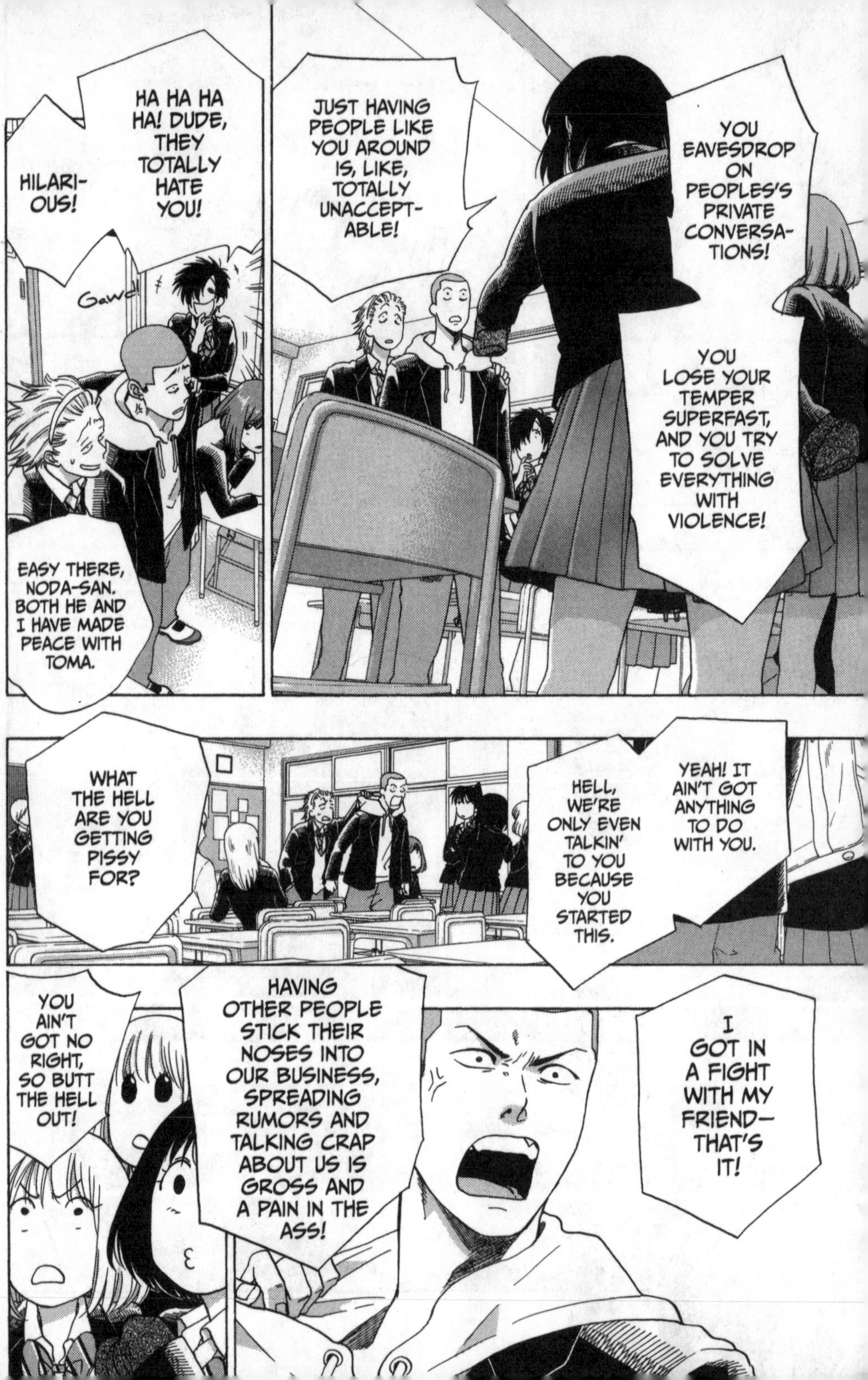
YOU EAVESDROP ON PEOPLES'S PRIVATE CONVERSATIONS!
YOU LOSE YOUR TEMPER SUPERFAST, AND YOU TRY TO SOLVE EVERYTHING WITH VIOLENCE!
JUST HAVING PEOPLE LIKE YOU AROUND IS, LIKE, TOTALLY UNACCEPTABLE!
HA HA HA HA! DUDE, THEY TOTALLY HATE YOU!
HILARIOUS!
Gawd!
EASY THERE, NODA-SAN. BOTH HE AND I HAVE MADE PEACE WITH TOMA.
YEAH! IT AIN'T GOT ANYTHING TO DO WITH YOU.
HELL, WE'RE ONLY EVEN TALKIN' TO YOU BECAUSE YOU STARTED THIS.
WHAT THE HELL ARE YOU GETTING PISSY FOR?
I GOT IN A FIGHT WITH MY FRIEND—THAT'S IT!
HAVING OTHER PEOPLE STICK THEIR NOSES INTO OUR BUSINESS, SPREADING RUMORS AND TALKING CRAP ABOUT US IS GROSS AND A PAIN IN THE ASS!
YOU AIN'T GOT NO RIGHT, SO BUTT THE HELL OUT!

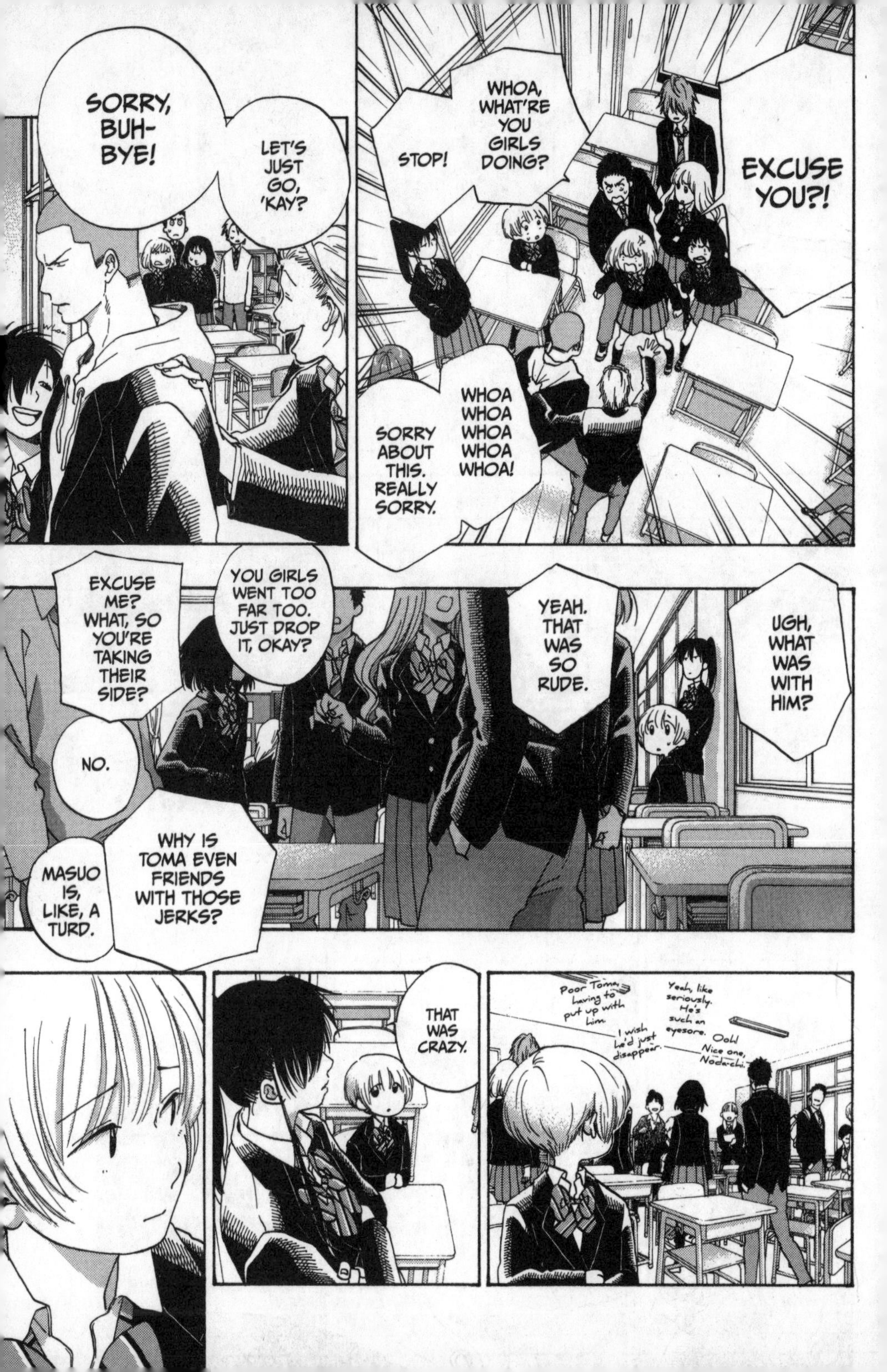
EXCUSE YOU?!
WHOA, WHAT'RE YOU GIRLS DOING?
STOP!
WHOA WHOA WHOA WHOA WHOA!
SORRY ABOUT THIS. REALLY SORRY.
LET'S JUST GO, 'KAY?
SORRY, BUH-BYE!
UGH, WHAT WAS WITH HIM?
YEAH. THAT WAS SO RUDE.
YOU GIRLS WENT TOO FAR TOO. JUST DROP IT, OKAY?
EXCUSE ME? WHAT, SO YOU'RE TAKING THEIR SIDE?
NO.
WHY IS TOMA EVEN FRIENDS WITH THOSE JERKS?
MASUO IS, LIKE, A TURD.
Yeah, like seriously. He's such an eyesore.
Poor Toma, having to put up with him.
Ooh! Nice one, Noda-chi.
I wish he'd just disappear.
THAT WAS CRAZY.

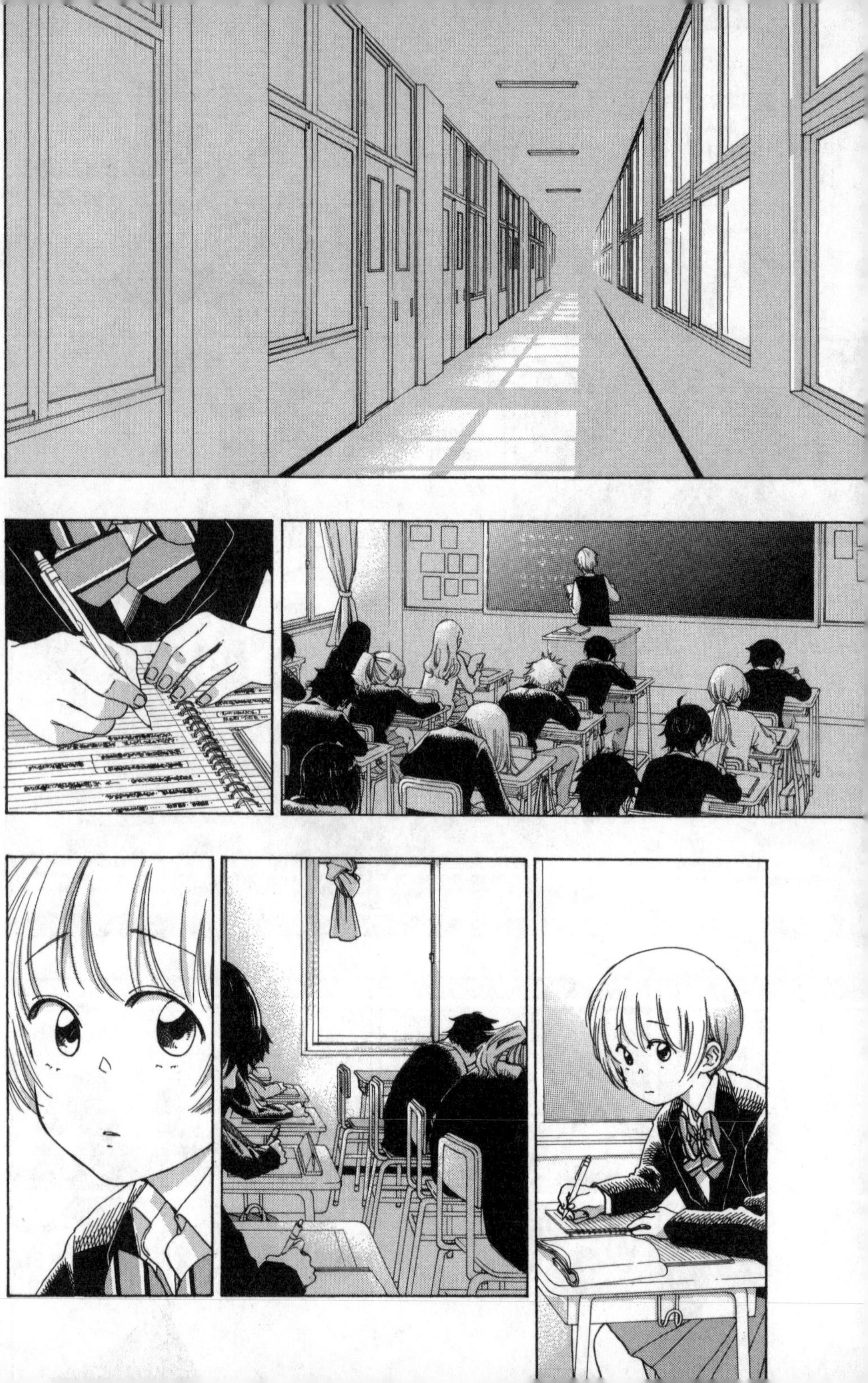

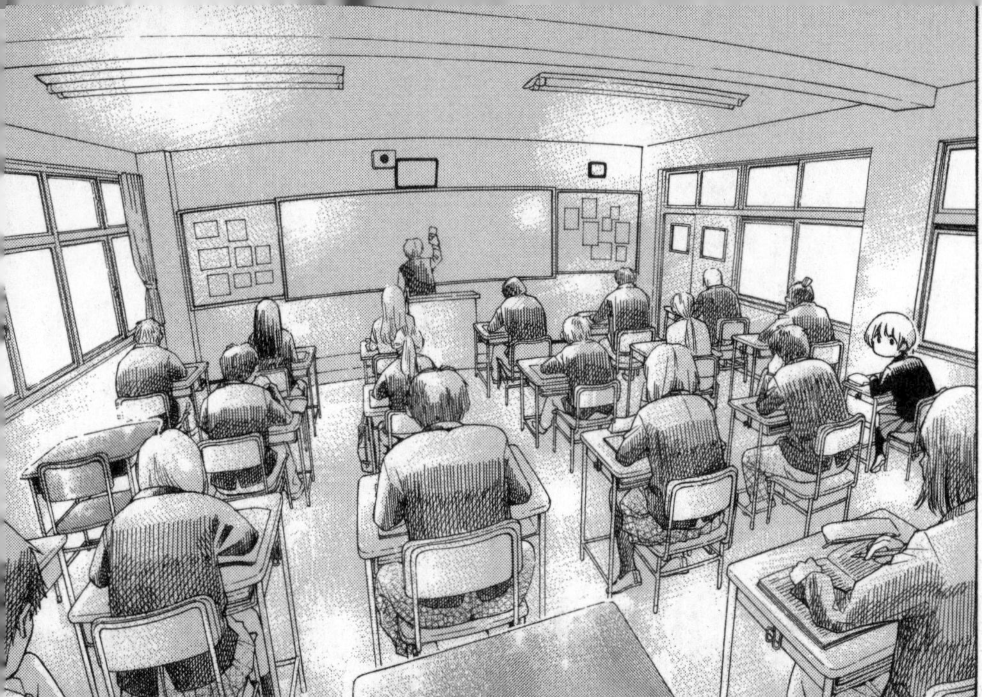
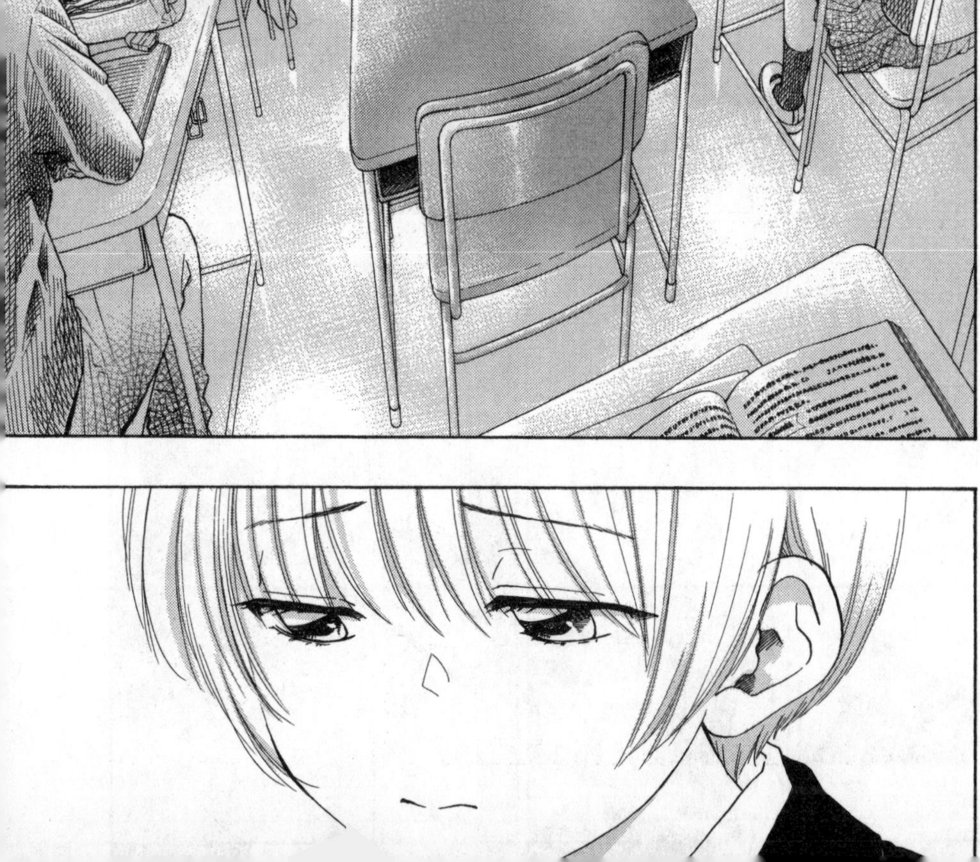

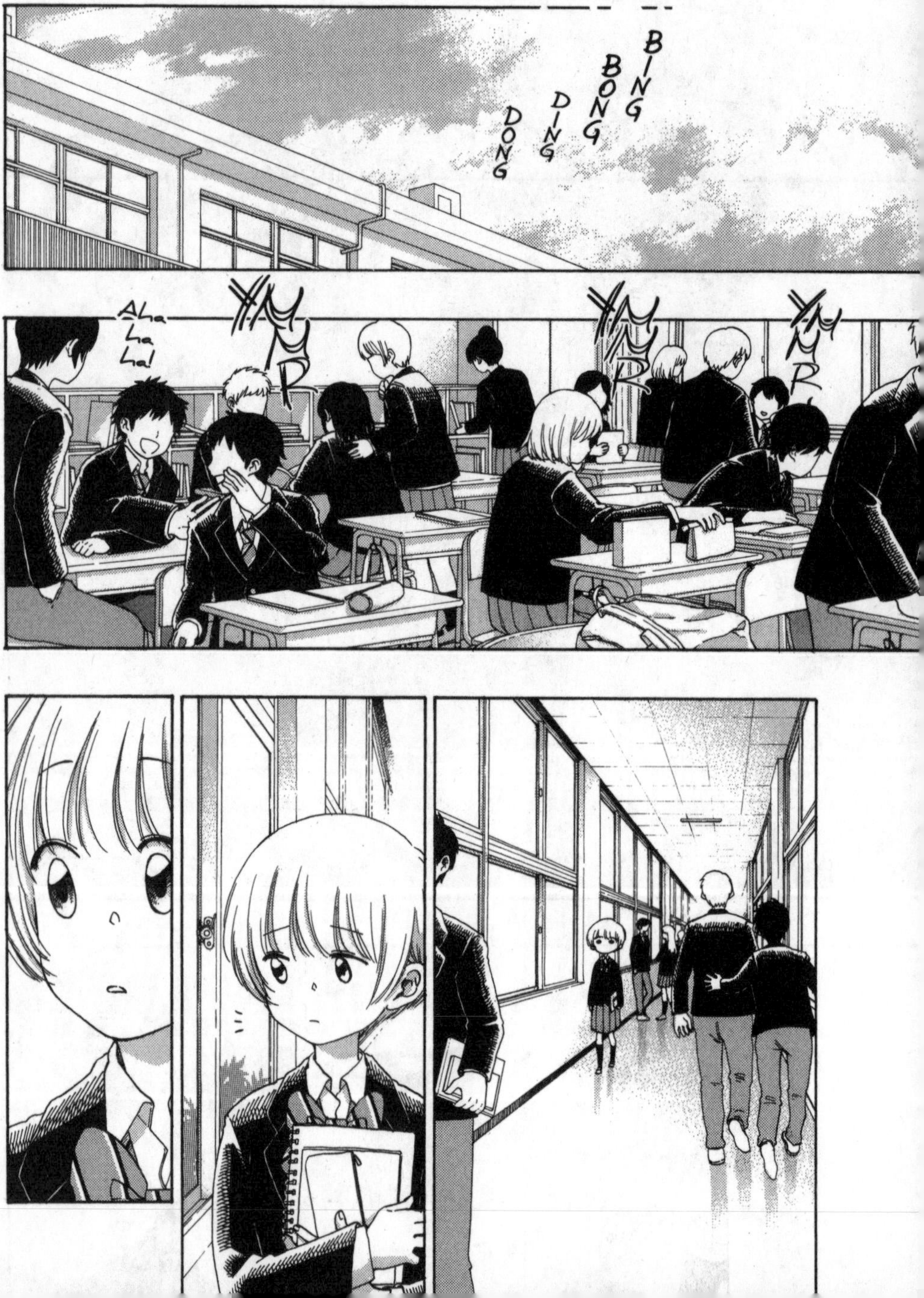
BING
BONG
DING
DONG
YMMR
YMMR
YMMR
Aha ha ha!

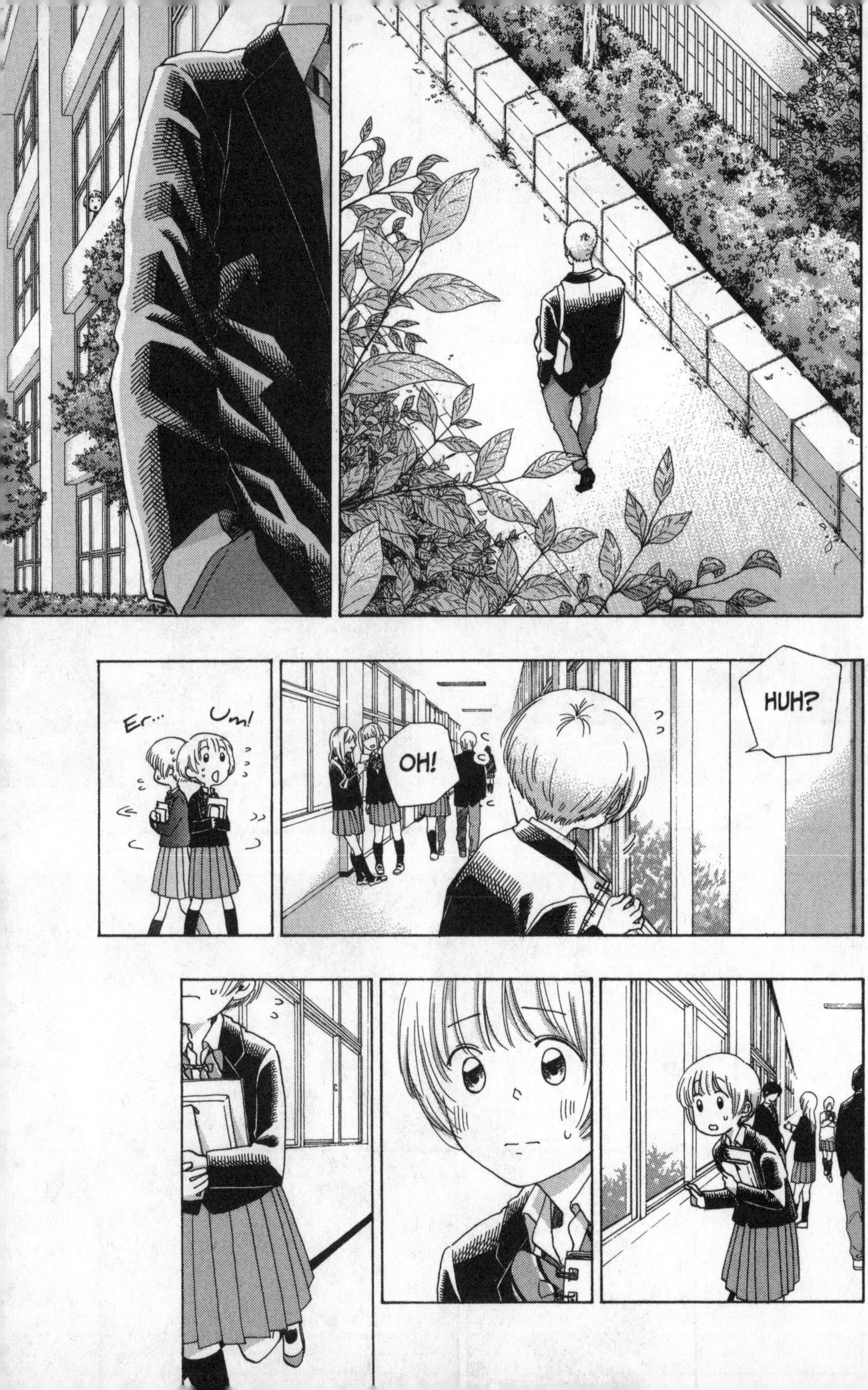
HUH?
OH!
Um!
Er...

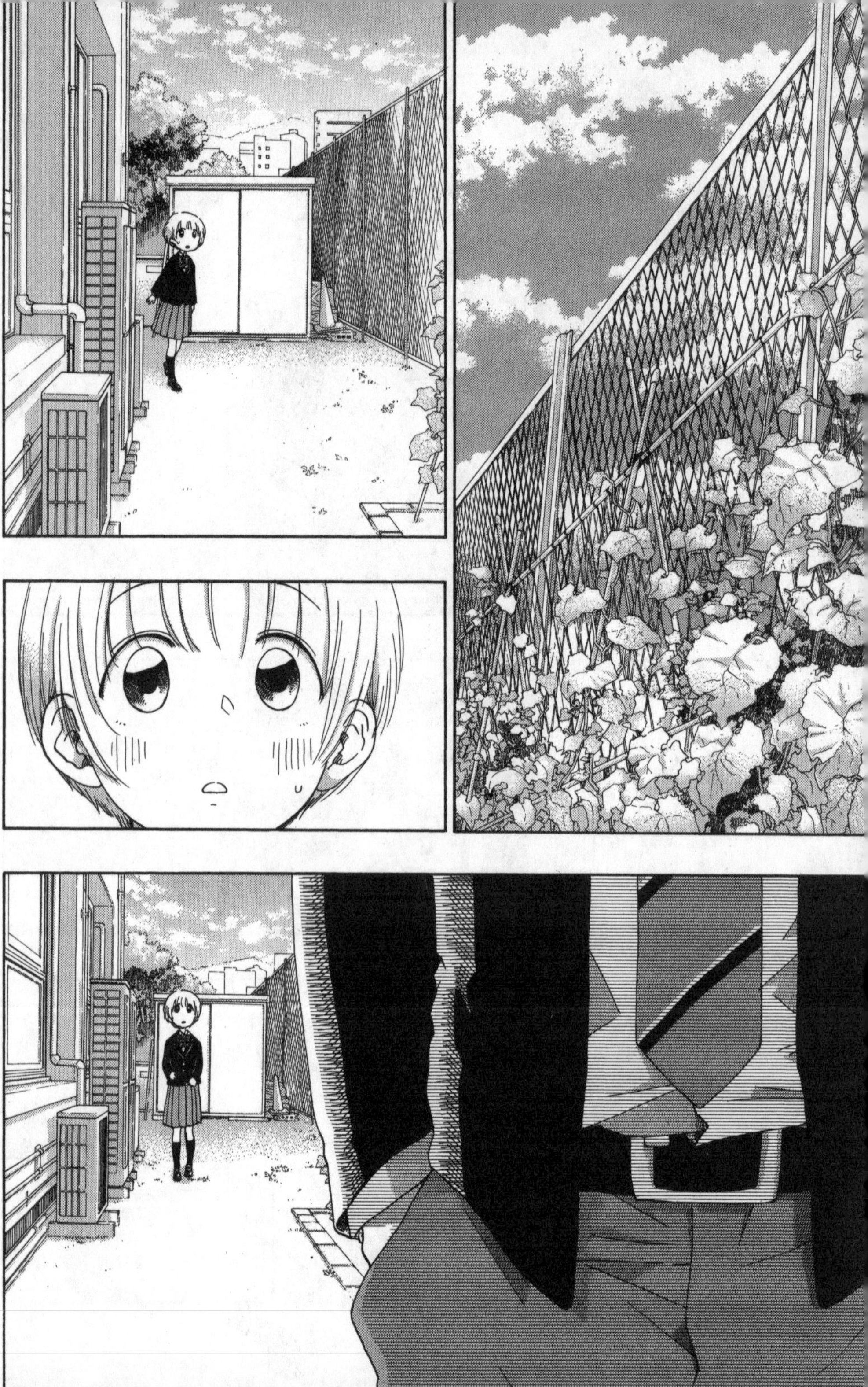

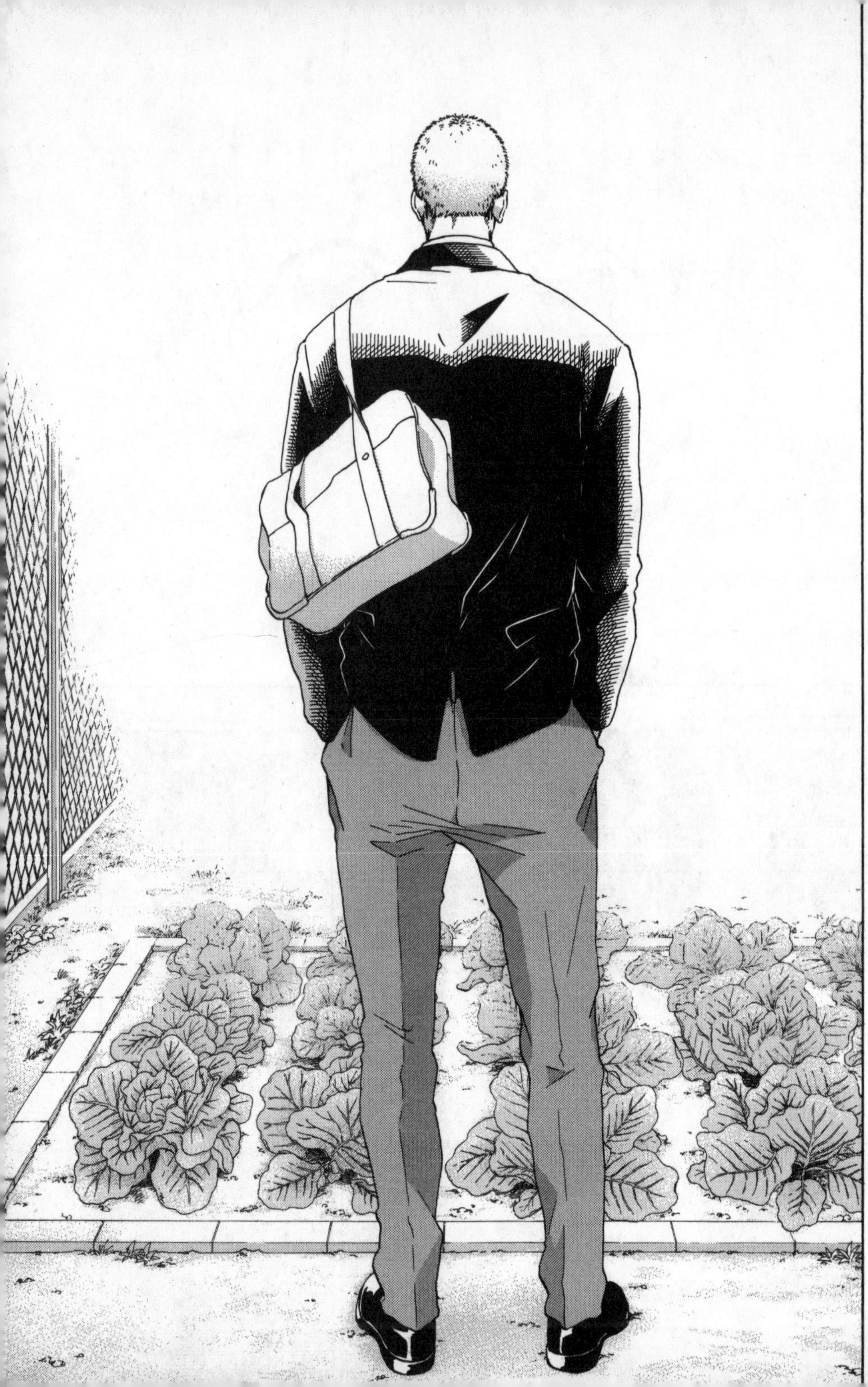

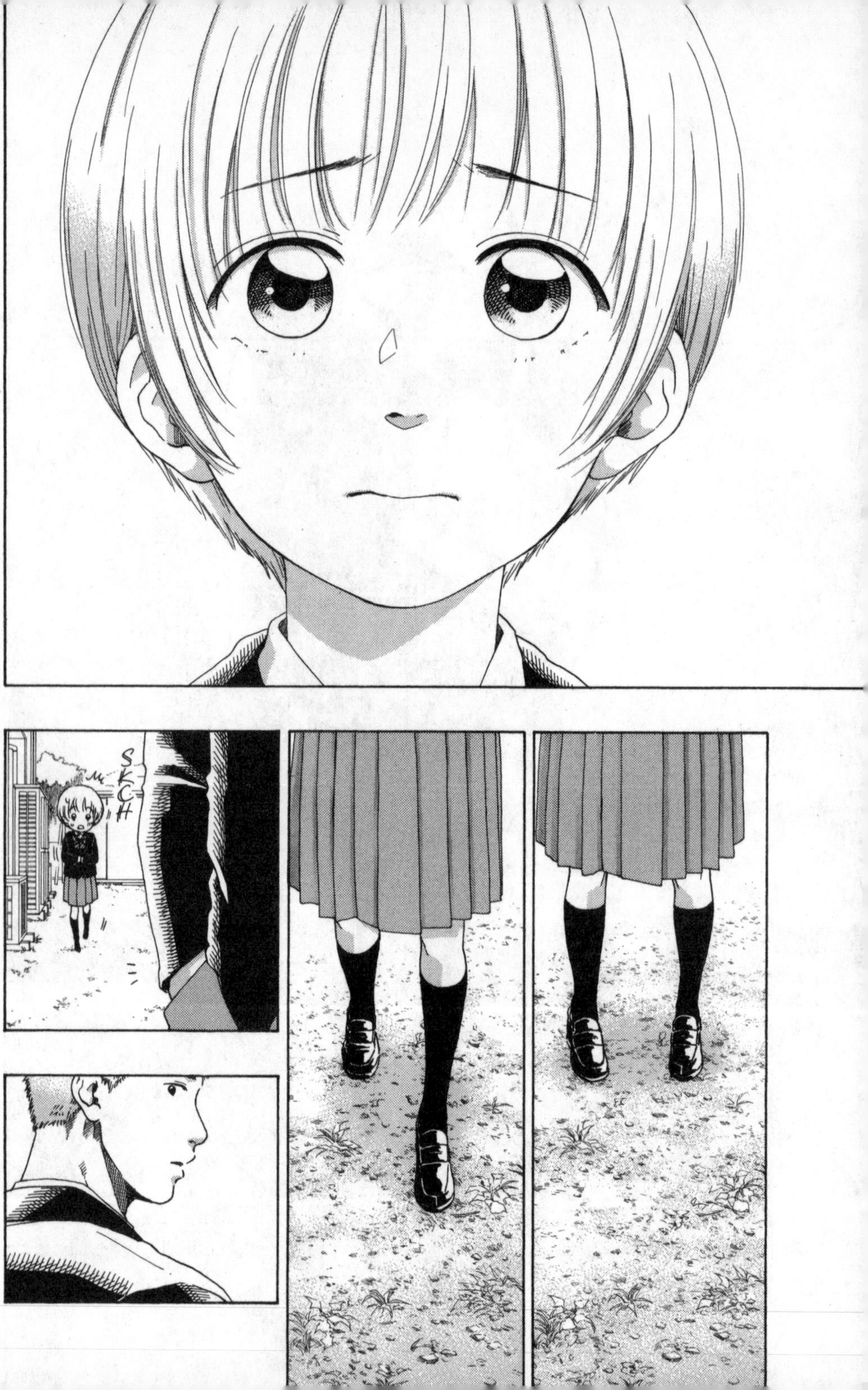
SKCH

UM...

G...

GOOD MORNING.

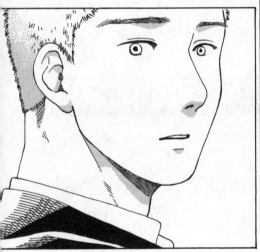

SO, UH...

MORNING.

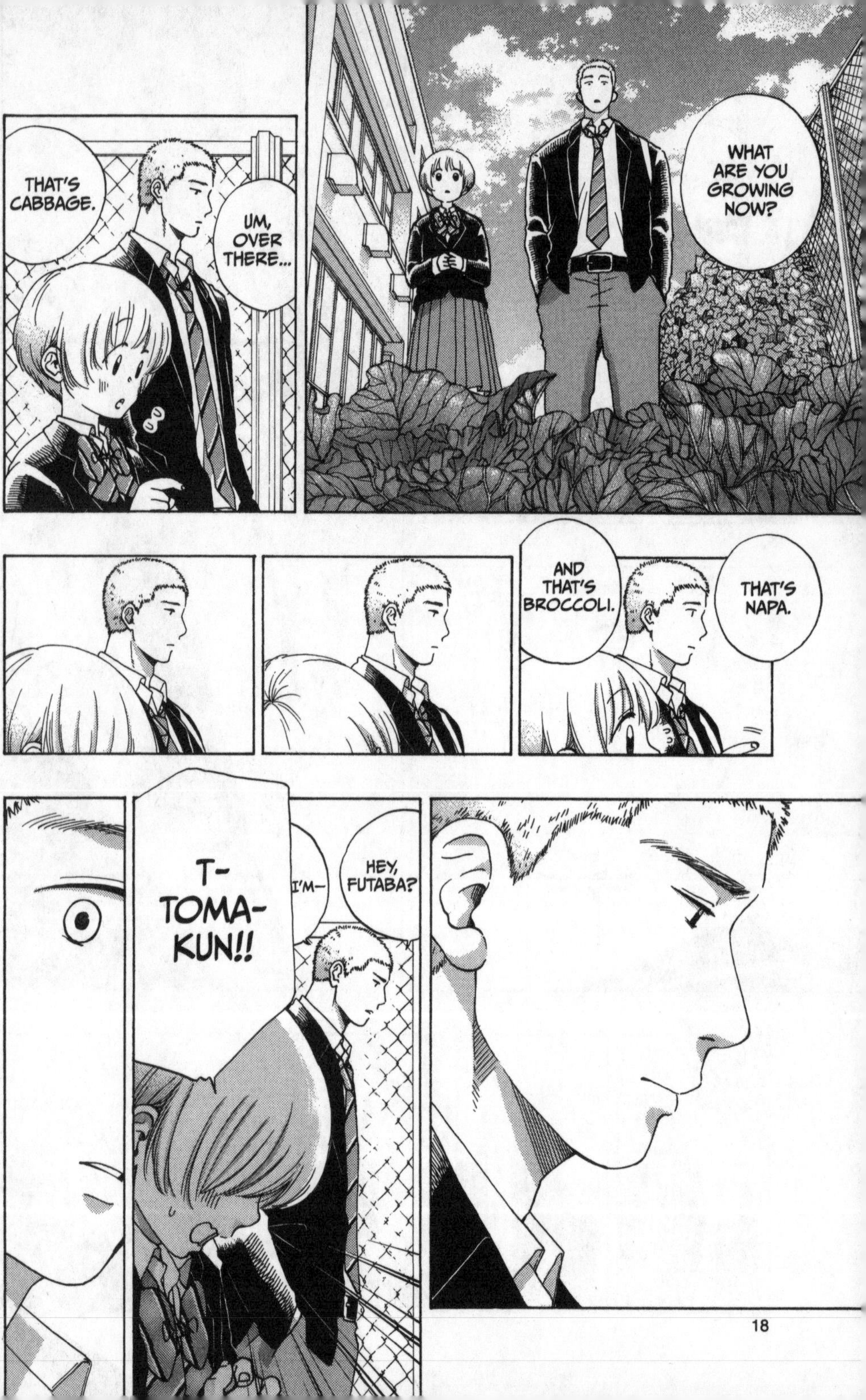
WHAT ARE YOU GROWING NOW?
UM, OVER THERE...
THAT'S CABBAGE.
THAT'S NAPA.
AND THAT'S BROCCOLI.
HEY, FUTABA?
I'M—
T-TOMA-KUN!!

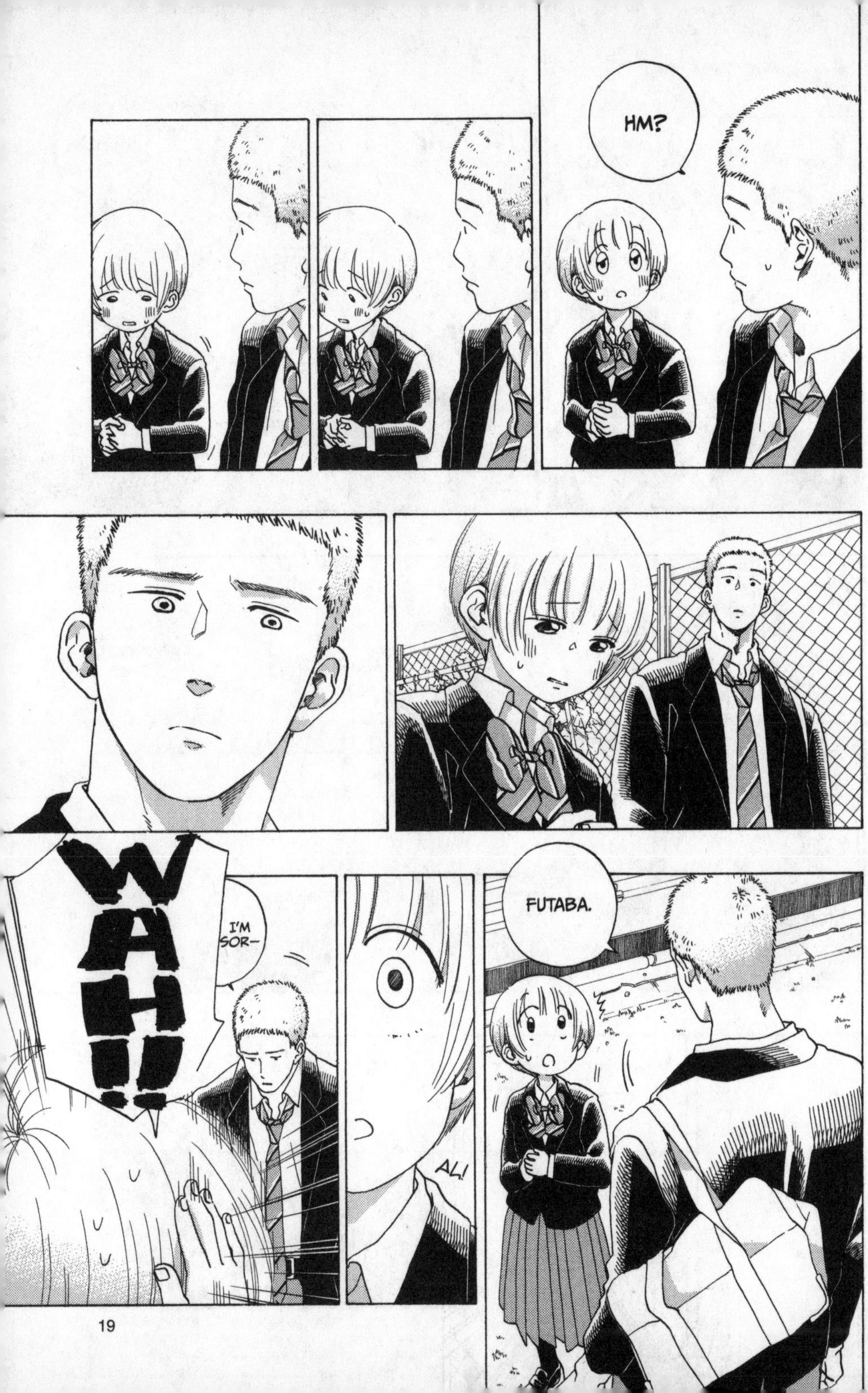
HM?
FUTABA.
AH!
I'M SOR—
WAH!!

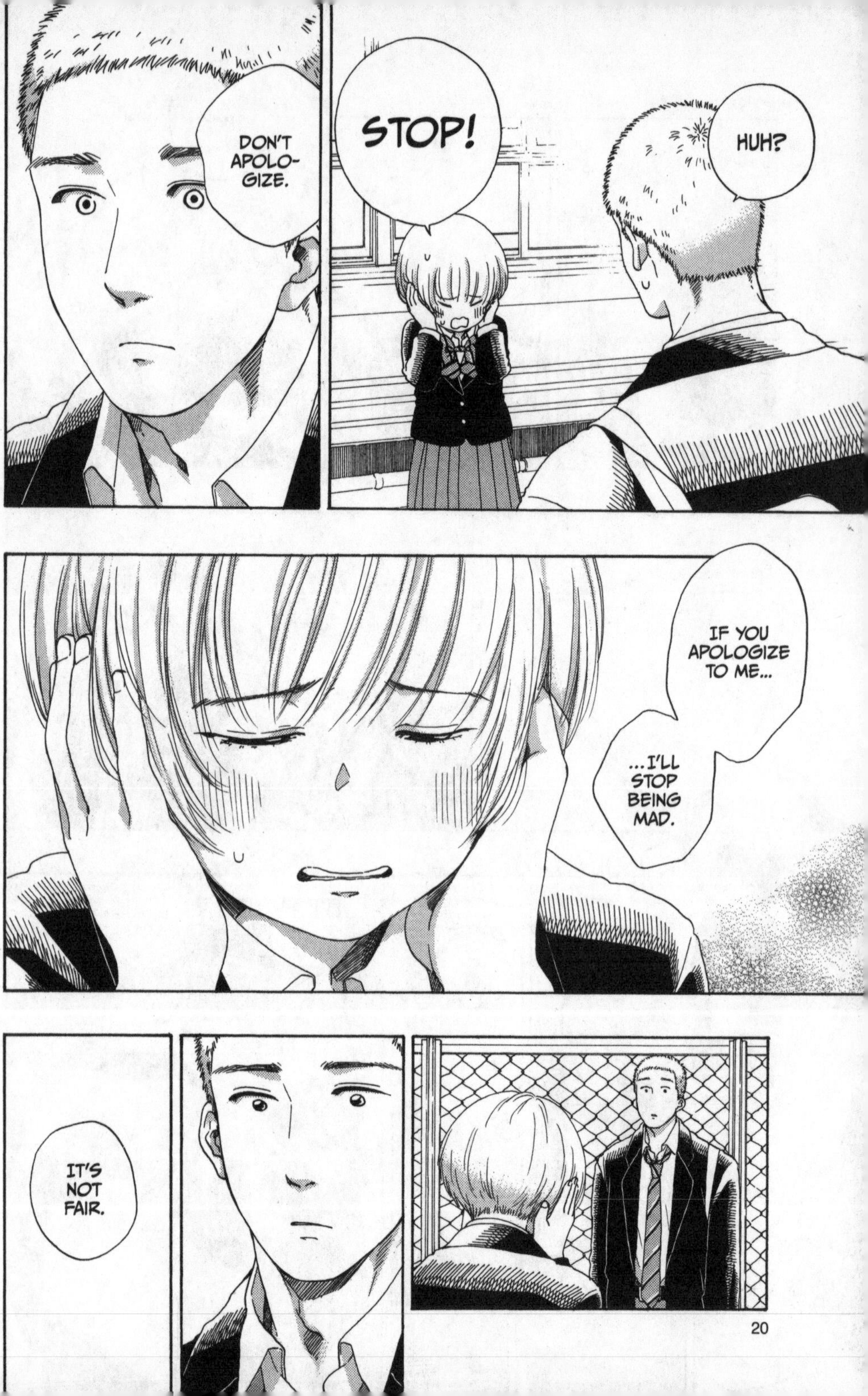
HUH?
STOP!
DON'T APOLOGIZE.
IF YOU APOLOGIZE TO ME...
...I'LL STOP BEING MAD.
IT'S NOT FAIR.

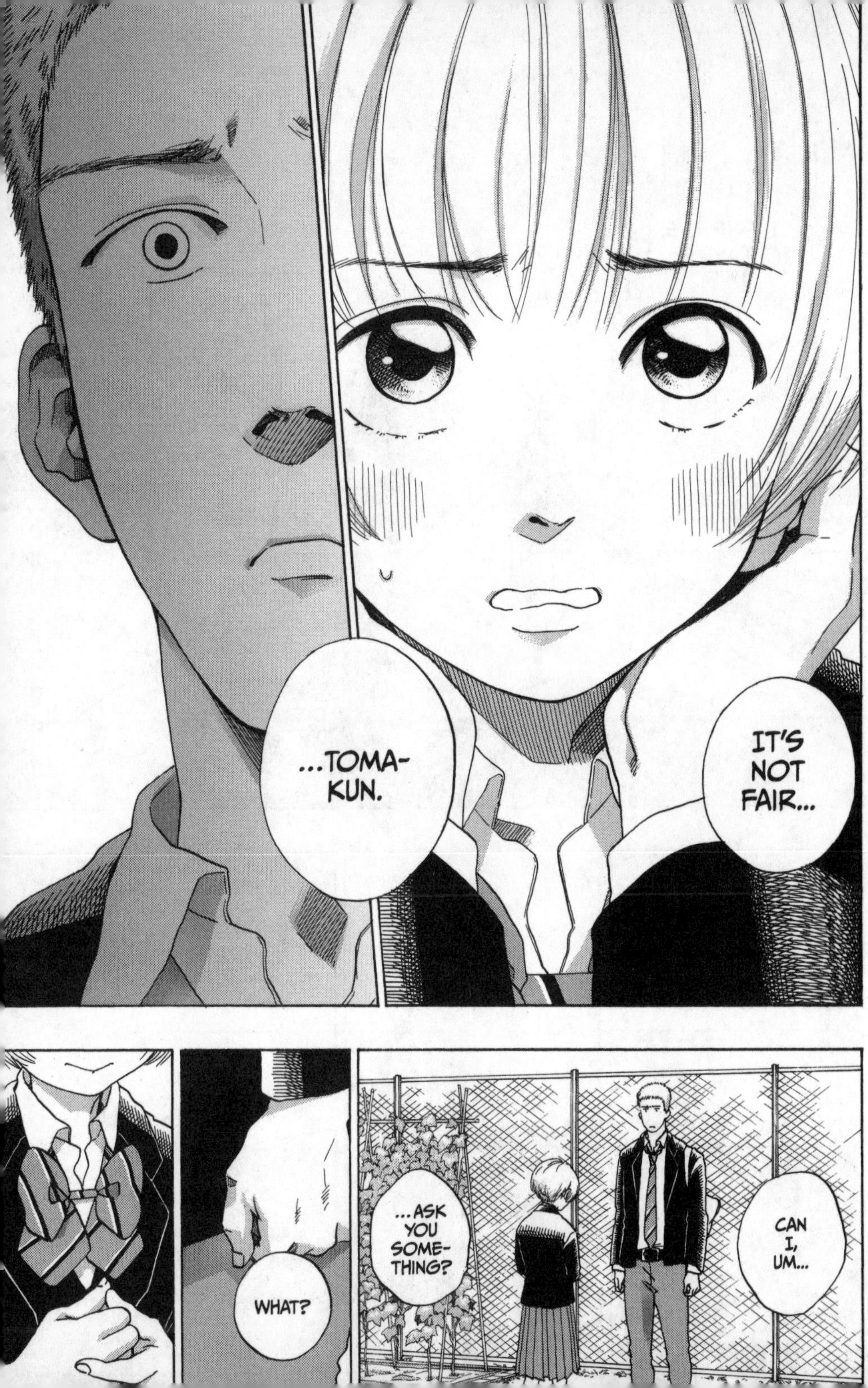
IT'S NOT FAIR...
...TOMA-KUN.
CAN I, UM...
...ASK YOU SOMETHING?
WHAT?

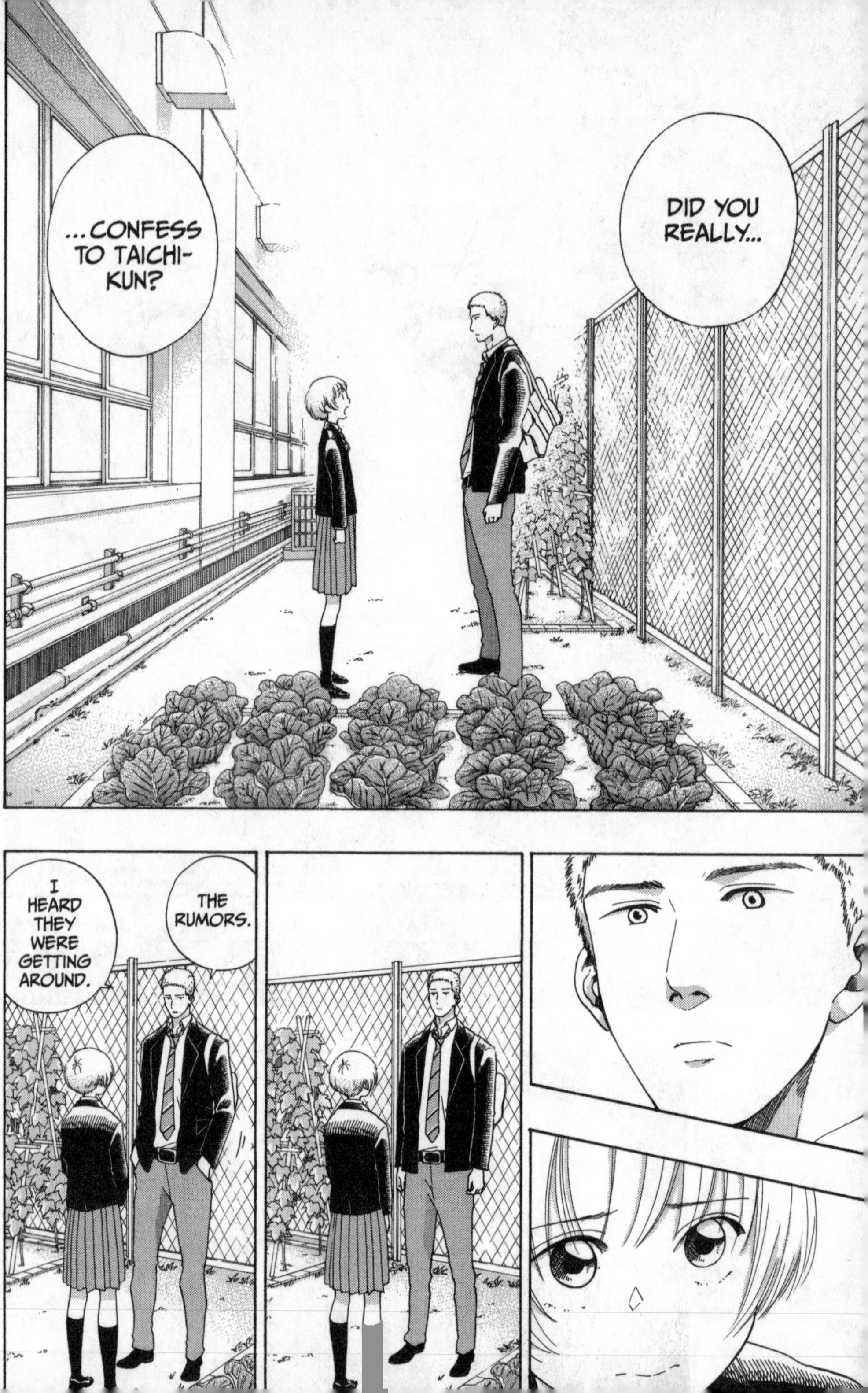
DID YOU REALLY...
...CONFESS TO TAICHI-KUN?
THE RUMORS.
I HEARD THEY WERE GETTING AROUND.

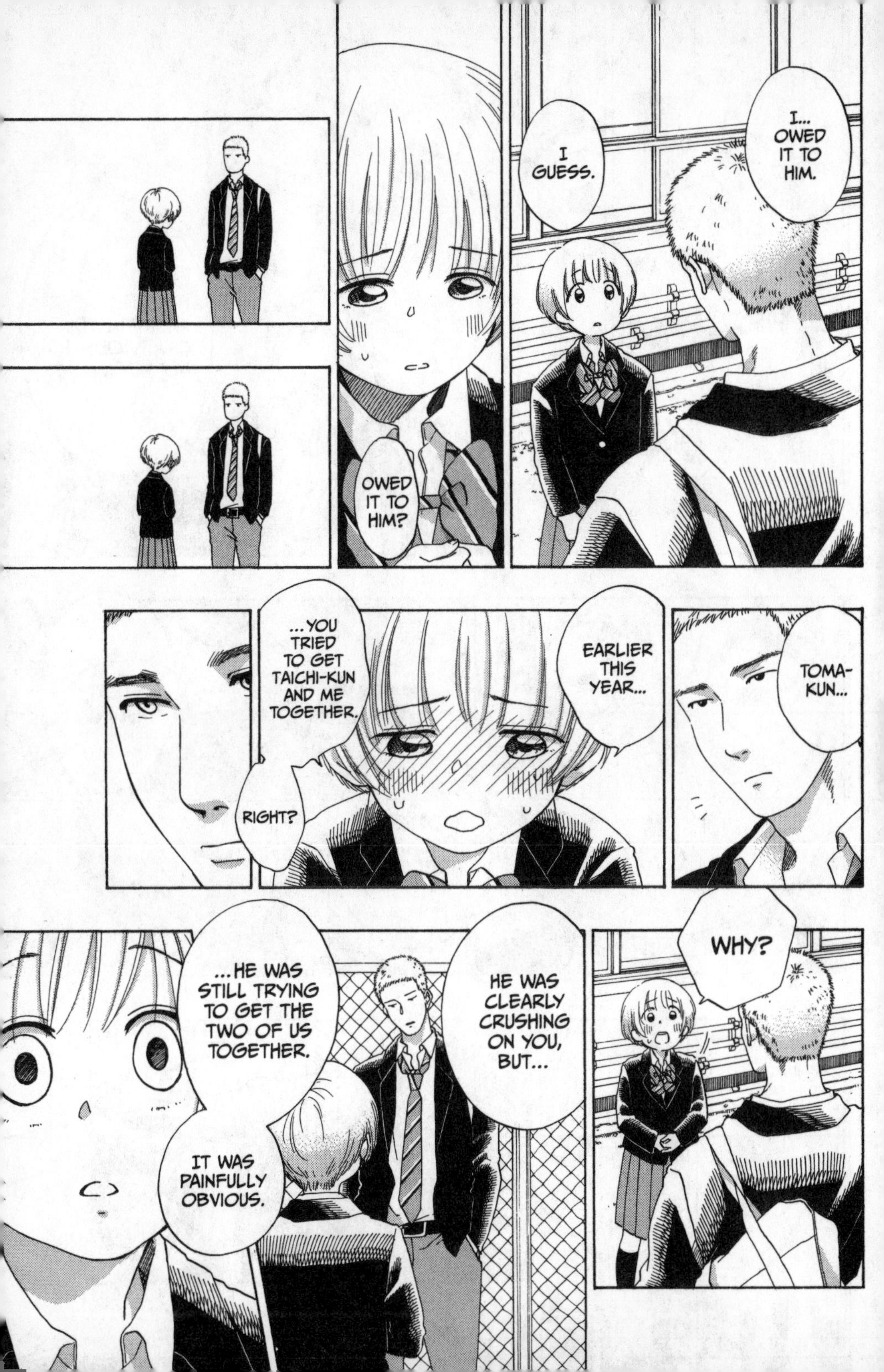
I... OWED IT TO HIM.
I GUESS.
OWED IT TO HIM?
TOMA-KUN...
EARLIER THIS YEAR...
...YOU TRIED TO GET TAICHI-KUN AND ME TOGETHER.
RIGHT?
WHY?
HE WAS CLEARLY CRUSHING ON YOU, BUT...
...HE WAS STILL TRYING TO GET THE TWO OF US TOGETHER.
IT WAS PAINFULLY OBVIOUS.

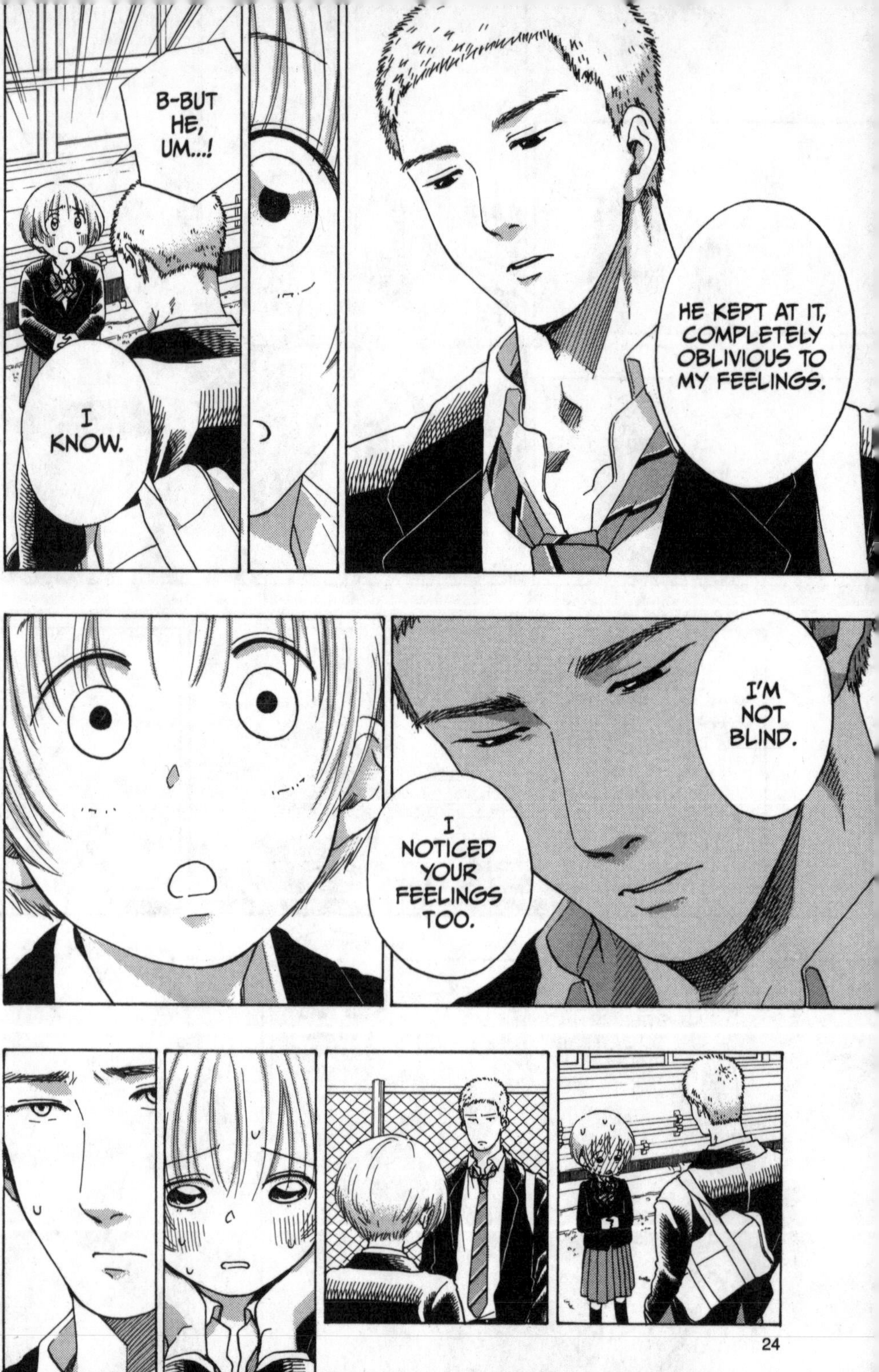

HE KEPT AT IT, COMPLETELY OBLIVIOUS TO MY FEELINGS.
B-BUT HE, UM...!
I KNOW.
I'M NOT BLIND.
I NOTICED YOUR FEELINGS TOO.

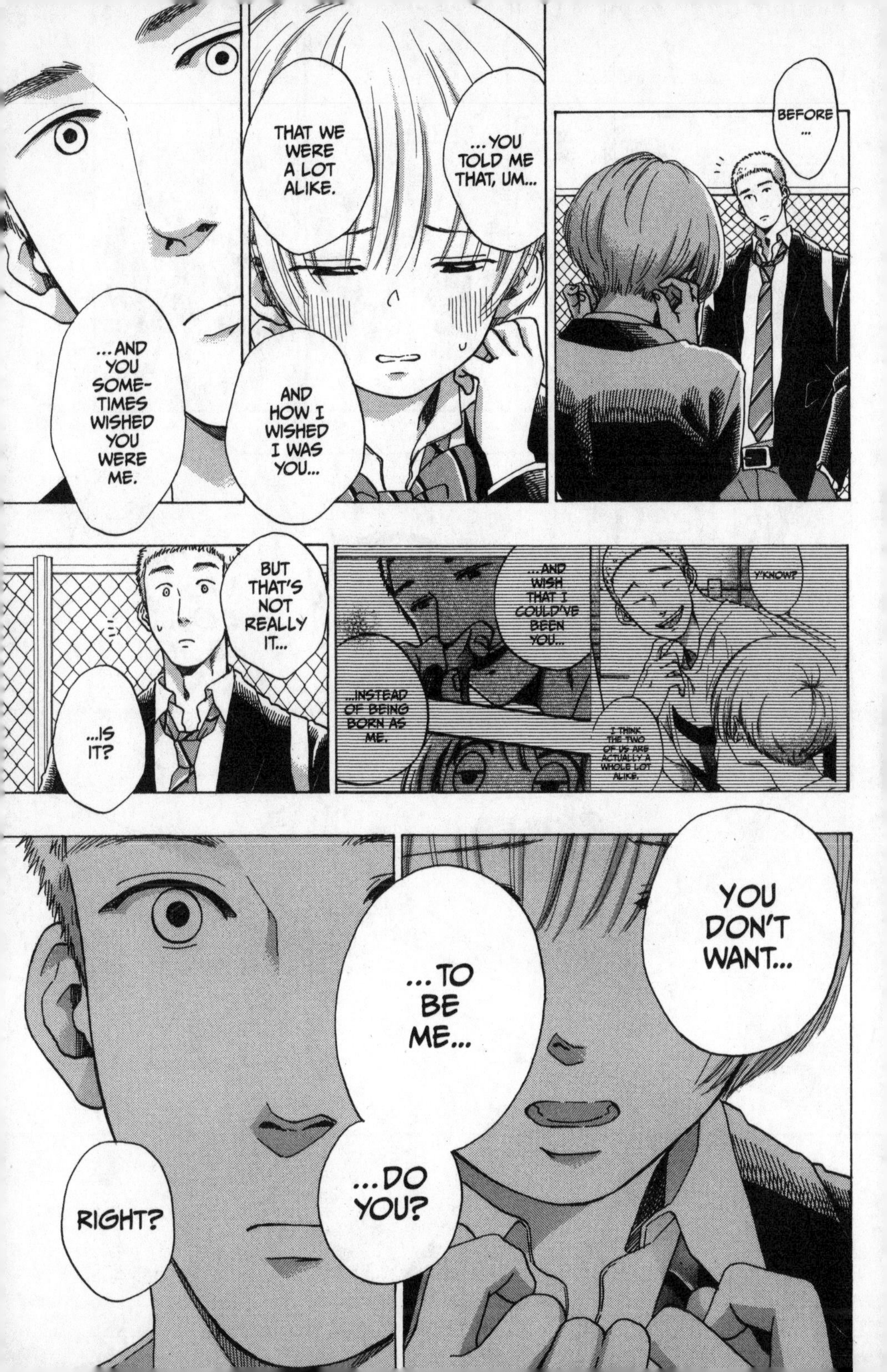
BEFORE...
...YOU TOLD ME THAT, UM...
THAT WE WERE A LOT ALIKE.
AND HOW I WISHED I WAS YOU...
...AND YOU SOMETIMES WISHED YOU WERE ME.
Y'KNOW?
I THINK THE TWO OF US ARE ACTUALLY A WHOLE LOT ALIKE.
...AND WISH THAT I COULD'VE BEEN YOU...
...INSTEAD OF BEING BORN AS ME.
BUT THAT'S NOT REALLY IT...
...IS IT?
YOU DON'T WANT...
...TO BE ME...
...DO YOU?
RIGHT?

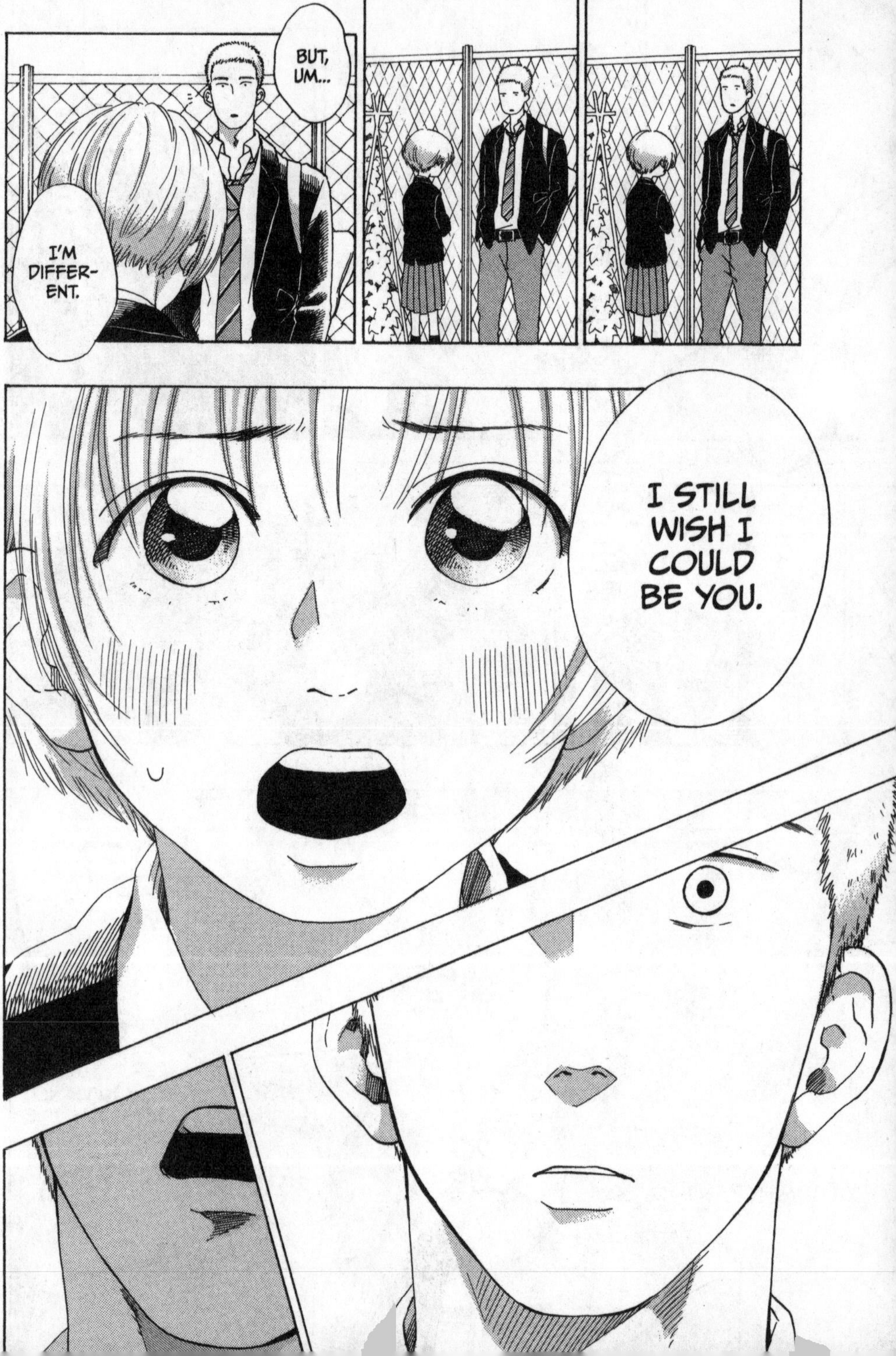
BUT, UM...
I'M DIFFER-ENT.
I STILL WISH I COULD BE YOU.

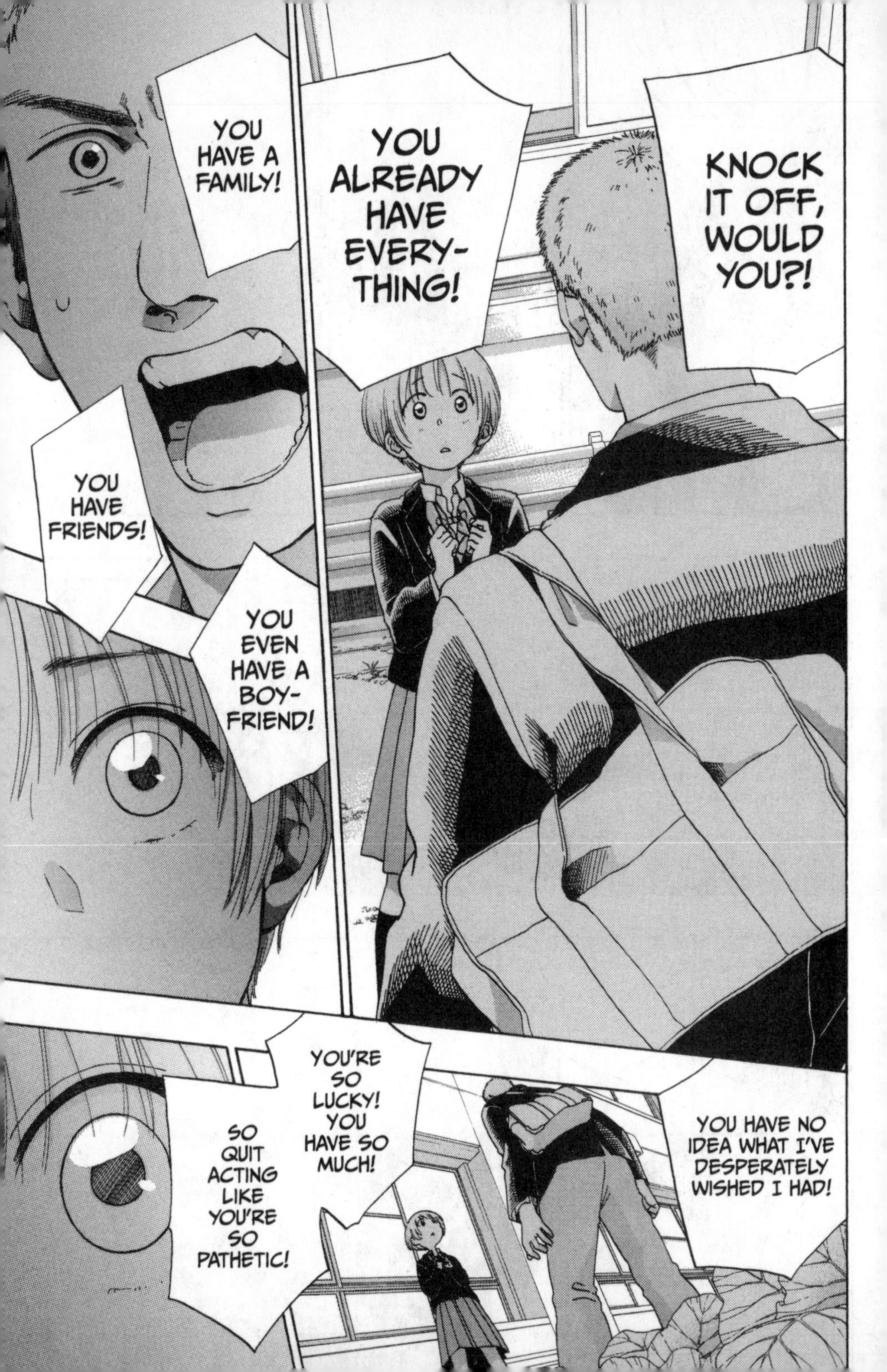
KNOCK IT OFF, WOULD YOU?!
YOU ALREADY HAVE EVERY-THING!
YOU HAVE A FAMILY!
YOU HAVE FRIENDS!
YOU EVEN HAVE A BOY-FRIEND!
YOU HAVE NO IDEA WHAT I'VE DESPERATELY WISHED I HAD!
YOU'RE SO LUCKY! YOU HAVE SO MUCH!
SO QUIT ACTING LIKE YOU'RE SO PATHETIC!

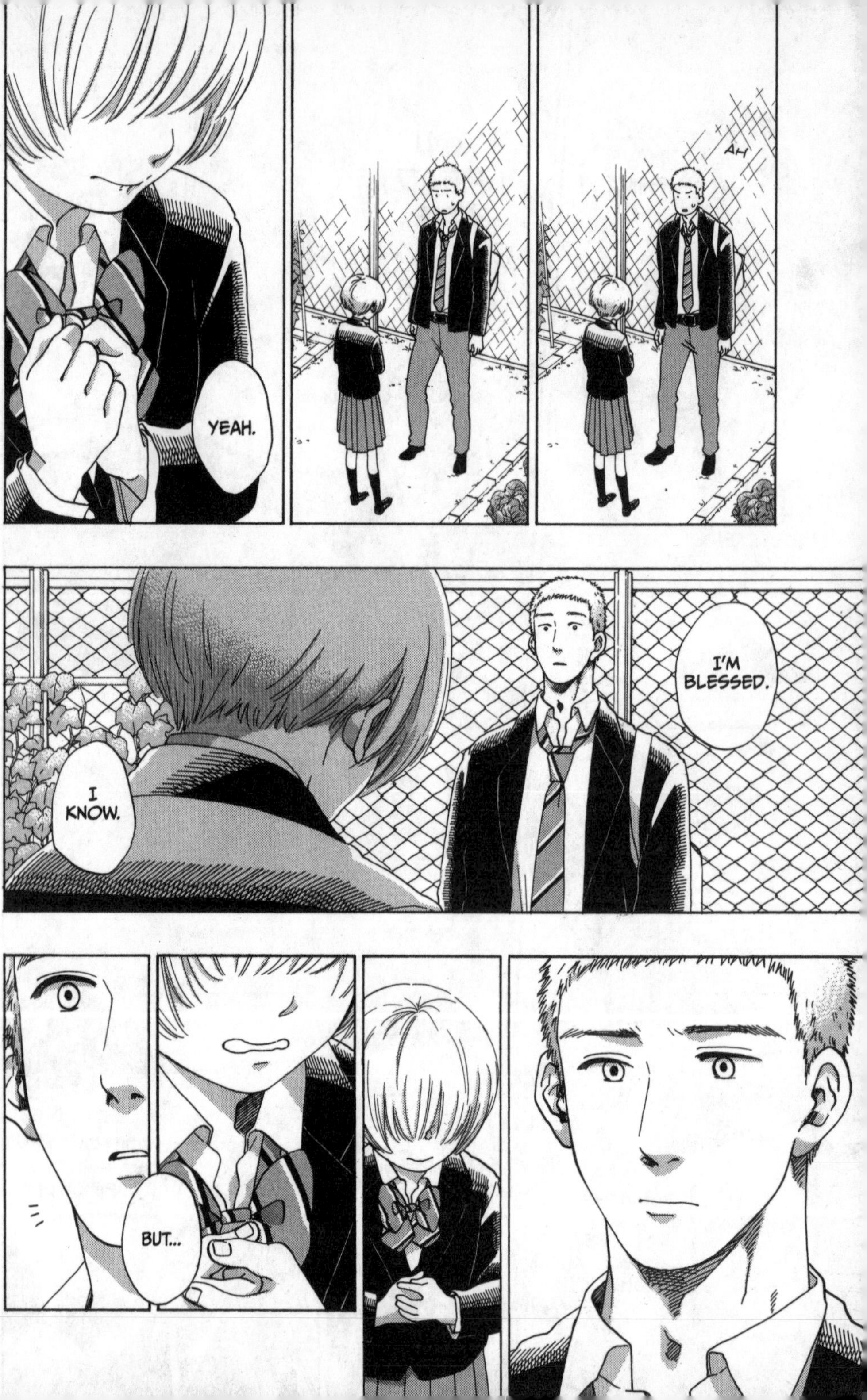
AH
YEAH.
I'M BLESSED.
I KNOW.
BUT...

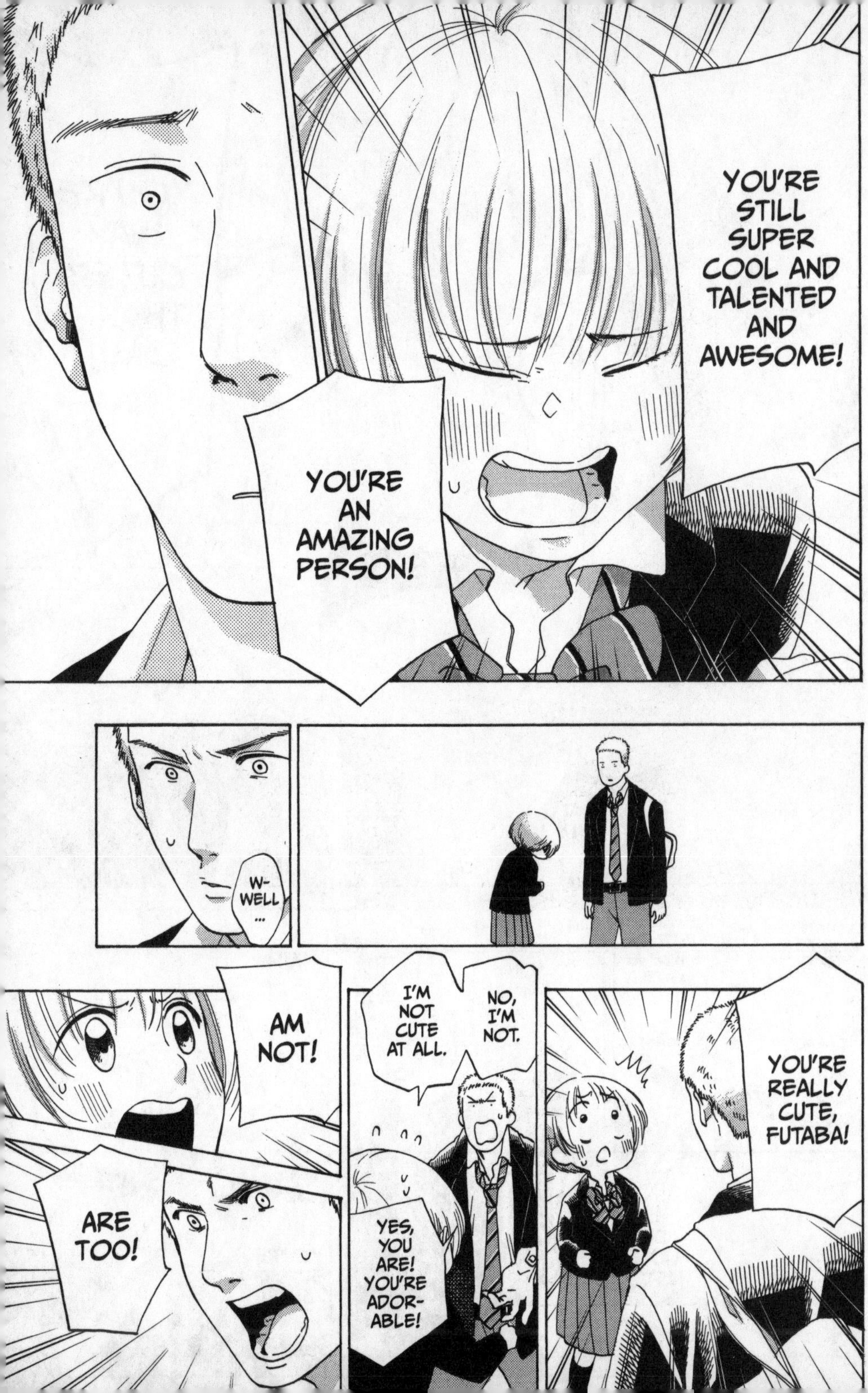
YOU'RE STILL SUPER COOL AND TALENTED AND AWESOME!
YOU'RE AN AMAZING PERSON!
W-WELL...
YOU'RE REALLY CUTE, FUTABA!
NO, I'M NOT.
I'M NOT CUTE AT ALL.
YES, YOU ARE! YOU'RE ADOR-ABLE!
AM NOT!
ARE TOO!

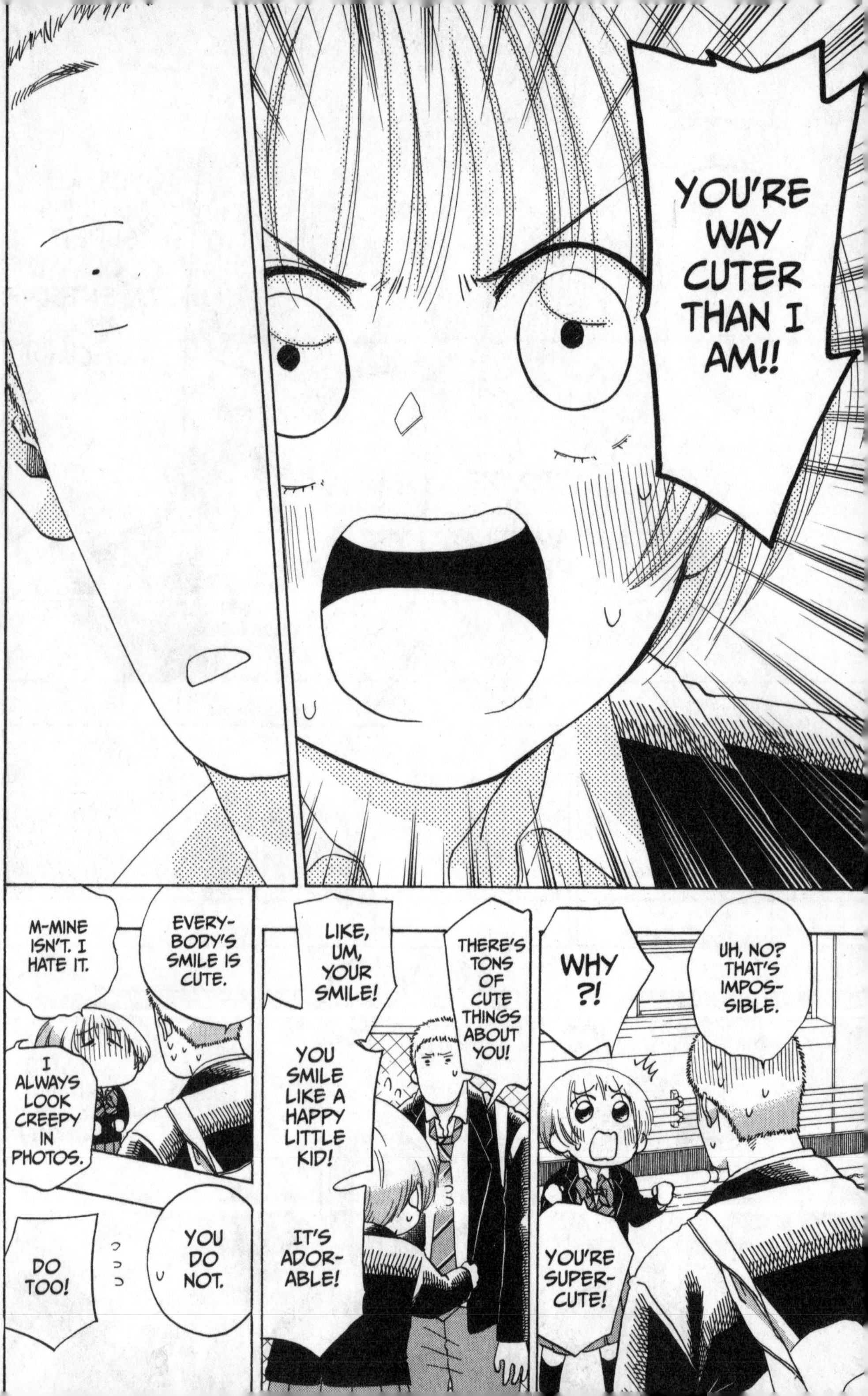
YOU'RE WAY CUTER THAN I AM!!
UH, NO? THAT'S IMPOS-SIBLE.
WHY ?!
YOU'RE SUPER-CUTE!
THERE'S TONS OF CUTE THINGS ABOUT YOU!
LIKE, UM, YOUR SMILE!
YOU SMILE LIKE A HAPPY LITTLE KID!
IT'S ADOR-ABLE!
EVERY-BODY'S SMILE IS CUTE.
M-MINE ISN'T. I HATE IT.
I ALWAYS LOOK CREEPY IN PHOTOS.
YOU DO NOT.
DO TOO!

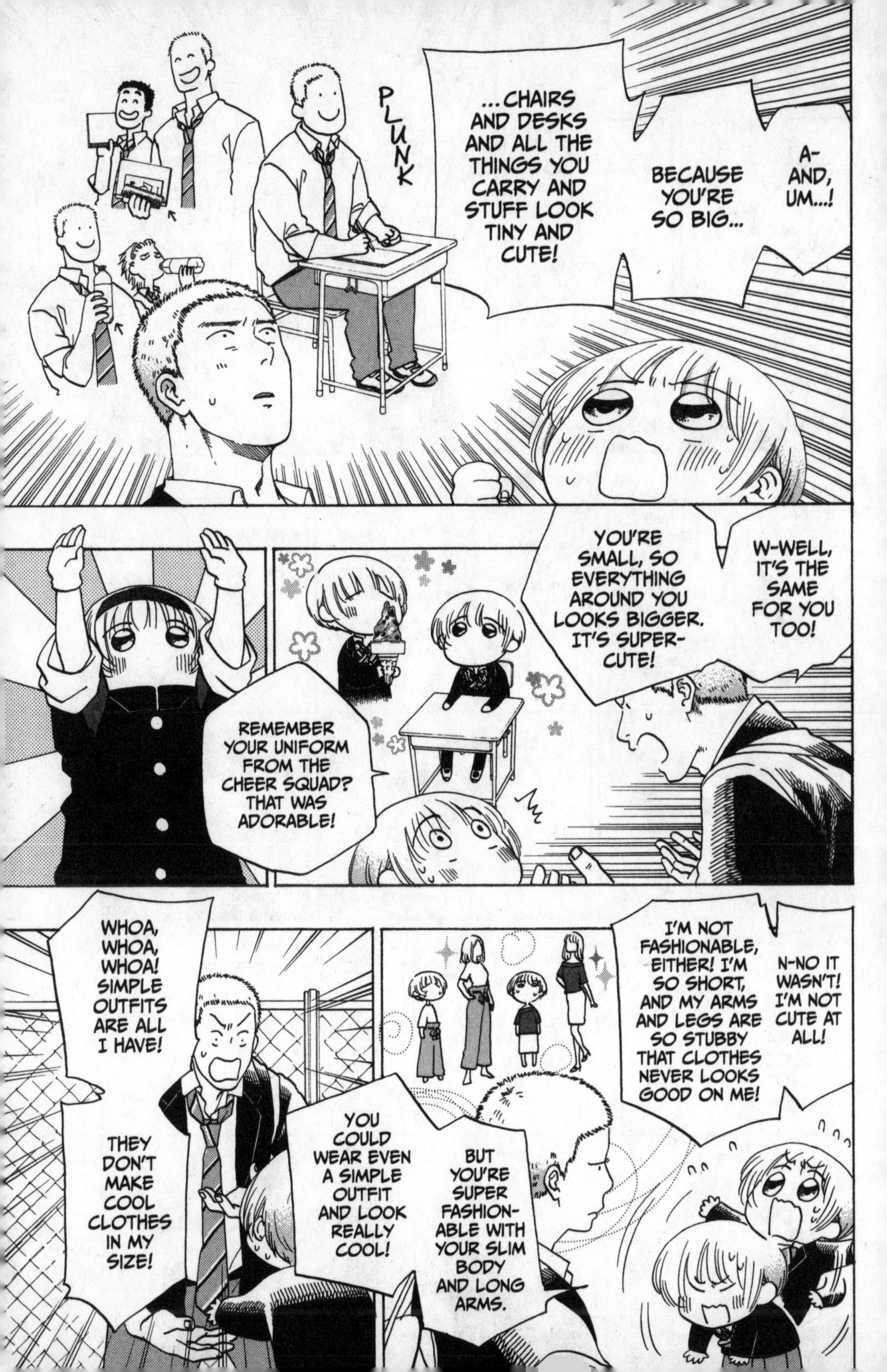
A- AND, UM...!
BECAUSE YOU'RE SO BIG...
...CHAIRS AND DESKS AND ALL THE THINGS YOU CARRY AND STUFF LOOK TINY AND CUTE!
PLUNK
W-WELL, IT'S THE SAME FOR YOU TOO!
YOU'RE SMALL, SO EVERYTHING AROUND YOU LOOKS BIGGER. IT'S SUPER-CUTE!
REMEMBER YOUR UNIFORM FROM THE CHEER SQUAD? THAT WAS ADORABLE!
N-NO IT WASN'T! I'M NOT CUTE AT ALL!
I'M NOT FASHIONABLE, EITHER! I'M SO SHORT, AND MY ARMS AND LEGS ARE SO STUBBY THAT CLOTHES NEVER LOOKS GOOD ON ME!
BUT YOU'RE SUPER FASHION-ABLE WITH YOUR SLIM BODY AND LONG ARMS.
YOU COULD WEAR EVEN A SIMPLE OUTFIT AND LOOK REALLY COOL!
WHOA, WHOA, WHOA! SIMPLE OUTFITS ARE ALL I HAVE!
THEY DON'T MAKE COOL CLOTHES IN MY SIZE!

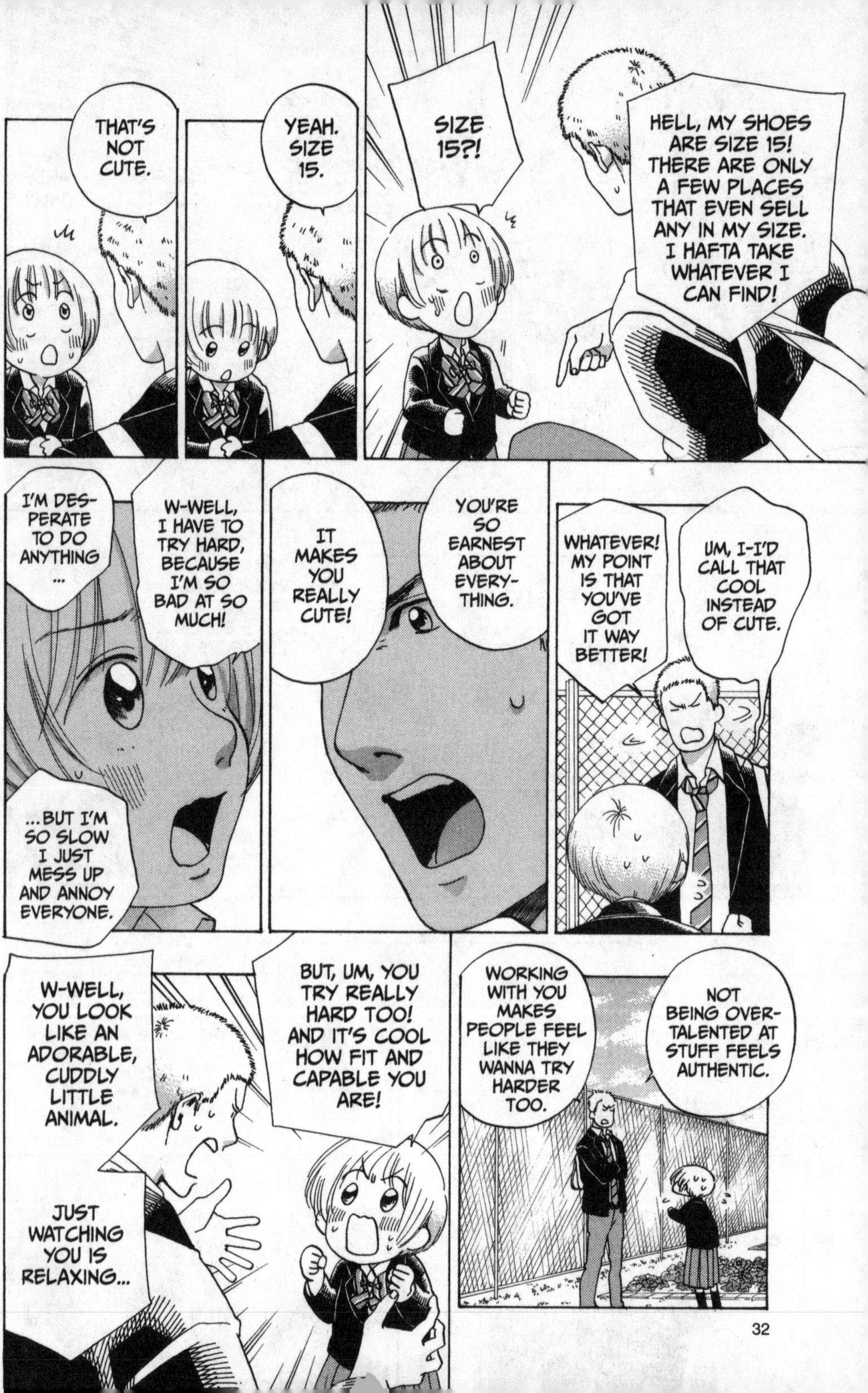
HELL, MY SHOES ARE SIZE 15! THERE ARE ONLY A FEW PLACES THAT EVEN SELL ANY IN MY SIZE. I HAFTA TAKE WHATEVER I CAN FIND!
SIZE 15?!
YEAH. SIZE 15.
THAT'S NOT CUTE.
UM, I-I'D CALL THAT COOL INSTEAD OF CUTE.
WHATEVER! MY POINT IS THAT YOU'VE GOT IT WAY BETTER!
YOU'RE SO EARNEST ABOUT EVERY-THING.
IT MAKES YOU REALLY CUTE!
W-WELL, I HAVE TO TRY HARD, BECAUSE I'M SO BAD AT SO MUCH!
I'M DES-PERATE TO DO ANYTHING ...
...BUT I'M SO SLOW I JUST MESS UP AND ANNOY EVERYONE.
NOT BEING OVER-TALENTED AT STUFF FEELS AUTHENTIC.
WORKING WITH YOU MAKES PEOPLE FEEL LIKE THEY WANNA TRY HARDER TOO.
BUT, UM, YOU TRY REALLY HARD TOO! AND IT'S COOL HOW FIT AND CAPABLE YOU ARE!
W-WELL, YOU LOOK LIKE AN ADORABLE, CUDDLY LITTLE ANIMAL.
JUST WATCHING YOU IS RELAXING...

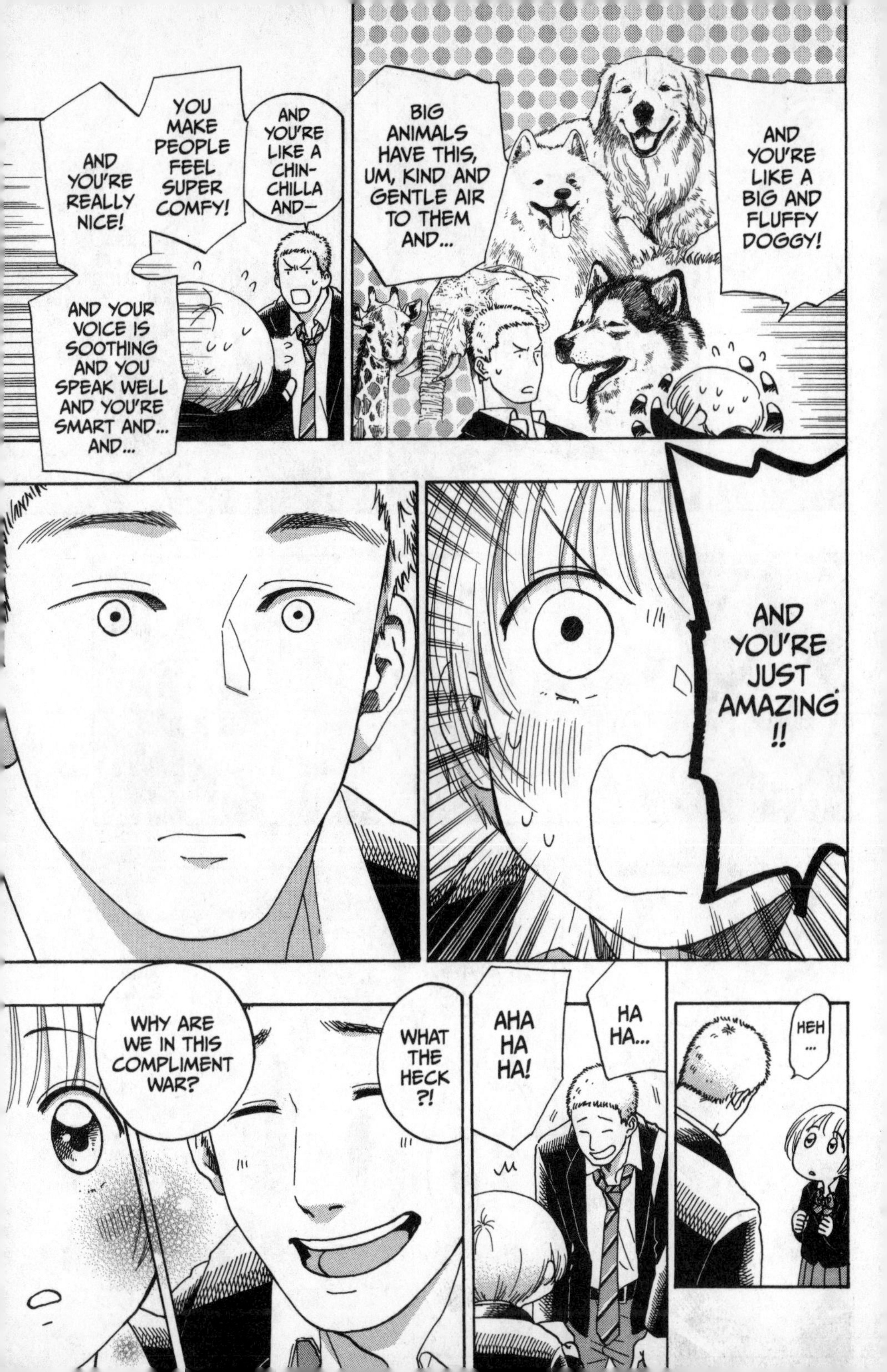

AND YOU'RE LIKE A BIG AND FLUFFY DOGGY!
BIG ANIMALS HAVE THIS, UM, KIND AND GENTLE AIR TO THEM AND...
AND YOU'RE LIKE A CHIN-CHILLA AND—
YOU MAKE PEOPLE FEEL SUPER COMFY!
AND YOU'RE REALLY NICE!
AND YOUR VOICE IS SOOTHING AND YOU SPEAK WELL AND YOU'RE SMART AND... AND...
AND YOU'RE JUST AMAZING!!
HEH ...
HA HA...
AHA HA HA!
WHAT THE HECK?!
WHY ARE WE IN THIS COMPLIMENT WAR?

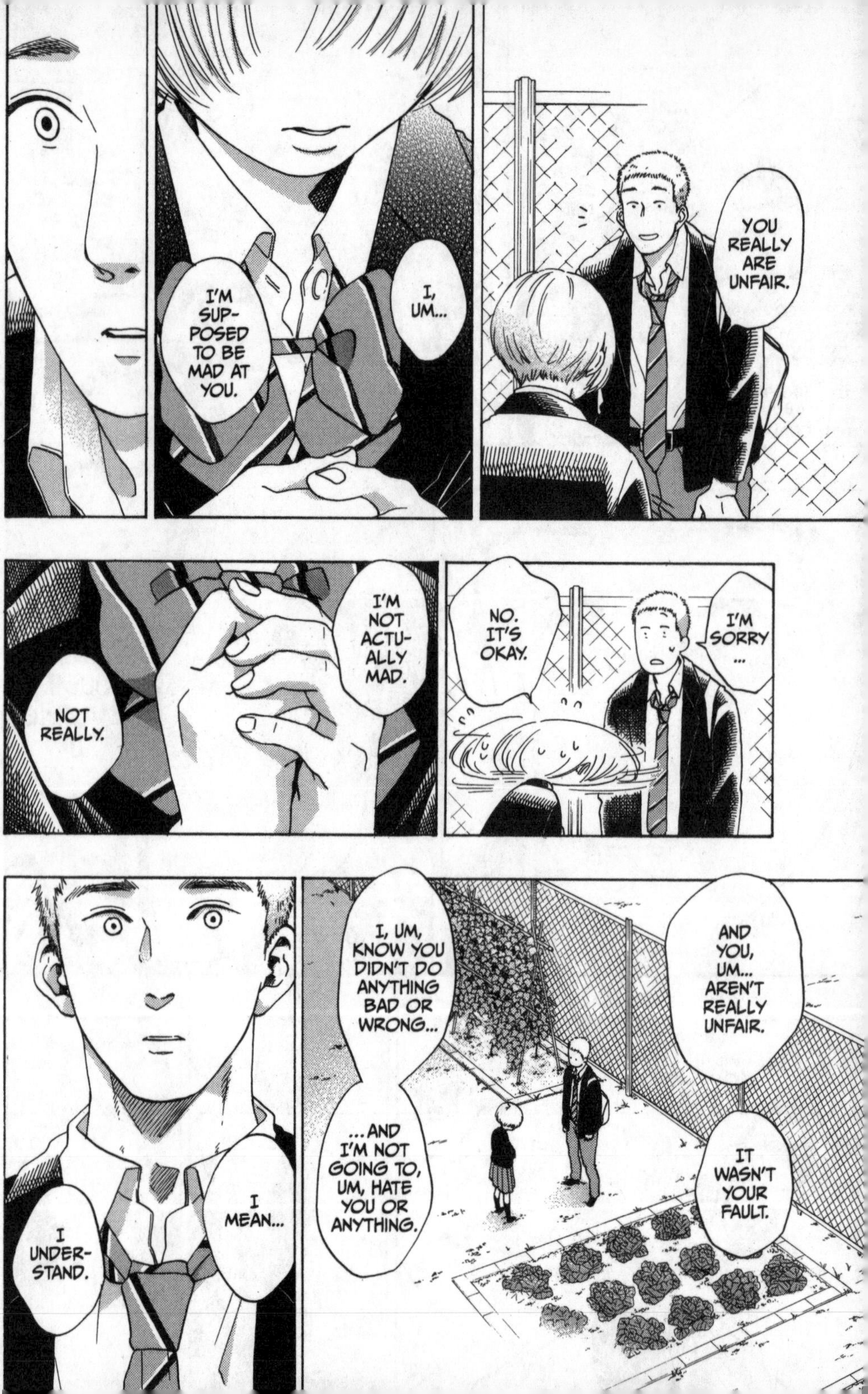
YOU REALLY ARE UNFAIR.
I, UM...
I'M SUP-POSED TO BE MAD AT YOU.
I'M SORRY...
NO. IT'S OKAY.
I'M NOT ACTU-ALLY MAD.
NOT REALLY.
AND YOU, UM... AREN'T REALLY UNFAIR.
IT WASN'T YOUR FAULT.
I, UM, KNOW YOU DIDN'T DO ANYTHING BAD OR WRONG...
...AND I'M NOT GOING TO, UM, HATE YOU OR ANYTHING.
I MEAN...
I UNDER-STAND.

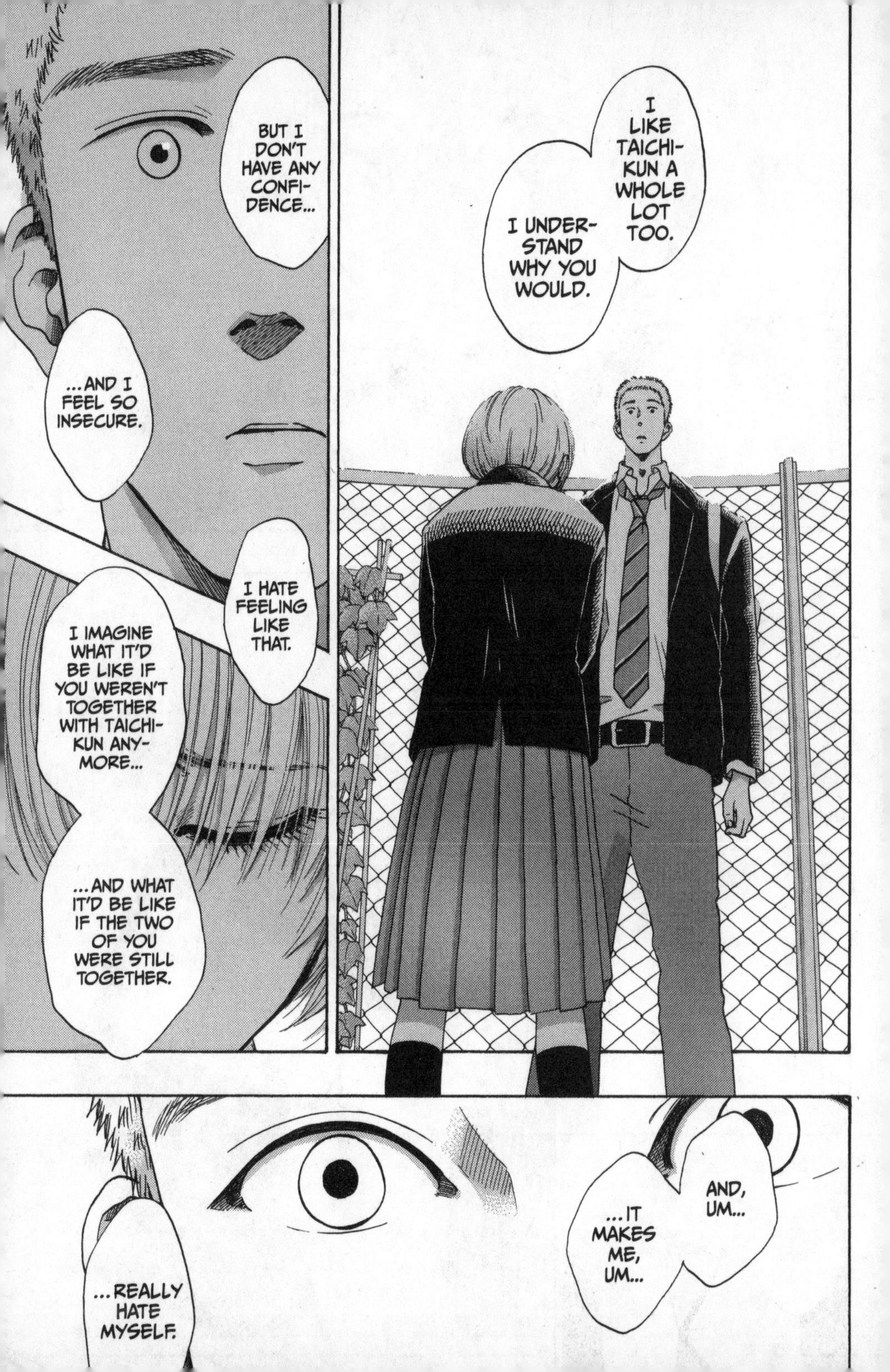
I LIKE TAICHI-KUN A WHOLE LOT TOO.
I UNDERSTAND WHY YOU WOULD.
BUT I DON'T HAVE ANY CONFIDENCE...
...AND I FEEL SO INSECURE.
I HATE FEELING LIKE THAT.
I IMAGINE WHAT IT'D BE LIKE IF YOU WEREN'T TOGETHER WITH TAICHI-KUN ANYMORE...
...AND WHAT IT'D BE LIKE IF THE TWO OF YOU WERE STILL TOGETHER.
AND, UM...
...IT MAKES ME, UM...
...REALLY HATE MYSELF.

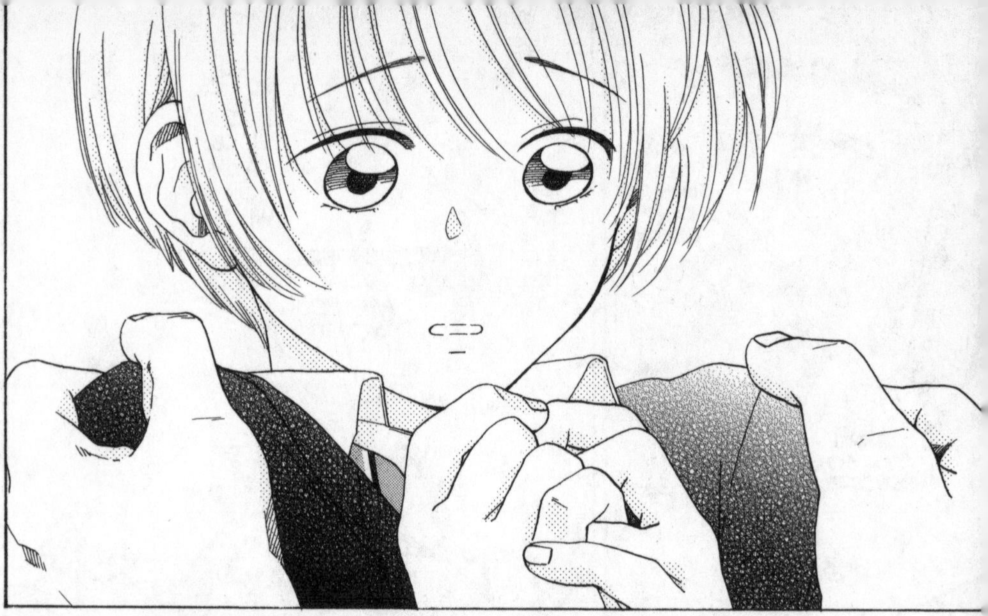
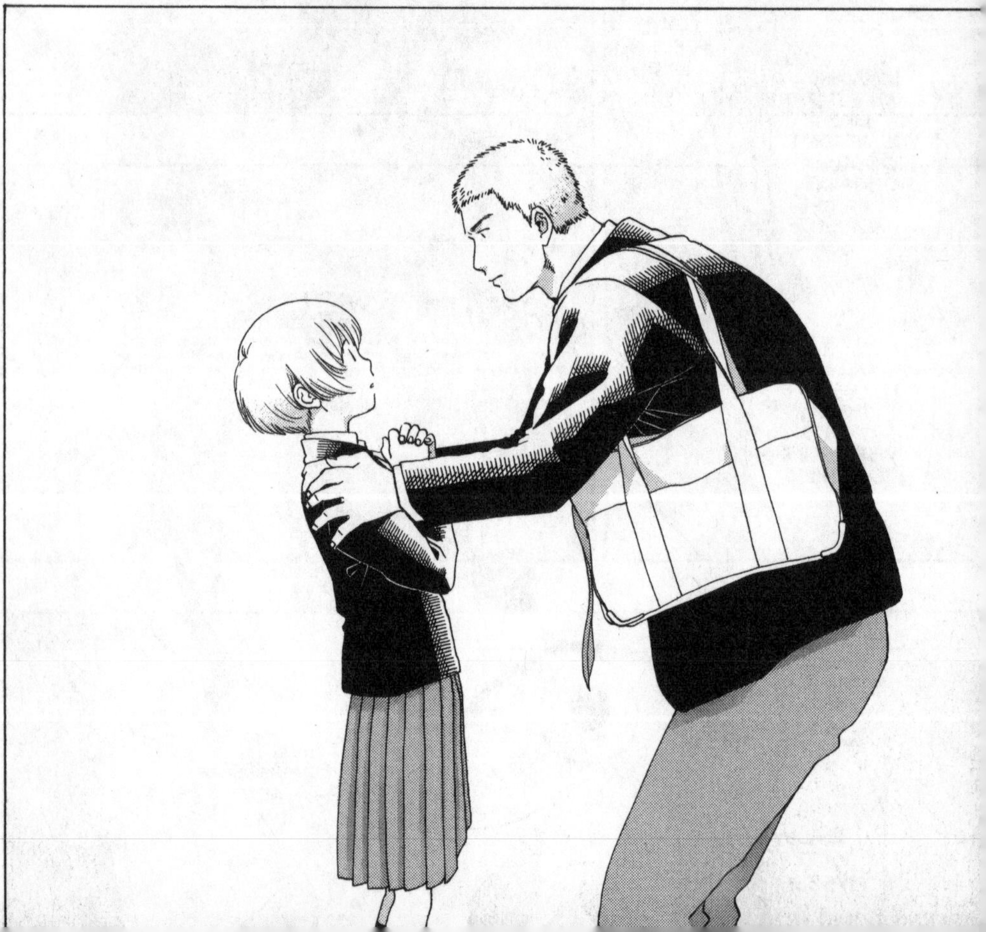

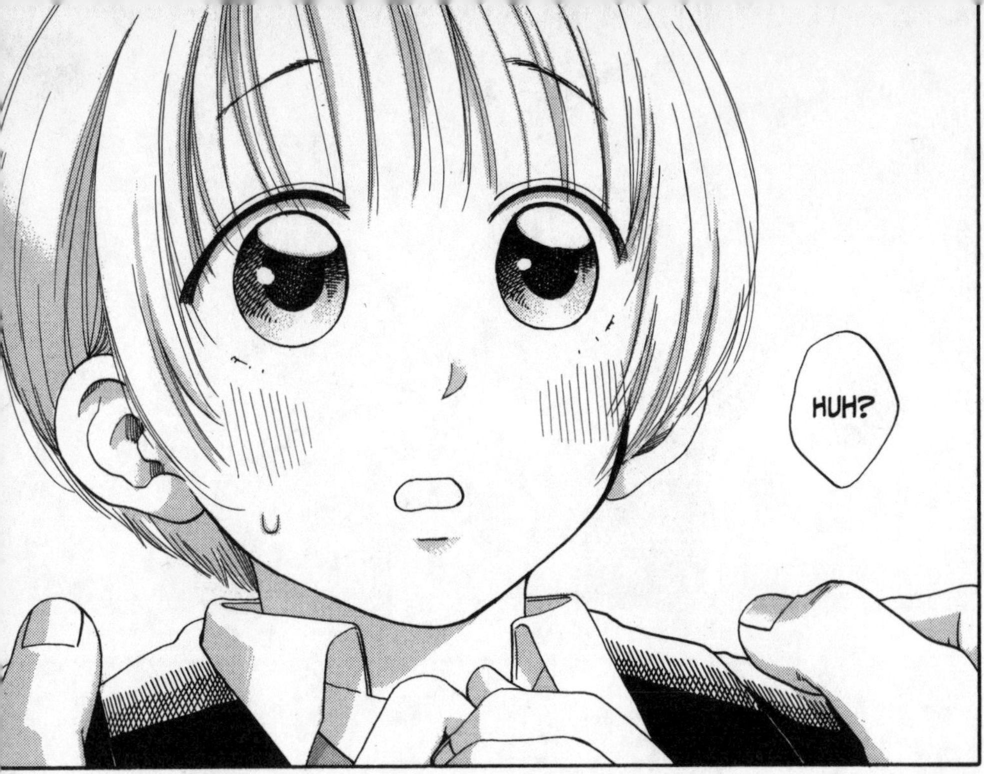
HUH?
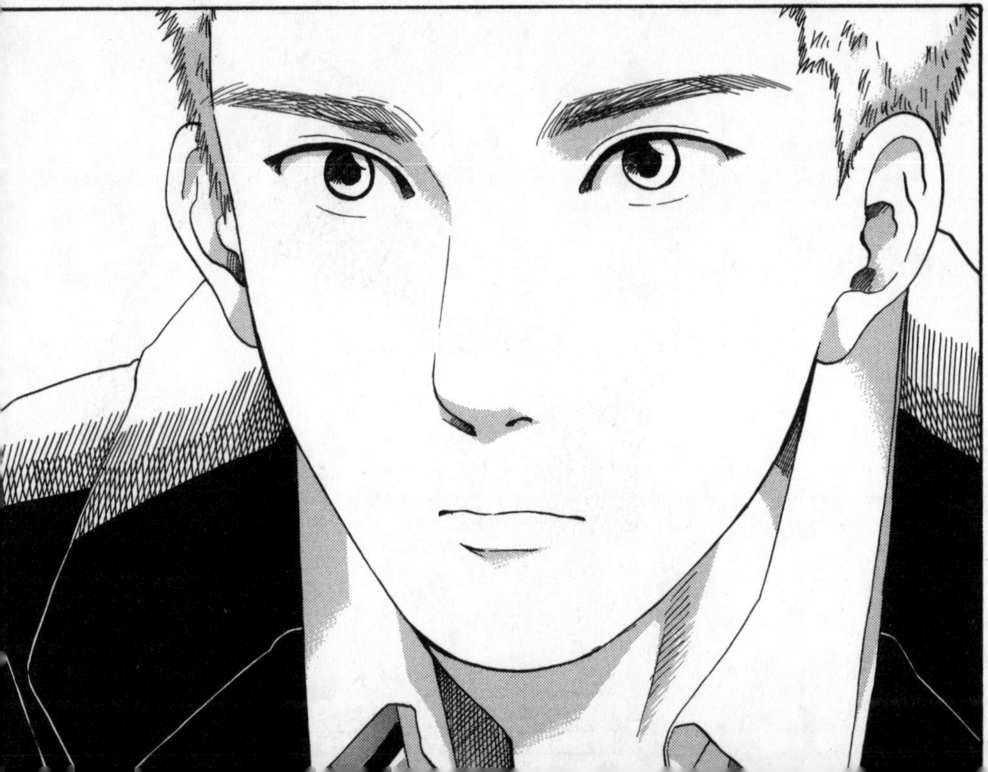

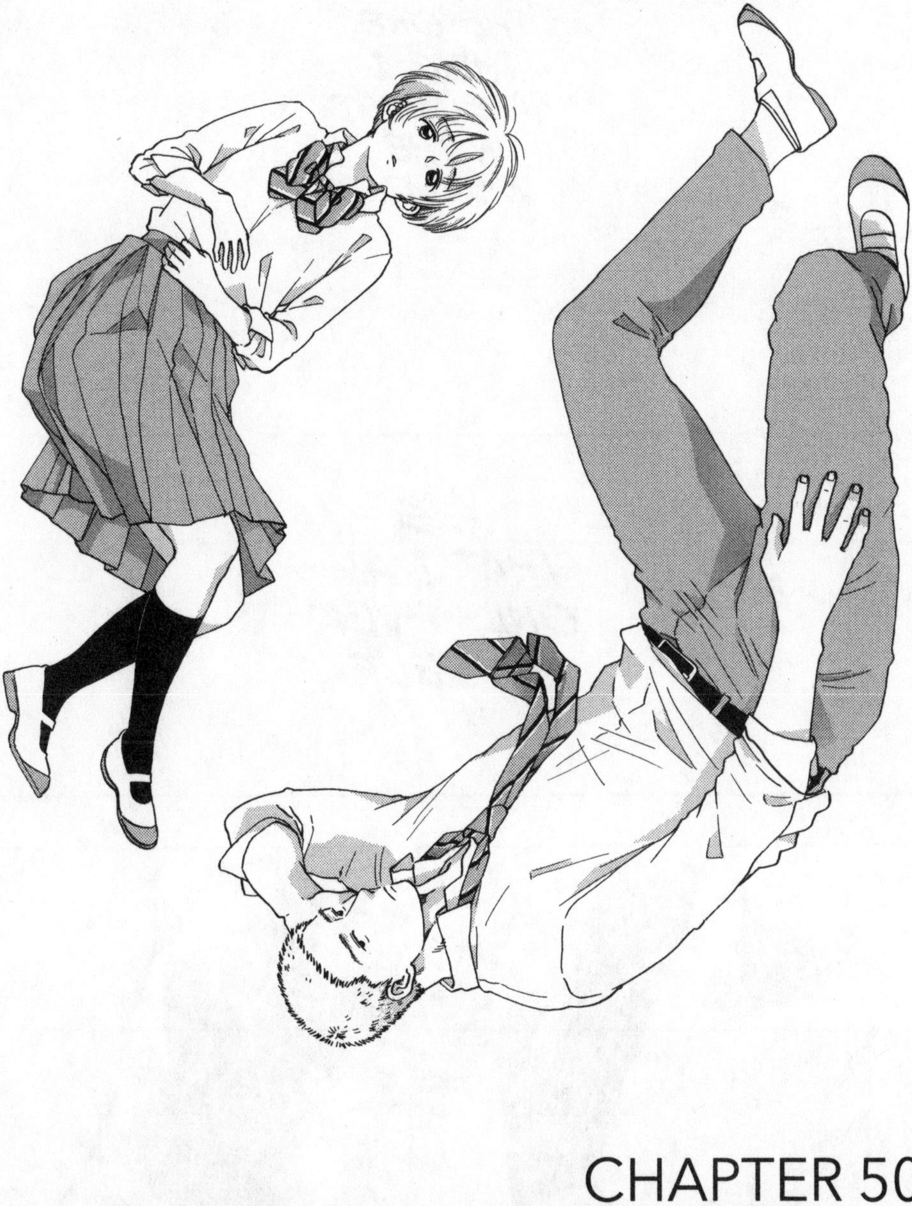

CHAPTER 50

THE ONE
THING I
HATE MOST
IN THE
WORLD...

...IS
THAT I AM
ONLY EVER
MYSELF.

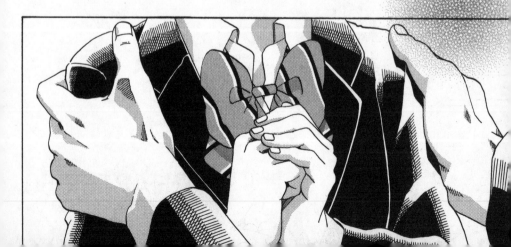

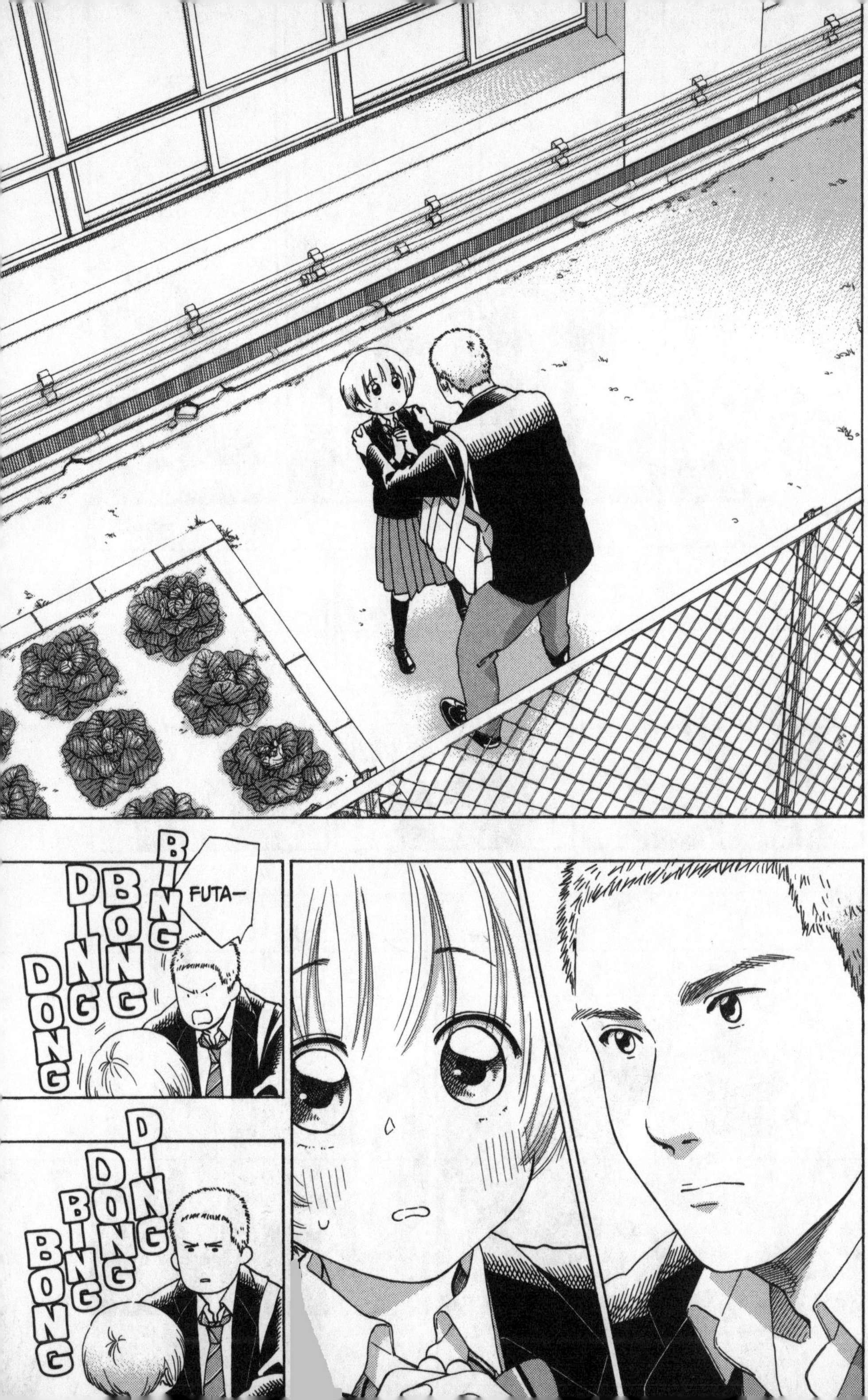
FUTA—
BING BONG DING DONG
DING DONG BING BONG

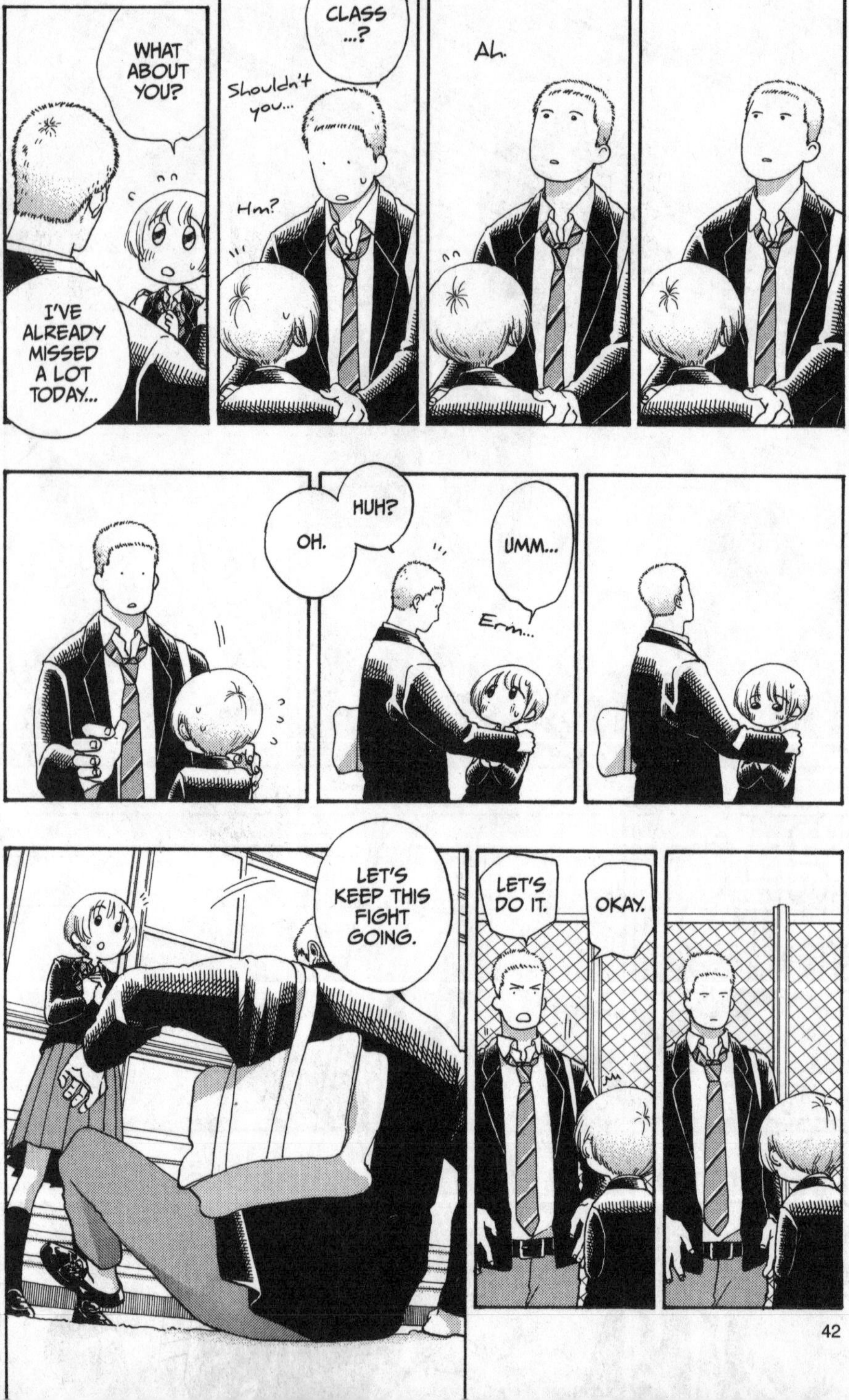
WHAT ABOUT YOU?
I'VE ALREADY MISSED A LOT TODAY...
CLASS ...?
Shouldn't you...
Hm?
Ah.
OH.
HUH?
UMM...
Erm...
LET'S KEEP THIS FIGHT GOING.
LET'S DO IT.
OKAY.

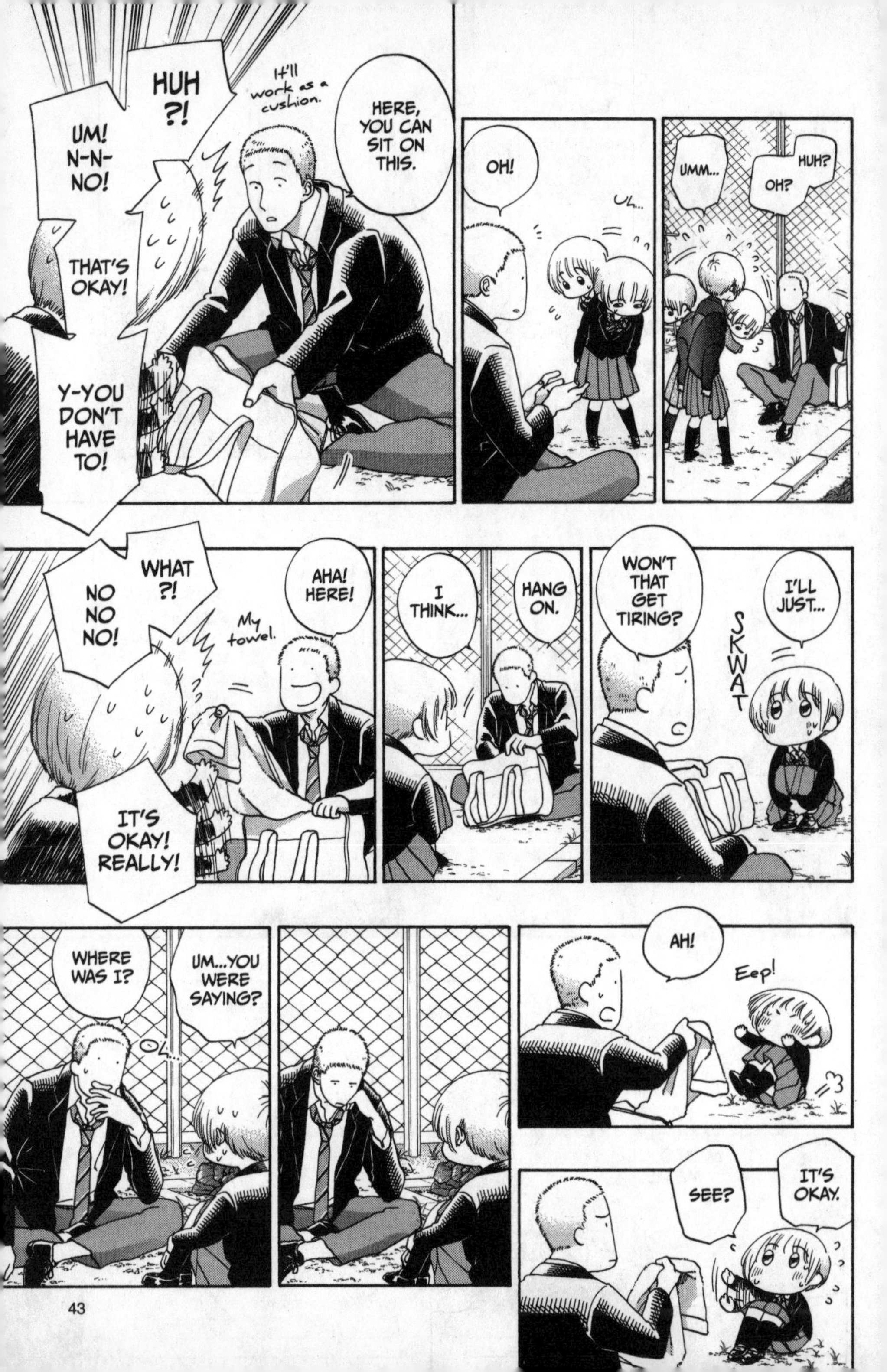
HUH?
OH?
UMM...
OH!
UL...
HERE, YOU CAN SIT ON THIS.
It'll work as a cushion.
HUH ?!
UM! N-N-NO!
THAT'S OKAY!
Y-YOU DON'T HAVE TO!
I'LL JUST...
SKWAT
WON'T THAT GET TIRING?
HANG ON.
I THINK...
AHA! HERE!
My towel.
WHAT ?!
NO NO NO!
IT'S OKAY! REALLY!
AH!
Eep!
IT'S OKAY.
SEE?
UM...YOU WERE SAYING?
WHERE WAS I?

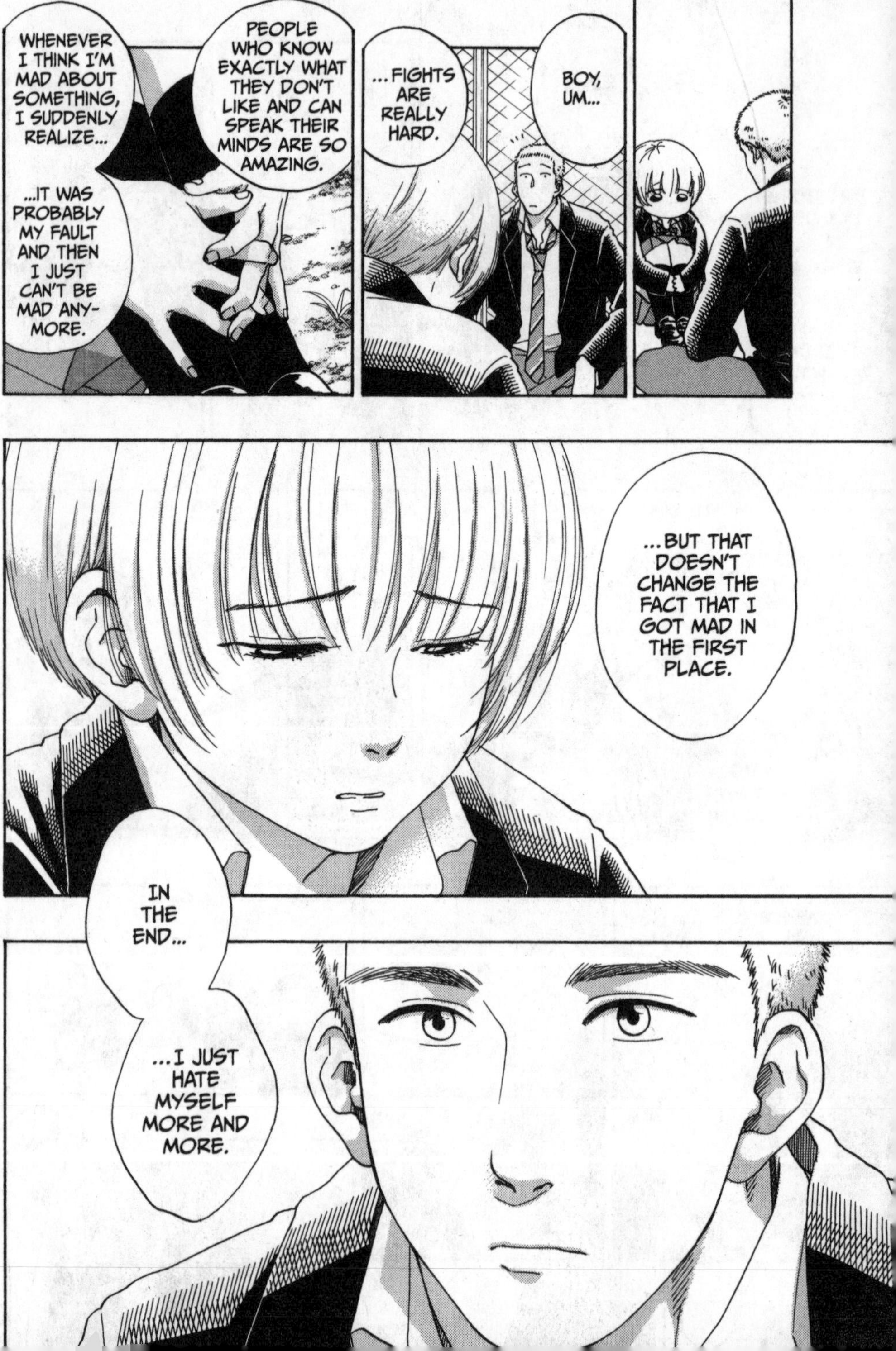
BOY, UM...
...FIGHTS ARE REALLY HARD.
PEOPLE WHO KNOW EXACTLY WHAT THEY DON'T LIKE AND CAN SPEAK THEIR MINDS ARE SO AMAZING.
WHENEVER I THINK I'M MAD ABOUT SOMETHING, I SUDDENLY REALIZE...
...IT WAS PROBABLY MY FAULT AND THEN I JUST CAN'T BE MAD ANYMORE.
...BUT THAT DOESN'T CHANGE THE FACT THAT I GOT MAD IN THE FIRST PLACE.
IN THE END...
...I JUST HATE MYSELF MORE AND MORE.

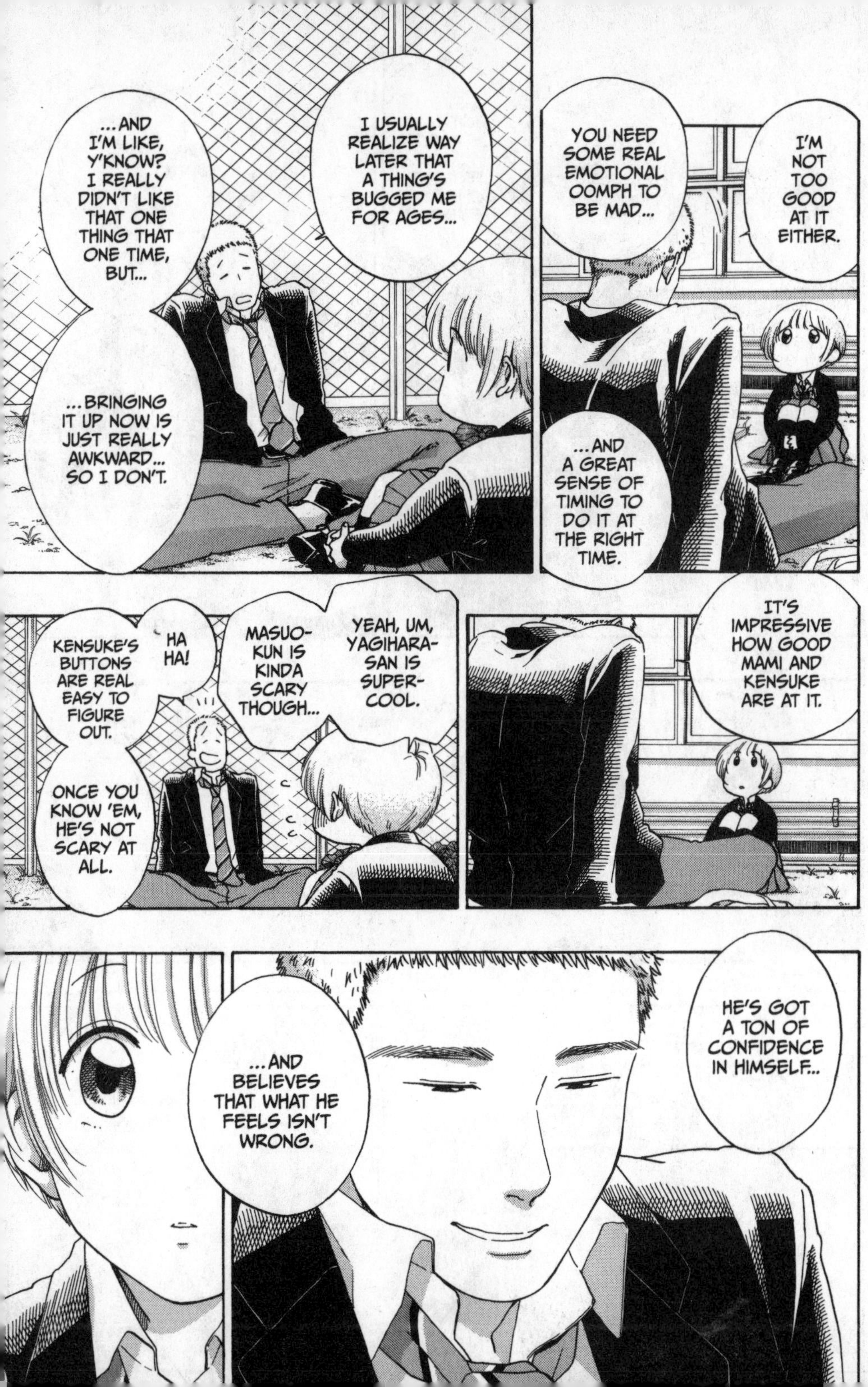
I'M NOT TOO GOOD AT IT EITHER.
YOU NEED SOME REAL EMOTIONAL OOMPH TO BE MAD...
...AND A GREAT SENSE OF TIMING TO DO IT AT THE RIGHT TIME.
I USUALLY REALIZE WAY LATER THAT A THING'S BUGGED ME FOR AGES...
...AND I'M LIKE, Y'KNOW? I REALLY DIDN'T LIKE THAT ONE THING THAT ONE TIME, BUT...
...BRINGING IT UP NOW IS JUST REALLY AWKWARD... SO I DON'T.
IT'S IMPRESSIVE HOW GOOD MAMI AND KENSUKE ARE AT IT.
YEAH, UM, YAGIHARA-SAN IS SUPER-COOL.
MASUO-KUN IS KINDA SCARY THOUGH...
HA HA!
KENSUKE'S BUTTONS ARE REAL EASY TO FIGURE OUT.
ONCE YOU KNOW 'EM, HE'S NOT SCARY AT ALL.
HE'S GOT A TON OF CONFIDENCE IN HIMSELF...
...AND BELIEVES THAT WHAT HE FEELS ISN'T WRONG.

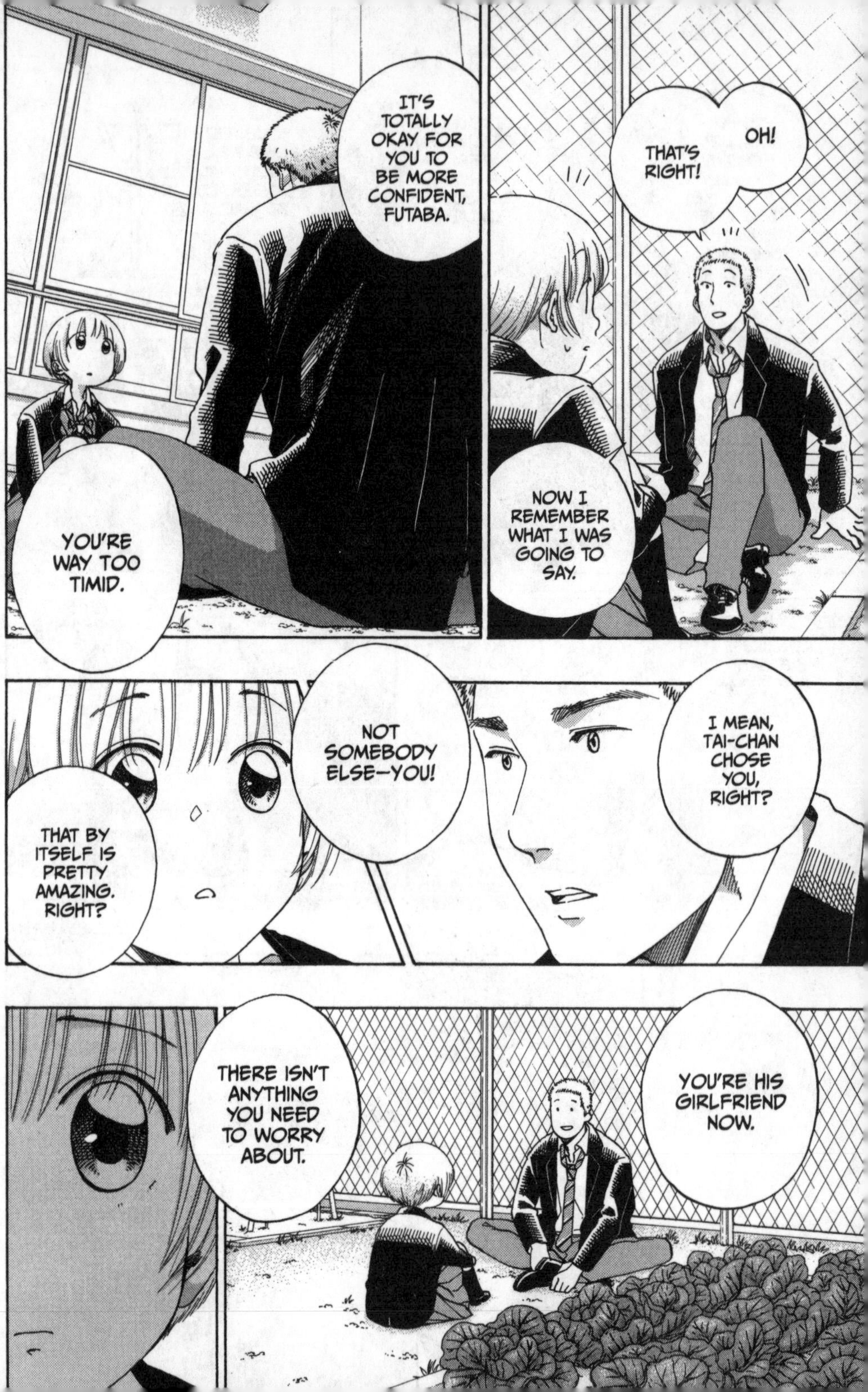
OH!
THAT'S RIGHT!
NOW I REMEMBER WHAT I WAS GOING TO SAY.
IT'S TOTALLY OKAY FOR YOU TO BE MORE CONFIDENT, FUTABA.
YOU'RE WAY TOO TIMID.
I MEAN, TAI-CHAN CHOSE YOU, RIGHT?
NOT SOMEBODY ELSE—YOU!
THAT BY ITSELF IS PRETTY AMAZING. RIGHT?
YOU'RE HIS GIRLFRIEND NOW.
THERE ISN'T ANYTHING YOU NEED TO WORRY ABOUT.

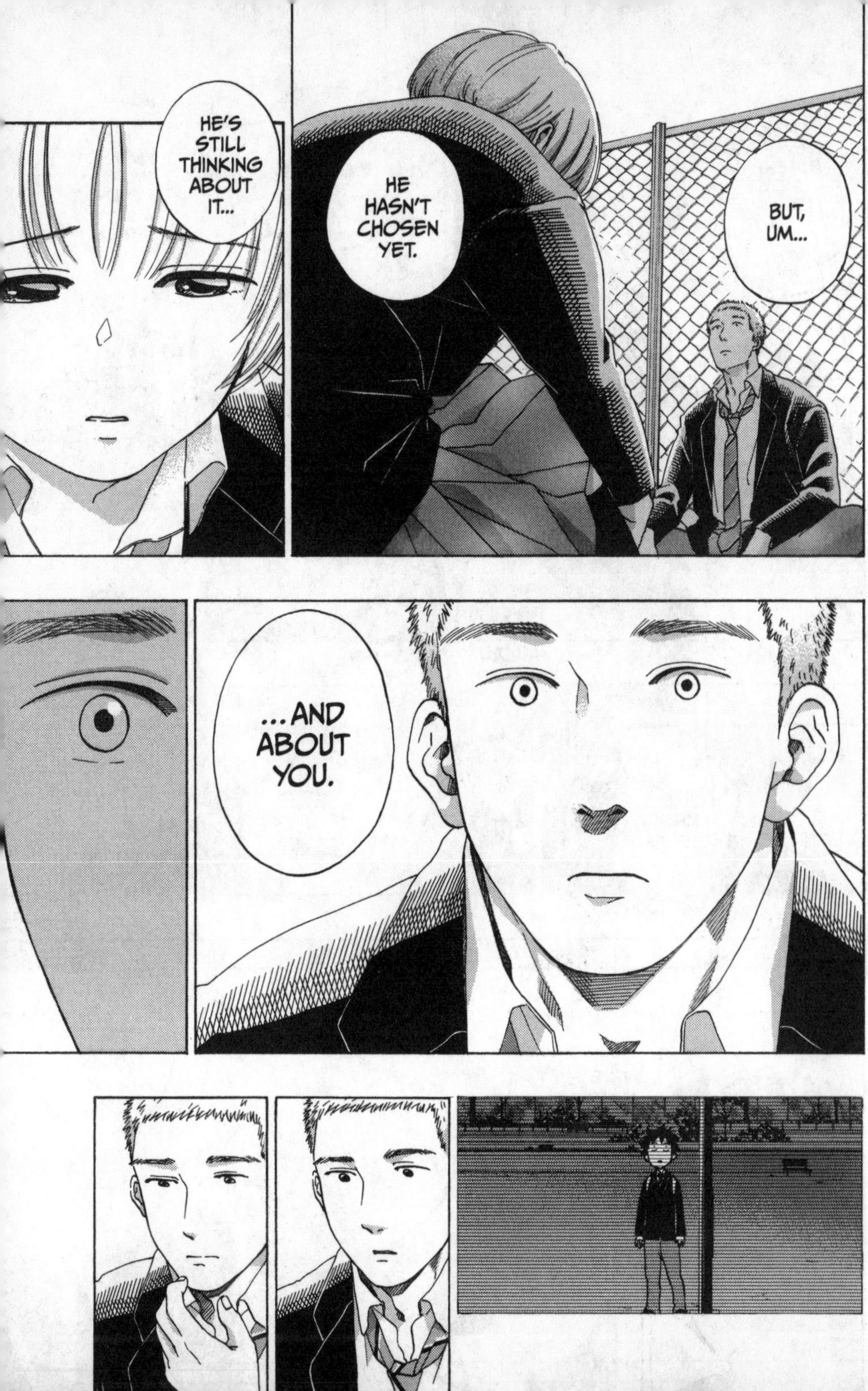
BUT, UM...
HE HASN'T CHOSEN YET.
HE'S STILL THINKING ABOUT IT...
...AND ABOUT YOU.

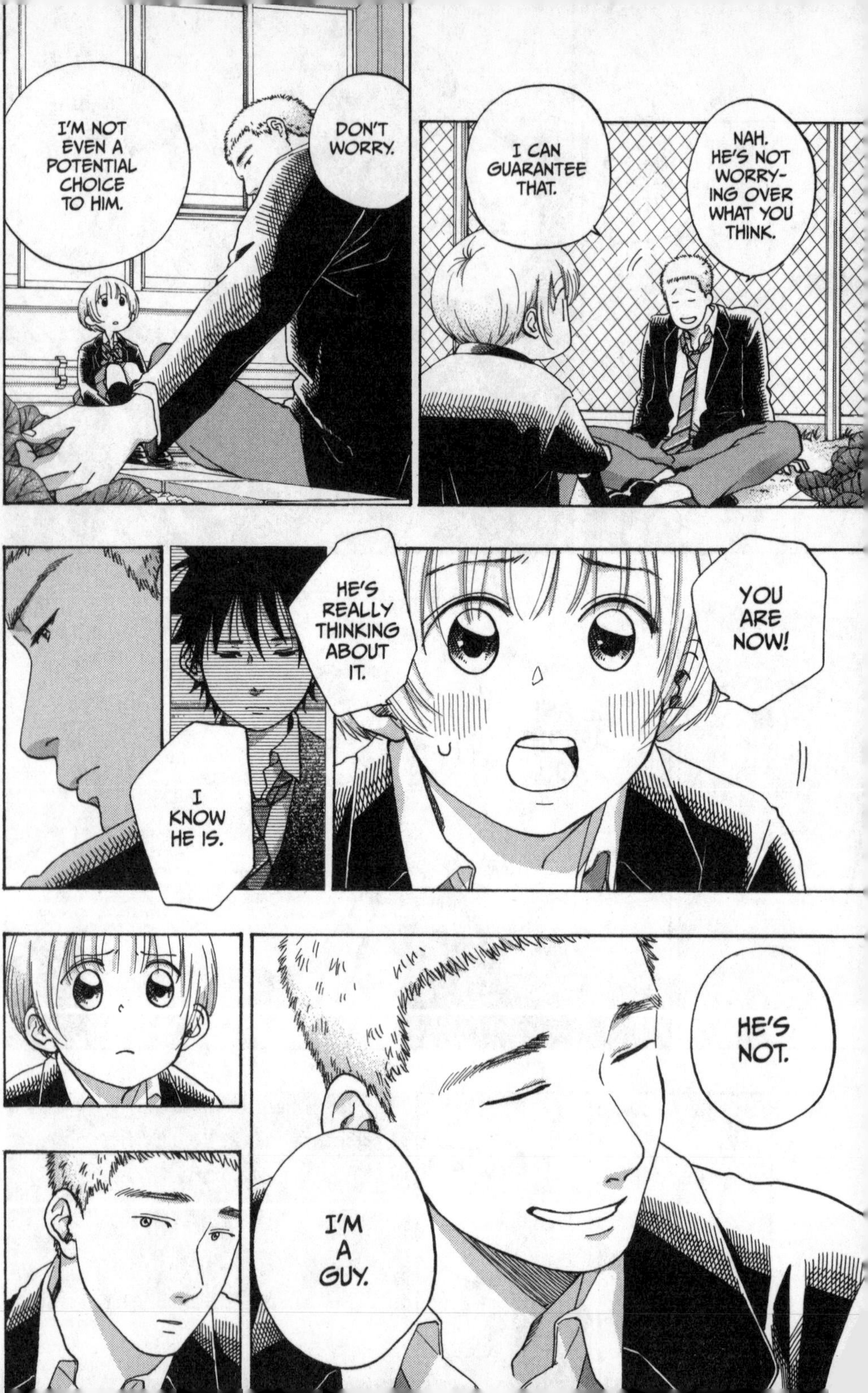
NAH. HE'S NOT WORRY-ING OVER WHAT YOU THINK.
I CAN GUARANTEE THAT.
DON'T WORRY.
I'M NOT EVEN A POTENTIAL CHOICE TO HIM.
YOU ARE NOW!
HE'S REALLY THINKING ABOUT IT.
I KNOW HE IS.
HE'S NOT.
I'M A GUY.

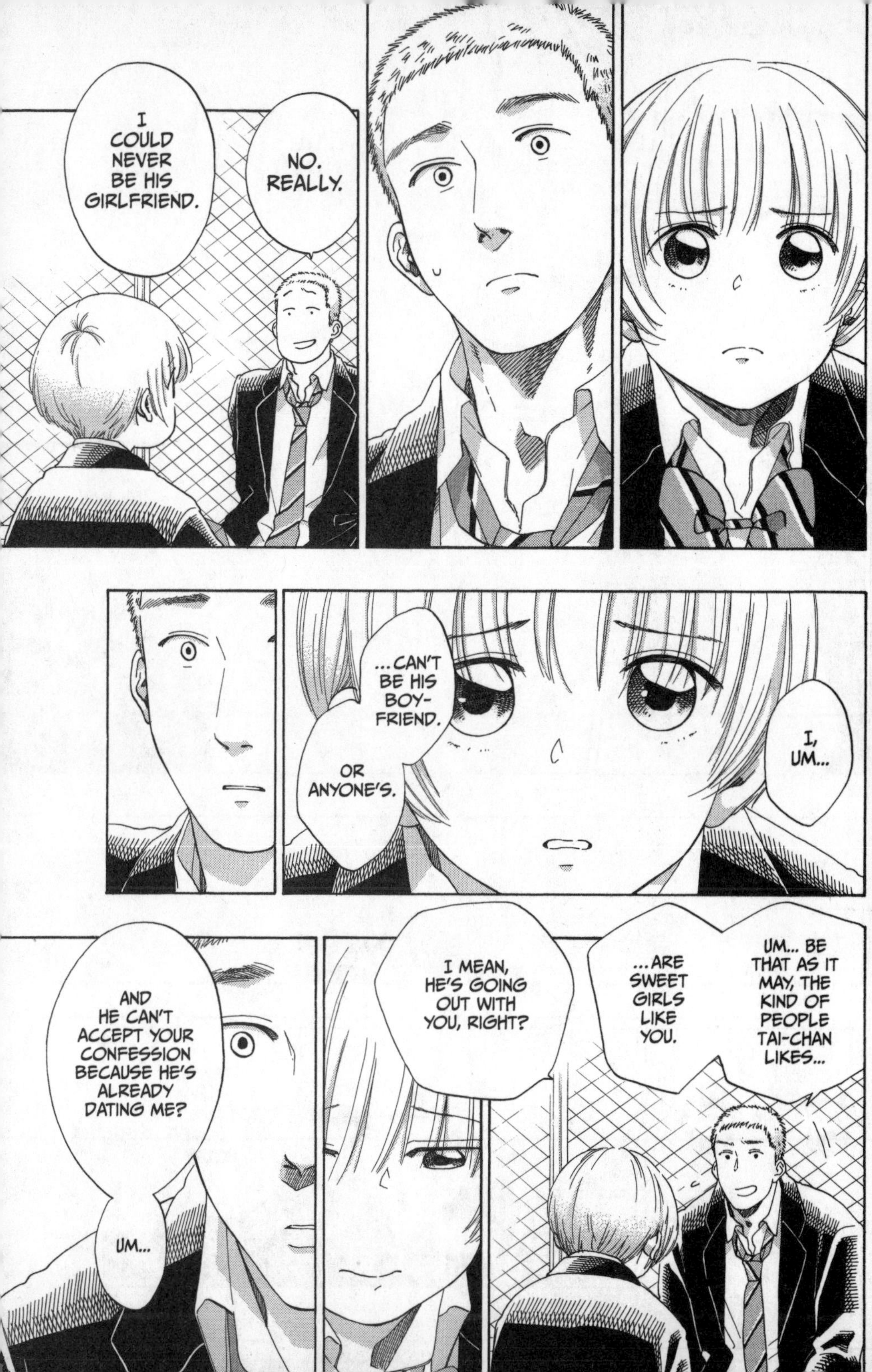
NO. REALLY.
I COULD NEVER BE HIS GIRLFRIEND.
I, UM...
...CAN'T BE HIS BOY-FRIEND.
OR ANYONE'S.
UM... BE THAT AS IT MAY, THE KIND OF PEOPLE TAI-CHAN LIKES...
...ARE SWEET GIRLS LIKE YOU.
I MEAN, HE'S GOING OUT WITH YOU, RIGHT?
AND HE CAN'T ACCEPT YOUR CONFESSION BECAUSE HE'S ALREADY DATING ME?
UM...

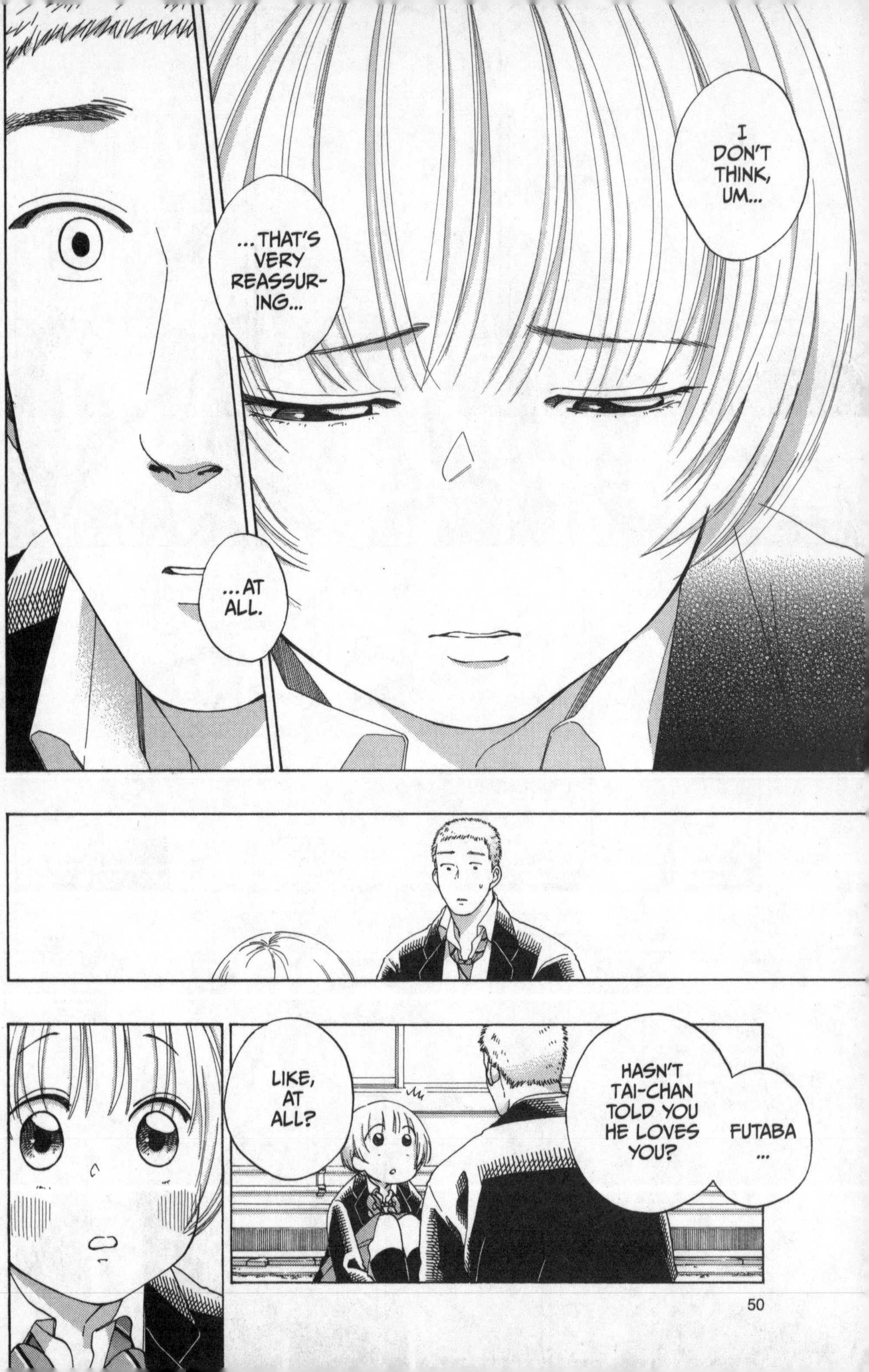
I DON'T THINK, UM...
...THAT'S VERY REASSURING...
...AT ALL.
FUTABA ...
HASN'T TAI-CHAN TOLD YOU HE LOVES YOU?
LIKE, AT ALL?

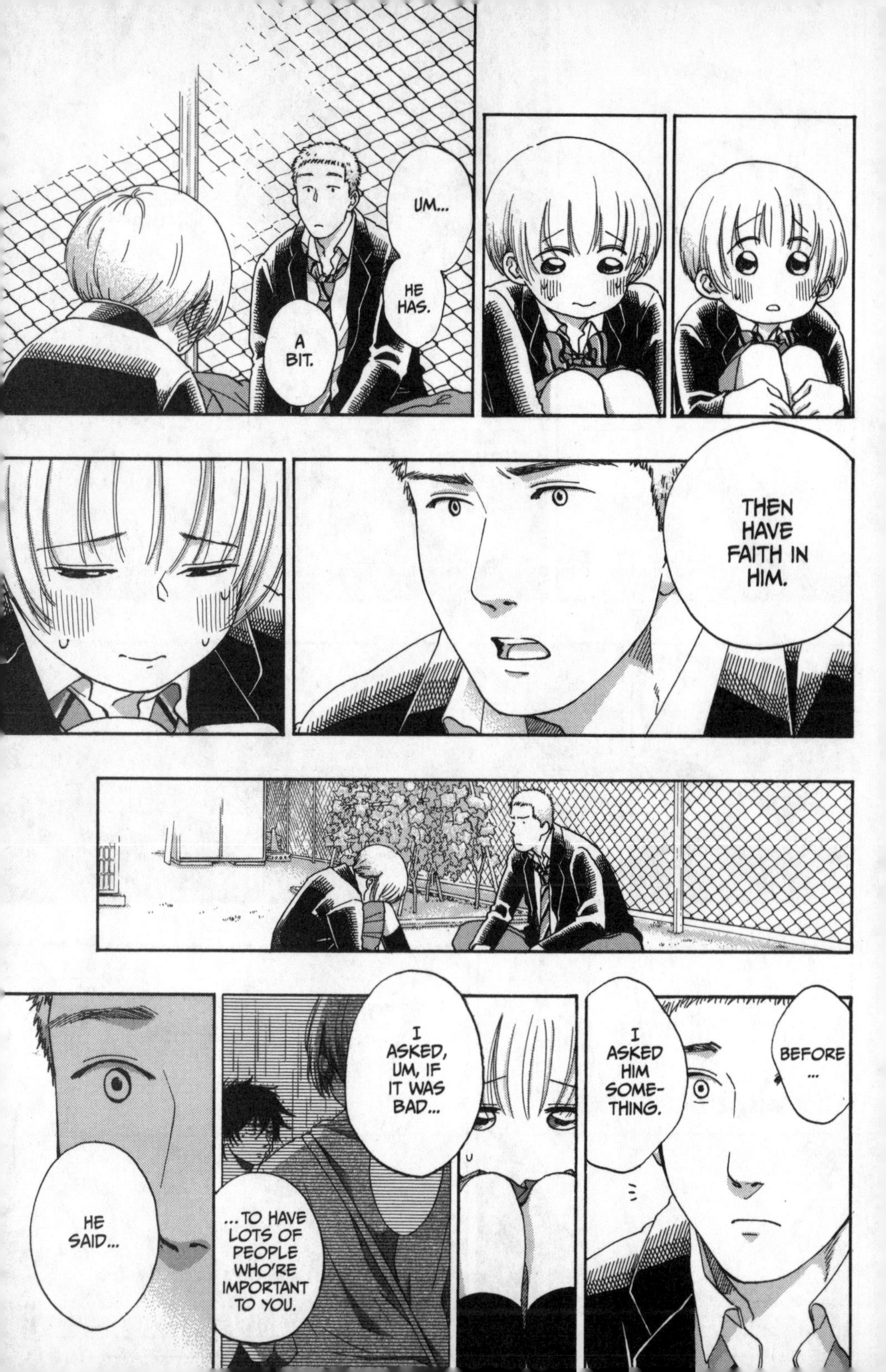
UM...
HE HAS.
A BIT.
THEN HAVE FAITH IN HIM.
BEFORE...
I ASKED HIM SOMETHING.
I ASKED, UM, IF IT WAS BAD...
...TO HAVE LOTS OF PEOPLE WHO'RE IMPORTANT TO YOU.
HE SAID...

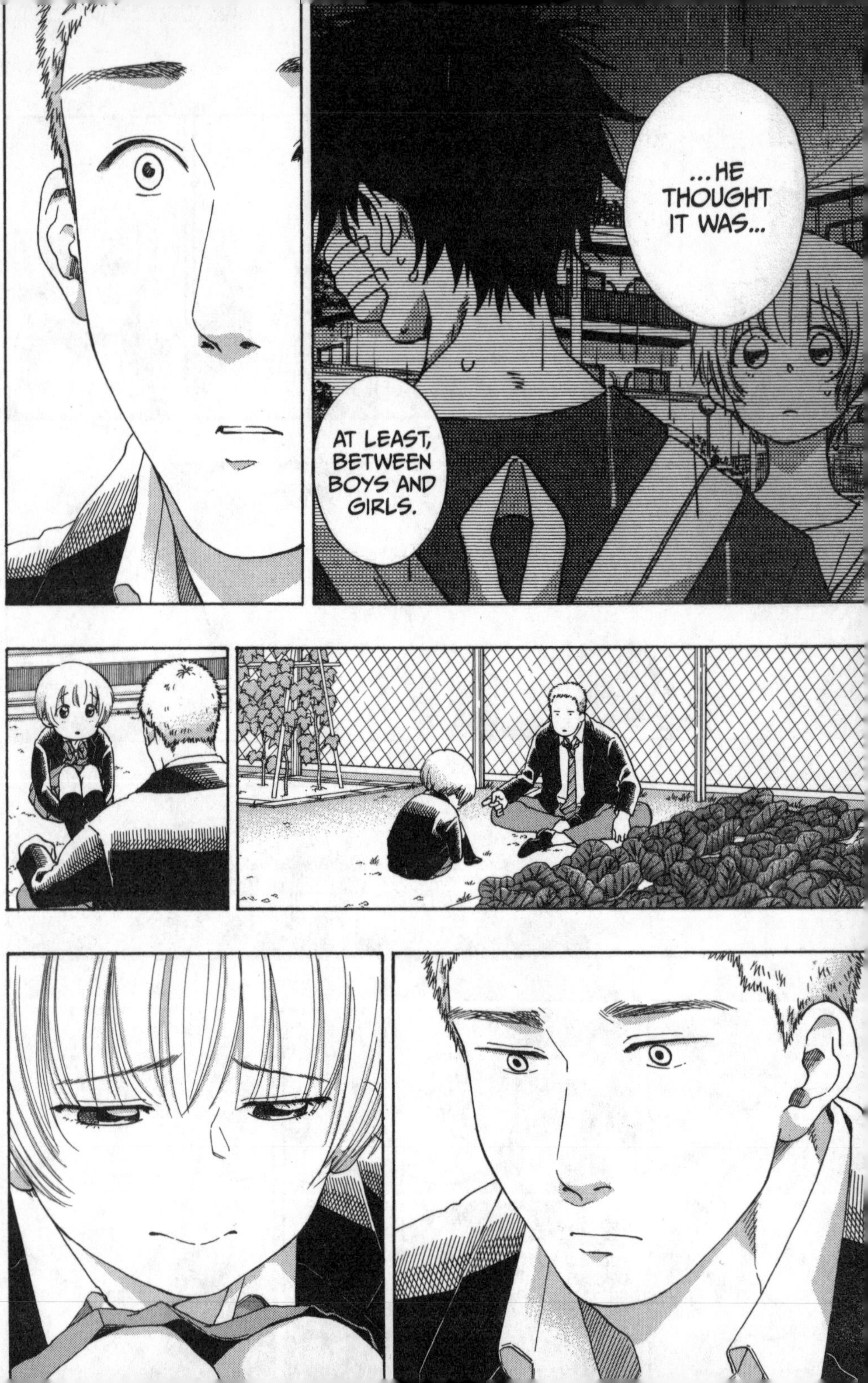
...HE THOUGHT IT WAS...
AT LEAST, BETWEEN BOYS AND GIRLS.

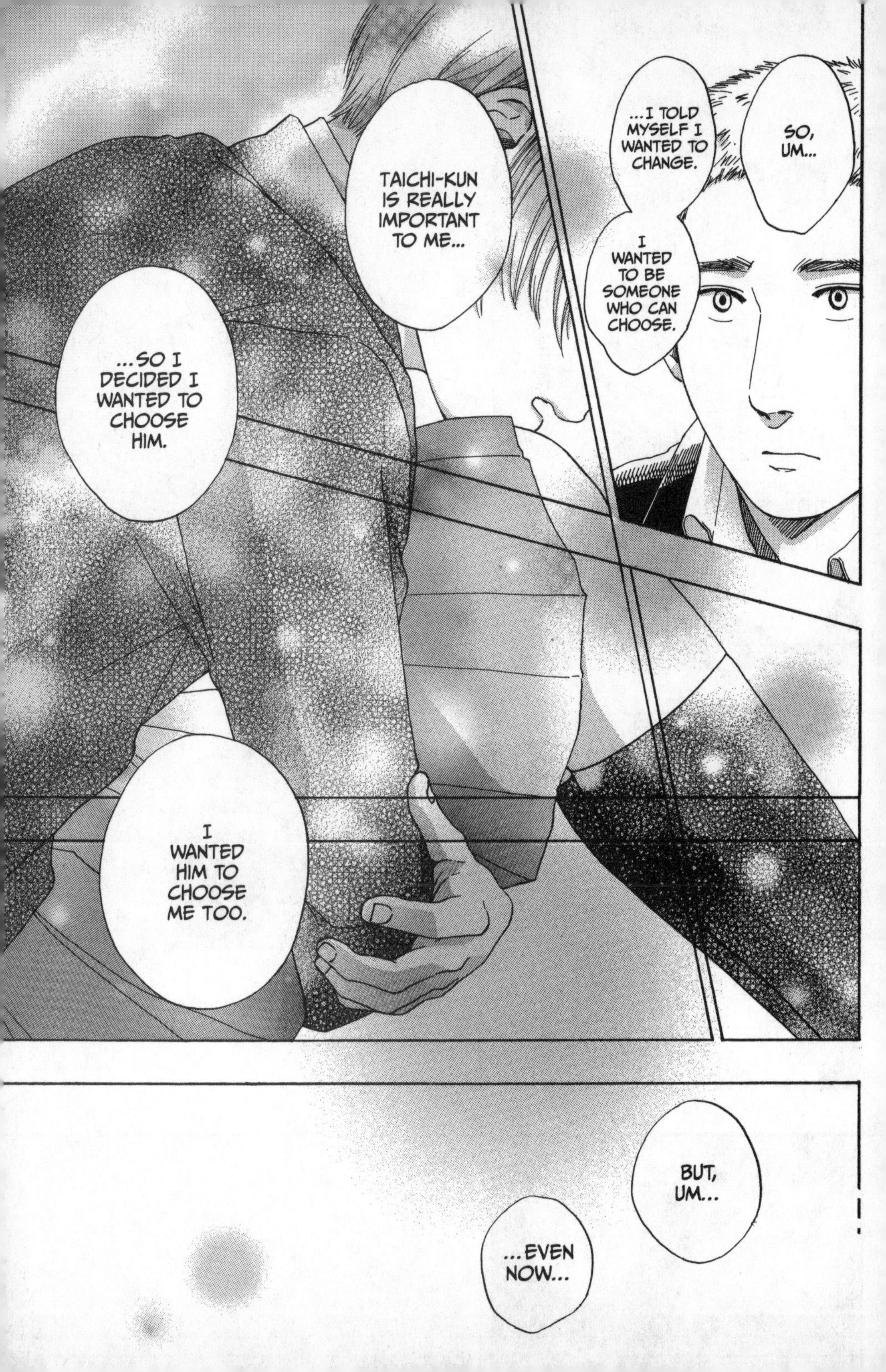
SO, UM...
...I TOLD MYSELF I WANTED TO CHANGE.
I WANTED TO BE SOMEONE WHO CAN CHOOSE.
TAICHI-KUN IS REALLY IMPORTANT TO ME...
...SO I DECIDED I WANTED TO CHOOSE HIM.
I WANTED HIM TO CHOOSE ME TOO.
BUT, UM...
...EVEN NOW...

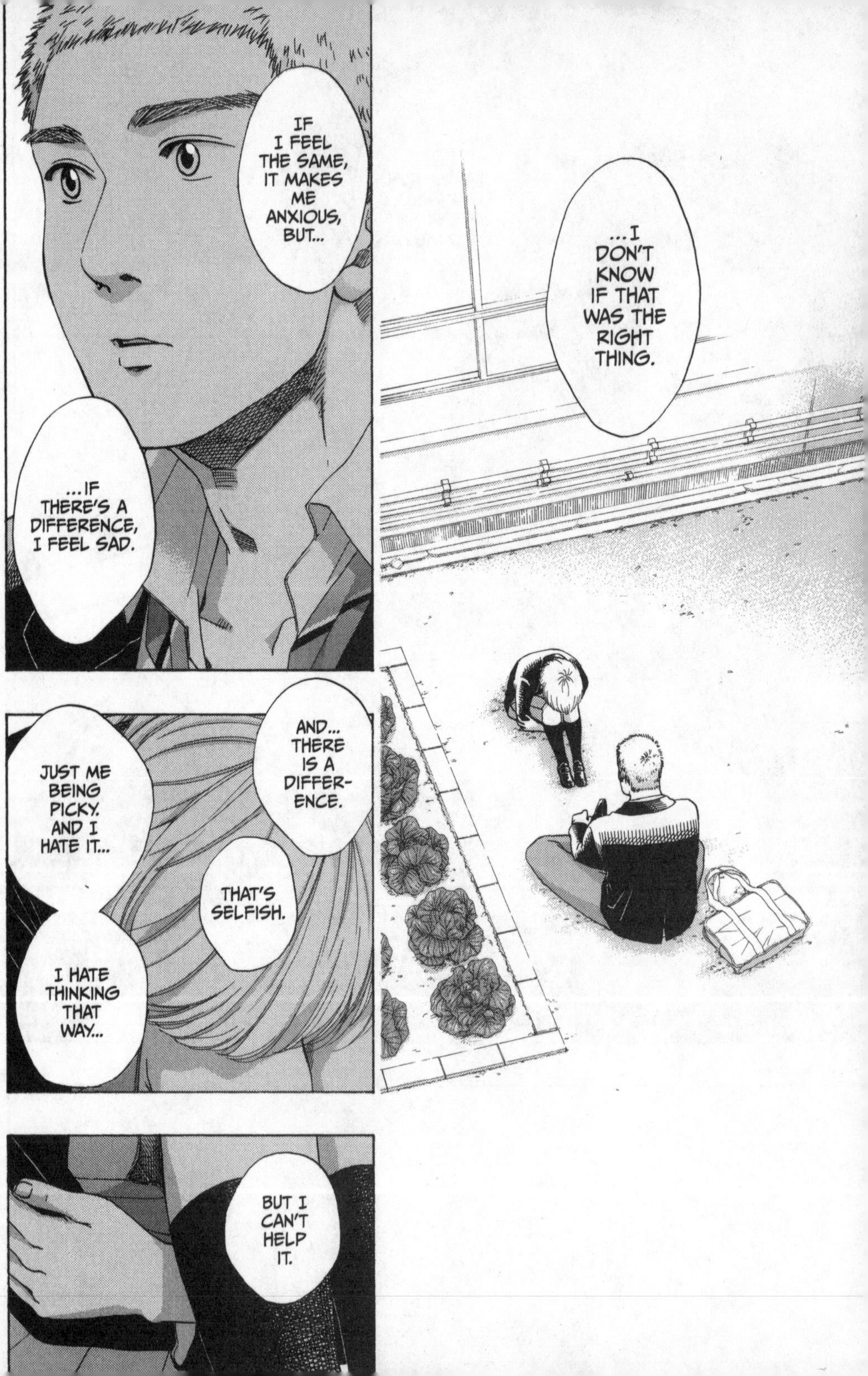
...I DON'T KNOW IF THAT WAS THE RIGHT THING.
IF I FEEL THE SAME, IT MAKES ME ANXIOUS, BUT...
...IF THERE'S A DIFFERENCE, I FEEL SAD.
AND... THERE IS A DIFFER-ENCE.
JUST ME BEING PICKY. AND I HATE IT...
THAT'S SELFISH.
I HATE THINKING THAT WAY...
BUT I CAN'T HELP IT.

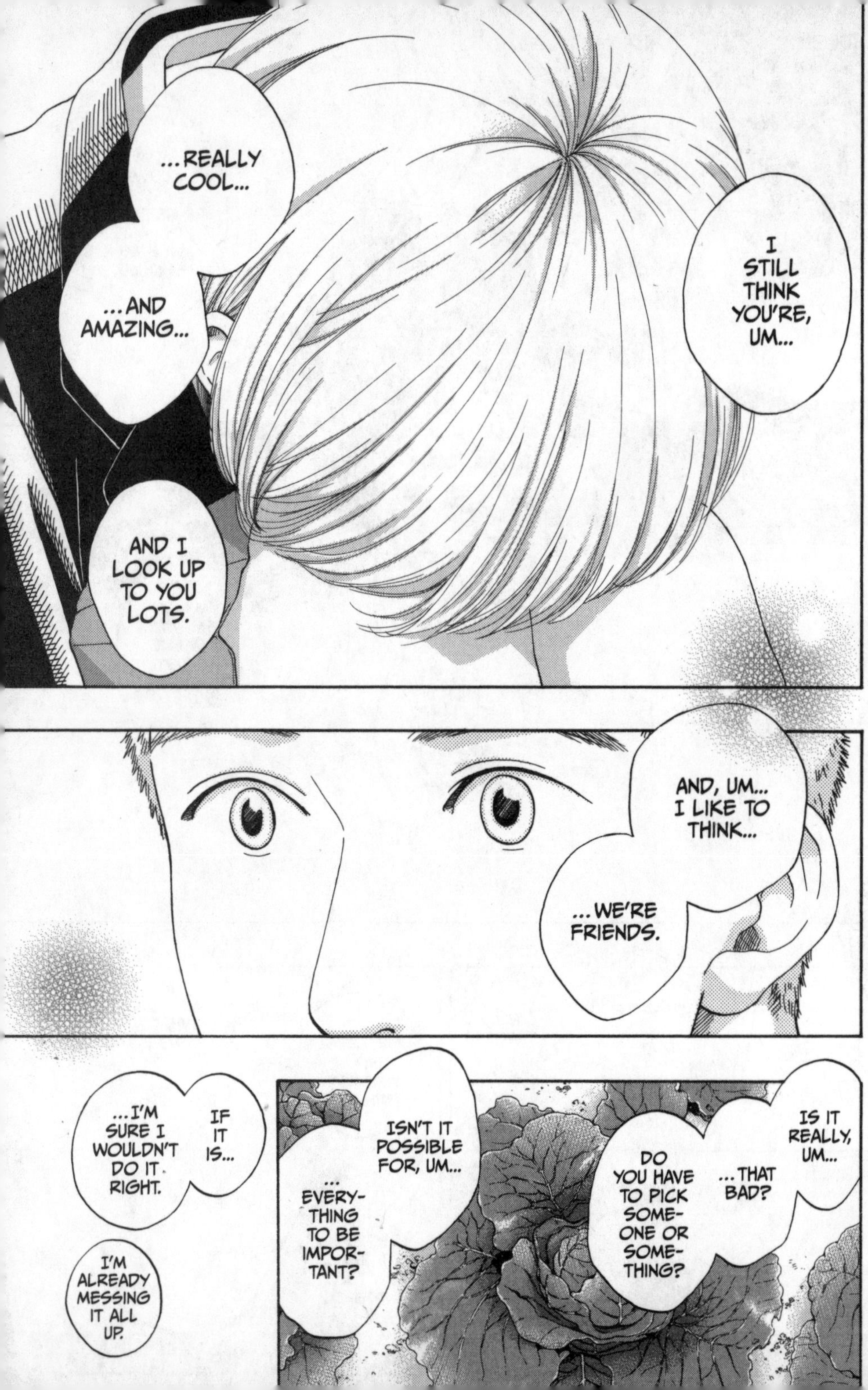
I STILL THINK YOU'RE, UM...
...REALLY COOL...
...AND AMAZING...
AND I LOOK UP TO YOU LOTS.
AND, UM... I LIKE TO THINK...
...WE'RE FRIENDS.
IS IT REALLY, UM...
...THAT BAD?
DO YOU HAVE TO PICK SOME-ONE OR SOME-THING?
ISN'T IT POSSIBLE FOR, UM...
...EVERY-THING TO BE IMPOR-TANT?
IF IT IS...
...I'M SURE I WOULDN'T DO IT RIGHT.
I'M ALREADY MESSING IT ALL UP.

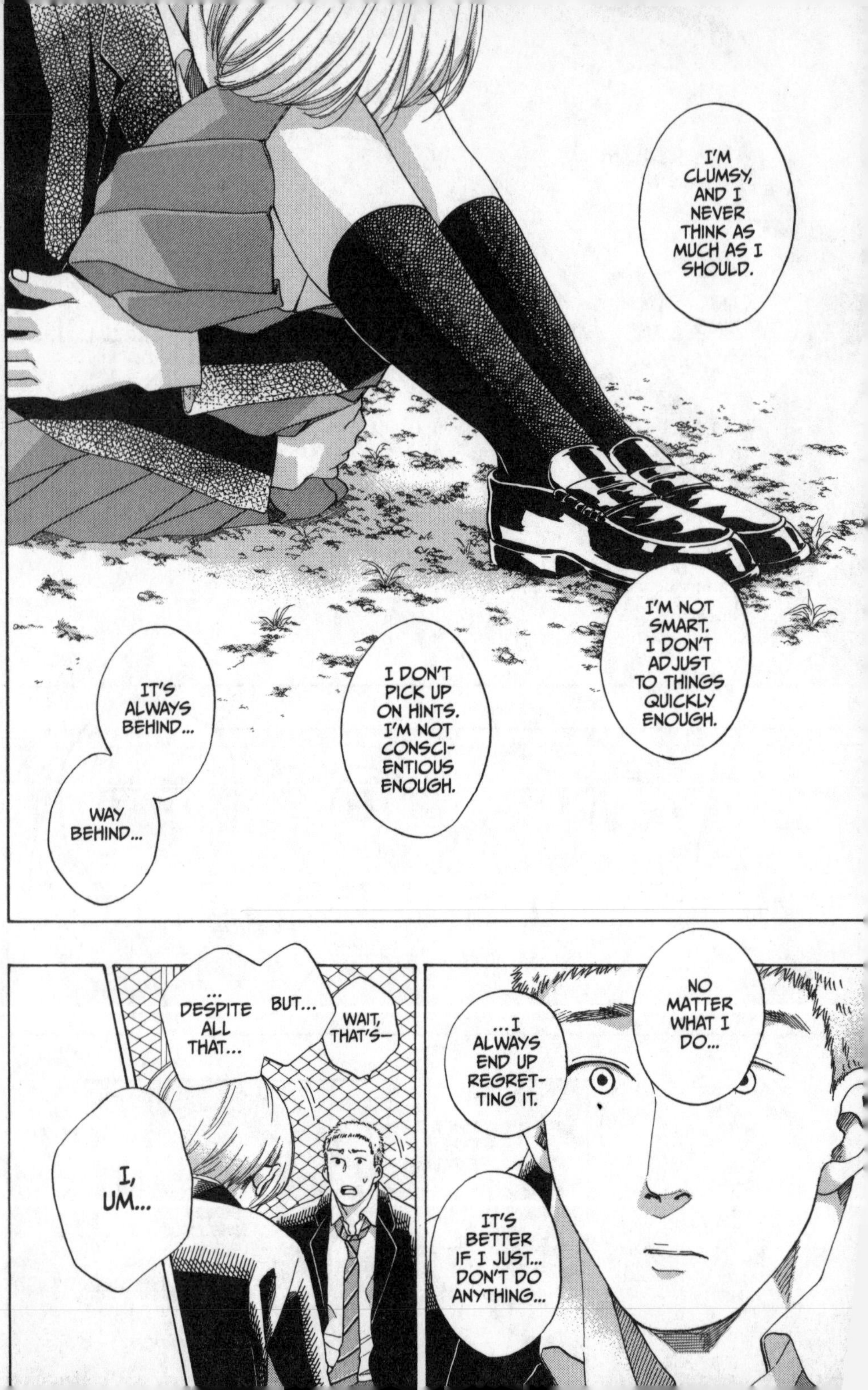
I'M CLUMSY, AND I NEVER THINK AS MUCH AS I SHOULD.
I'M NOT SMART. I DON'T ADJUST TO THINGS QUICKLY ENOUGH.
I DON'T PICK UP ON HINTS. I'M NOT CONSCI-ENTIOUS ENOUGH.
IT'S ALWAYS BEHIND...
WAY BEHIND...
NO MATTER WHAT I DO...
...I ALWAYS END UP REGRET-TING IT.
IT'S BETTER IF I JUST... DON'T DO ANYTHING...
WAIT, THAT'S—
BUT...
...DESPITE ALL THAT...
I, UM...

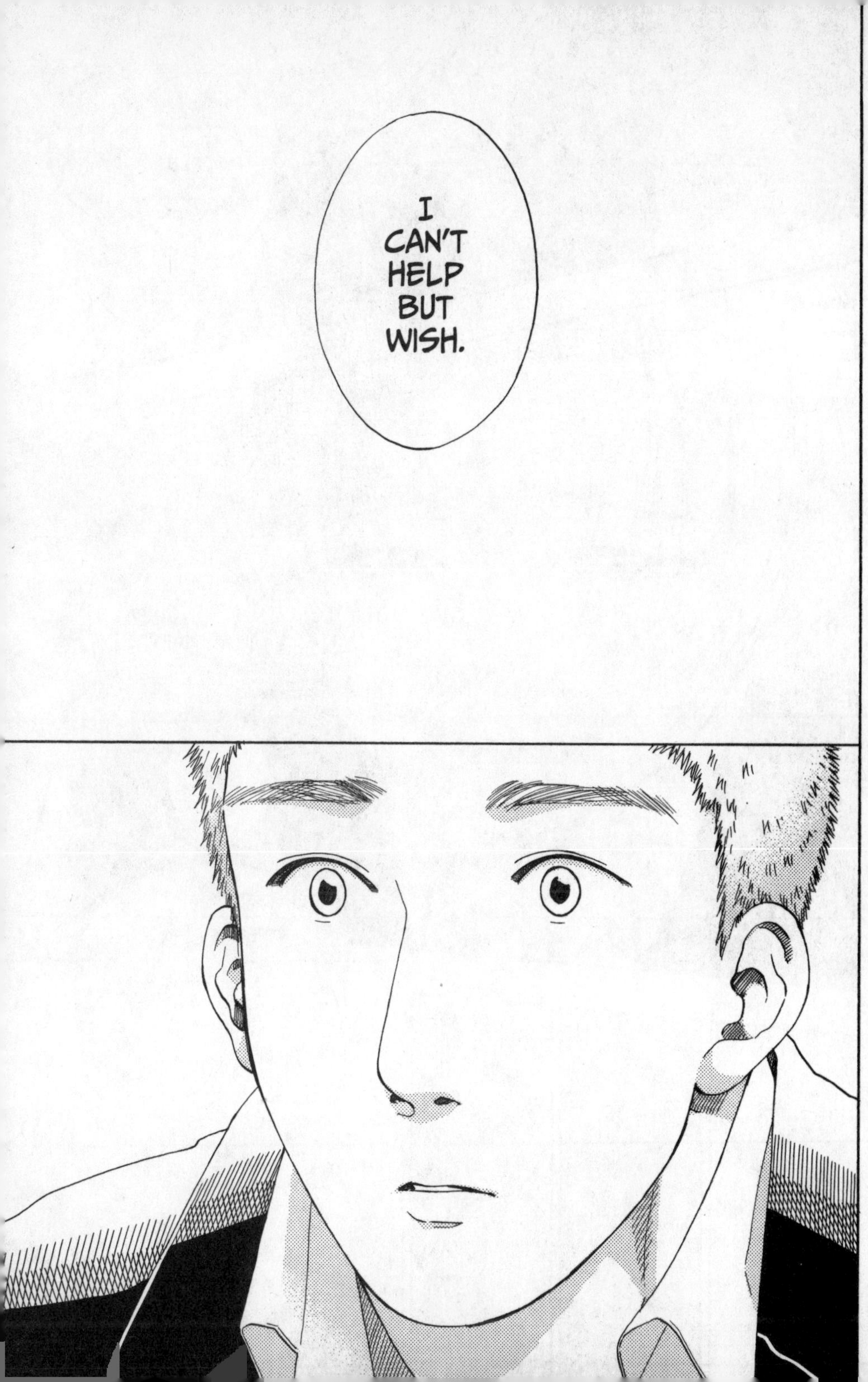
I CAN'T HELP BUT WISH.

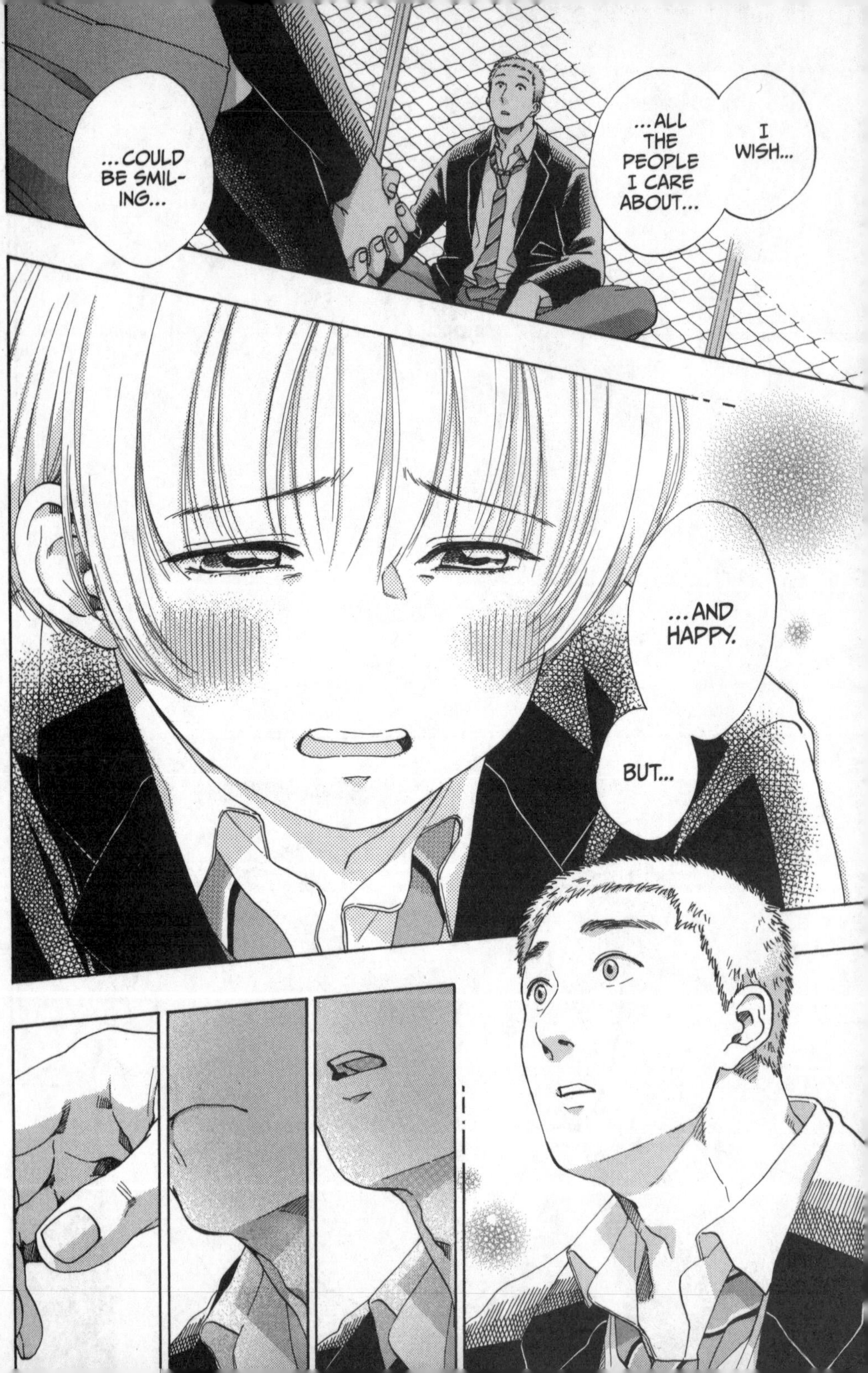
I WISH...
...ALL THE PEOPLE I CARE ABOUT...
...COULD BE SMIL-ING...
...AND HAPPY.
BUT...

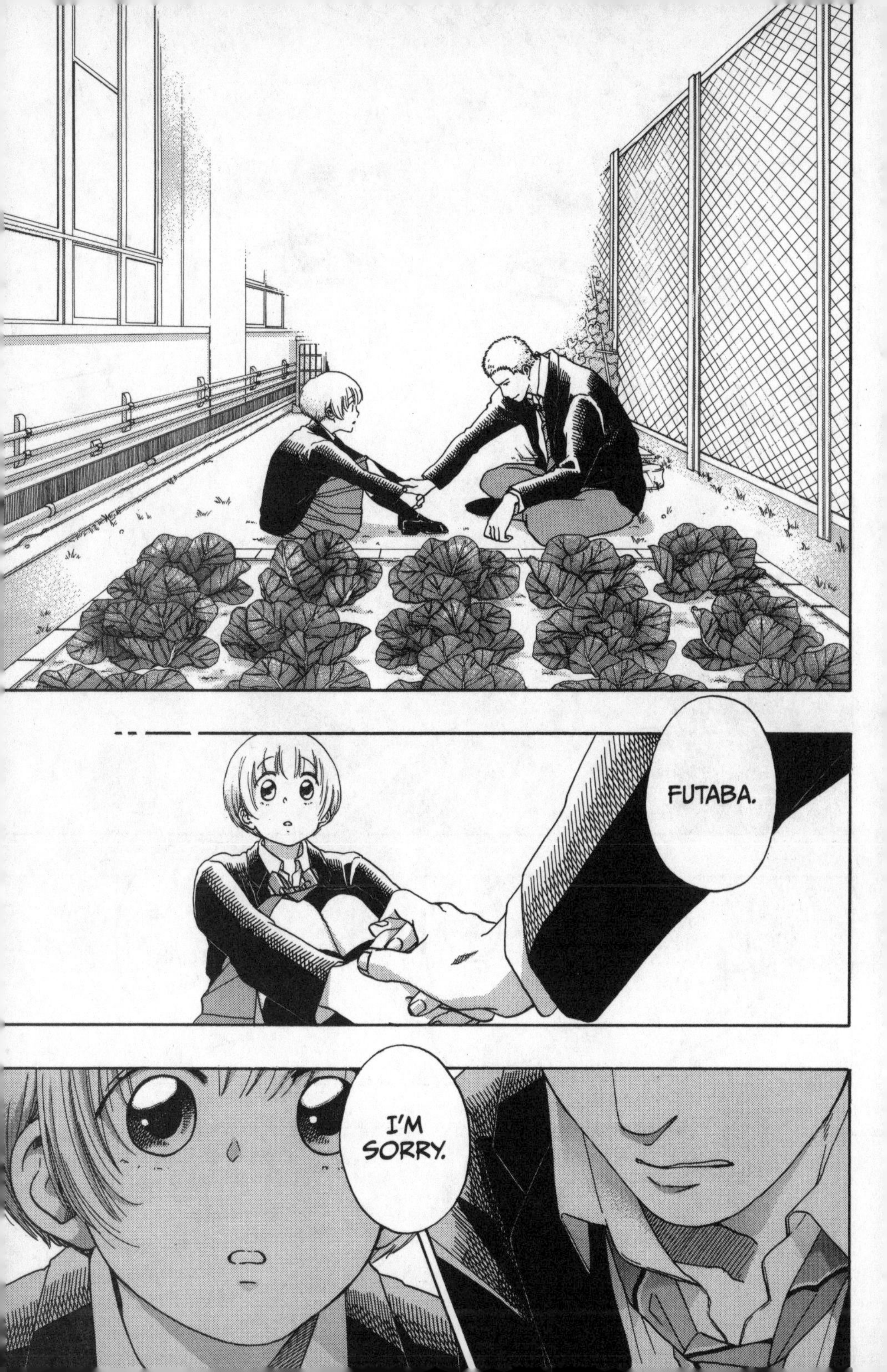
FUTABA.
I'M SORRY.

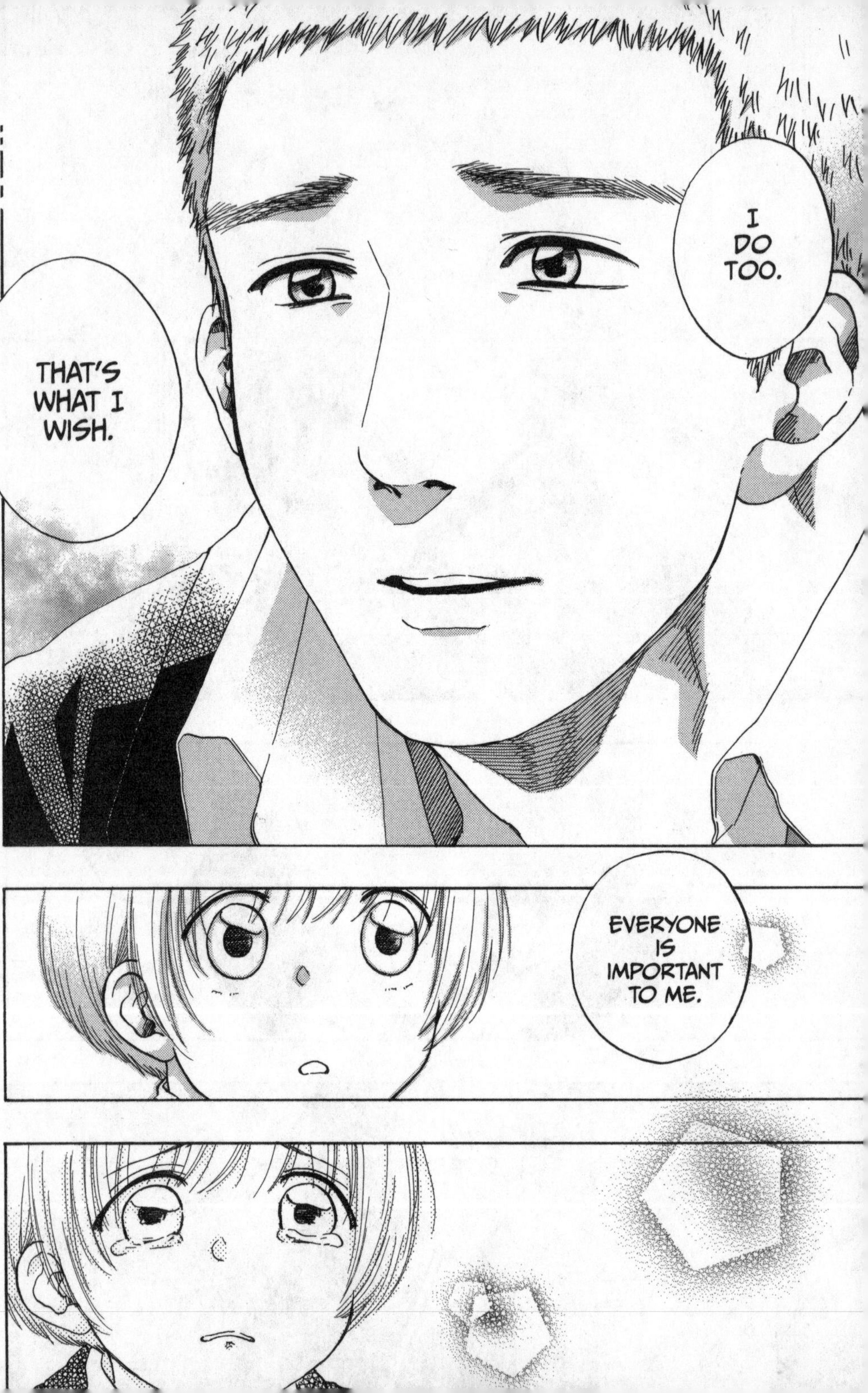
I DO TOO.
THAT'S WHAT I WISH.
EVERYONE IS IMPORTANT TO ME.

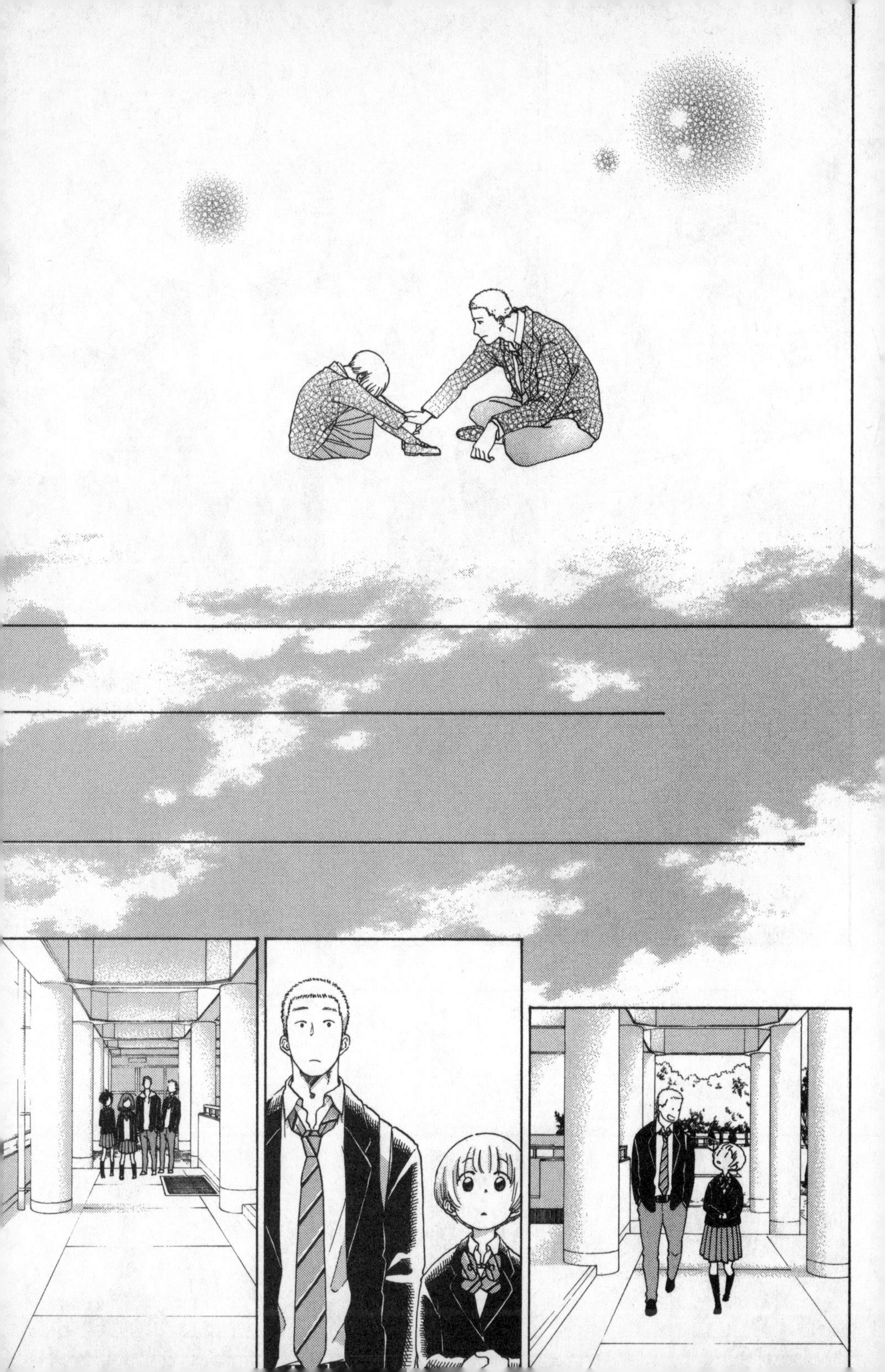

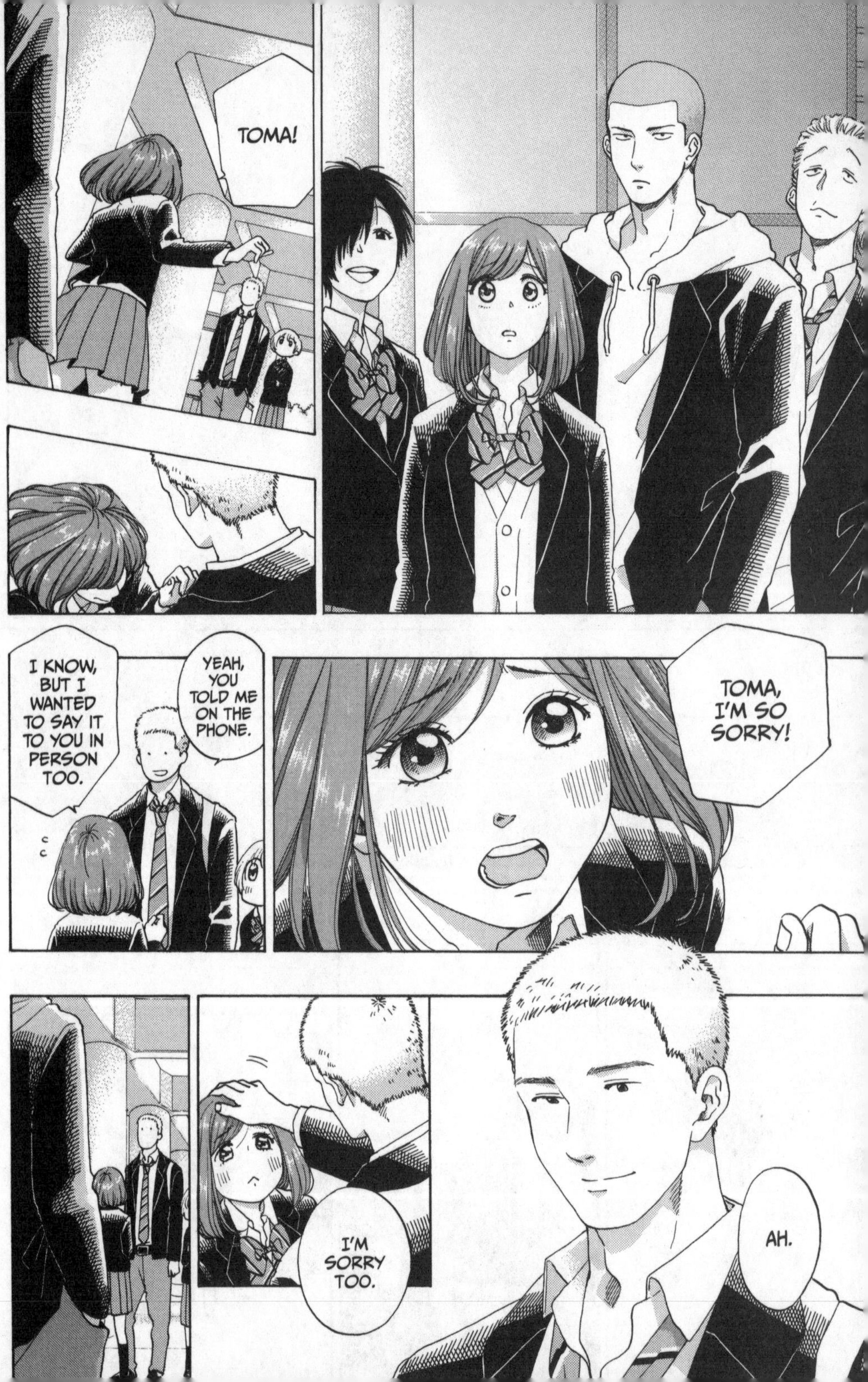
TOMA!
TOMA, I'M SO SORRY!
YEAH, YOU TOLD ME ON THE PHONE.
I KNOW, BUT I WANTED TO SAY IT TO YOU IN PERSON TOO.
AH.
I'M SORRY TOO.

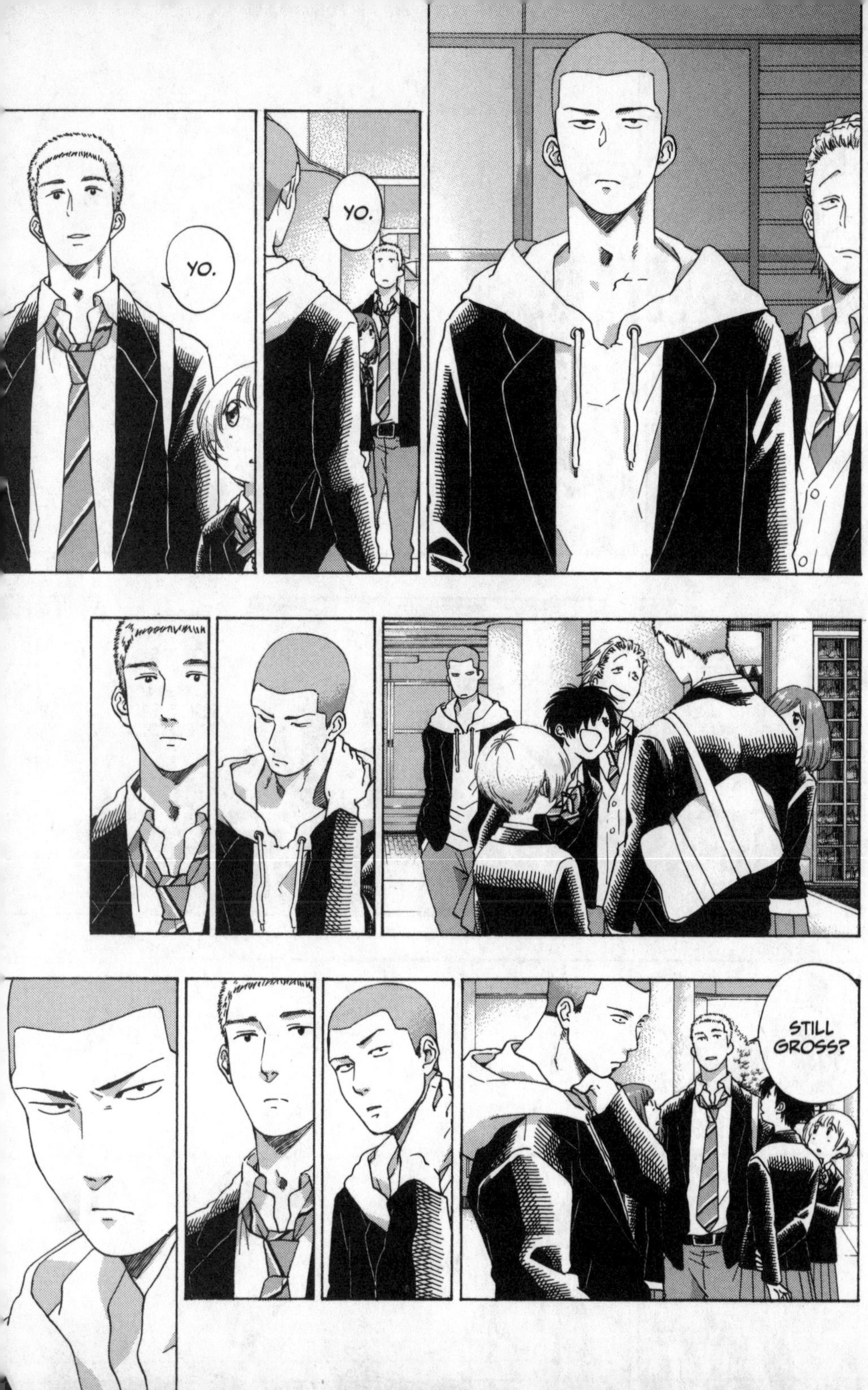
YO.
YO.
STILL GROSS?

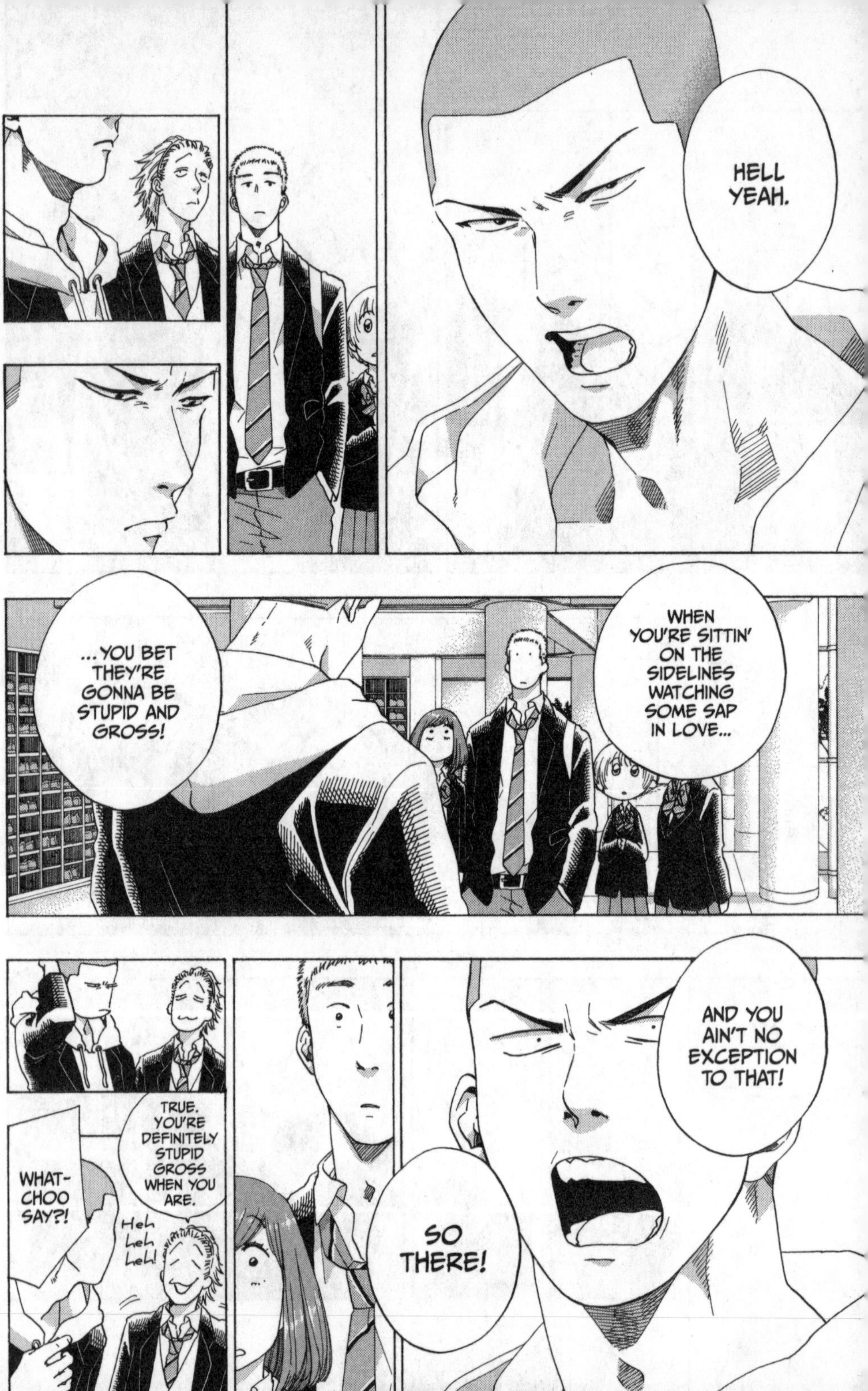
HELL YEAH.
WHEN YOU'RE SITTIN' ON THE SIDELINES WATCHING SOME SAP IN LOVE...
...YOU BET THEY'RE GONNA BE STUPID AND GROSS!
AND YOU AIN'T NO EXCEPTION TO THAT!
SO THERE!
TRUE. YOU'RE DEFINITELY STUPID GROSS WHEN YOU ARE.
Heh heh heh!
WHAT-CHOO SAY?!

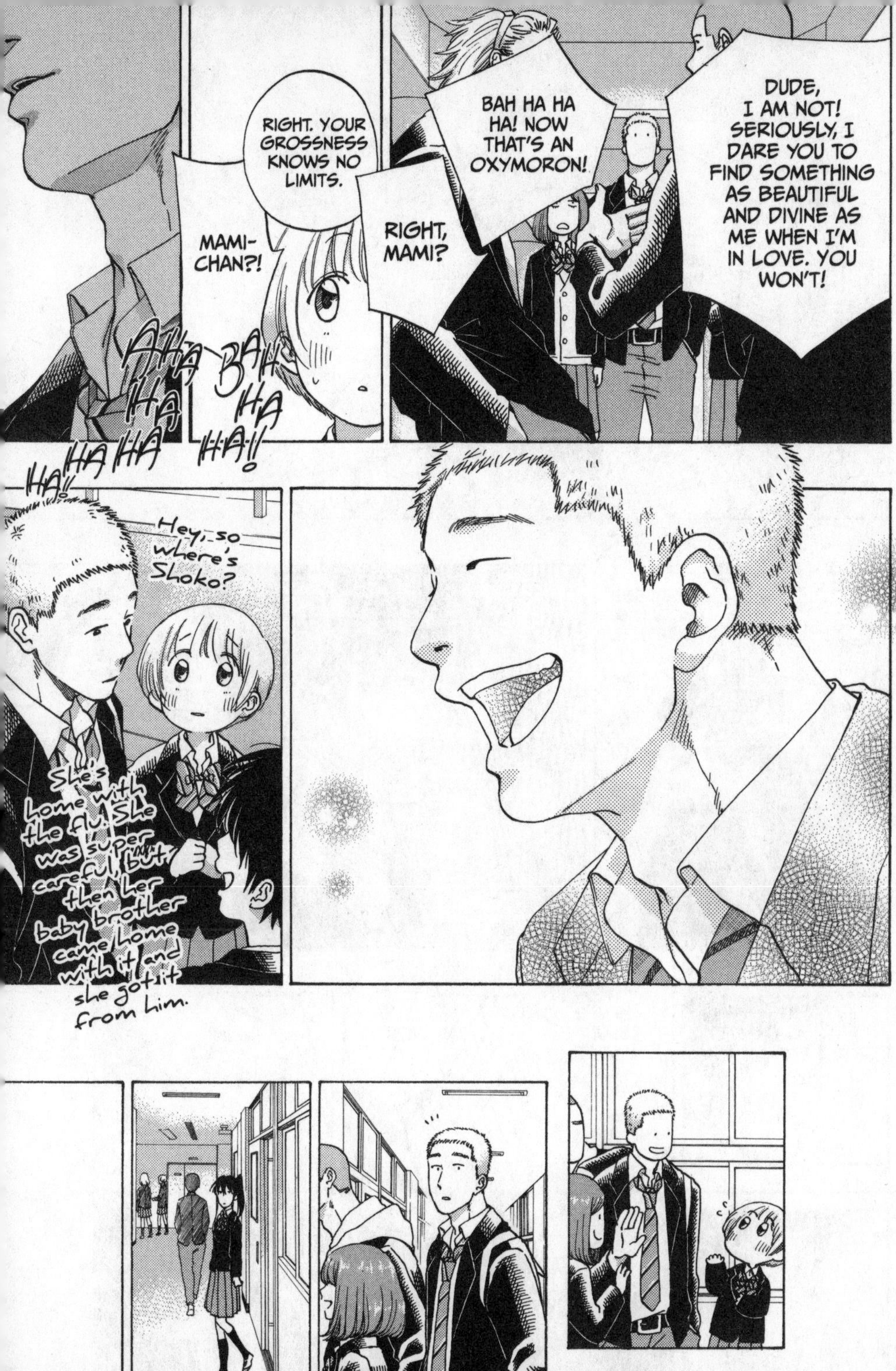
DUDE, I AM NOT! SERIOUSLY, I DARE YOU TO FIND SOMETHING AS BEAUTIFUL AND DIVINE AS ME WHEN I'M IN LOVE. YOU WON'T!
BAH HA HA HA! NOW THAT'S AN OXYMORON!
RIGHT, MAMI?
RIGHT. YOUR GROSSNESS KNOWS NO LIMITS.
MAMI-CHAN?!
BAH HA HA!!
AHA HA HA HA HA HA!!
Hey, so where's Shoko?
She's home with the flu. She was super careful, but then her baby brother came home with it and she got it from him.

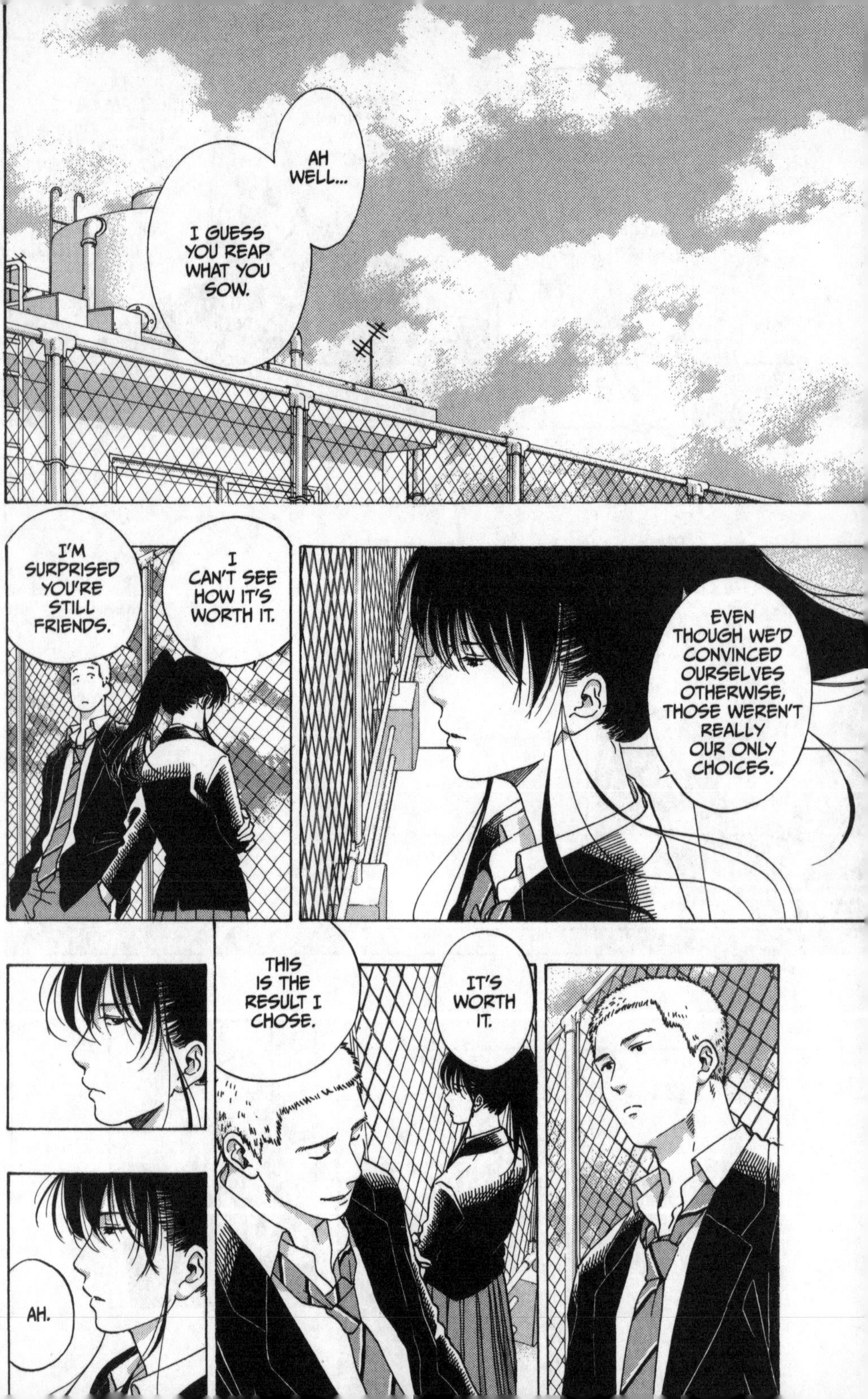
AH WELL...
I GUESS YOU REAP WHAT YOU SOW.
EVEN THOUGH WE'D CONVINCED OURSELVES OTHERWISE, THOSE WEREN'T REALLY OUR ONLY CHOICES.
I CAN'T SEE HOW IT'S WORTH IT.
I'M SURPRISED YOU'RE STILL FRIENDS.
IT'S WORTH IT.
THIS IS THE RESULT I CHOSE.
AH.

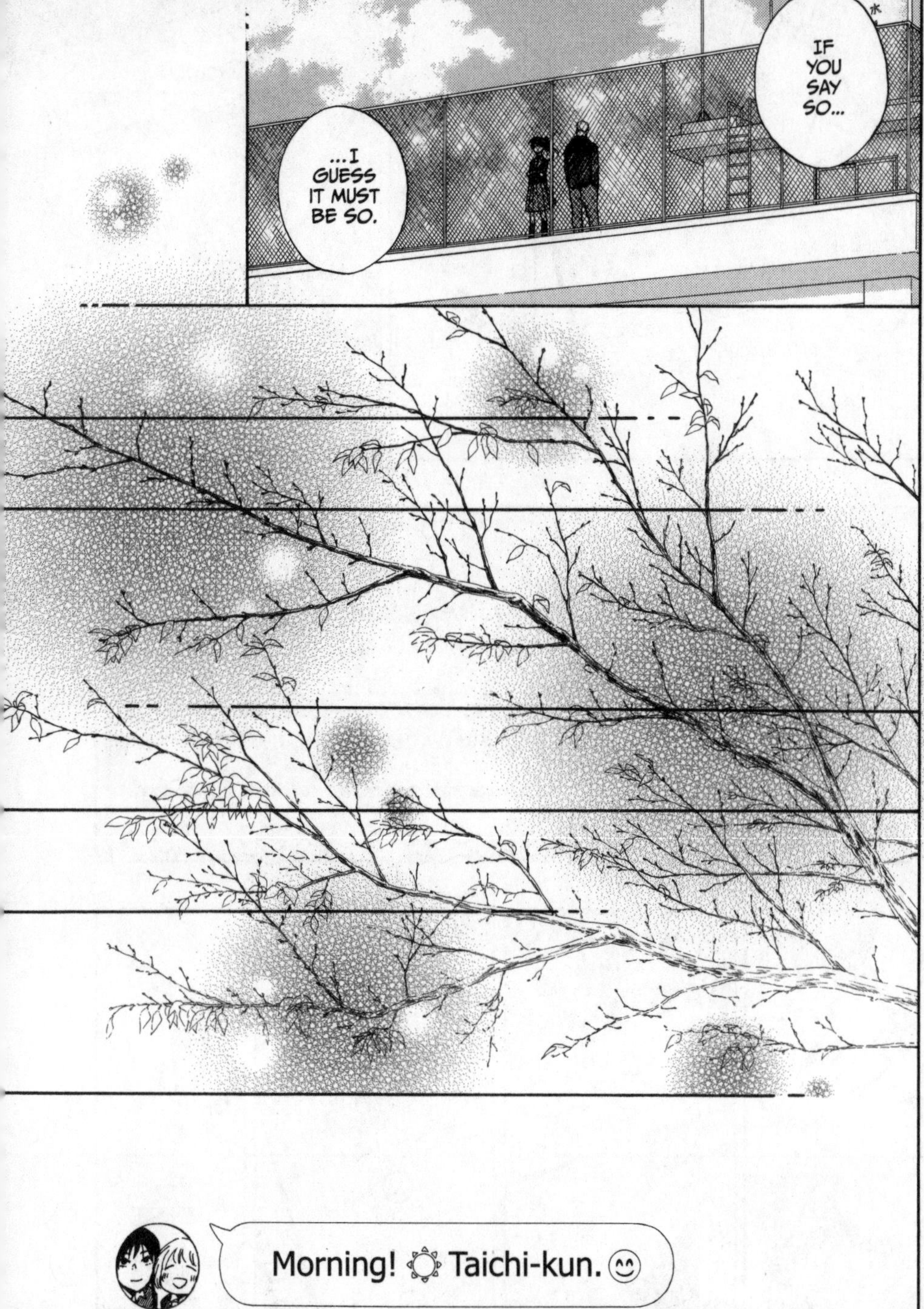
IF YOU SAY SO...
...I GUESS IT MUST BE SO.
Morning! Taichi-kun.

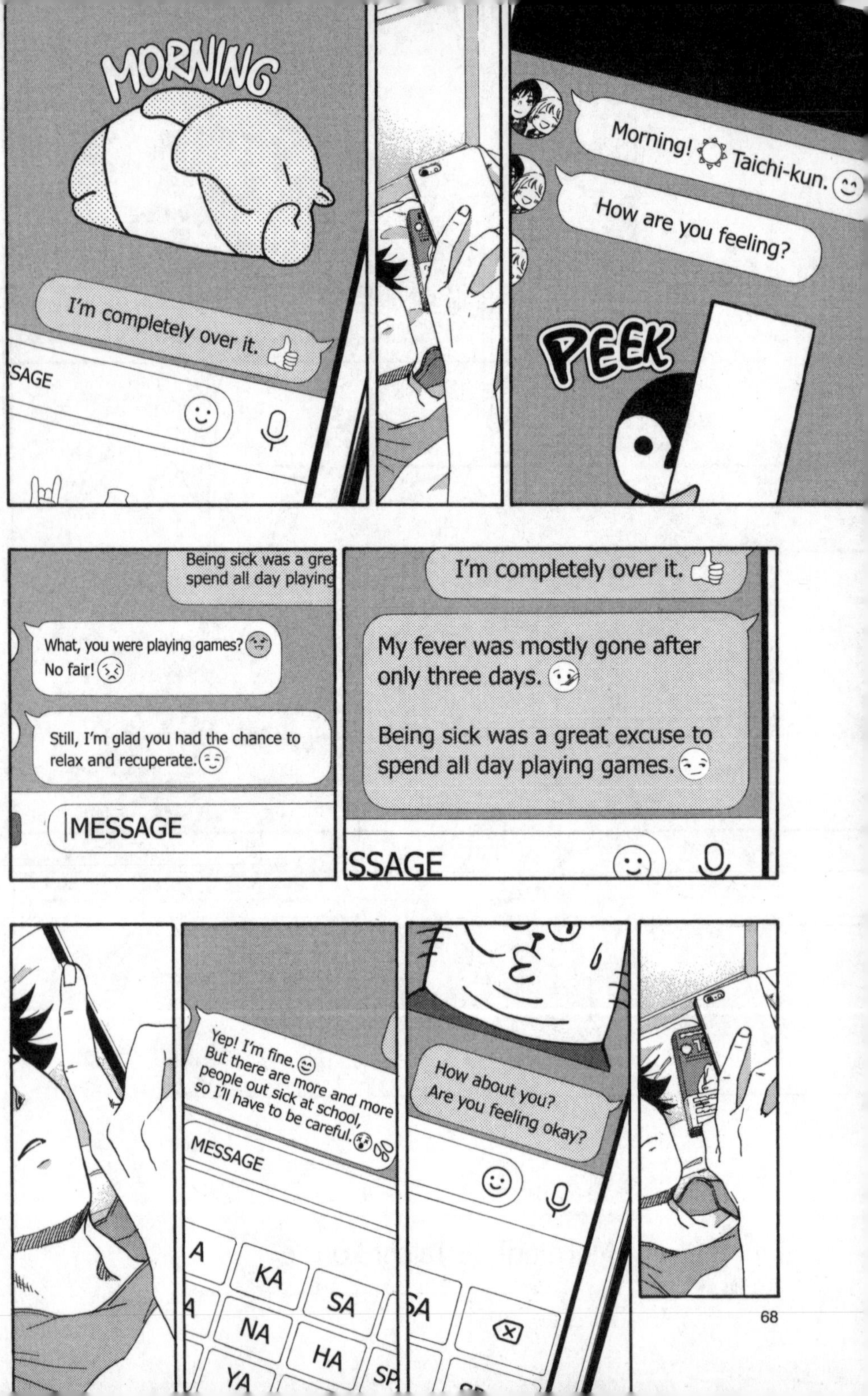
Morning! Taichi-kun.
How are you feeling?
PEEK
MORNING
I'm completely over it.
I'm completely over it.
My fever was mostly gone after only three days.

Being sick was a great excuse to spend all day playing games.
What, you were playing games? No fair!
Still, I'm glad you had the chance to relax and recuperate.
MESSAGE
How about you? Are you feeling okay?
Yep! I'm fine. But there are more and more people out sick at school, so I'll have to be careful.
MESSAGE

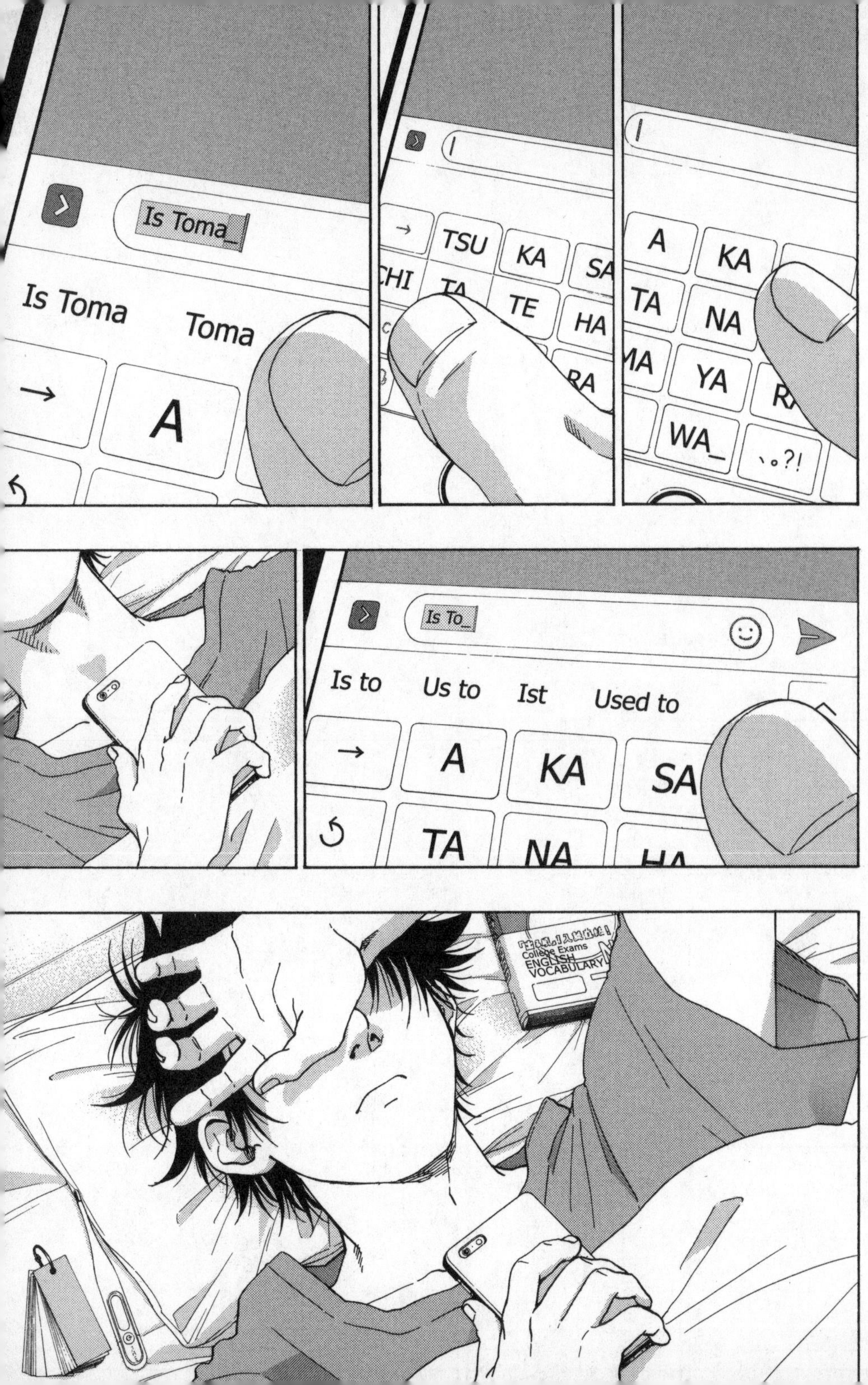
A
KA
TA
NA
MA
YA
RA
WA_
、。?!
→
TSU
KA
SA
CHI
TA
TE
HA
RA
Is Toma_
Is Toma
Toma
→
A
Is To_
Is to
Us to
Ist
Used to
→
A
KA
SA
TA
NA
College Exams
ENGLISH
VOCABULARY

CHAPTER 51

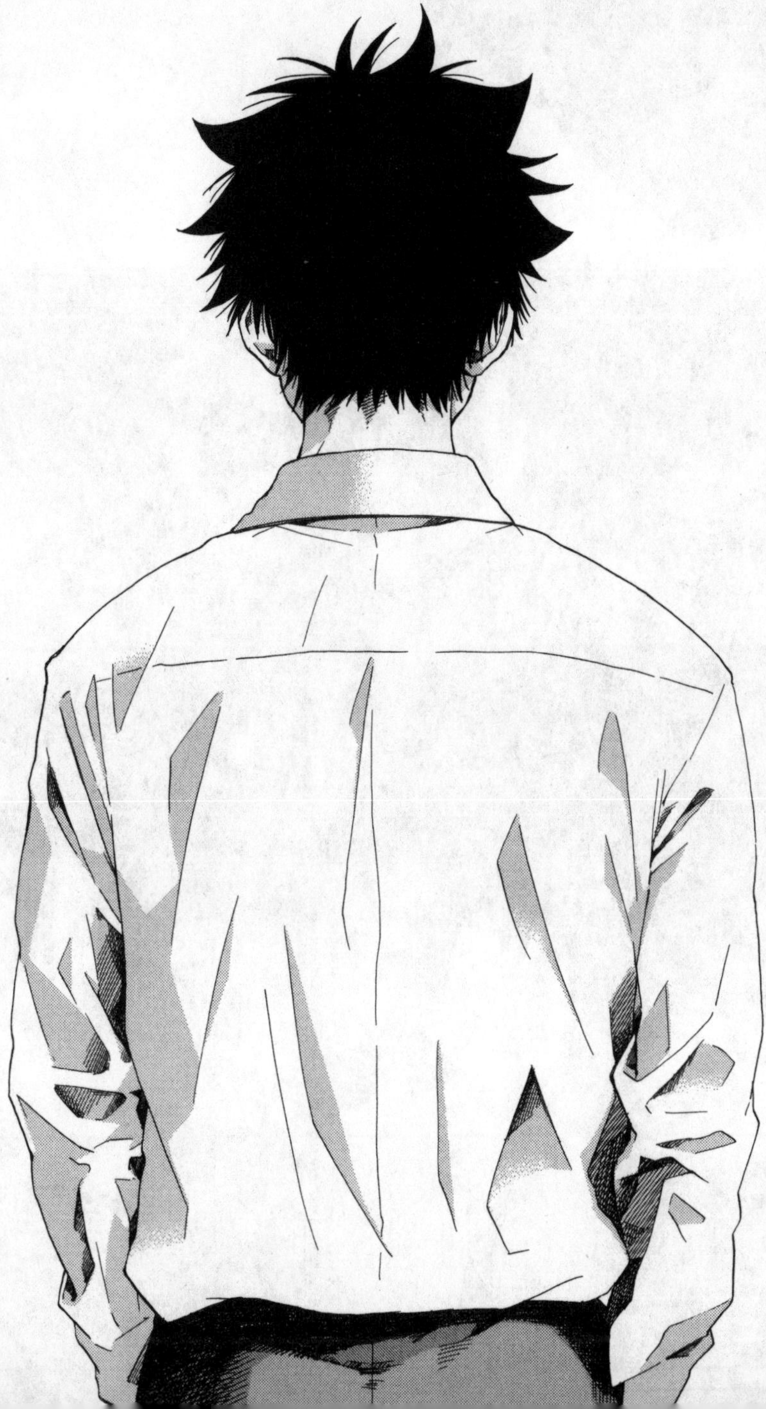

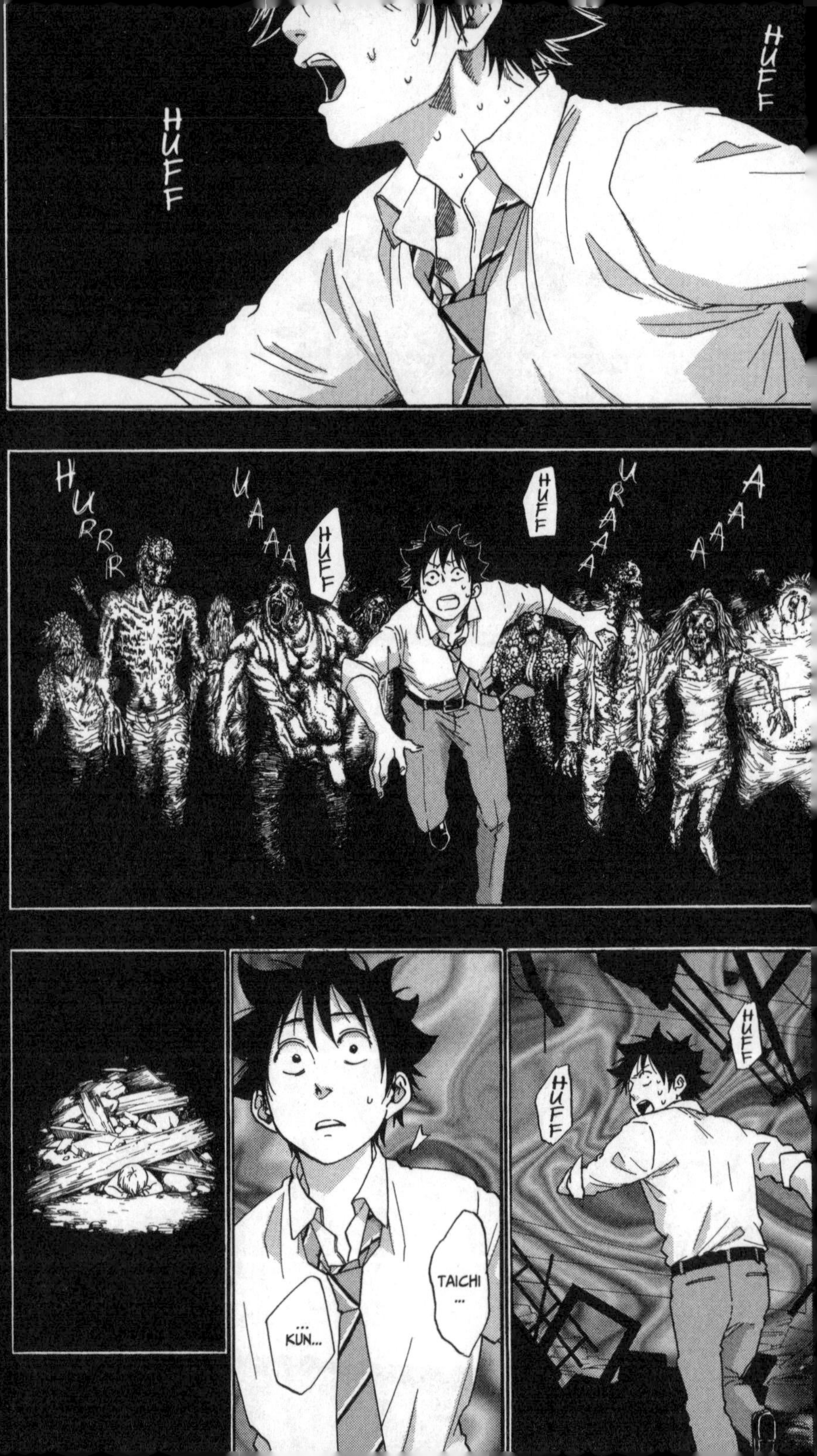
HUFF
HUFF
AAAAA
URAAAA
HUFF
HUFF
UAAAA
HURRR
HUFF
HUFF
TAICHI ...
... KUN...

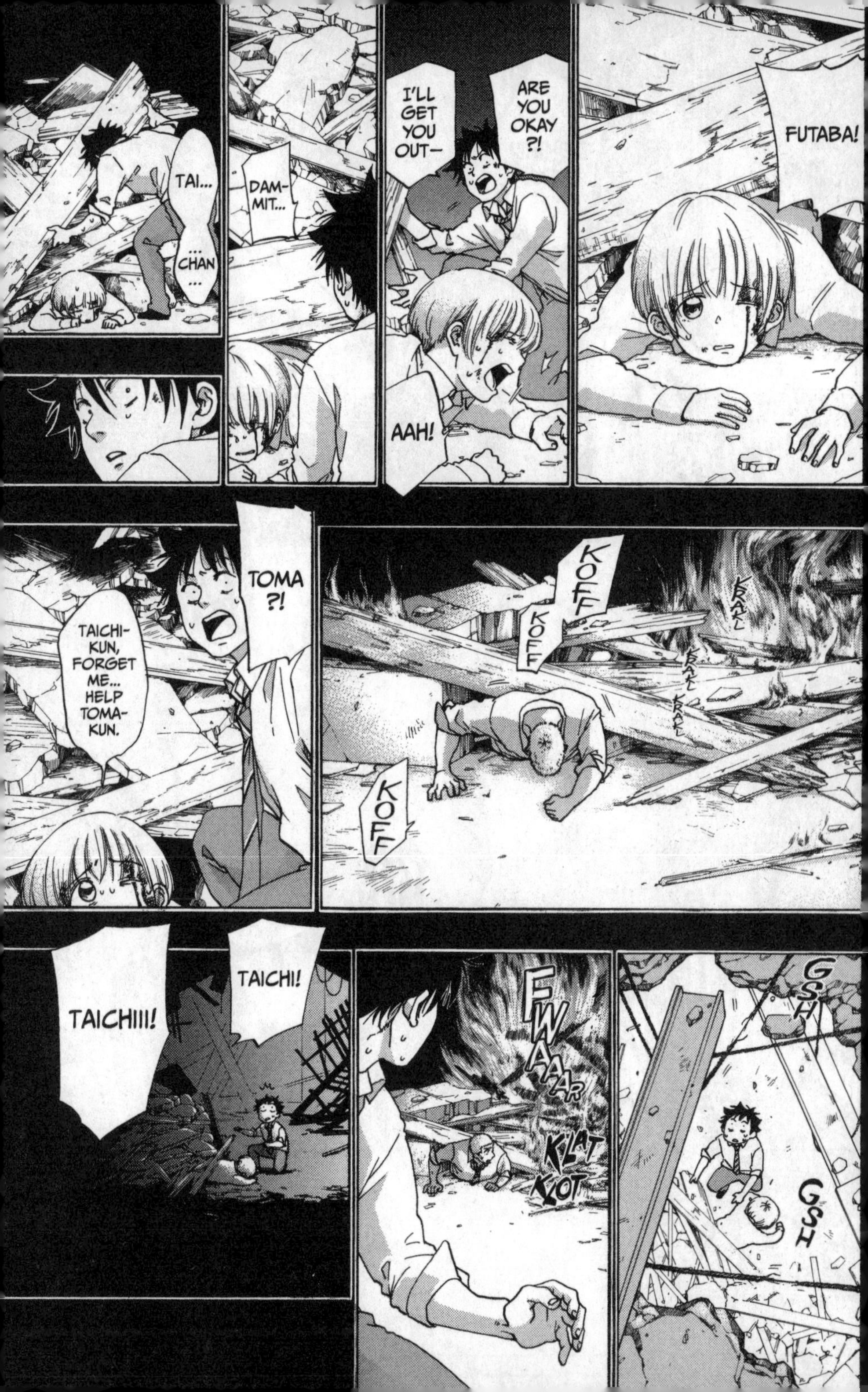
FUTABA!
ARE YOU OKAY?!
I'LL GET YOU OUT—
AAH!
DAM-MIT...
TAI...
...CHAN...
KOFF
KOFF
KRAKL
KRAKL
KRAKL
KOFF
TOMA?!
TAICHI-KUN, FORGET ME... HELP TOMA-KUN.
GSH
GSH
FWAAAAR
KLAT
KLOT
TAICHI!
TAICHIII!

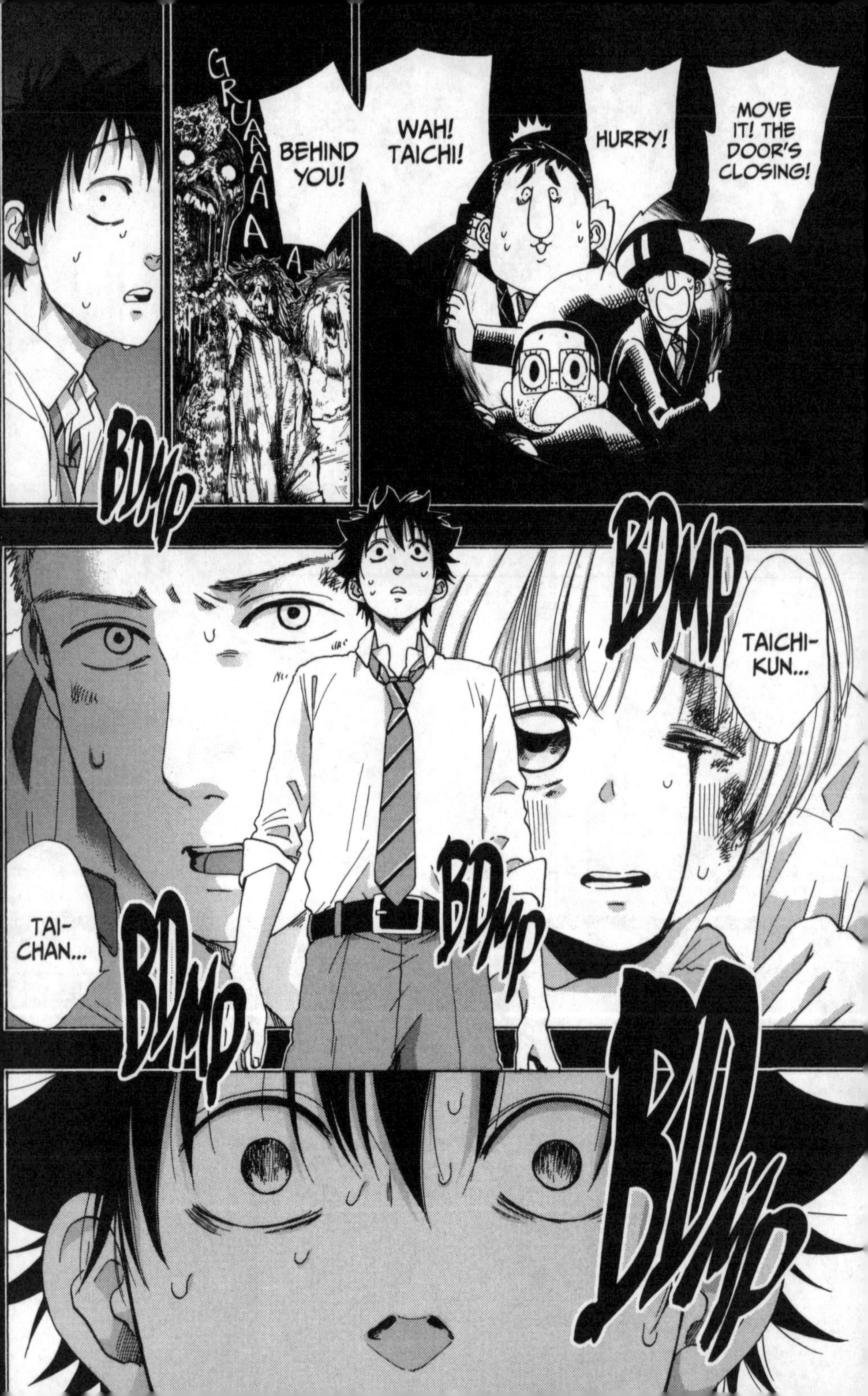
MOVE IT! THE DOOR'S CLOSING!
HURRY!
WAH! TAICHI!
BEHIND YOU!
GRUAAAAAAA
BDMP
BDMP
TAICHI-KUN...
BDMP
TAI-CHAN...
BDMP
BADUMP

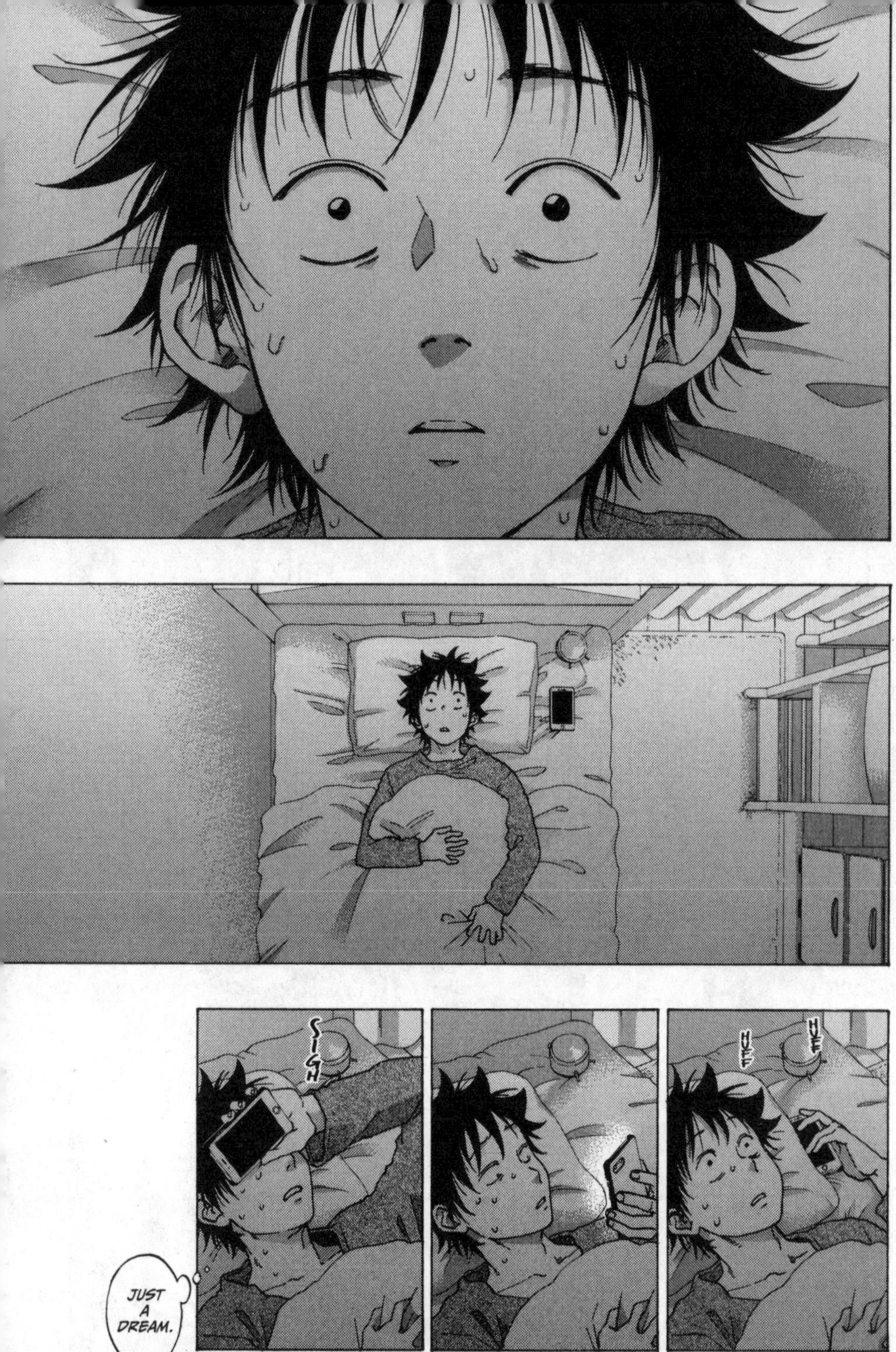
HUFF
HUFF
SIGH
JUST A DREAM.

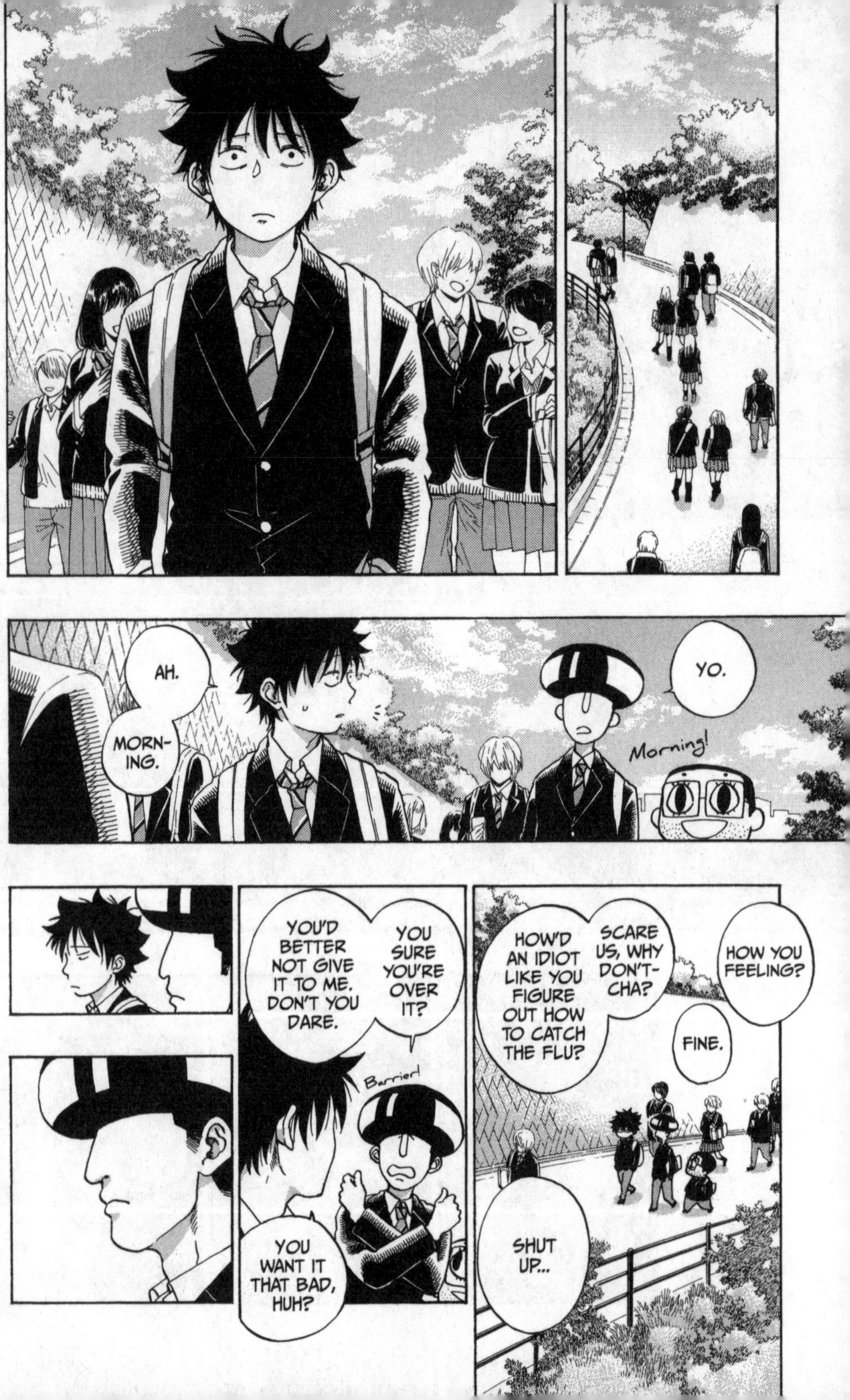
YO.
AH.
MORN-ING.
Morning!
HOW YOU FEELING?
FINE.
HOW'D AN IDIOT LIKE YOU FIGURE OUT HOW TO CATCH THE FLU?
SCARE US, WHY DON'T-CHA?
SHUT UP...
YOU SURE YOU'RE OVER IT?
YOU'D BETTER NOT GIVE IT TO ME. DON'T YOU DARE.
Barrier!
YOU WANT IT THAT BAD, HUH?

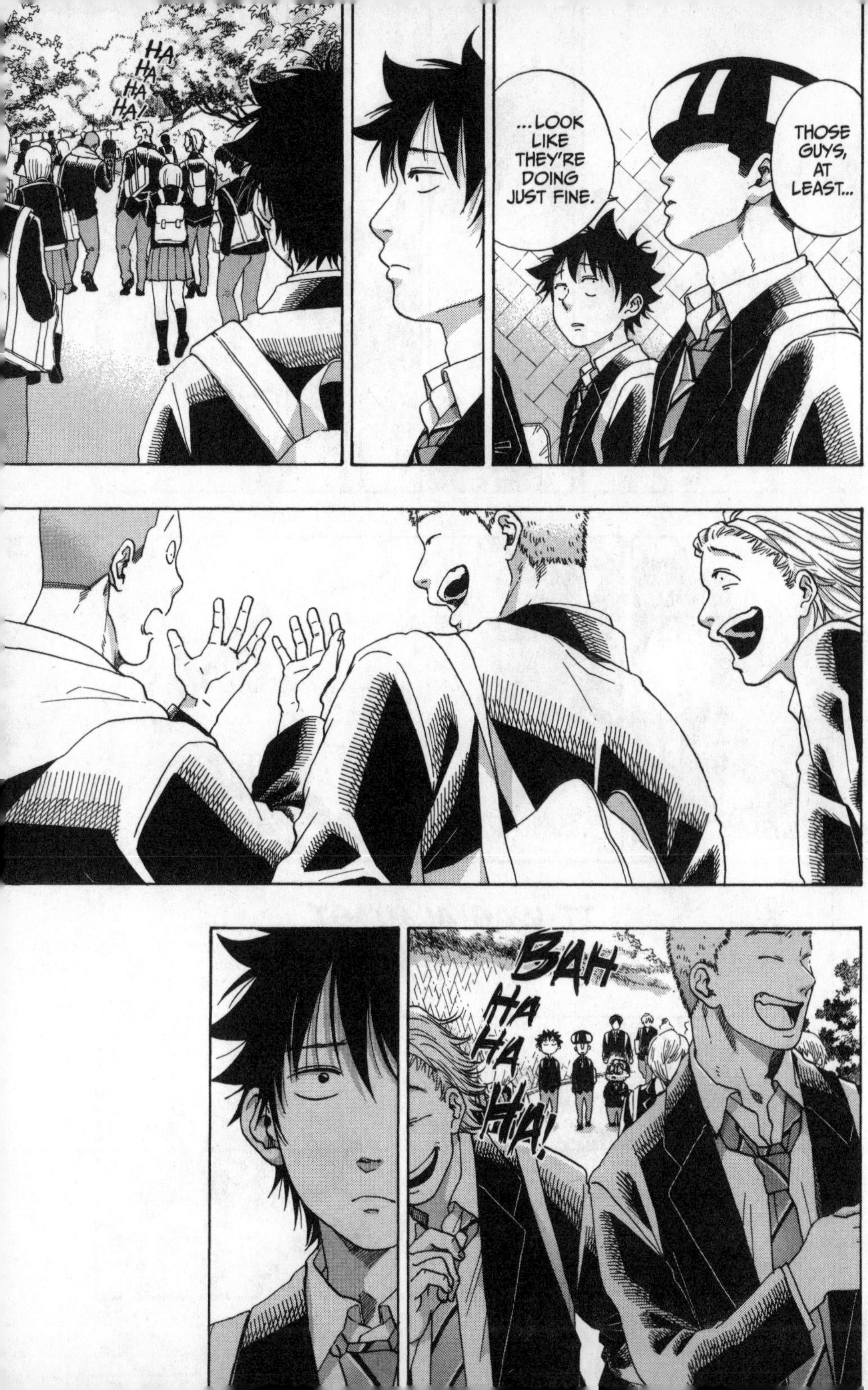
THOSE GUYS, AT LEAST...
...LOOK LIKE THEY'RE DOING JUST FINE.
HA HA HA HA!
BAH HA HA HA HA!

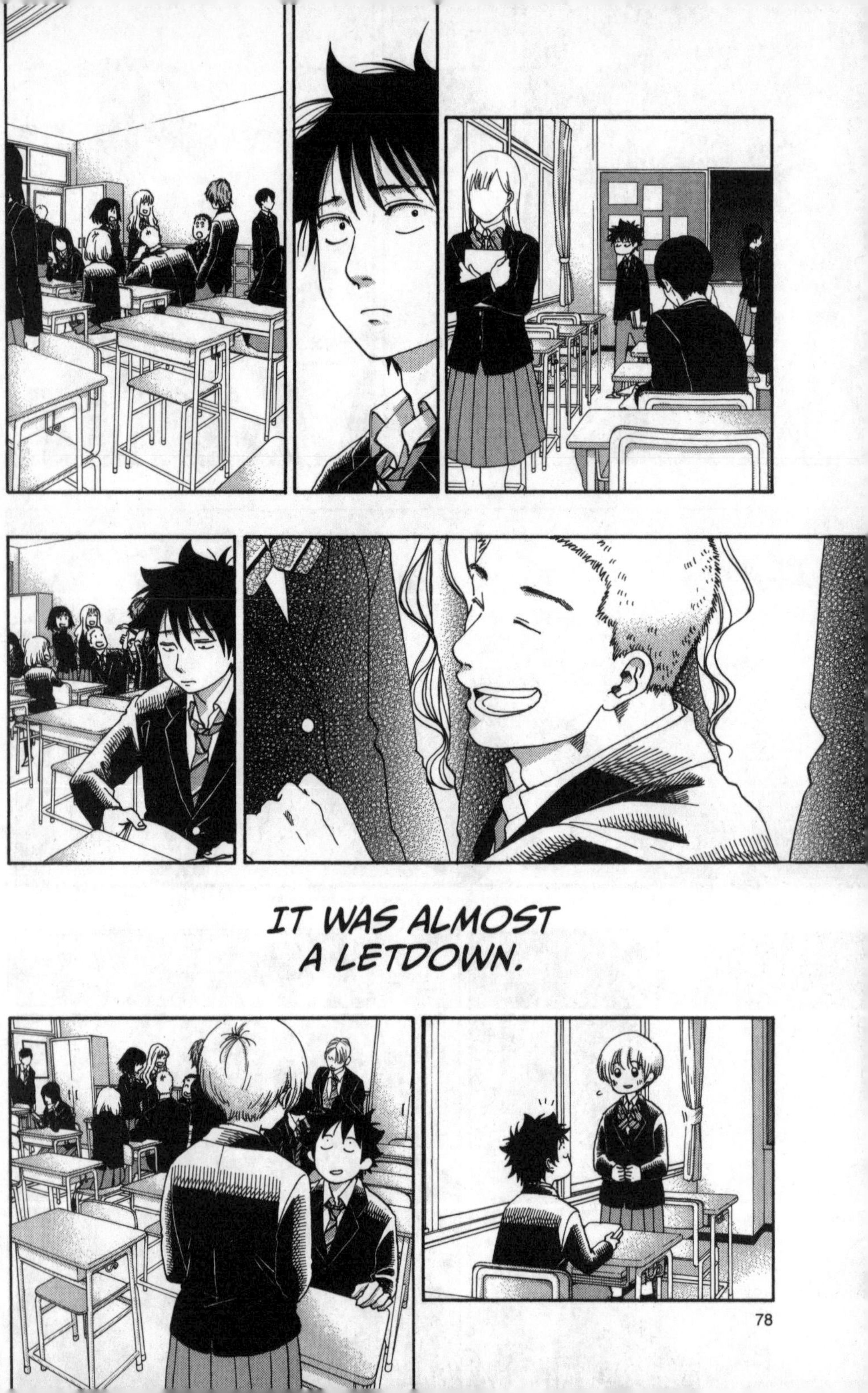
IT WAS ALMOST
A LETDOWN.

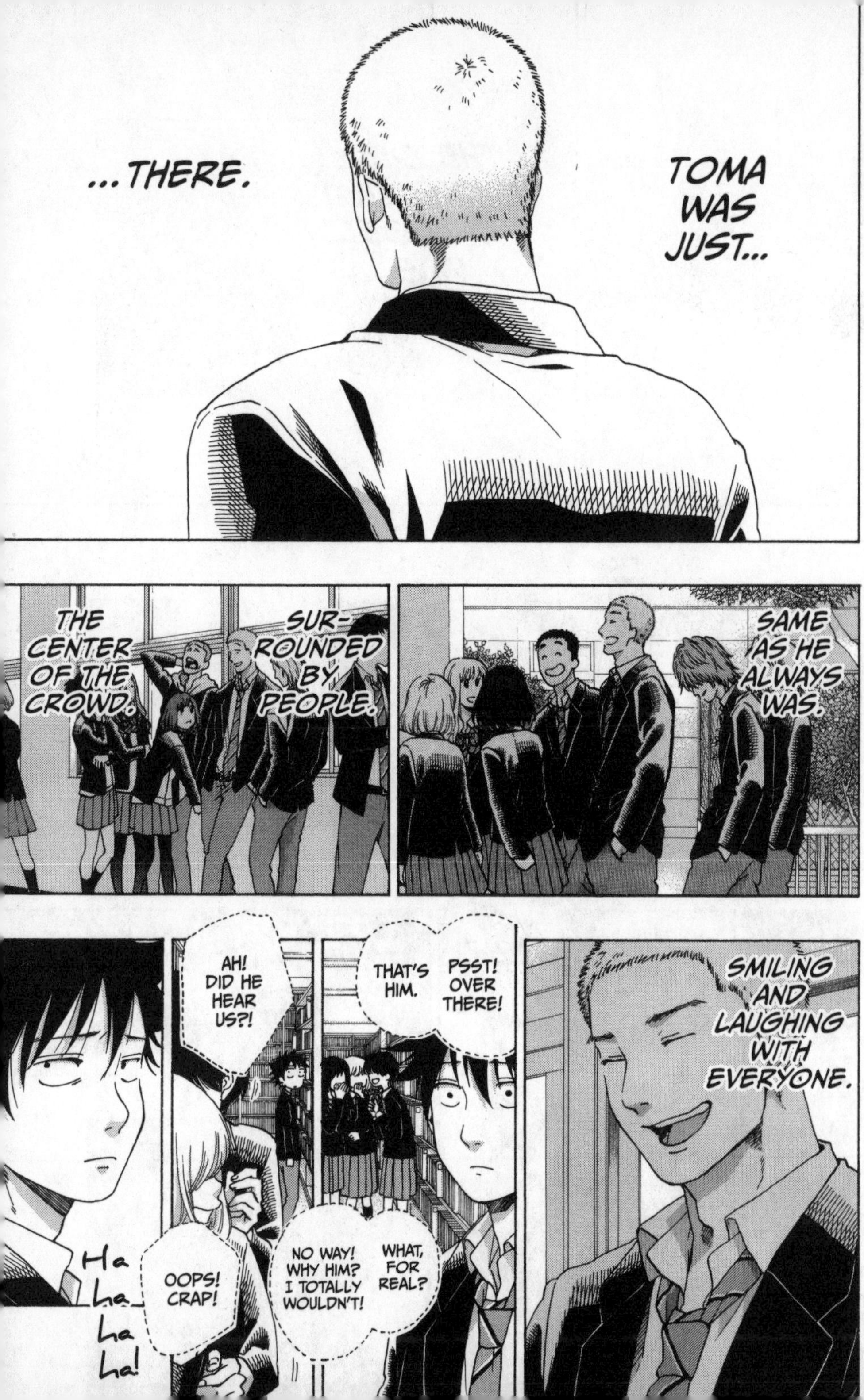
TOMA WAS JUST...
...THERE.
SAME AS HE ALWAYS WAS.
SUR-ROUNDED BY PEOPLE.
THE CENTER OF THE CROWD.
SMILING AND LAUGHING WITH EVERYONE.
PSST! OVER THERE!
THAT'S HIM.
WHAT, FOR REAL?
NO WAY! WHY HIM? I TOTALLY WOULDN'T!
AH! DID HE HEAR US?!
OOPS! CRAP!
Ha ha ha ha!

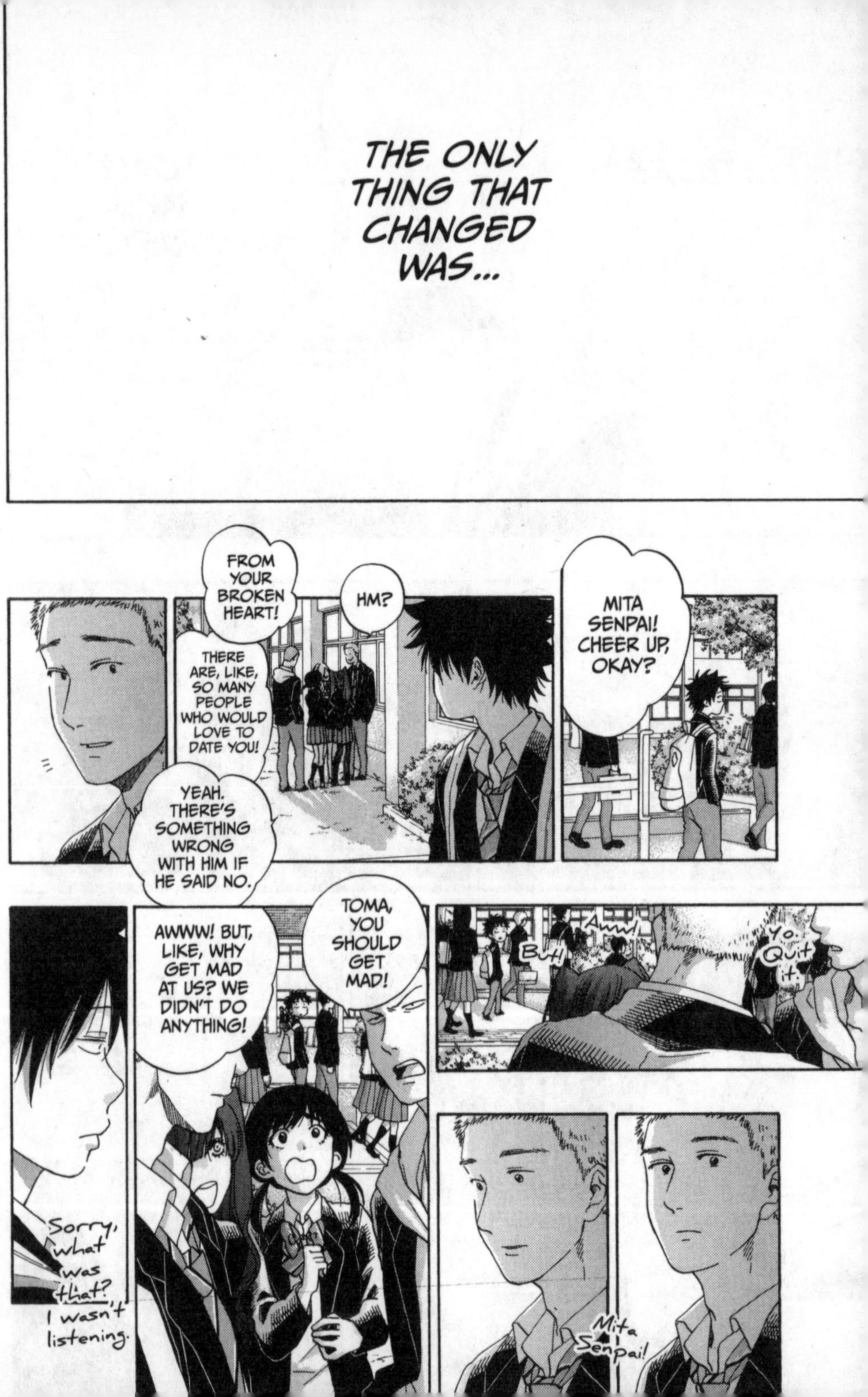
THE ONLY THING THAT CHANGED WAS...
MITA SENPAI! CHEER UP, OKAY?
HM?
FROM YOUR BROKEN HEART!
THERE ARE, LIKE, SO MANY PEOPLE WHO WOULD LOVE TO DATE YOU!
YEAH. THERE'S SOMETHING WRONG WITH HIM IF HE SAID NO.
Yo. Quit it.
Aww!
But!
Mita Senpai!
TOMA, YOU SHOULD GET MAD!
AWWW! BUT, LIKE, WHY GET MAD AT US? WE DIDN'T DO ANYTHING!
Sorry, what was that? I wasn't listening.

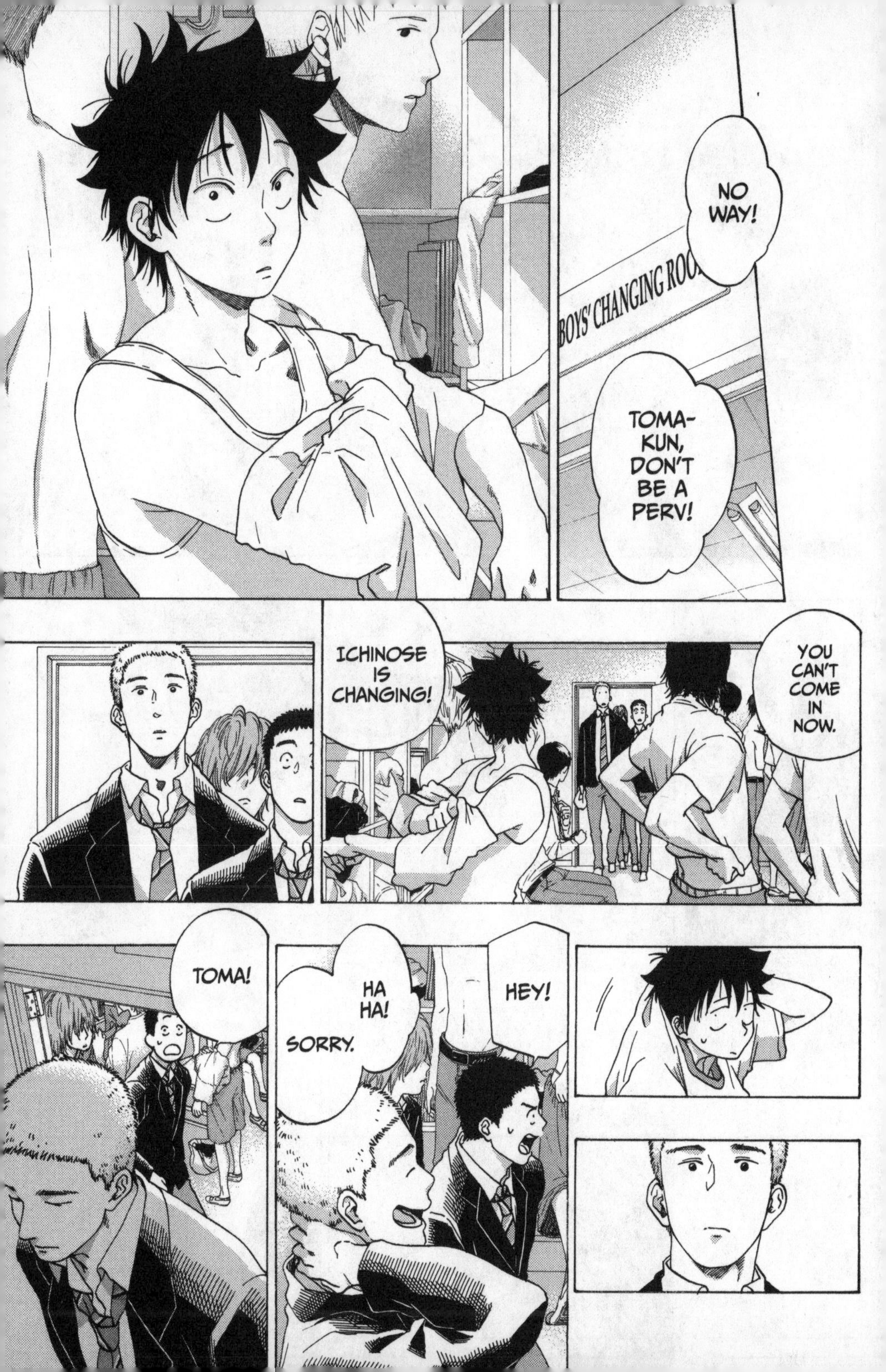
NO WAY!
BOYS' CHANGING ROO
TOMA-KUN, DON'T BE A PERV!
ICHINOSE IS CHANGING!
YOU CAN'T COME IN NOW.
HEY!
HA HA!
SORRY.
TOMA!

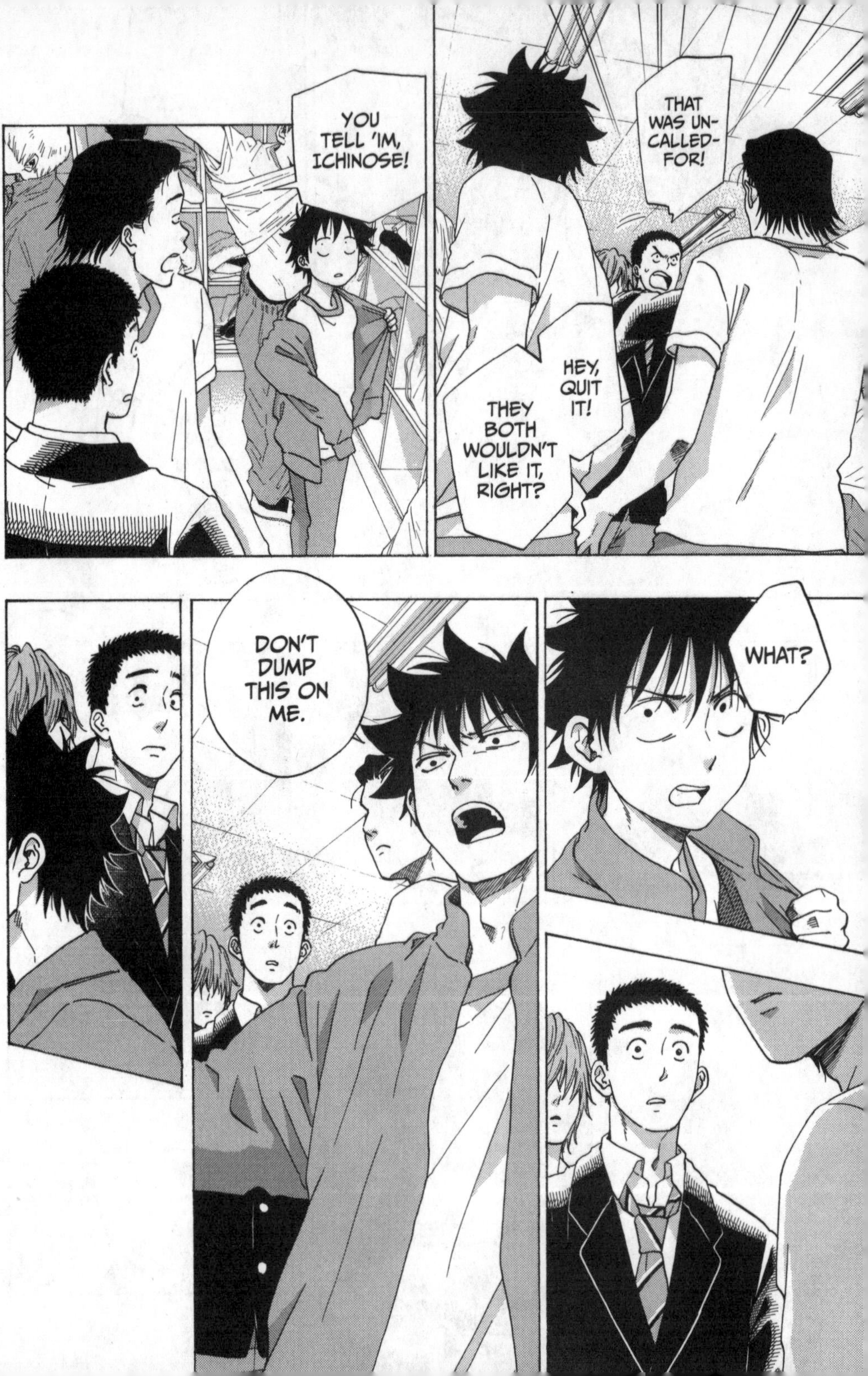
THAT WAS UN-CALLED-FOR!
HEY, QUIT IT!
THEY BOTH WOULDN'T LIKE IT, RIGHT?
YOU TELL 'IM, ICHINOSE!
WHAT?
DON'T DUMP THIS ON ME.

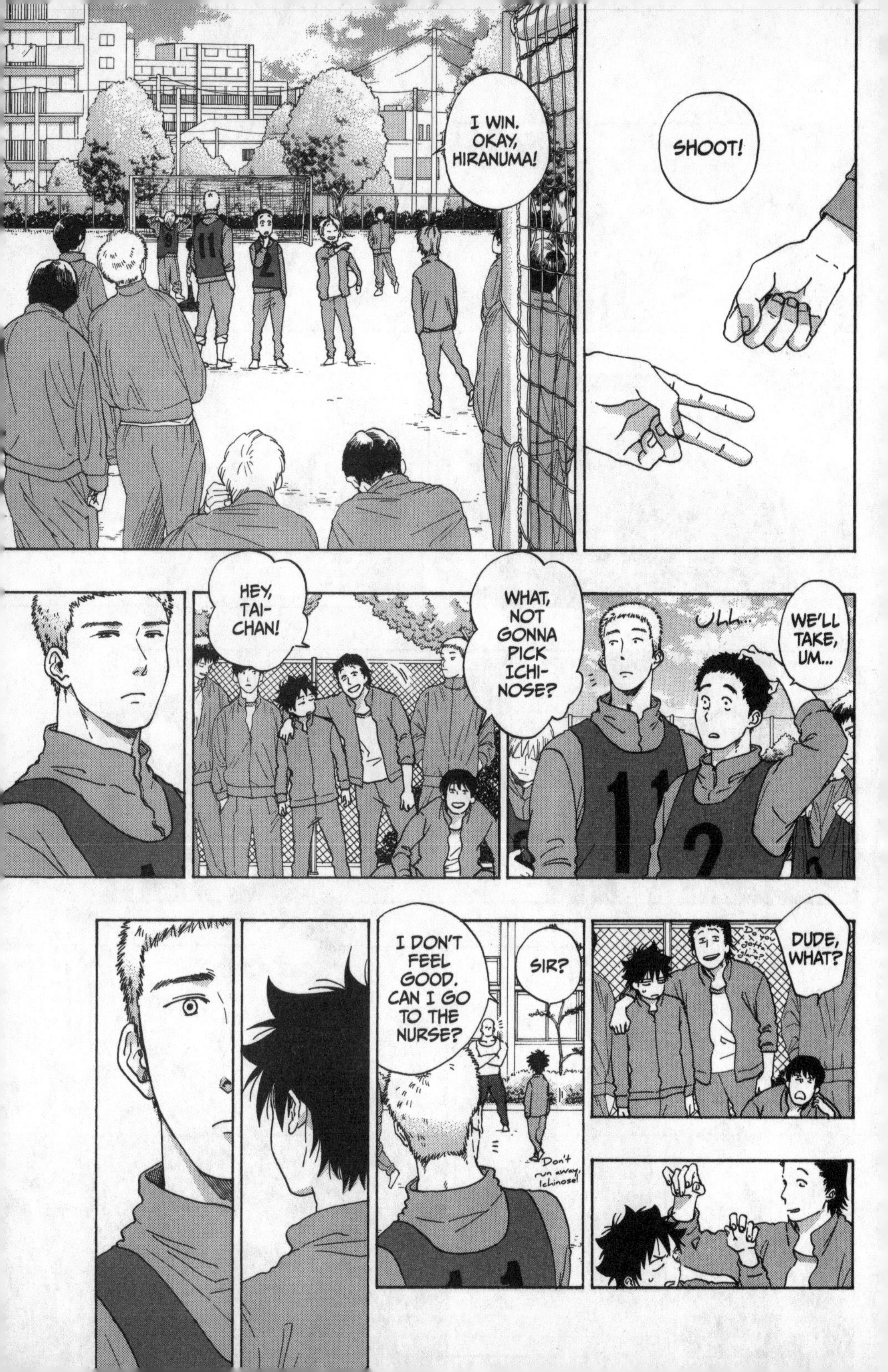
SHOOT!
I WIN. OKAY, HIRANUMA!
WE'LL TAKE, UM...
ULL...
WHAT, NOT GONNA PICK ICHINOSE?
HEY, TAI-CHAN!
DUDE, WHAT?
Do you gotta glare?
SIR?
I DON'T FEEL GOOD. CAN I GO TO THE NURSE?
Don't run away, Ichinose!

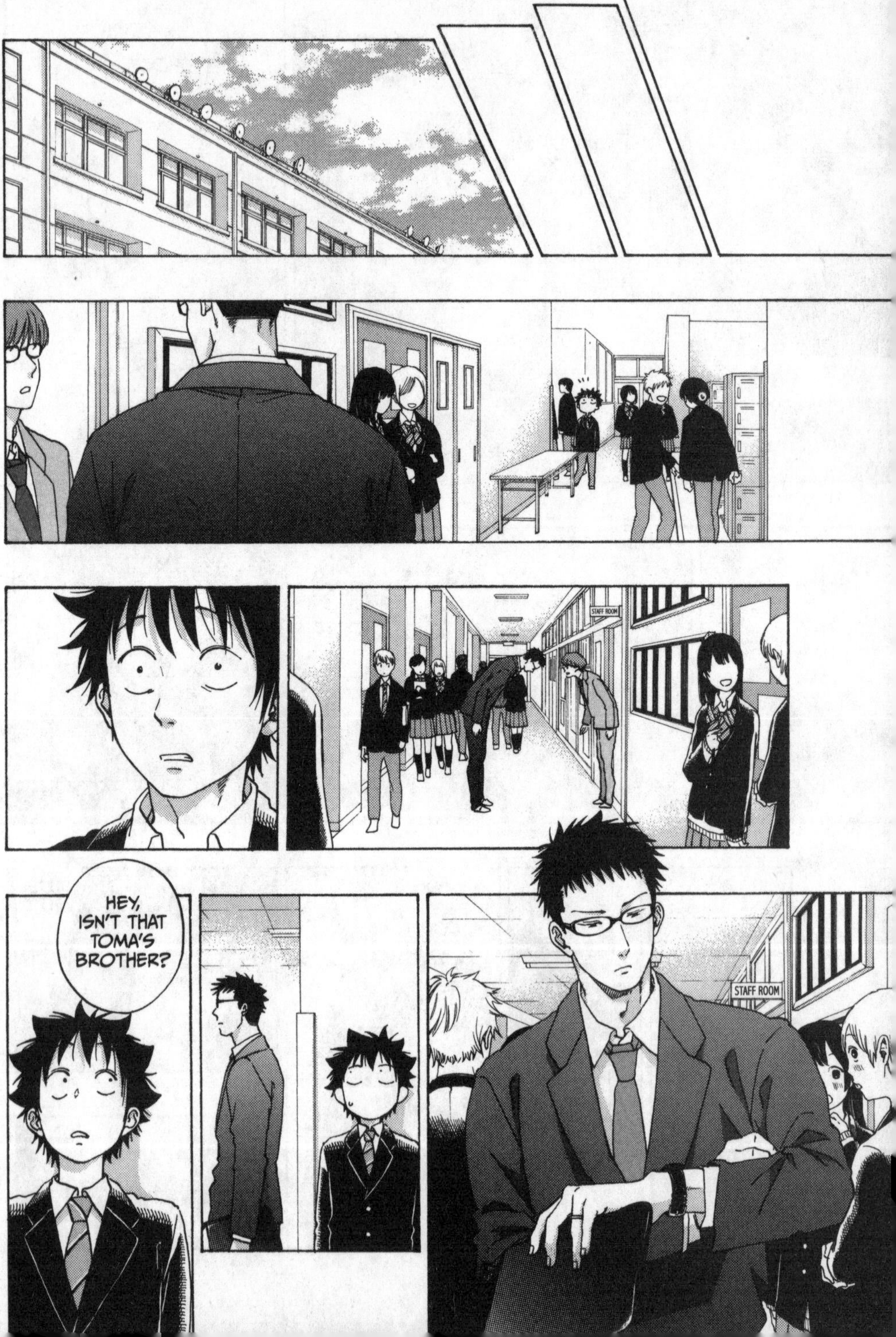
STAFF ROOM
STAFF ROOM
HEY, ISN'T THAT TOMA'S BROTHER?

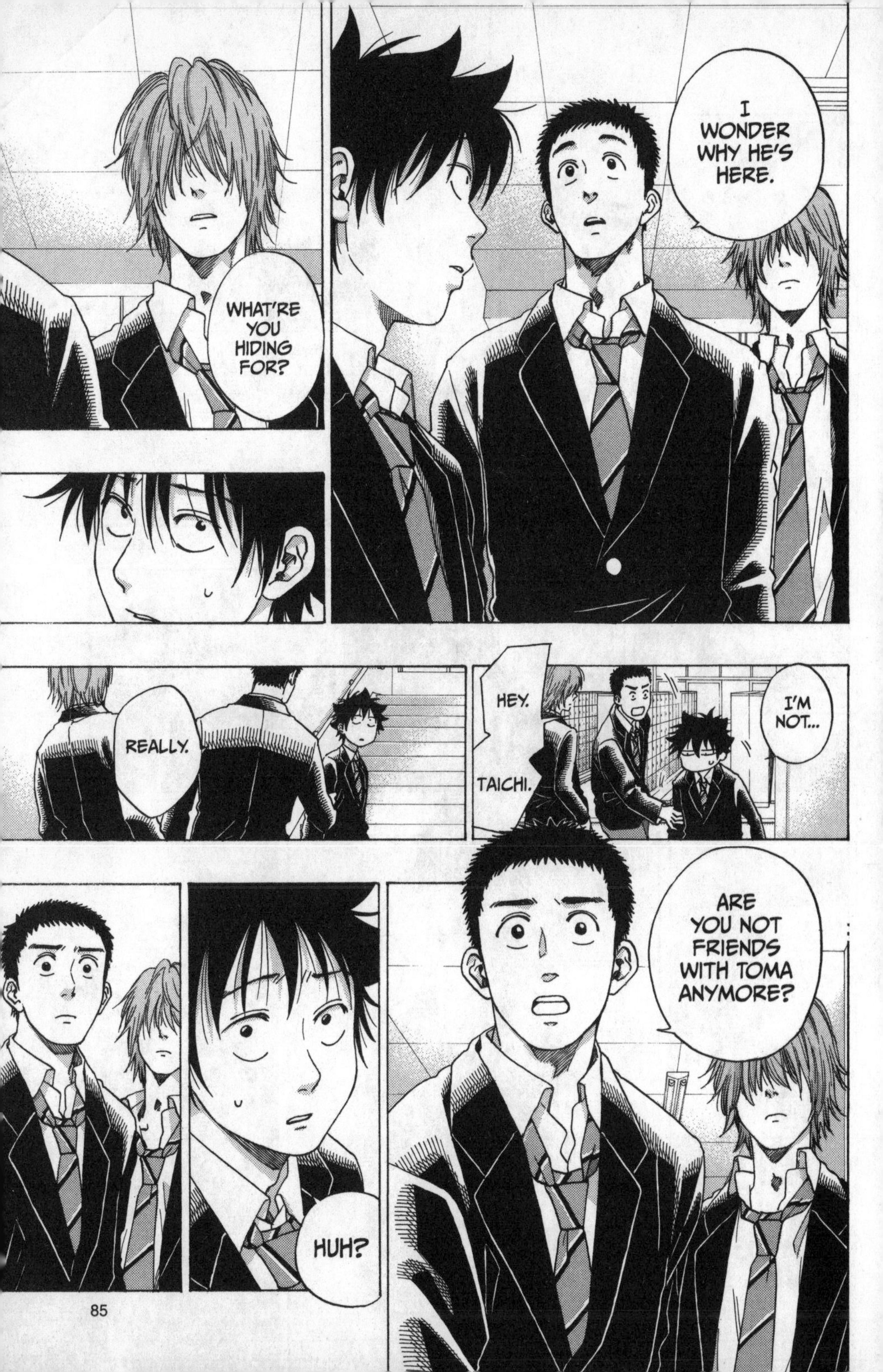
I WONDER WHY HE'S HERE.
WHAT'RE YOU HIDING FOR?
I'M NOT...
HEY.
TAICHI.
REALLY.
ARE YOU NOT FRIENDS WITH TOMA ANYMORE?
HUH?

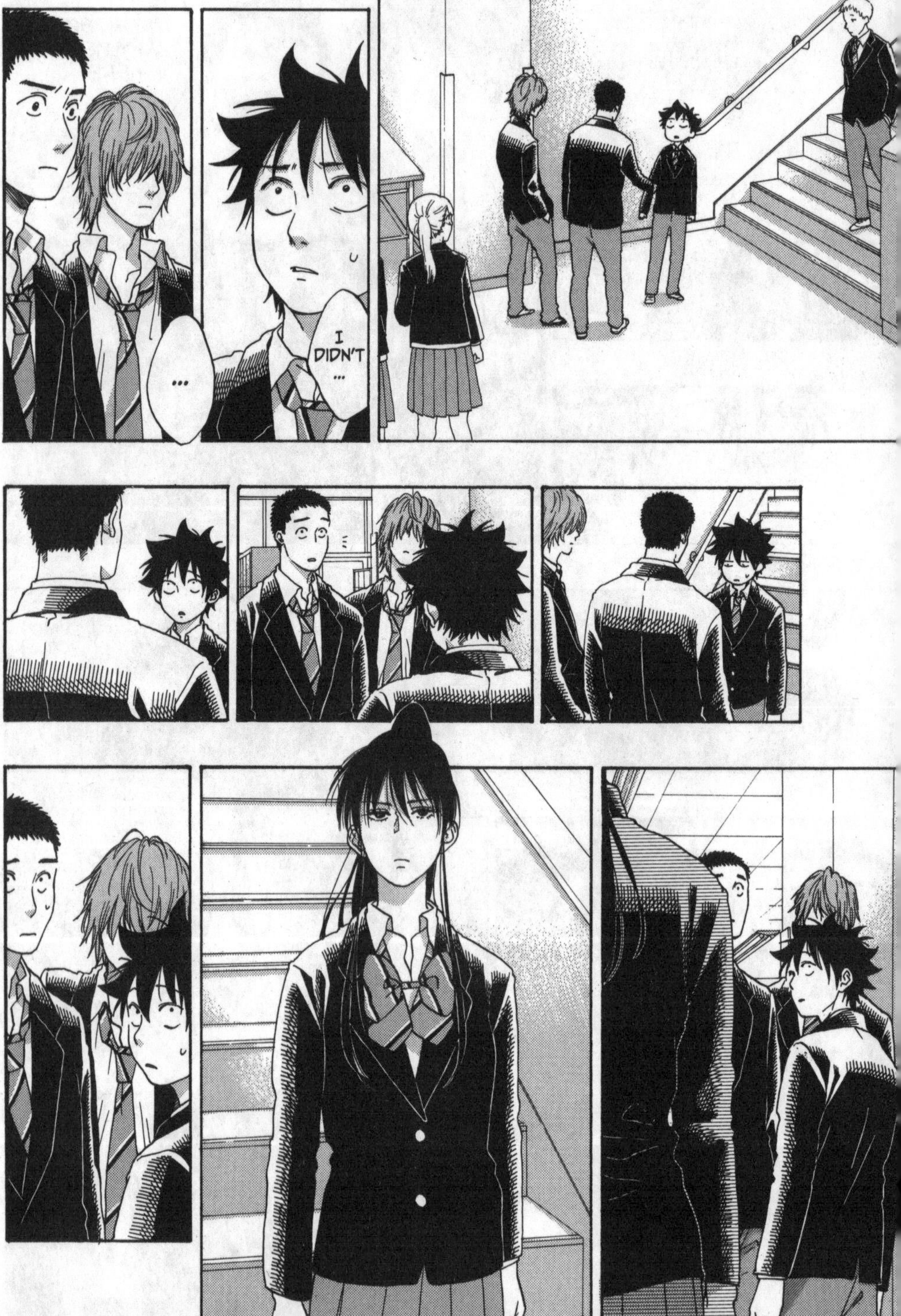
I DIDN'T ...
...

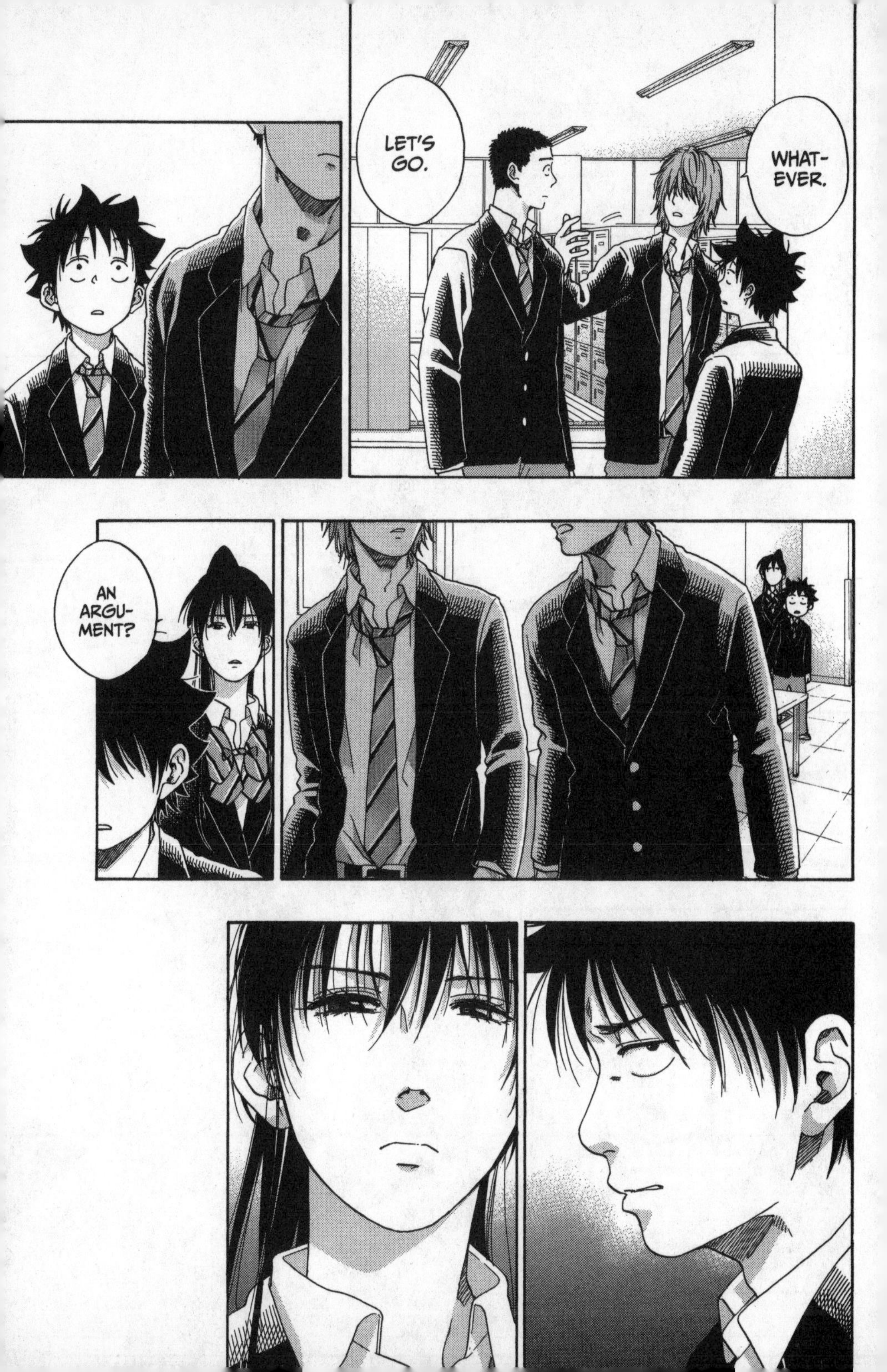
LET'S GO.
WHAT-EVER.
AN ARGU-MENT?

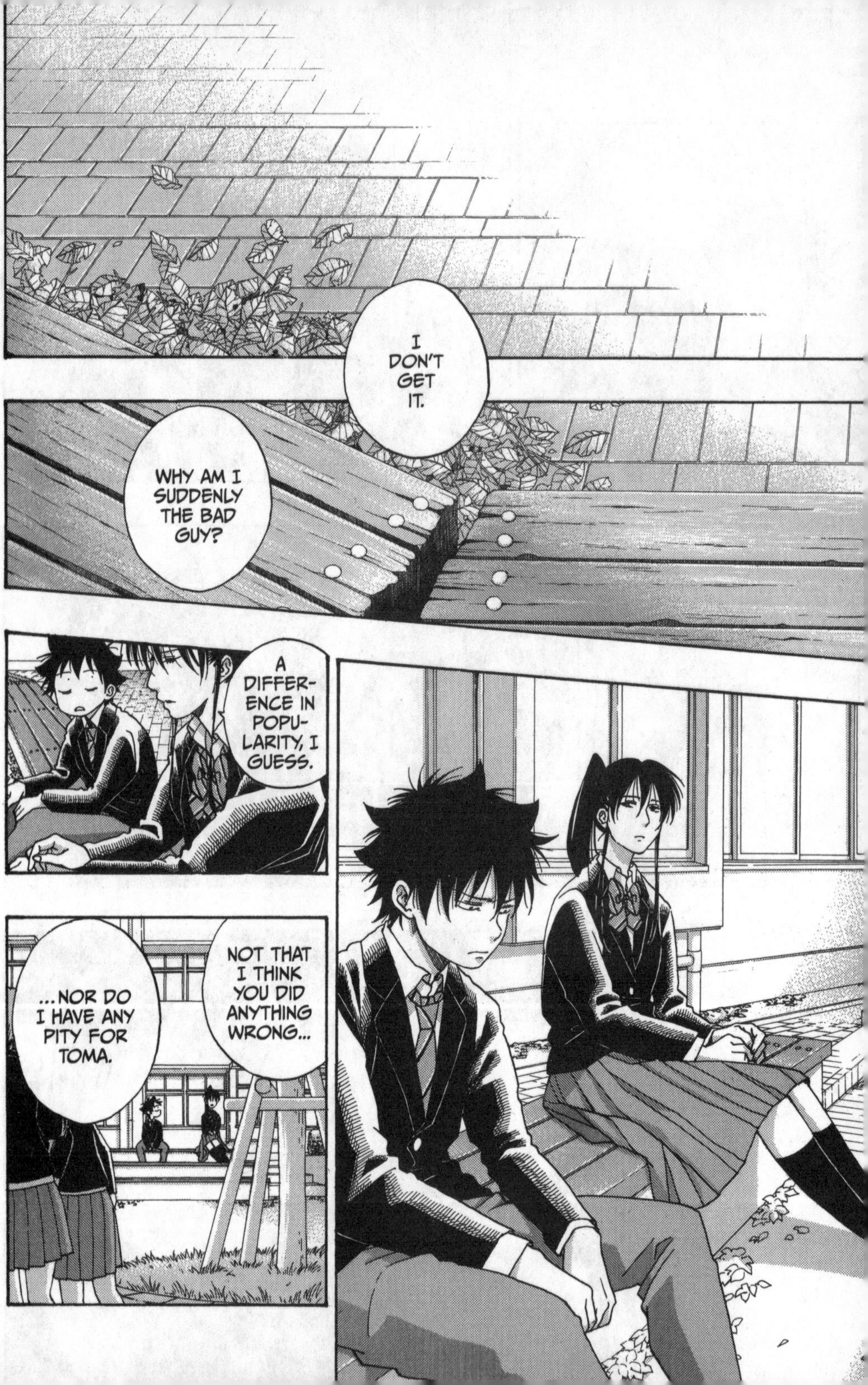
I DON'T GET IT.
WHY AM I SUDDENLY THE BAD GUY?
A DIFFERENCE IN POPULARITY, I GUESS.
NOT THAT I THINK YOU DID ANYTHING WRONG...
...NOR DO I HAVE ANY PITY FOR TOMA.

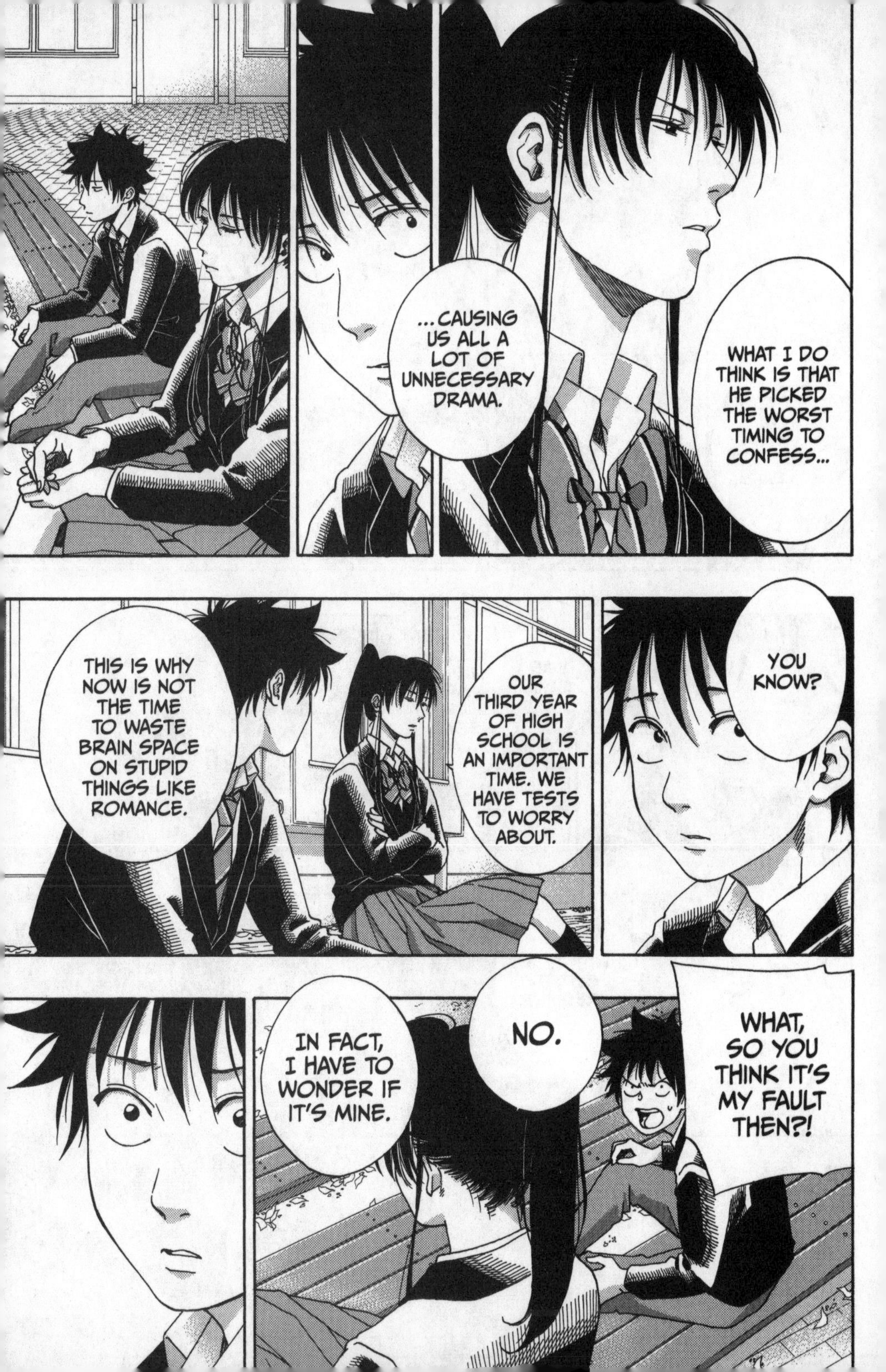
WHAT I DO THINK IS THAT HE PICKED THE WORST TIMING TO CONFESS...
...CAUSING US ALL A LOT OF UNNECESSARY DRAMA.
YOU KNOW?
OUR THIRD YEAR OF HIGH SCHOOL IS AN IMPORTANT TIME. WE HAVE TESTS TO WORRY ABOUT.
THIS IS WHY NOW IS NOT THE TIME TO WASTE BRAIN SPACE ON STUPID THINGS LIKE ROMANCE.
WHAT, SO YOU THINK IT'S MY FAULT THEN?!
NO.
IN FACT, I HAVE TO WONDER IF IT'S MINE.

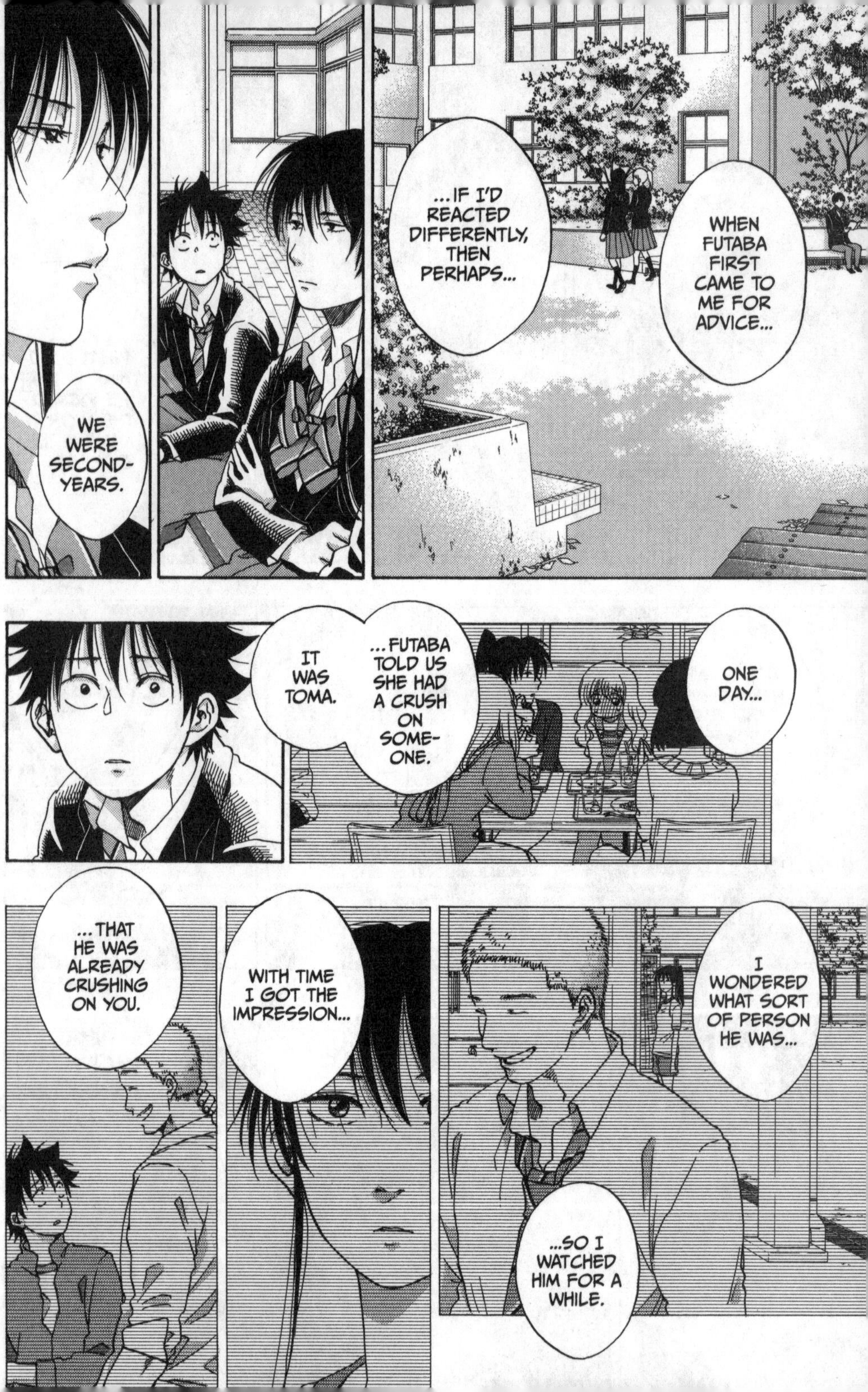
WHEN FUTABA FIRST CAME TO ME FOR ADVICE...
...IF I'D REACTED DIFFERENTLY, THEN PERHAPS...
WE WERE SECOND-YEARS.
ONE DAY...
...FUTABA TOLD US SHE HAD A CRUSH ON SOME-ONE.
IT WAS TOMA.
I WONDERED WHAT SORT OF PERSON HE WAS...
...SO I WATCHED HIM FOR A WHILE.
WITH TIME I GOT THE IMPRESSION...
...THAT HE WAS ALREADY CRUSHING ON YOU.

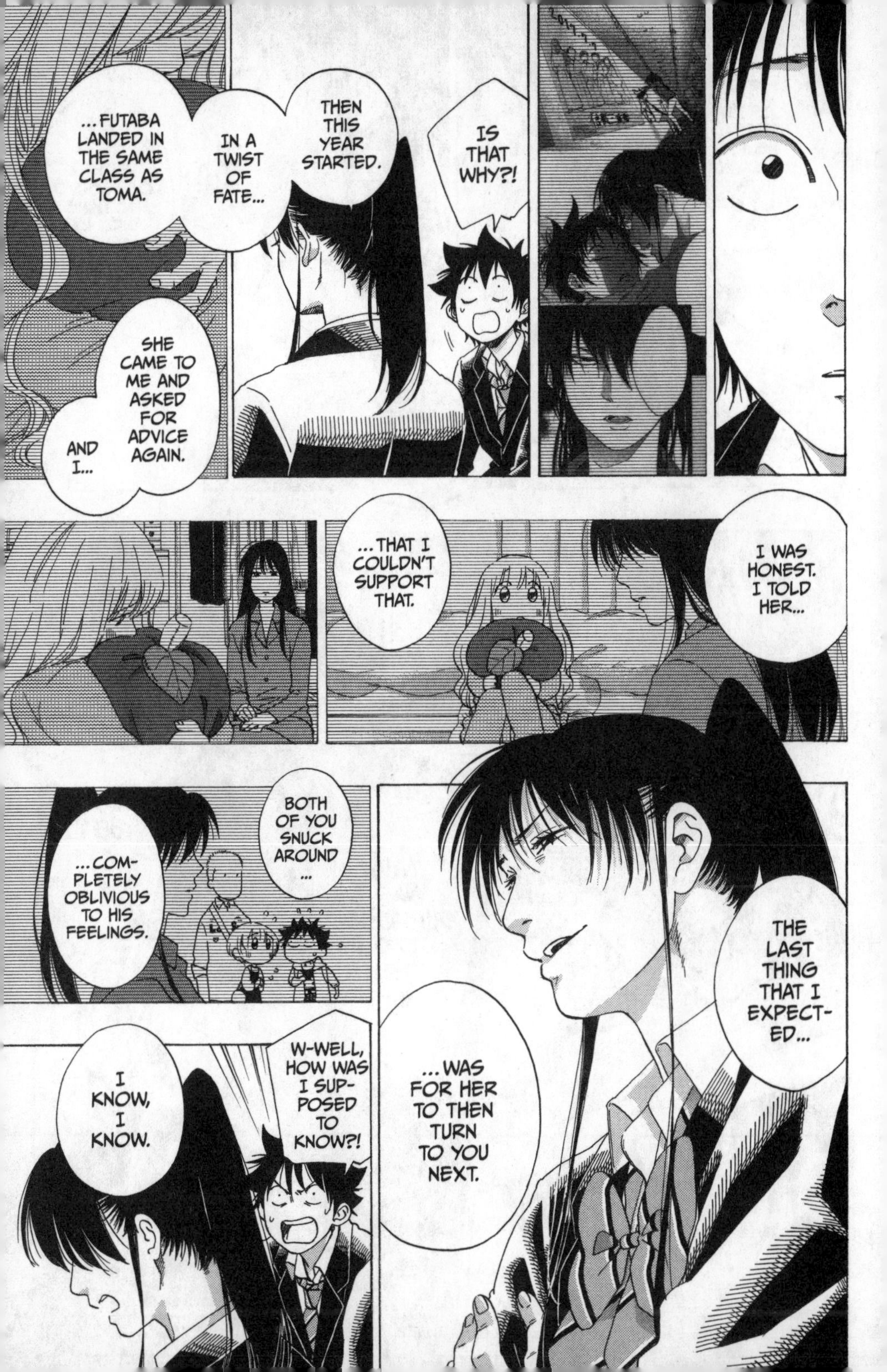
IS THAT WHY?!
THEN THIS YEAR STARTED.
IN A TWIST OF FATE...
...FUTABA LANDED IN THE SAME CLASS AS TOMA.
SHE CAME TO ME AND ASKED FOR ADVICE AGAIN.
AND I...
I WAS HONEST. I TOLD HER...
...THAT I COULDN'T SUPPORT THAT.
THE LAST THING THAT I EXPECTED...
...WAS FOR HER TO THEN TURN TO YOU NEXT.
BOTH OF YOU SNUCK AROUND...
...COMPLETELY OBLIVIOUS TO HIS FEELINGS.
W-WELL, HOW WAS I SUPPOSED TO KNOW?!
I KNOW, I KNOW.

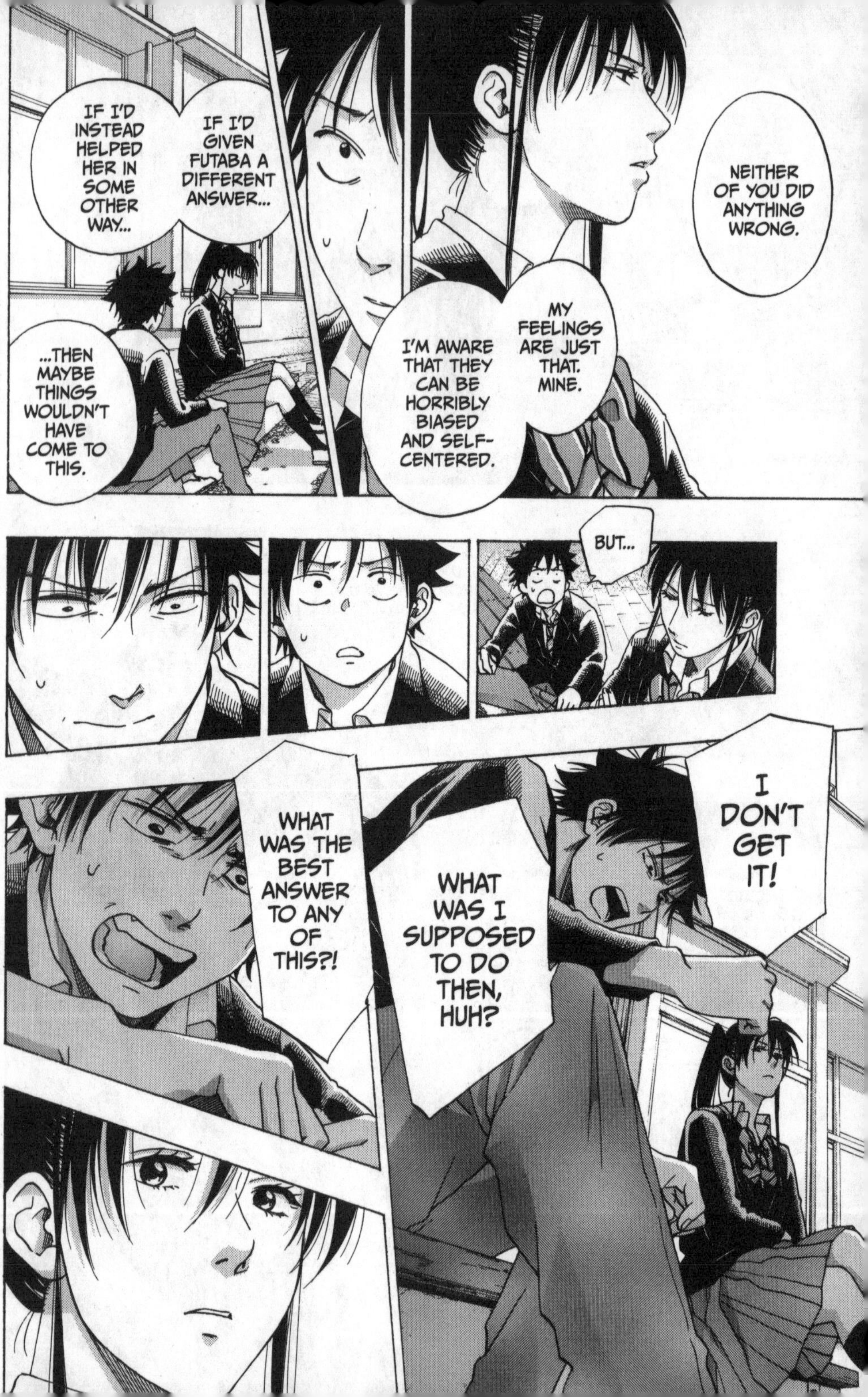
NEITHER OF YOU DID ANYTHING WRONG.
MY FEELINGS ARE JUST THAT. MINE.
I'M AWARE THAT THEY CAN BE HORRIBLY BIASED AND SELF-CENTERED.
IF I'D GIVEN FUTABA A DIFFERENT ANSWER...
IF I'D INSTEAD HELPED HER IN SOME OTHER WAY...
...THEN MAYBE THINGS WOULDN'T HAVE COME TO THIS.
BUT...
I DON'T GET IT!
WHAT WAS I SUPPOSED TO DO THEN, HUH?
WHAT WAS THE BEST ANSWER TO ANY OF THIS?!

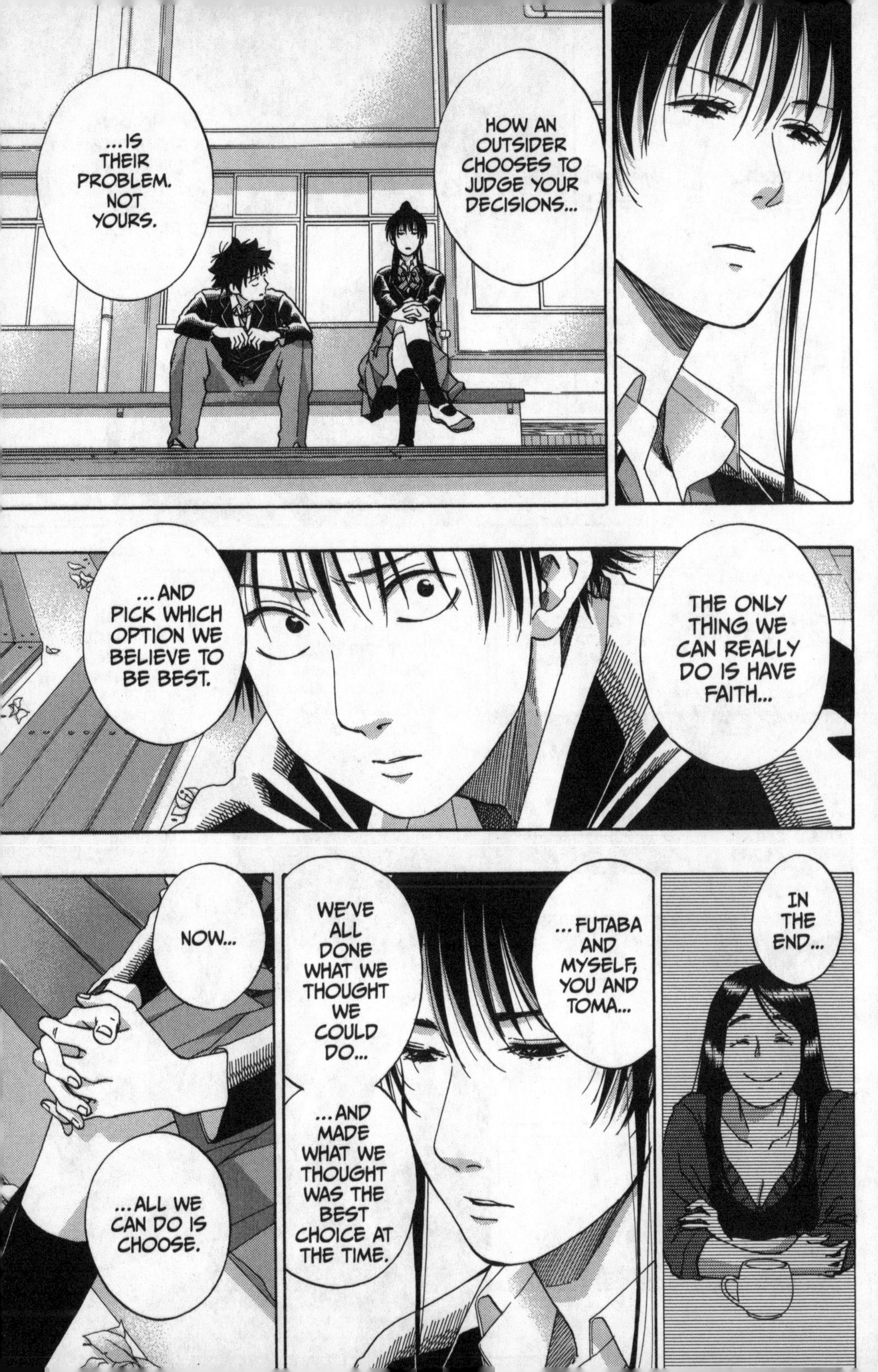
HOW AN OUTSIDER CHOOSES TO JUDGE YOUR DECISIONS...
...IS THEIR PROBLEM. NOT YOURS.
THE ONLY THING WE CAN REALLY DO IS HAVE FAITH...
...AND PICK WHICH OPTION WE BELIEVE TO BE BEST.
IN THE END...
...FUTABA AND MYSELF, YOU AND TOMA...
WE'VE ALL DONE WHAT WE THOUGHT WE COULD DO...
...AND MADE WHAT WE THOUGHT WAS THE BEST CHOICE AT THE TIME.
NOW...
...ALL WE CAN DO IS CHOOSE.

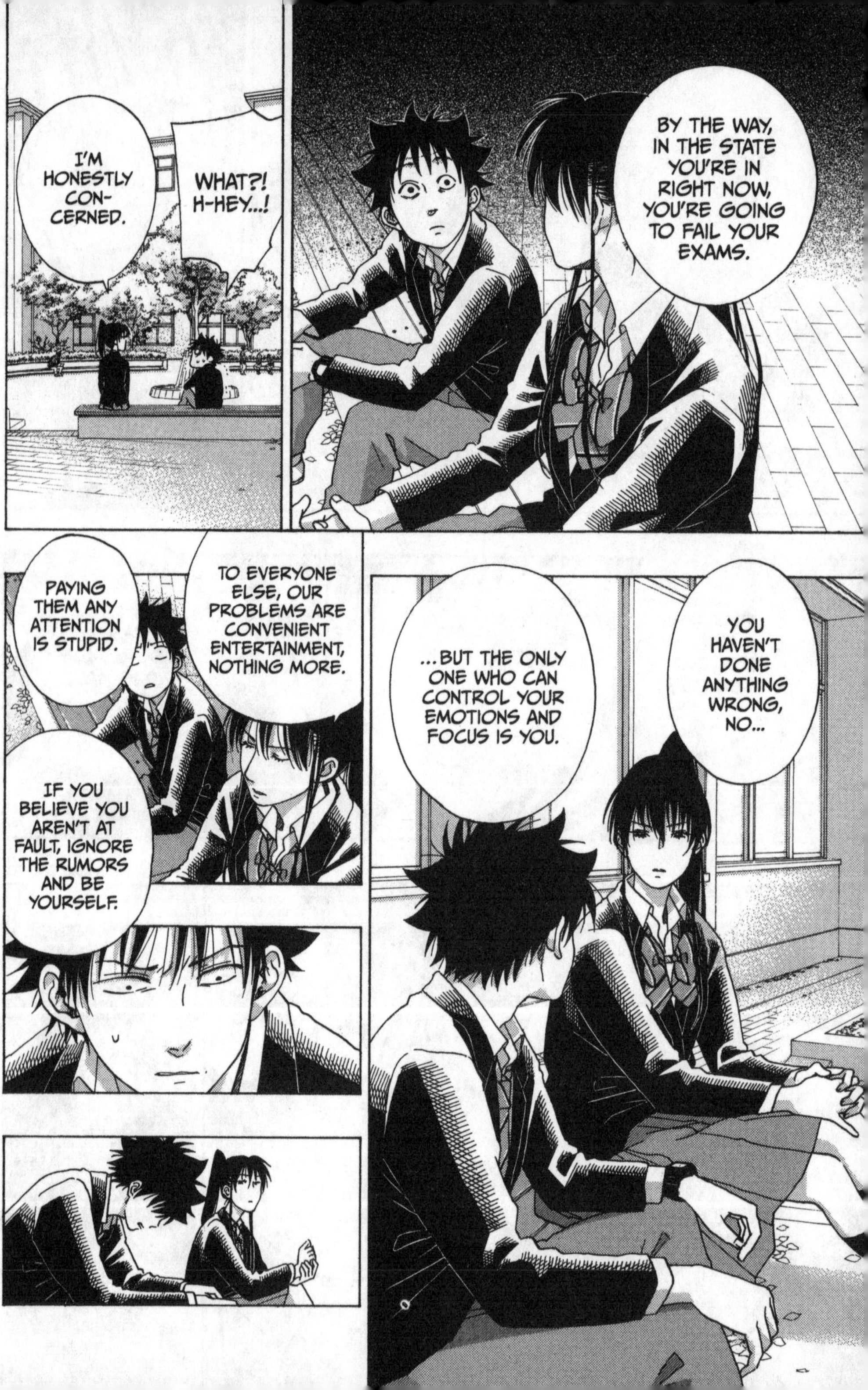

BY THE WAY, IN THE STATE YOU'RE IN RIGHT NOW, YOU'RE GOING TO FAIL YOUR EXAMS.
WHAT?! H-HEY...!
I'M HONESTLY CON-CERNED.
YOU HAVEN'T DONE ANYTHING WRONG, NO...
...BUT THE ONLY ONE WHO CAN CONTROL YOUR EMOTIONS AND FOCUS IS YOU.
TO EVERYONE ELSE, OUR PROBLEMS ARE CONVENIENT ENTERTAINMENT, NOTHING MORE.
PAYING THEM ANY ATTENTION IS STUPID.
IF YOU BELIEVE YOU AREN'T AT FAULT, IGNORE THE RUMORS AND BE YOURSELF.

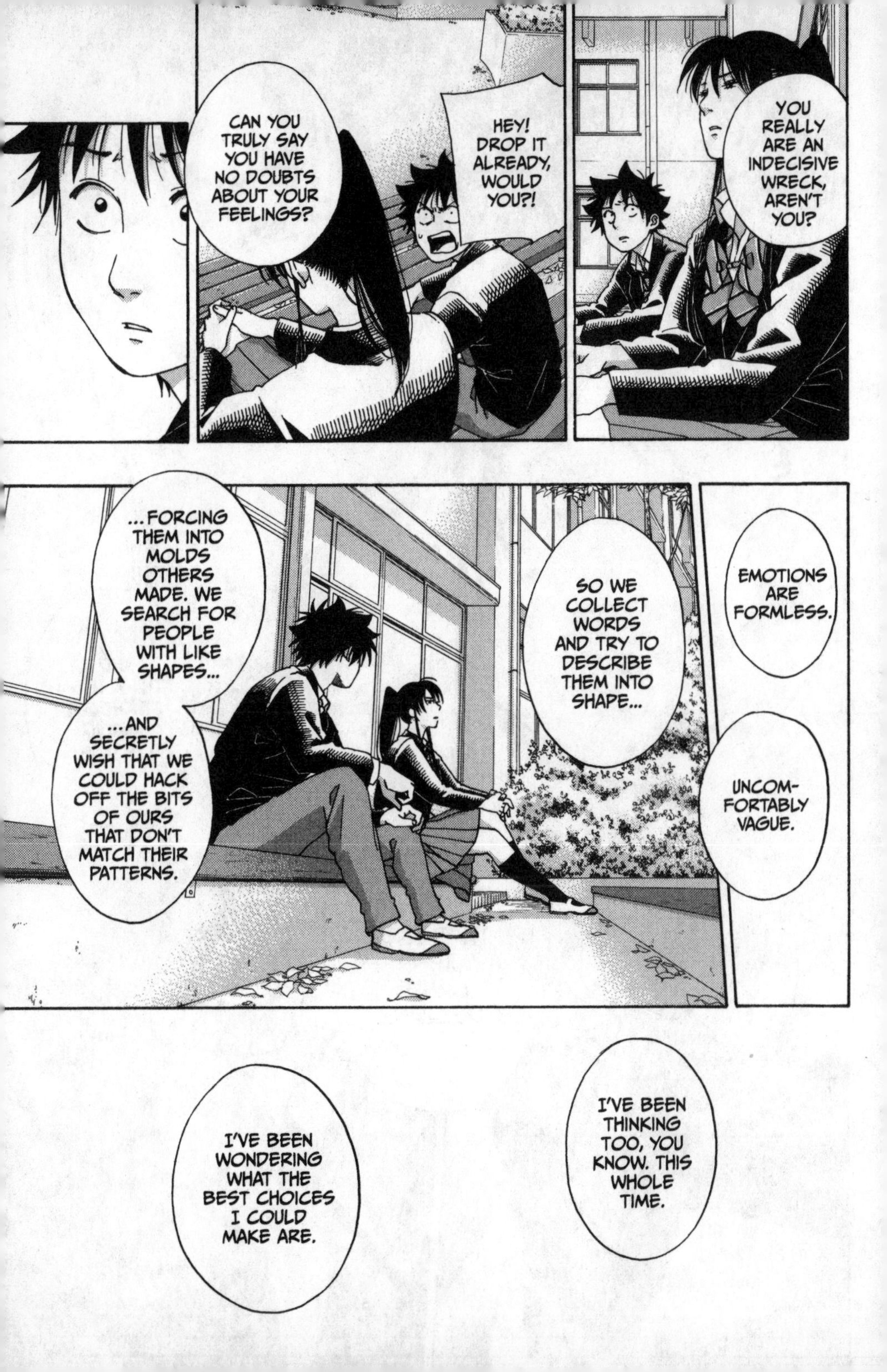
YOU REALLY ARE AN INDECISIVE WRECK, AREN'T YOU?
HEY! DROP IT ALREADY, WOULD YOU?!
CAN YOU TRULY SAY YOU HAVE NO DOUBTS ABOUT YOUR FEELINGS?
EMOTIONS ARE FORMLESS.
UNCOM-FORTABLY VAGUE.
SO WE COLLECT WORDS AND TRY TO DESCRIBE THEM INTO SHAPE...
...FORCING THEM INTO MOLDS OTHERS MADE. WE SEARCH FOR PEOPLE WITH LIKE SHAPES...
...AND SECRETLY WISH THAT WE COULD HACK OFF THE BITS OF OURS THAT DON'T MATCH THEIR PATTERNS.
I'VE BEEN THINKING TOO, YOU KNOW. THIS WHOLE TIME.
I'VE BEEN WONDERING WHAT THE BEST CHOICES I COULD MAKE ARE.

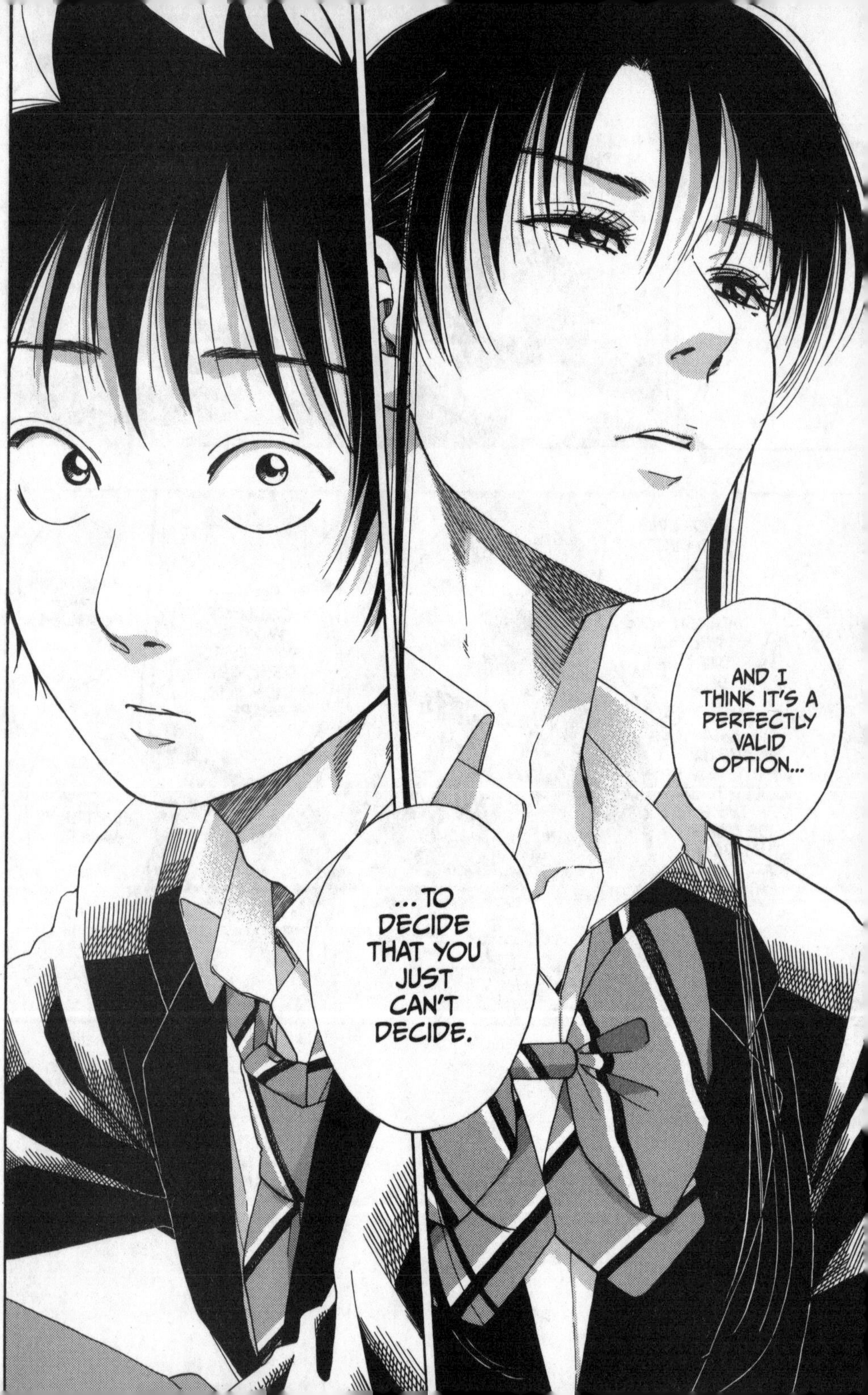
AND I THINK IT'S A PERFECTLY VALID OPTION...
...TO DECIDE THAT YOU JUST CAN'T DECIDE.

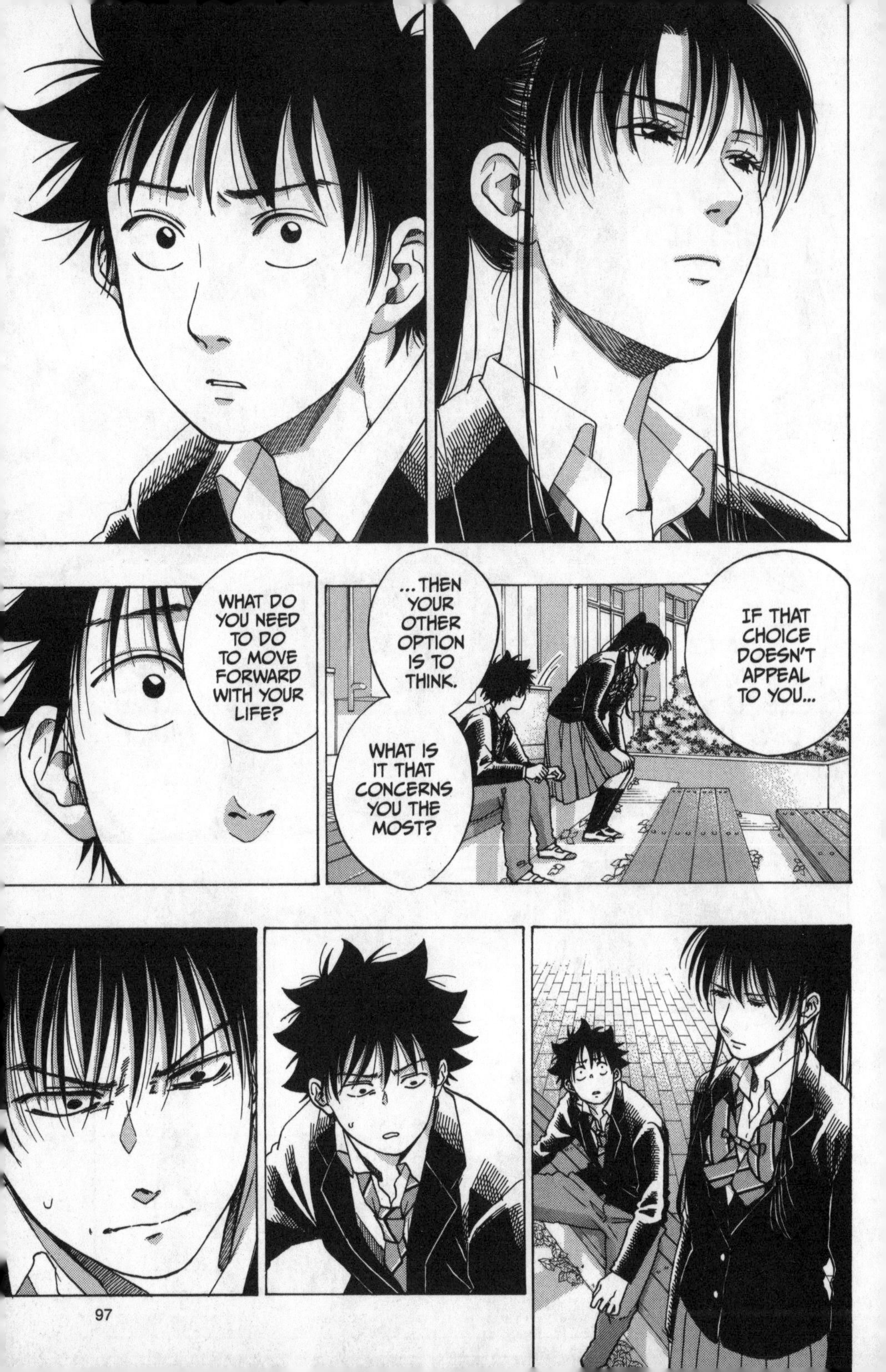
IF THAT CHOICE DOESN'T APPEAL TO YOU...
...THEN YOUR OTHER OPTION IS TO THINK.
WHAT IS IT THAT CONCERNS YOU THE MOST?
WHAT DO YOU NEED TO DO TO MOVE FORWARD WITH YOUR LIFE?

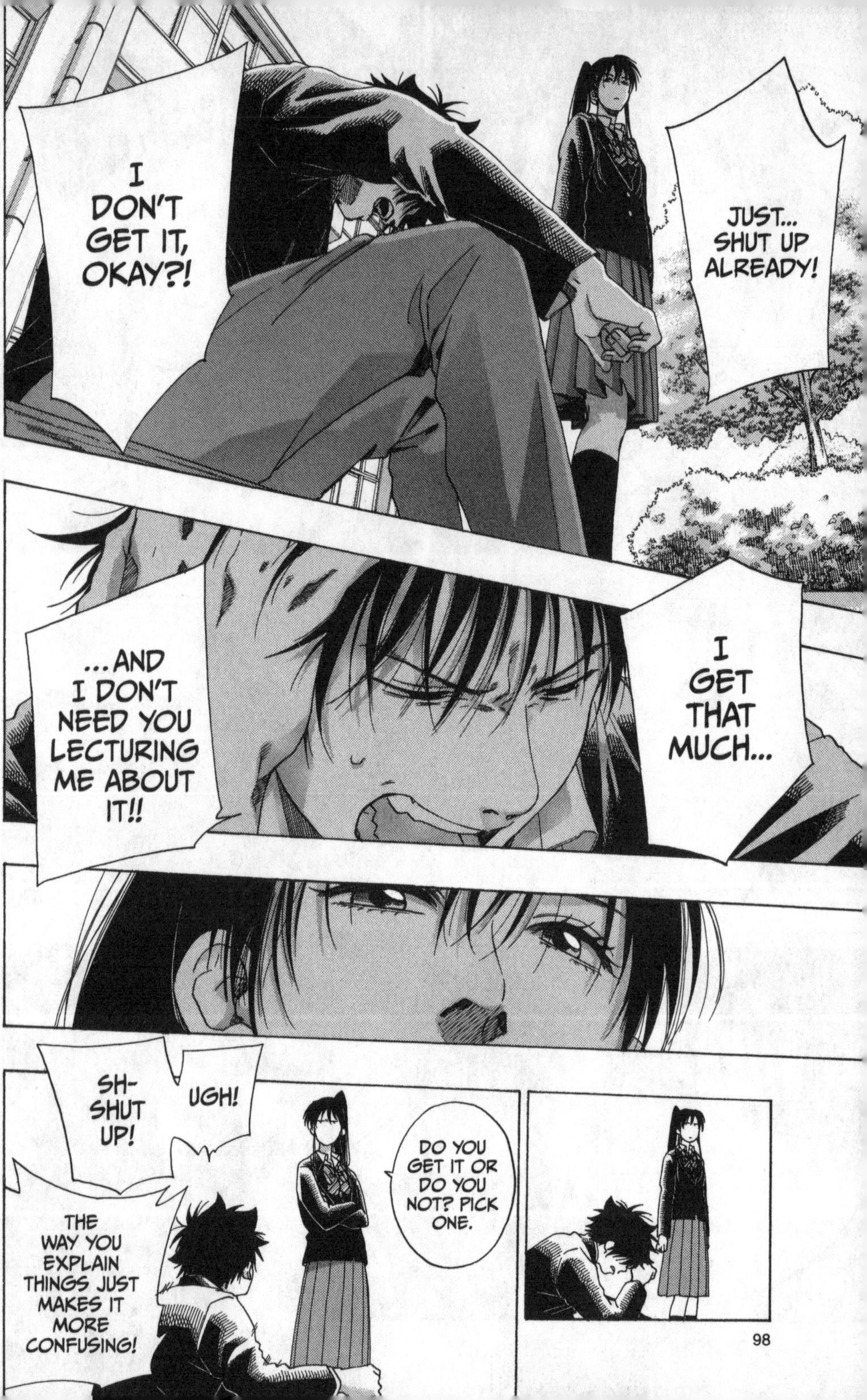
JUST... SHUT UP ALREADY!
I DON'T GET IT, OKAY?!
I GET THAT MUCH...
...AND I DON'T NEED YOU LECTURING ME ABOUT IT!!
DO YOU GET IT OR DO YOU NOT? PICK ONE.
UGH!
SH- SHUT UP!
THE WAY YOU EXPLAIN THINGS JUST MAKES IT MORE CONFUSING!

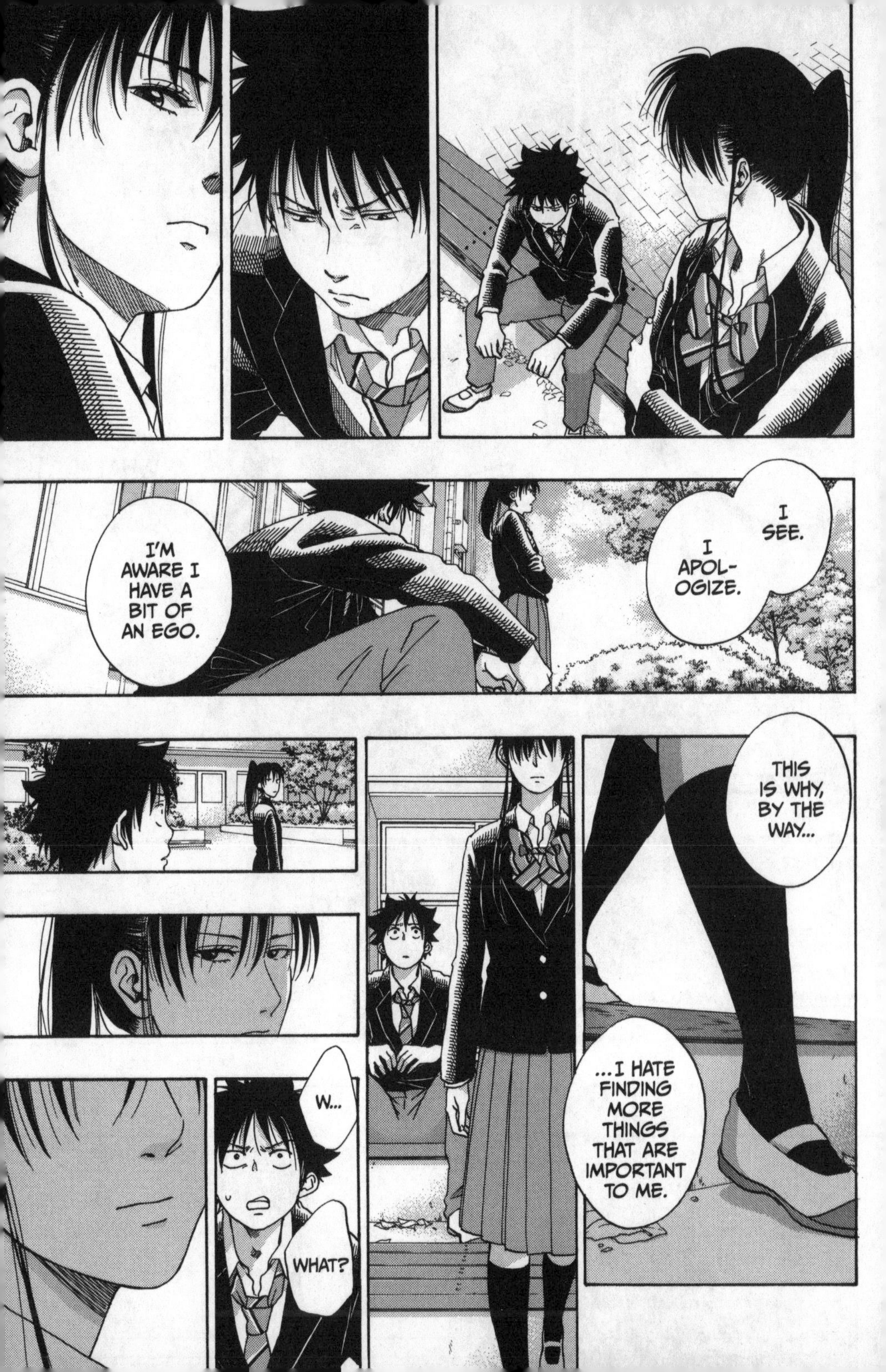
I SEE.
I APOLOGIZE.
I'M AWARE I HAVE A BIT OF AN EGO.
THIS IS WHY, BY THE WAY...
...I HATE FINDING MORE THINGS THAT ARE IMPORTANT TO ME.
W...
WHAT?

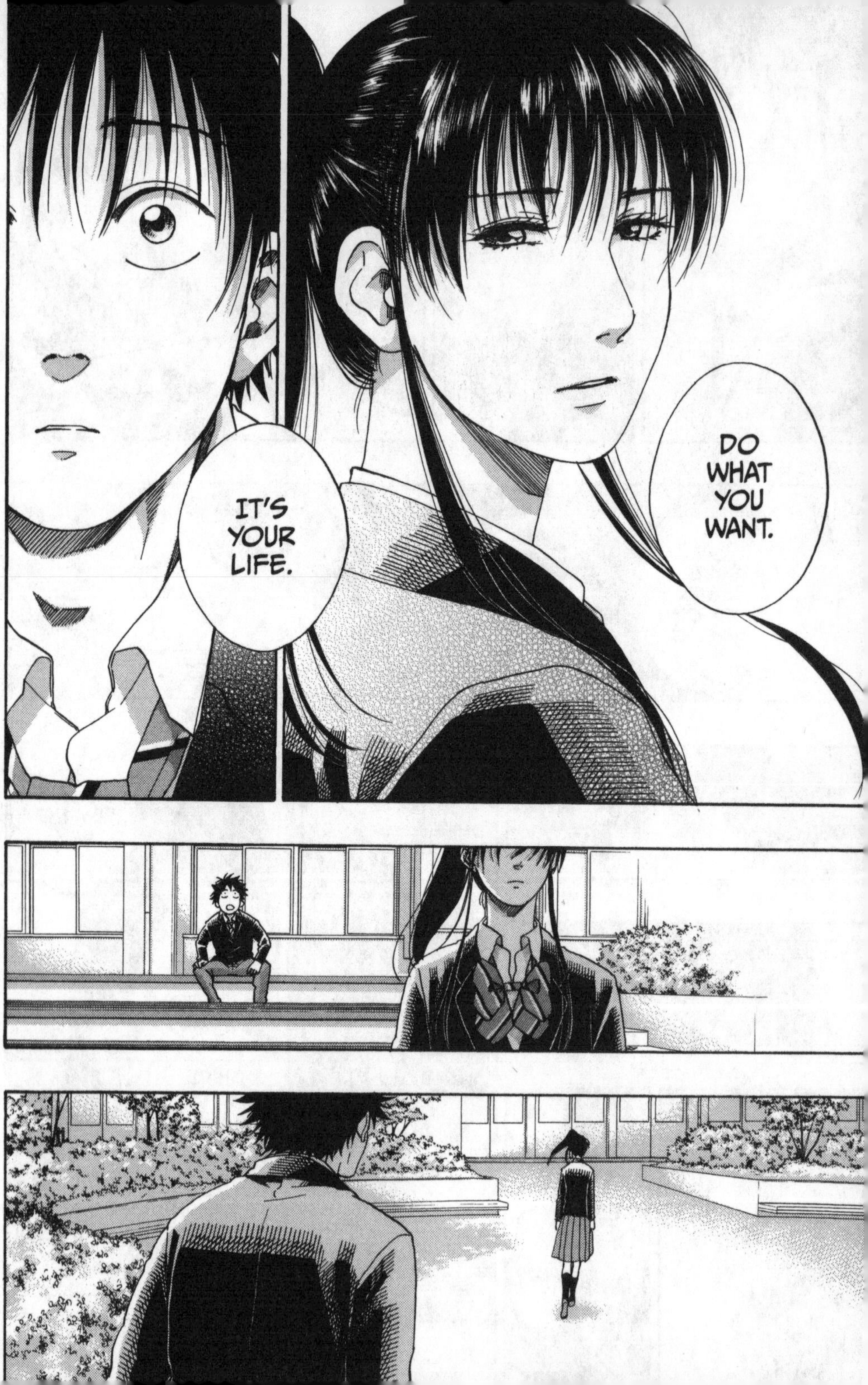
DO WHAT YOU WANT.
IT'S YOUR LIFE.

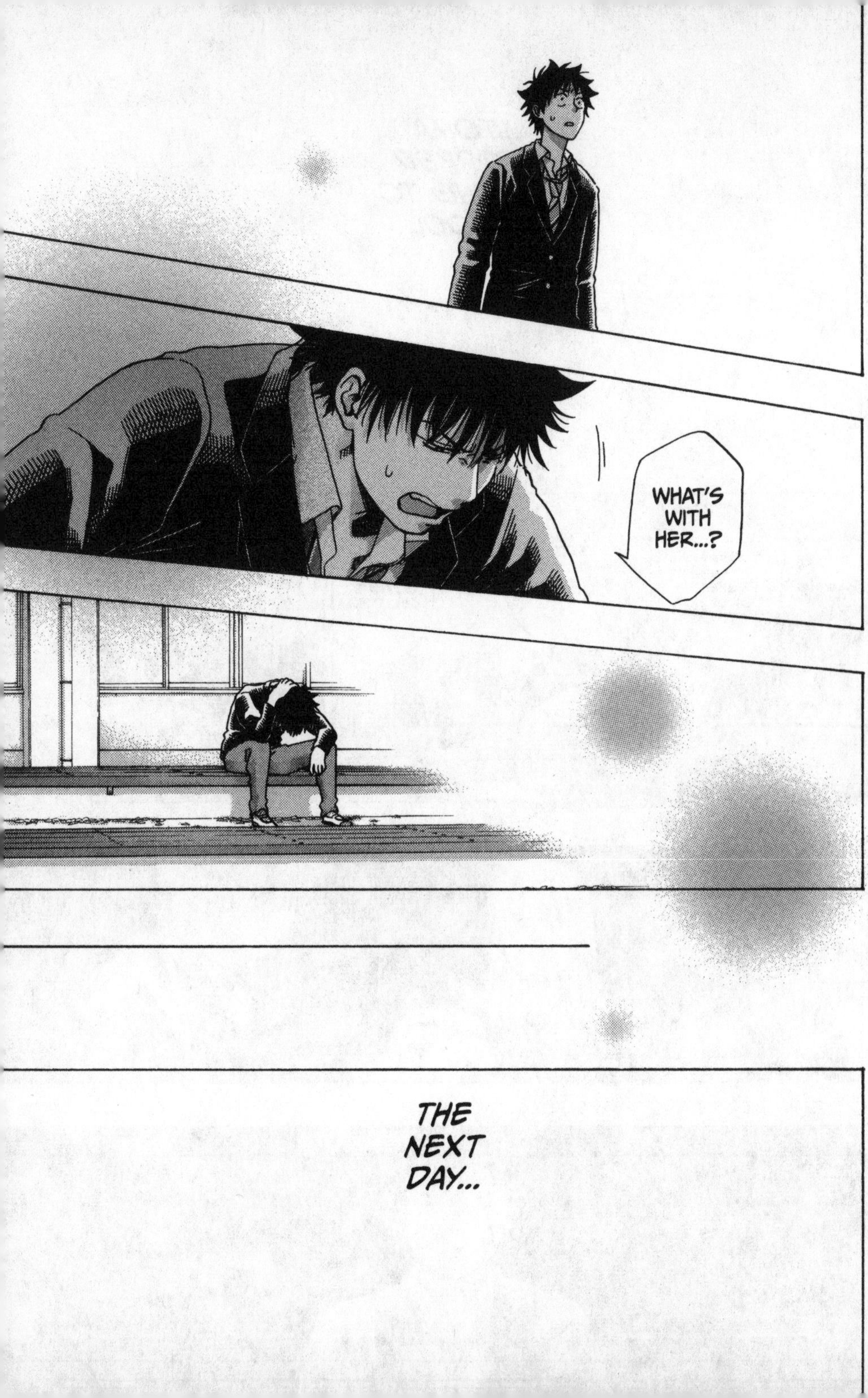
WHAT'S WITH HER...?
THE NEXT DAY...

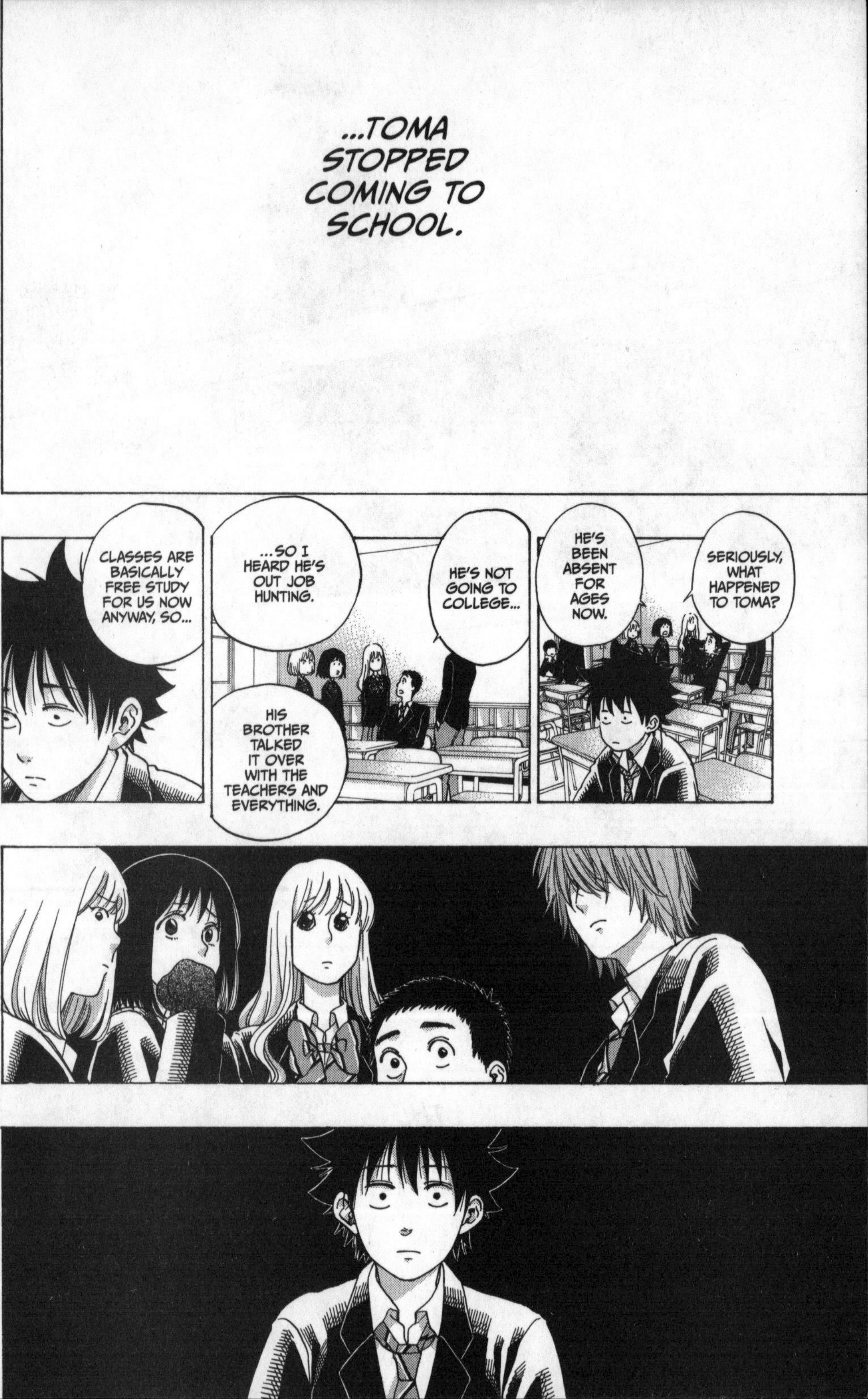
...TOMA STOPPED COMING TO SCHOOL.
SERIOUSLY, WHAT HAPPENED TO TOMA?
HE'S BEEN ABSENT FOR AGES NOW.
HE'S NOT GOING TO COLLEGE...
...SO I HEARD HE'S OUT JOB HUNTING.
HIS BROTHER TALKED IT OVER WITH THE TEACHERS AND EVERYTHING.
CLASSES ARE BASICALLY FREE STUDY FOR US NOW ANYWAY, SO...

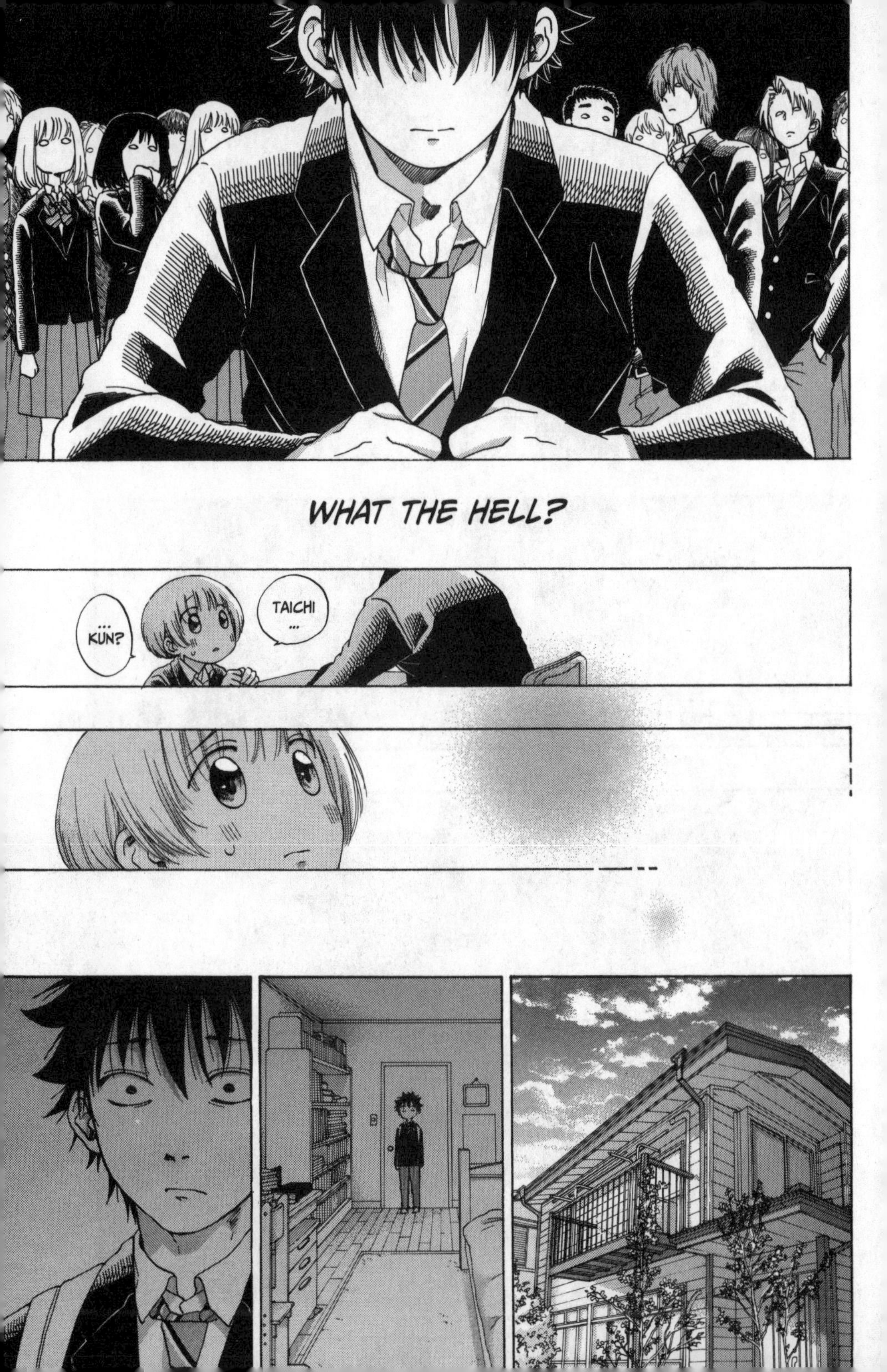
WHAT THE HELL?
TAICHI ...
... KUN?

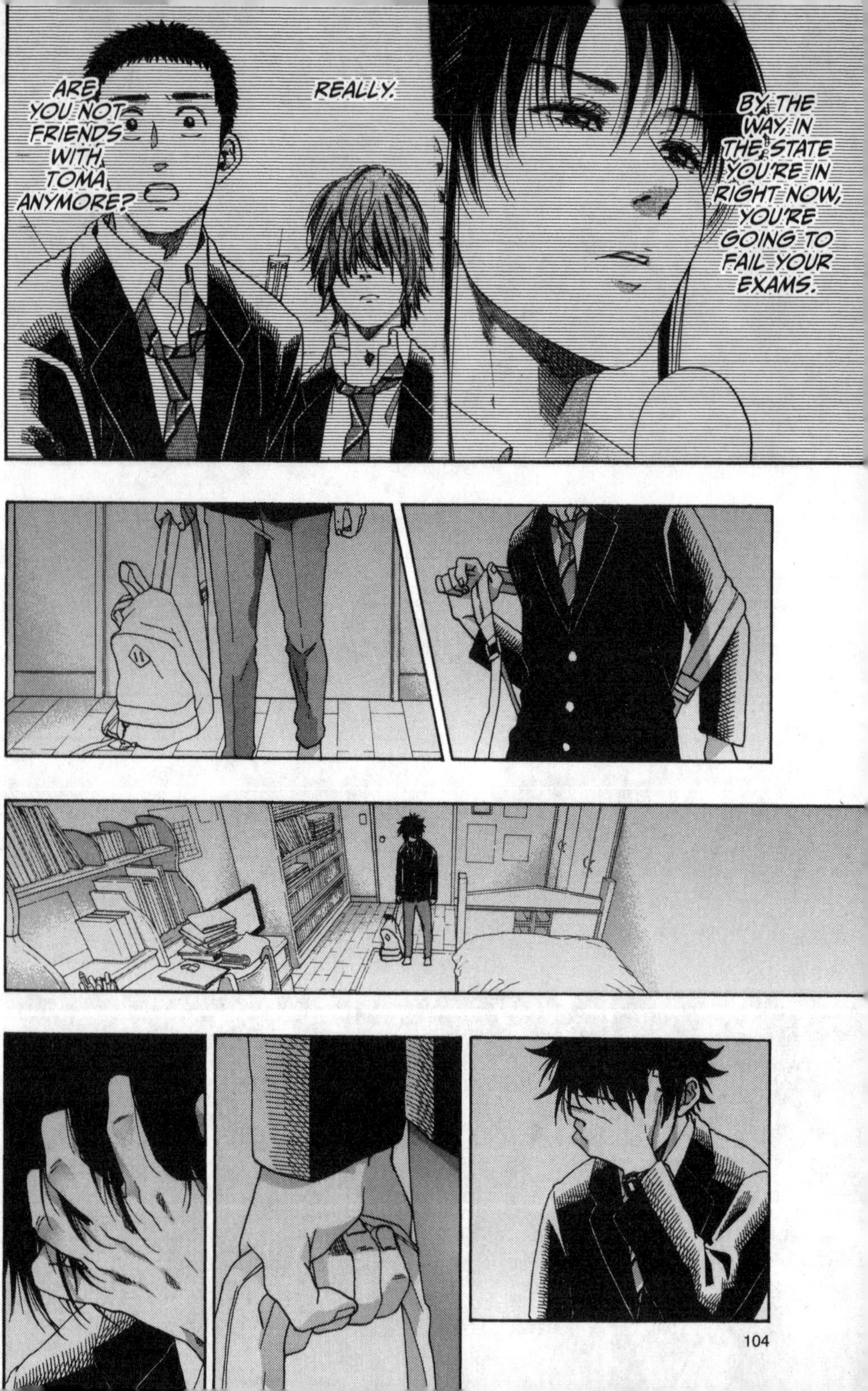
BY THE WAY, IN THE STATE YOU'RE IN RIGHT NOW, YOU'RE GOING TO FAIL YOUR EXAMS.
REALLY.
ARE YOU NOT FRIENDS WITH TOMA ANYMORE?

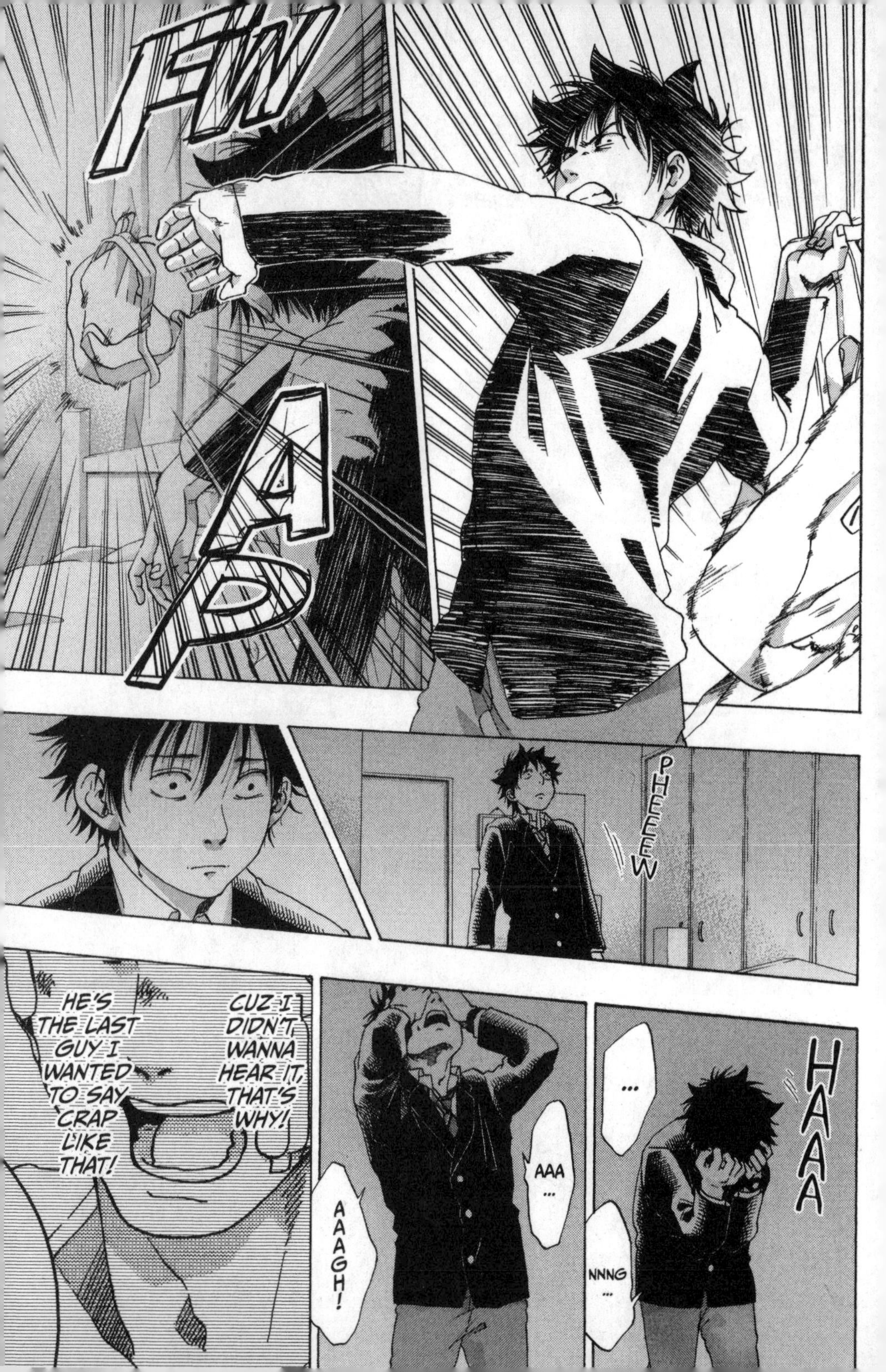
FWAP
PHEEEW
HAAA
...
NNNG ...
AAA ...
AAAAGH!
CUZ I DIDN'T WANNA HEAR IT, THAT'S WHY!
HE'S THE LAST GUY I WANTED TO SAY CRAP LIKE THAT!

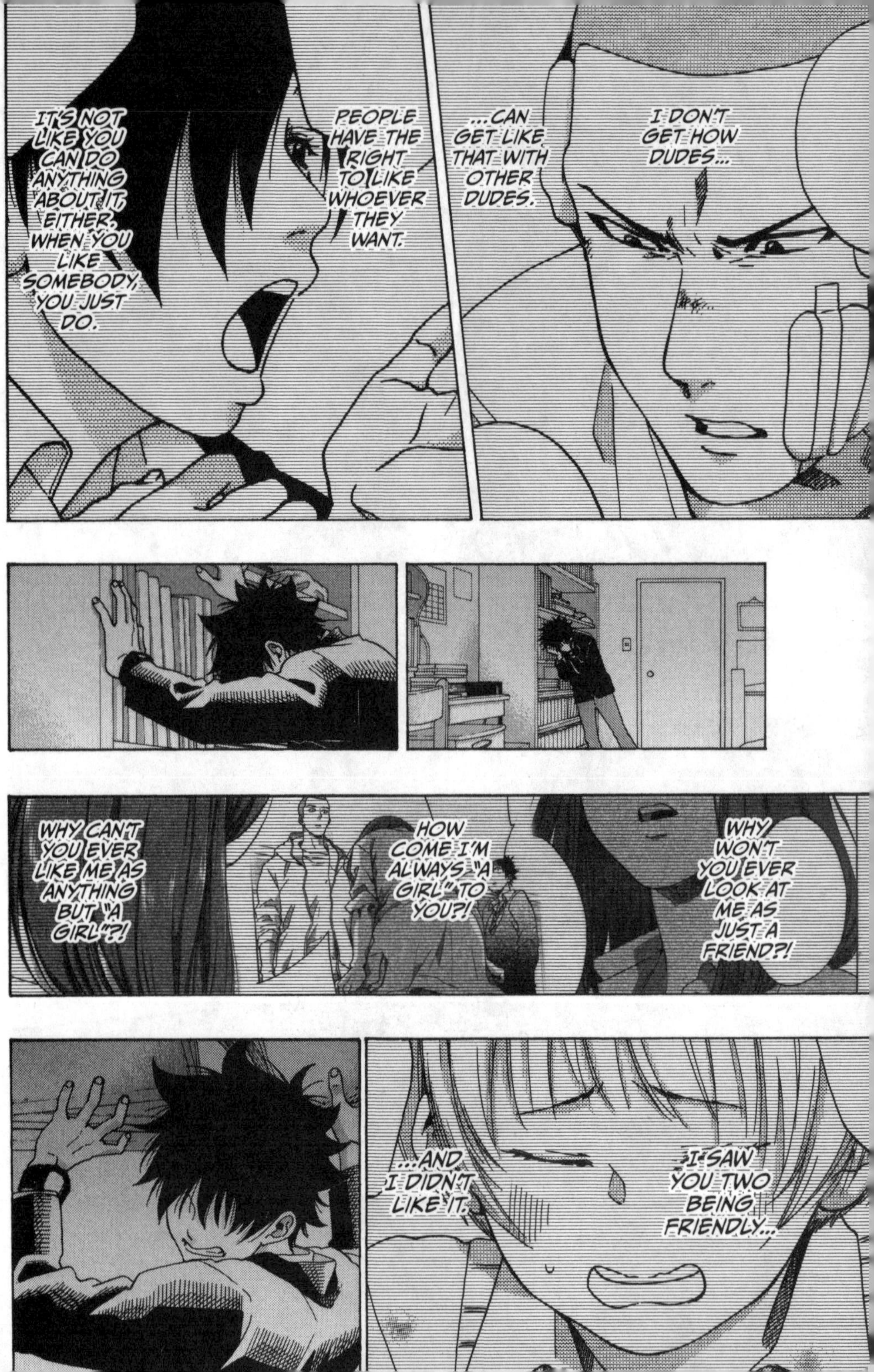
I DON'T GET HOW DUDES...
...CAN GET LIKE THAT WITH OTHER DUDES.
PEOPLE HAVE THE RIGHT TO LIKE WHOEVER THEY WANT.
IT'S NOT LIKE YOU CAN DO ANYTHING ABOUT IT, EITHER. WHEN YOU LIKE SOMEBODY, YOU JUST DO.
WHY WON'T YOU EVER LOOK AT ME AS JUST A FRIEND?!
HOW COME I'M ALWAYS "A GIRL" TO YOU?!
WHY CAN'T YOU EVER LIKE ME AS ANYTHING BUT "A GIRL"?!
I SAW YOU TWO BEING FRIENDLY...
...AND I DIDN'T LIKE IT.

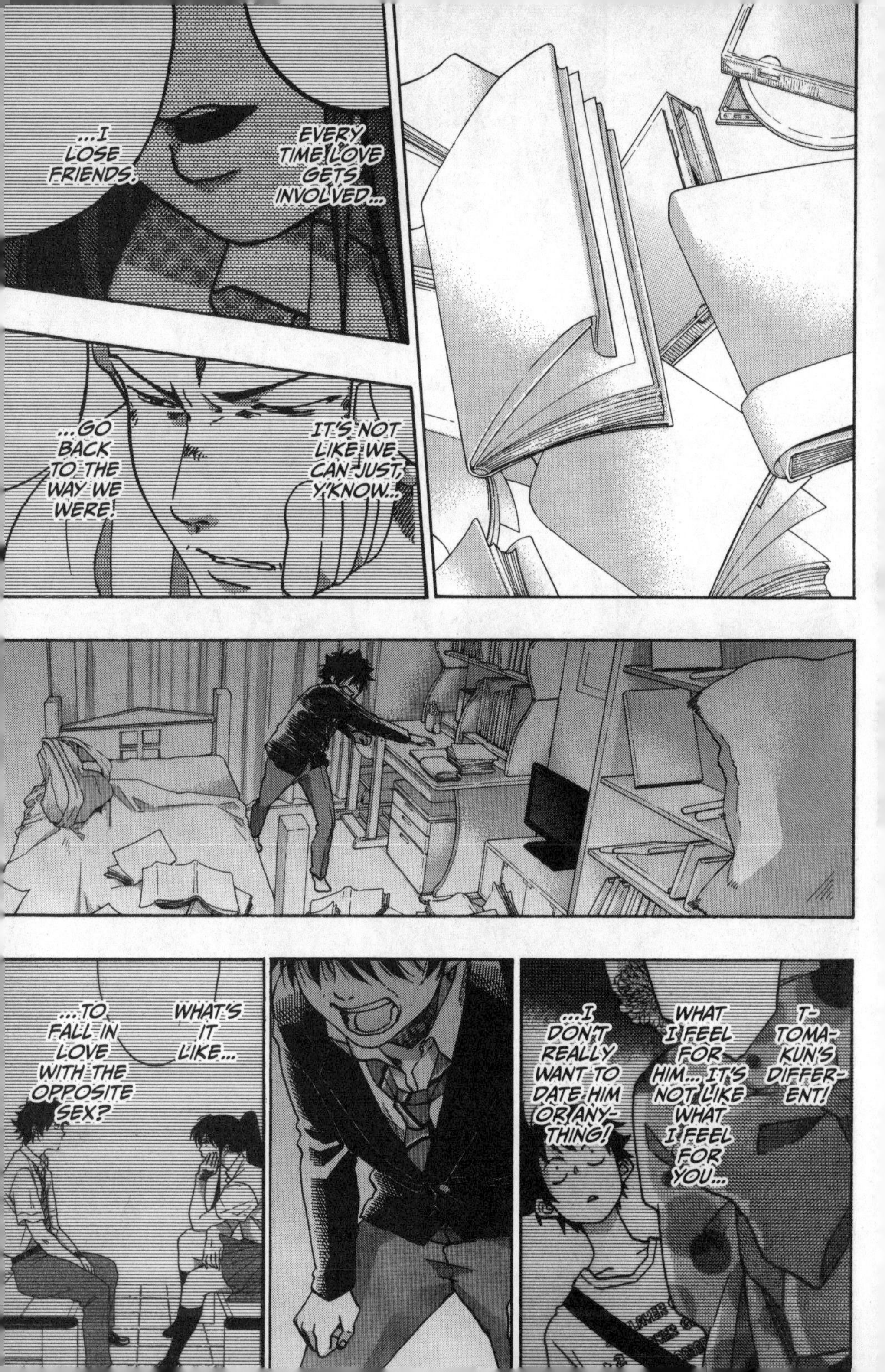
EVERY TIME LOVE GETS INVOLVED...
...I LOSE FRIENDS.
IT'S NOT LIKE WE CAN JUST, Y'KNOW...
...GO BACK TO THE WAY WE WERE!
T-TOMA-KUN'S DIFFERENT!
WHAT I FEEL FOR HIM... IT'S NOT LIKE WHAT I FEEL FOR YOU...
...I DON'T REALLY WANT TO DATE HIM OR ANYTHING!
WHAT'S IT LIKE...
...TO FALL IN LOVE WITH THE OPPOSITE SEX?

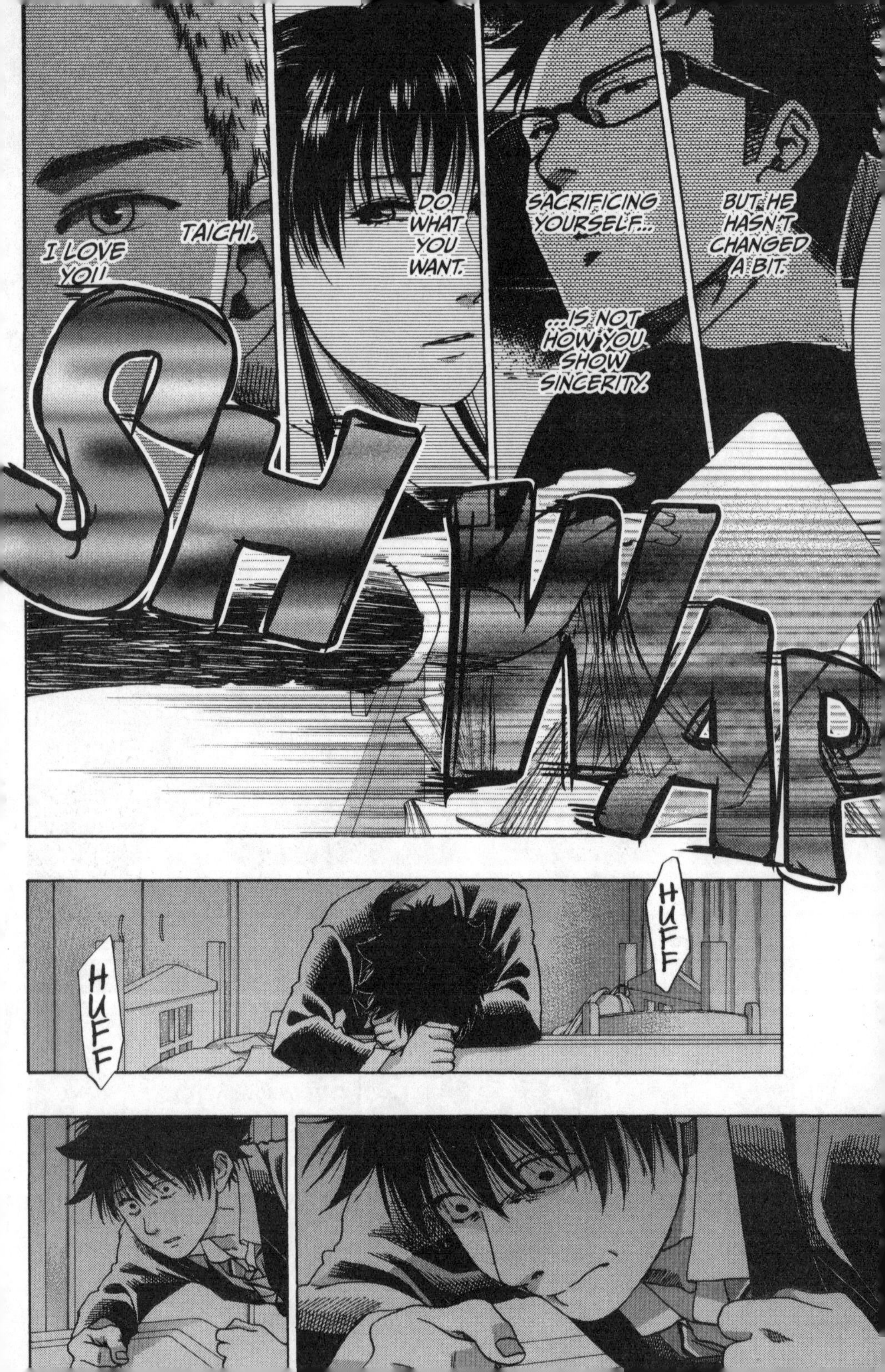
BUT HE HASN'T CHANGED A BIT.
SACRIFICING YOURSELF...
...IS NOT HOW YOU SHOW SINCERITY.
DO WHAT YOU WANT.
TAICHI.
I LOVE YOU.
SHWAP
HUFF
HUFF

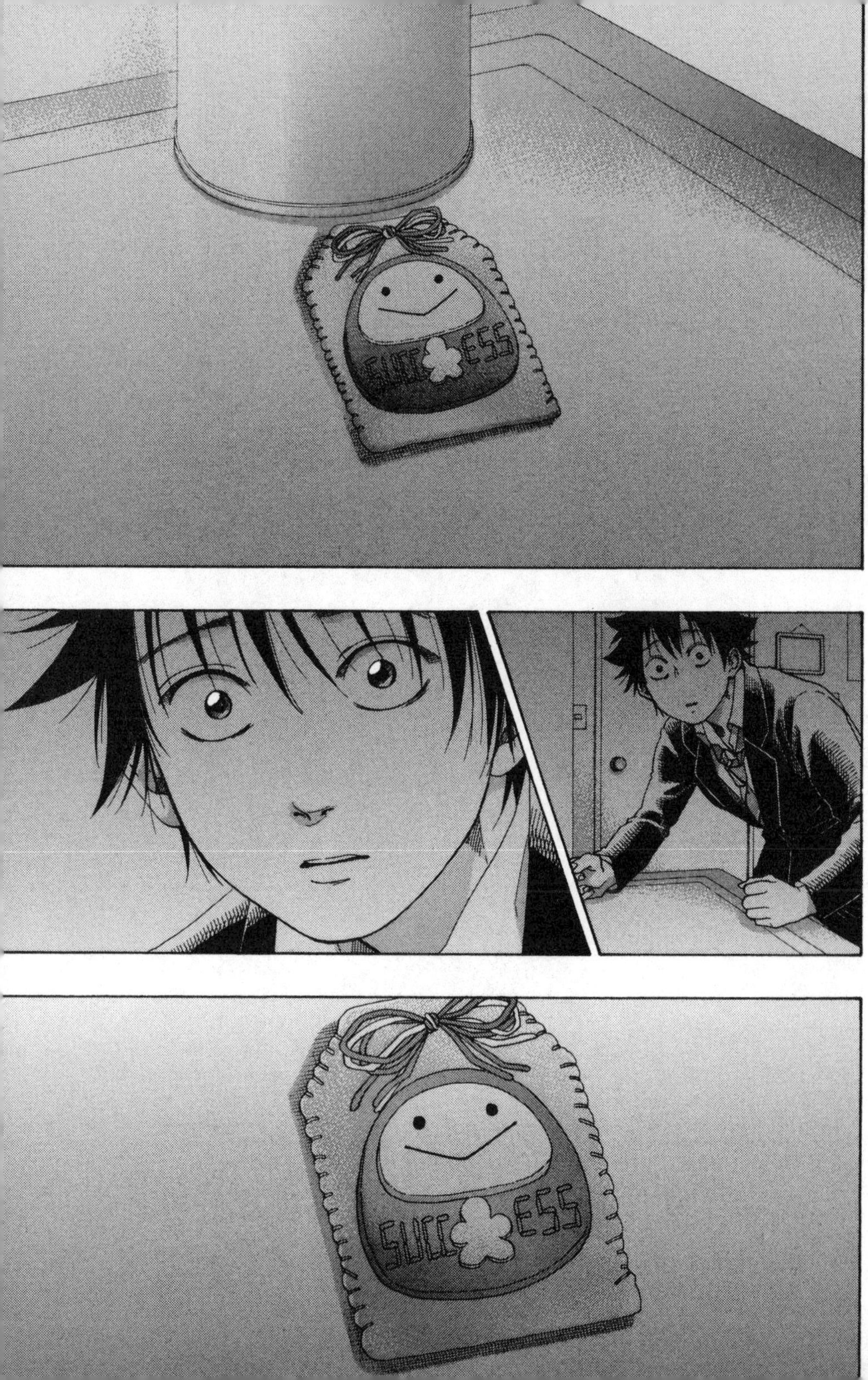
SUCC ESS
SUCC ESS

CHAPTER 52

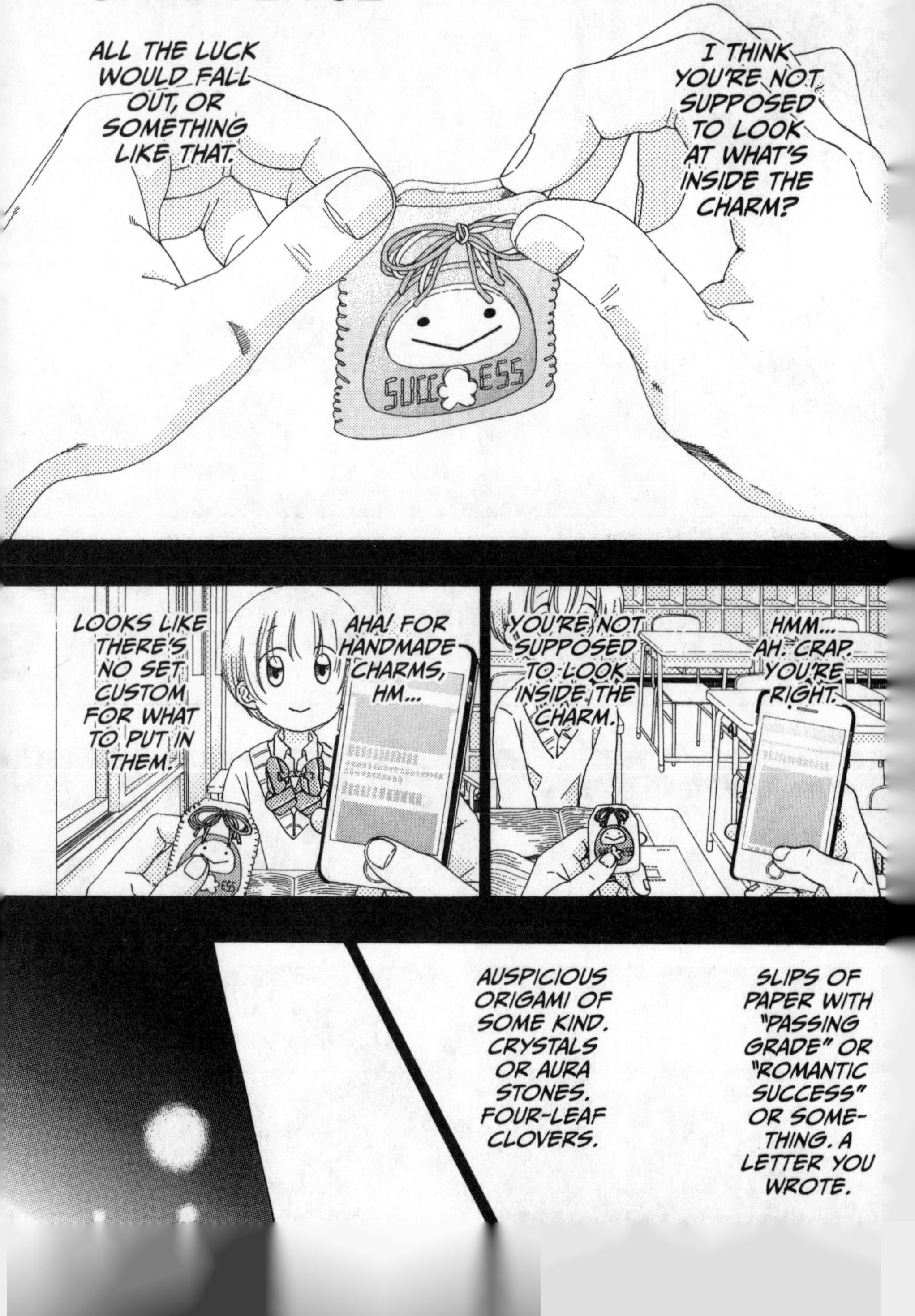
I THINK YOU'RE NOT SUPPOSED TO LOOK AT WHAT'S INSIDE THE CHARM?
ALL THE LUCK WOULD FALL OUT, OR SOMETHING LIKE THAT.
HMM... AH. CRAP. YOU'RE RIGHT.
YOU'RE NOT SUPPOSED TO LOOK INSIDE THE CHARM.
AHA! FOR HANDMADE CHARMS, HM...
LOOKS LIKE THERE'S NO SET CUSTOM FOR WHAT TO PUT IN THEM.
SLIPS OF PAPER WITH "PASSING GRADE" OR "ROMANTIC SUCCESS" OR SOME-THING. A LETTER YOU WROTE.
AUSPICIOUS ORIGAMI OF SOME KIND. CRYSTALS OR AURA STONES. FOUR-LEAF CLOVERS.

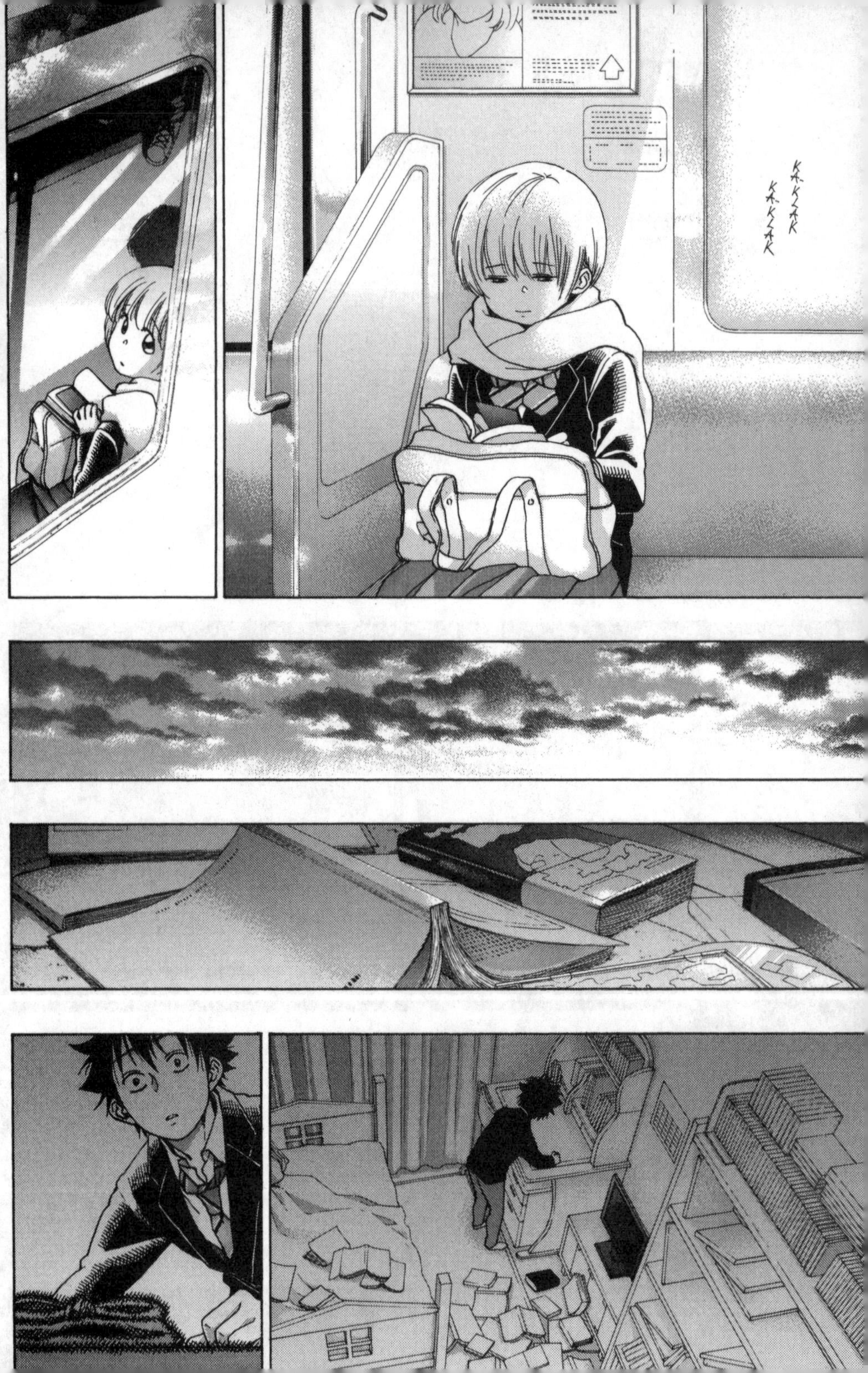
KA-KLAK
KA-KLAK

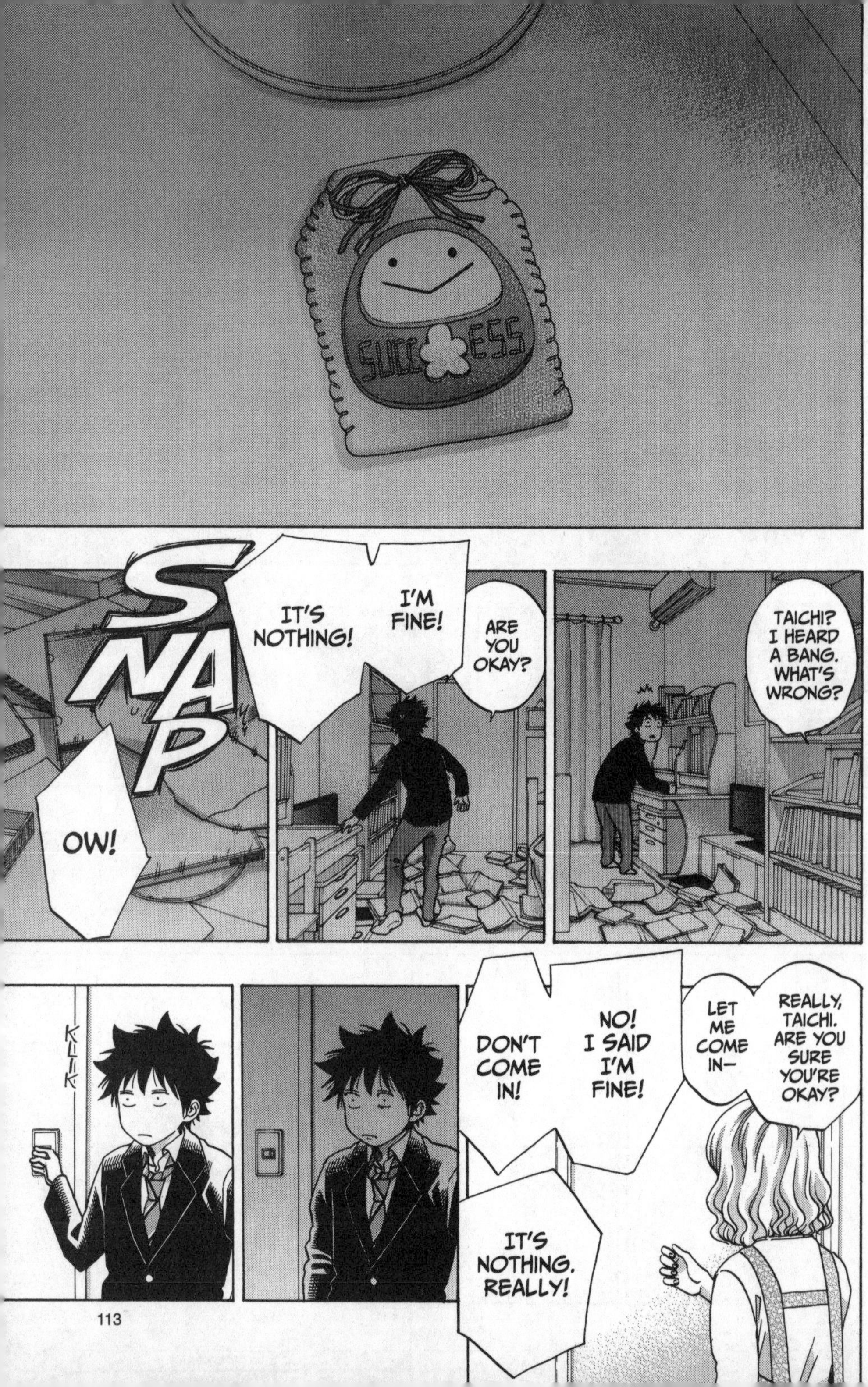
SUCC ESS
TAICHI? I HEARD A BANG. WHAT'S WRONG?
ARE YOU OKAY?
I'M FINE!
IT'S NOTHING!
SNAP
OW!
REALLY, TAICHI. ARE YOU SURE YOU'RE OKAY?
LET ME COME IN—
NO! I SAID I'M FINE!
DON'T COME IN!
IT'S NOTHING. REALLY!
KLIK

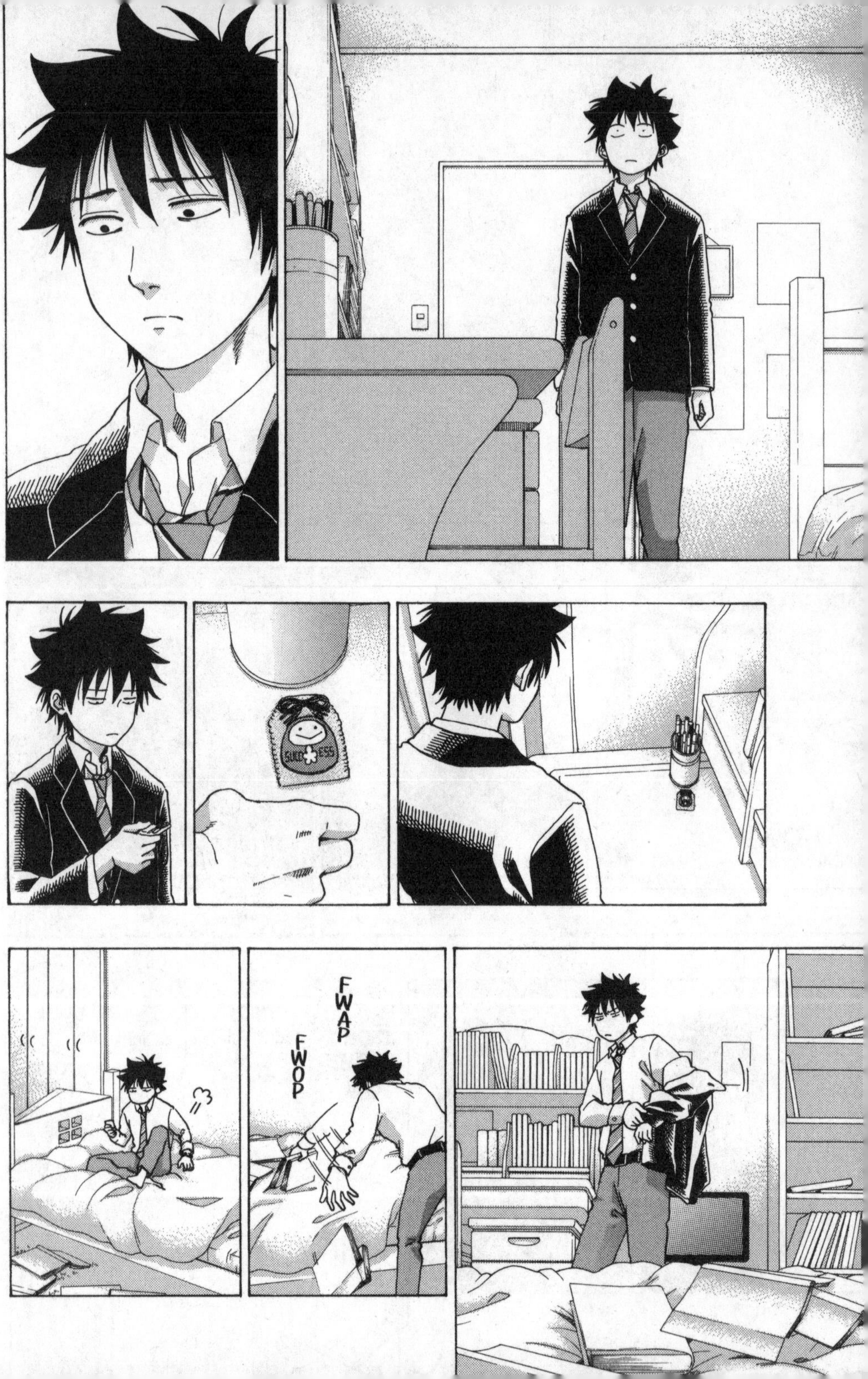
SUCCESS
FWAP
FWOP

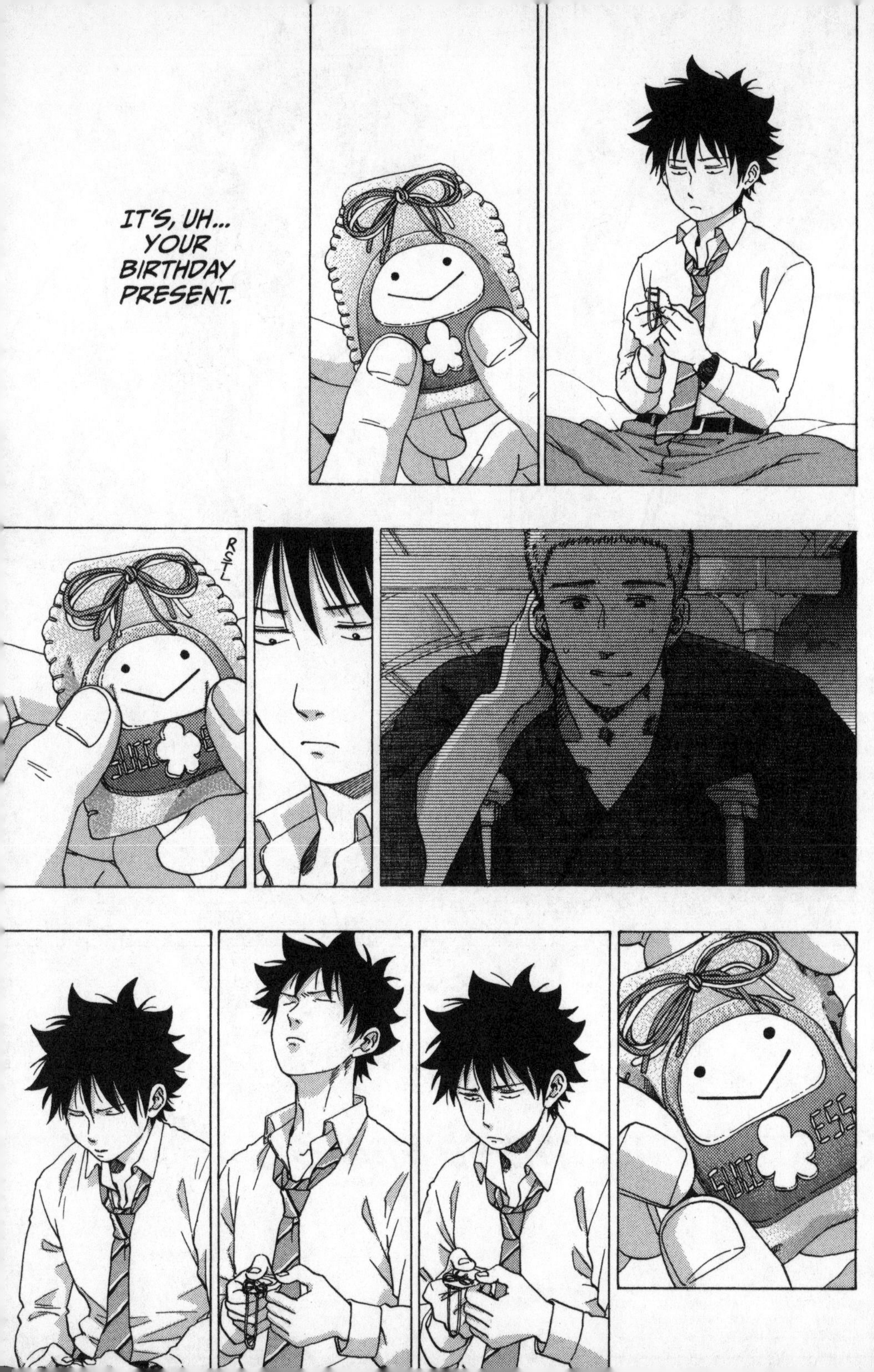
IT'S, UH... YOUR BIRTHDAY PRESENT.
RSTL
ESS

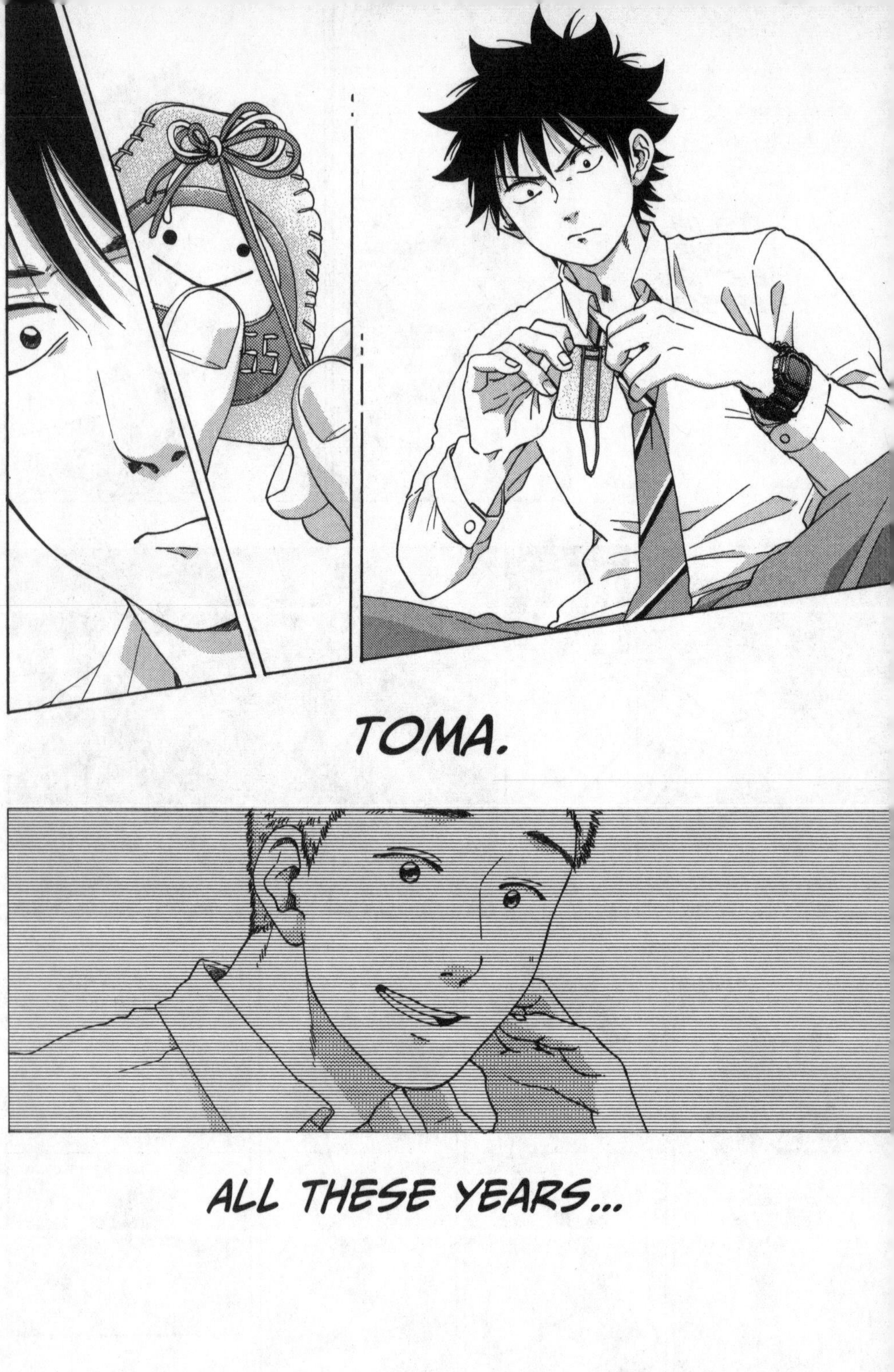
TOMA.
ALL THESE YEARS...

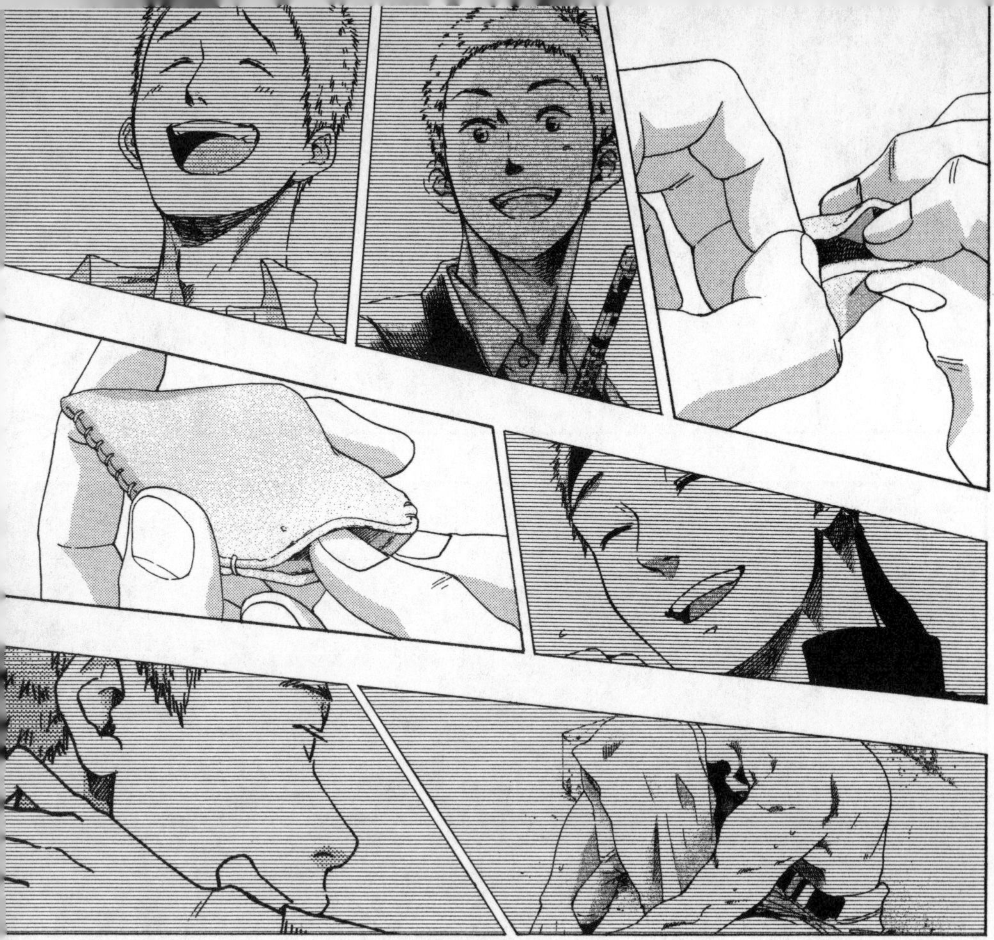

...WHAT HAVE YOU BEEN THINKING?

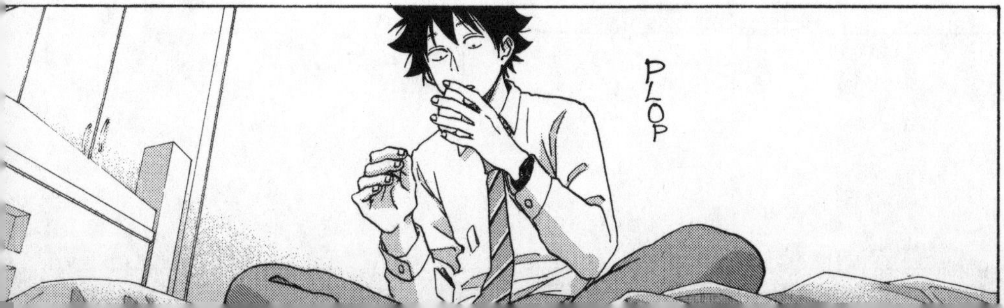
PLOP

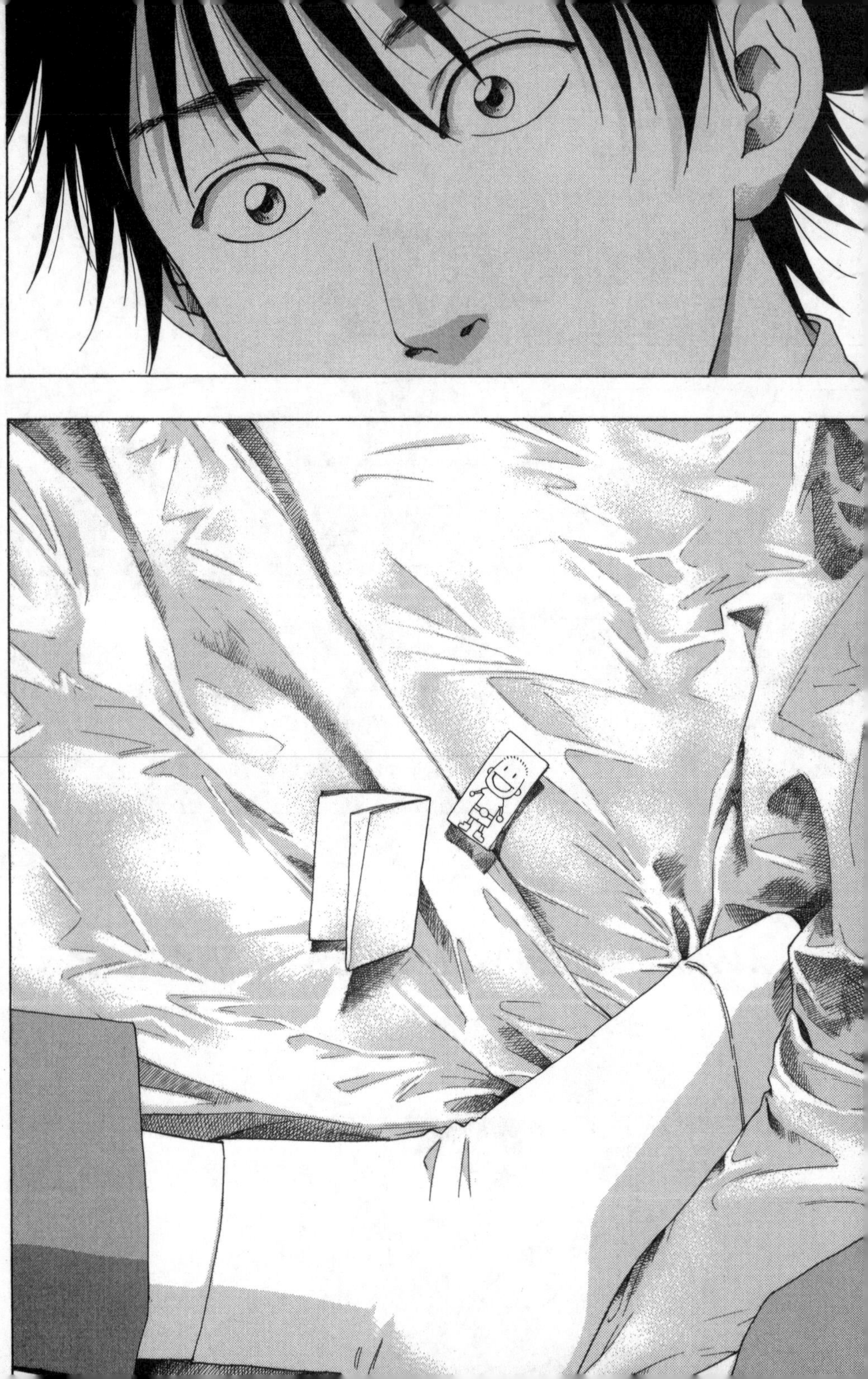

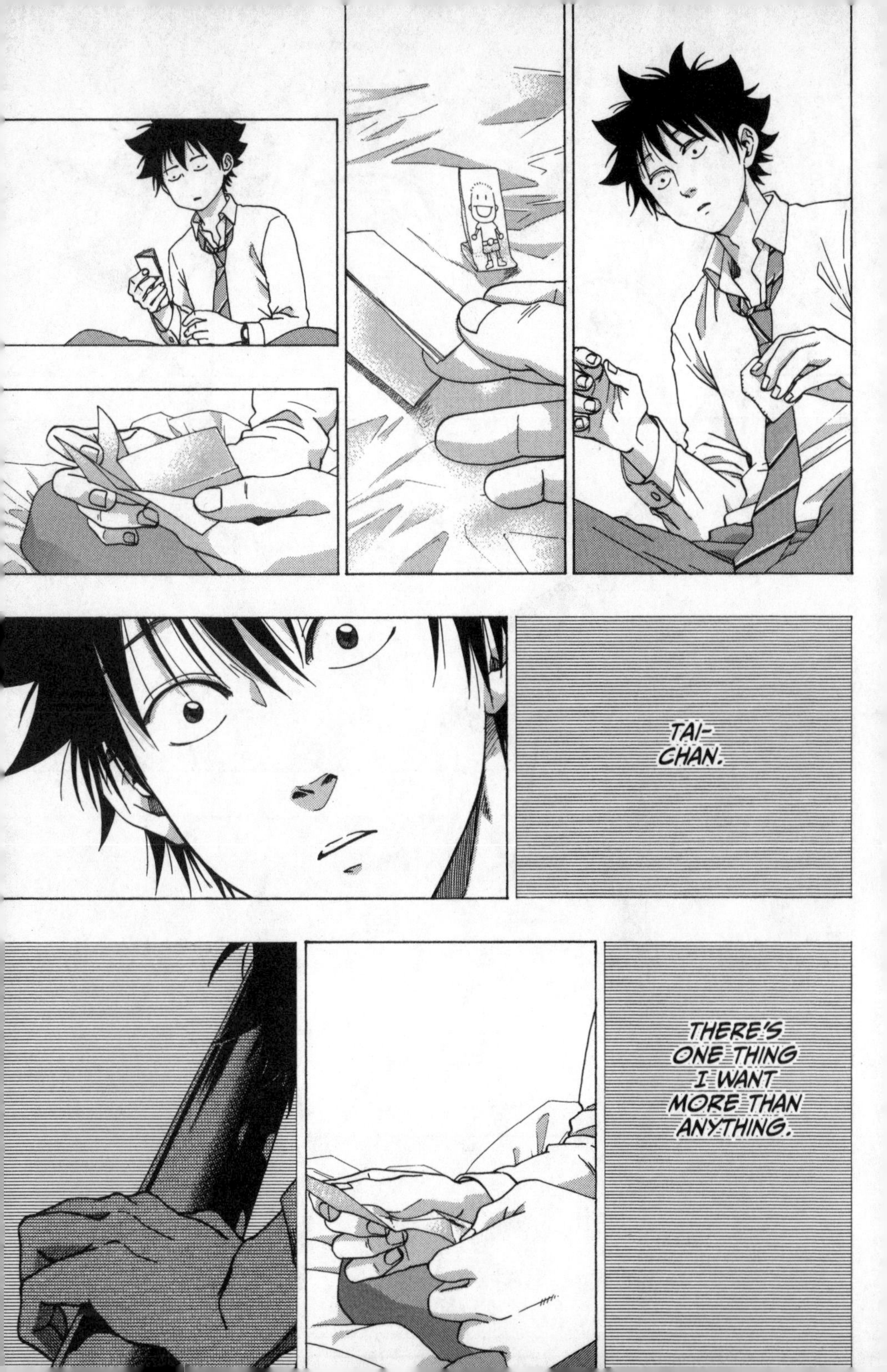
TAI-
CHAN.
THERE'S ONE THING I WANT MORE THAN ANYTHING.

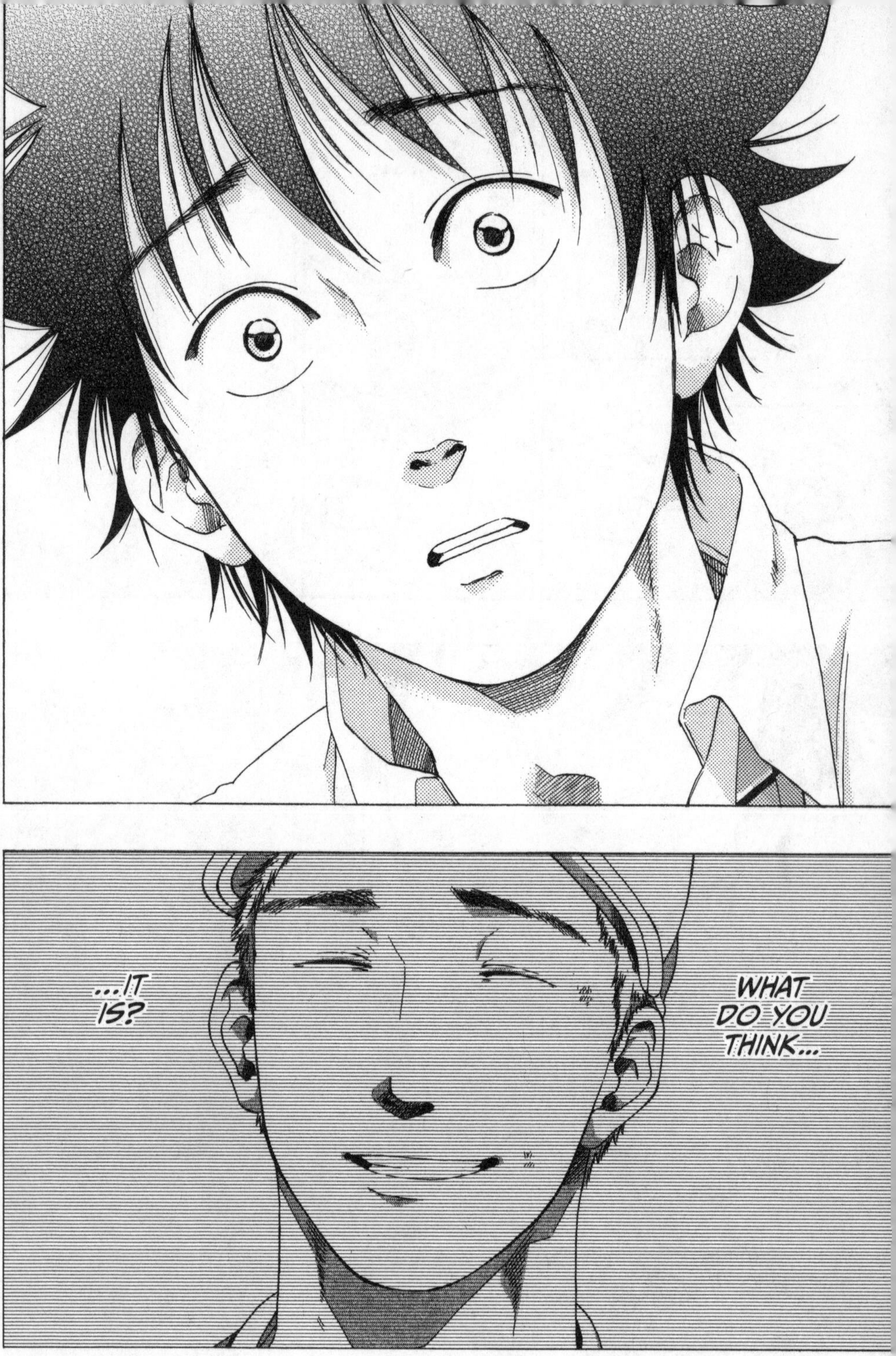
WHAT DO YOU THINK...
...IT IS?

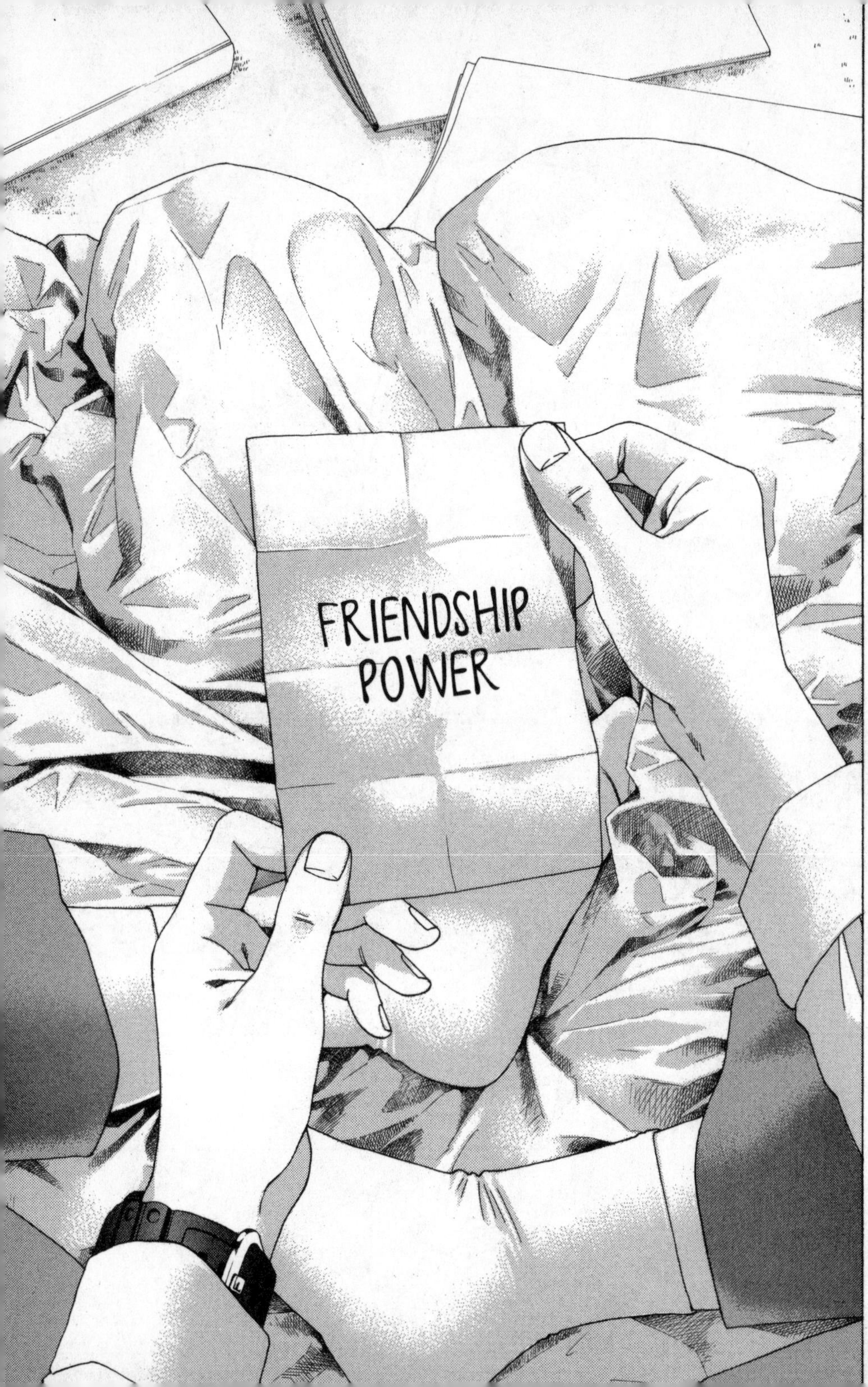
FRIENDSHIP
POWER

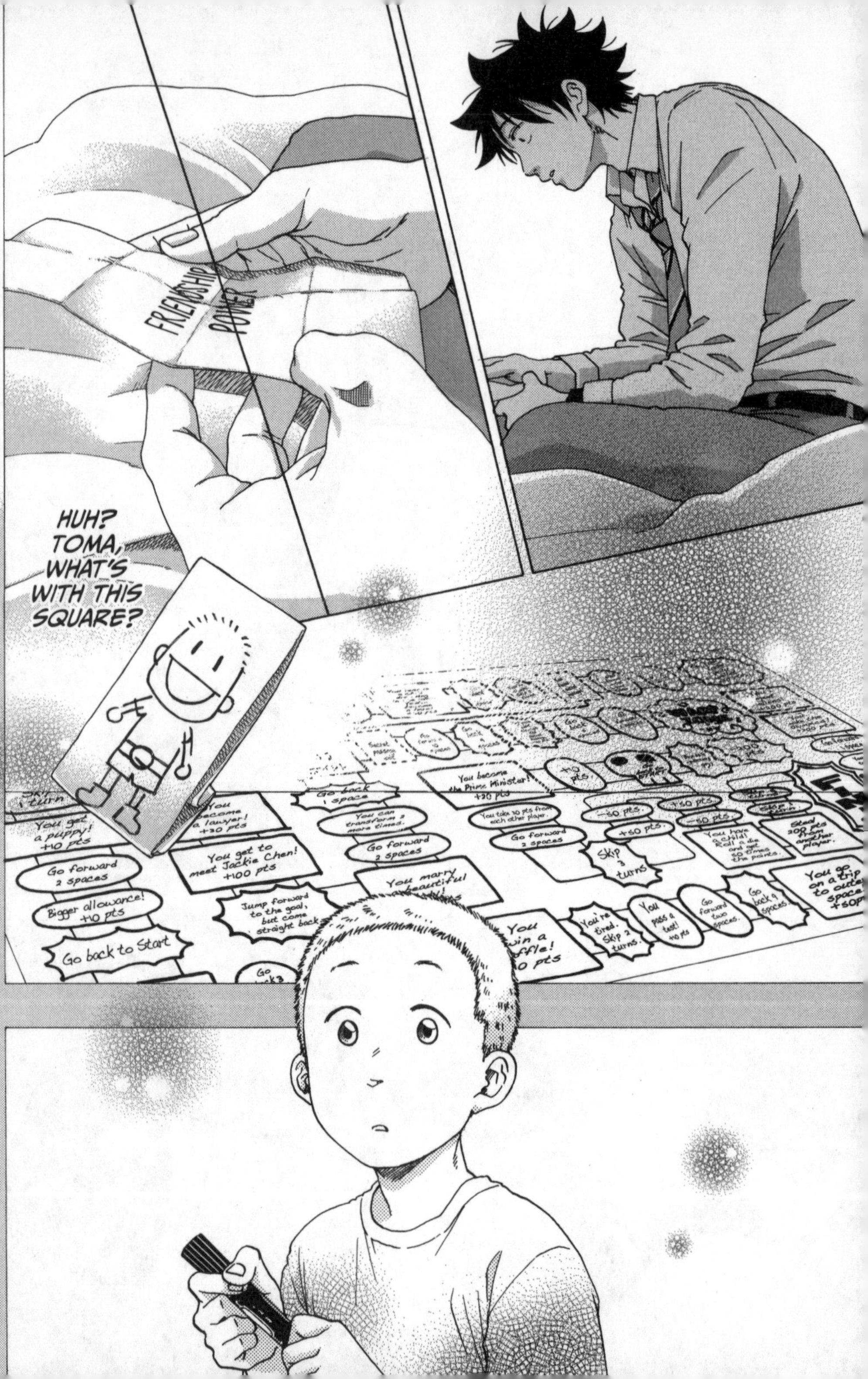
FRIENDSHIP POWER
HUH? TOMA, WHAT'S WITH THIS SQUARE?
You become the Prime Minister! +20 pts
Go back 1 space
You become a lawyer! +30 pts
You get a puppy! +10 pts
You can transform 2 more times.
You take 30 pts from each other player.
Go forward 2 spaces
+50 pts.
-50 pts.
Skip 3 turns
You get to meet Jackie Chen! +100 pts
Go forward 2 spaces
Go forward 2 spaces
You marry a beautiful
Bigger allowance! +10 pts
Jump forward to the goal, but come straight back.
Go back to Start
You're tired. Skip 2 turns.
You pass a test! +10 pts
Go forward two spaces.
Go back 4 spaces.
You go on a trip to outer space

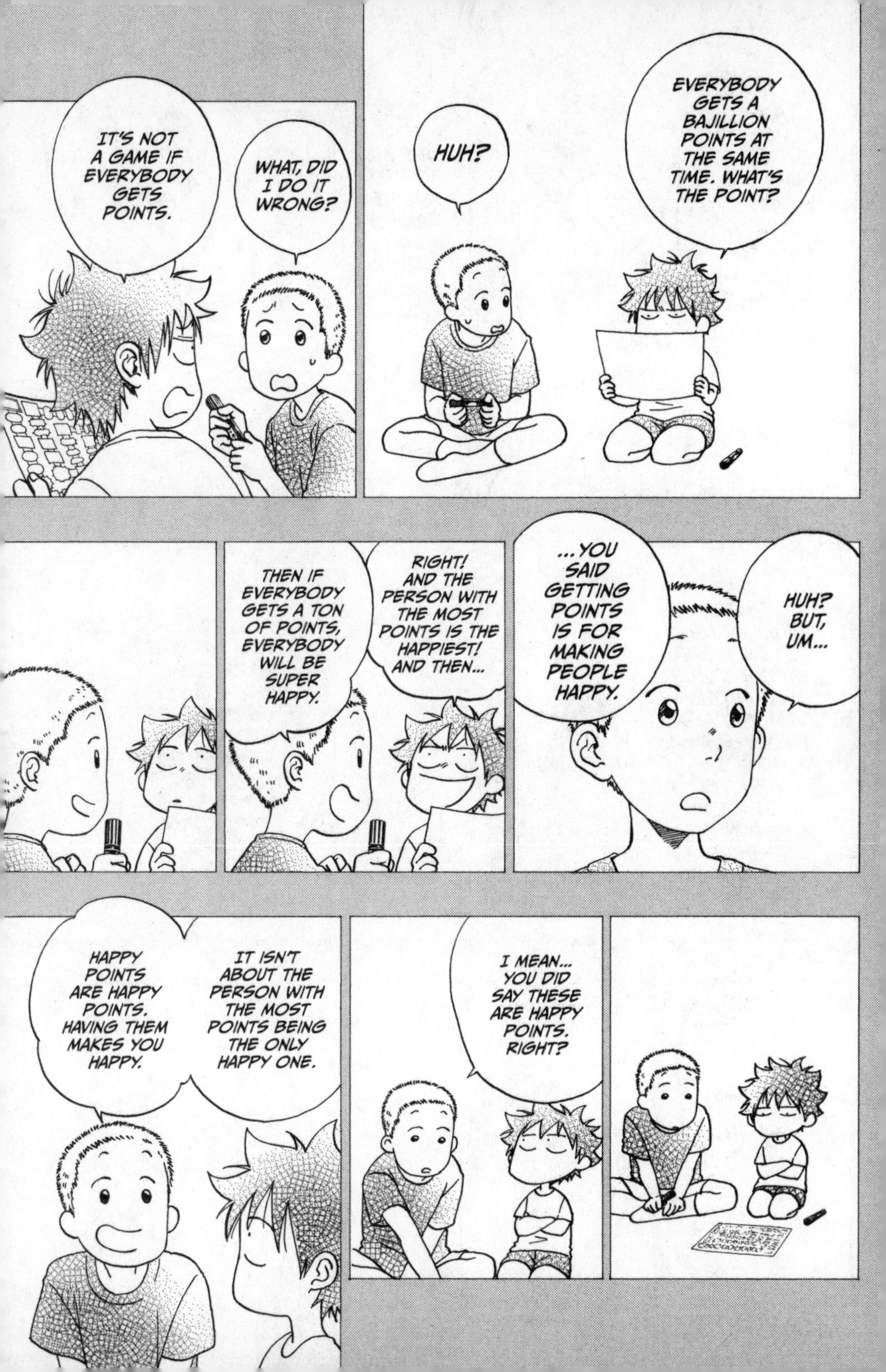
IT'S NOT A GAME IF EVERYBODY GETS POINTS.
WHAT, DID I DO IT WRONG?
HUH?
EVERYBODY GETS A BAJILLION POINTS AT THE SAME TIME. WHAT'S THE POINT?
THEN IF EVERYBODY GETS A TON OF POINTS, EVERYBODY WILL BE SUPER HAPPY.
RIGHT! AND THE PERSON WITH THE MOST POINTS IS THE HAPPIEST! AND THEN...
...YOU SAID GETTING POINTS IS FOR MAKING PEOPLE HAPPY.
HUH? BUT, UM...
HAPPY POINTS ARE HAPPY POINTS. HAVING THEM MAKES YOU HAPPY.
IT ISN'T ABOUT THE PERSON WITH THE MOST POINTS BEING THE ONLY HAPPY ONE.
I MEAN... YOU DID SAY THESE ARE HAPPY POINTS. RIGHT?

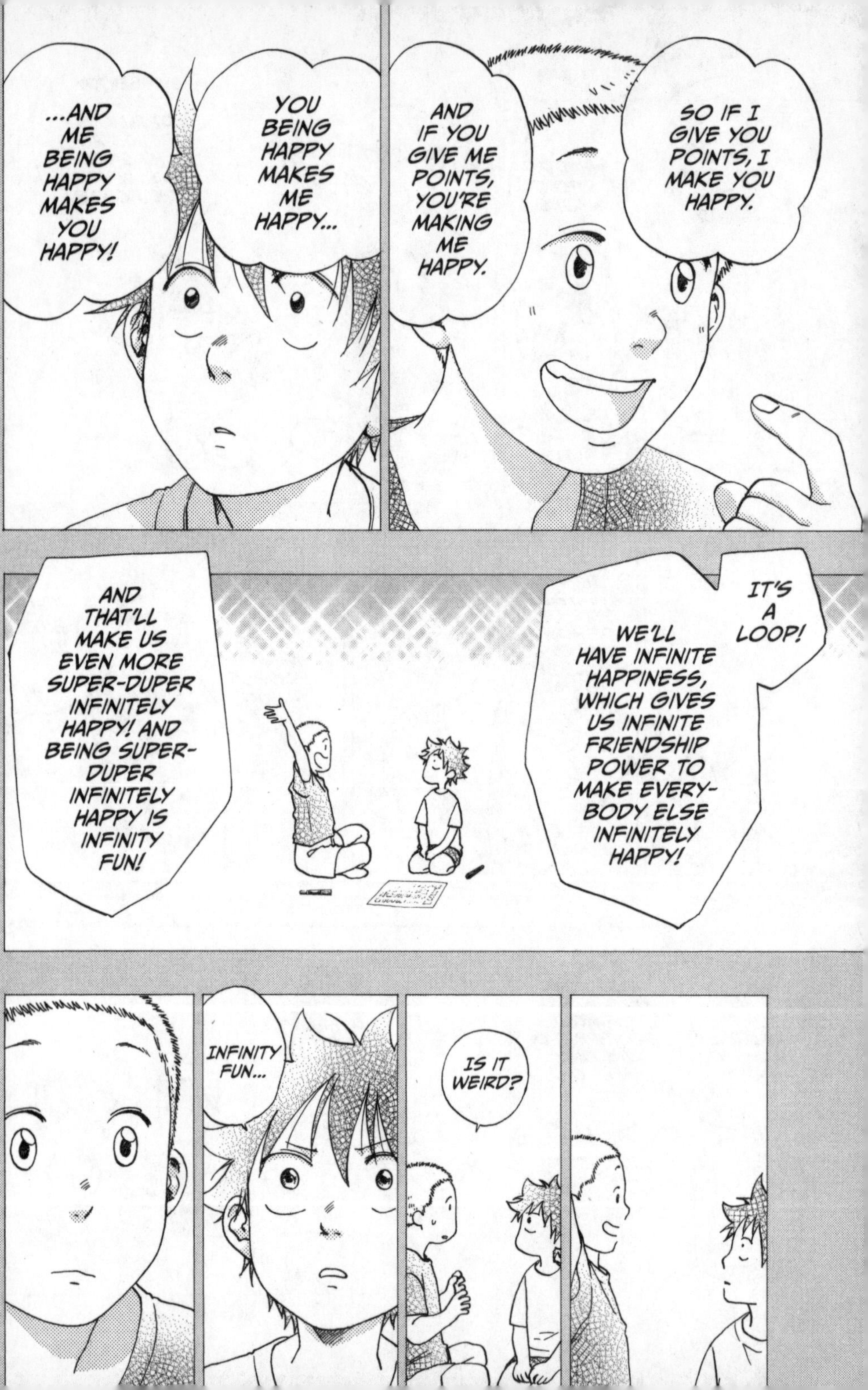
SO IF I GIVE YOU POINTS, I MAKE YOU HAPPY.
AND IF YOU GIVE ME POINTS, YOU'RE MAKING ME HAPPY.
YOU BEING HAPPY MAKES ME HAPPY...
...AND ME BEING HAPPY MAKES YOU HAPPY!
IT'S A LOOP!
WE'LL HAVE INFINITE HAPPINESS, WHICH GIVES US INFINITE FRIENDSHIP POWER TO MAKE EVERY-BODY ELSE INFINITELY HAPPY!
AND THAT'LL MAKE US EVEN MORE SUPER-DUPER INFINITELY HAPPY! AND BEING SUPER-DUPER INFINITELY HAPPY IS INFINITY FUN!
IS IT WEIRD?
INFINITY FUN...

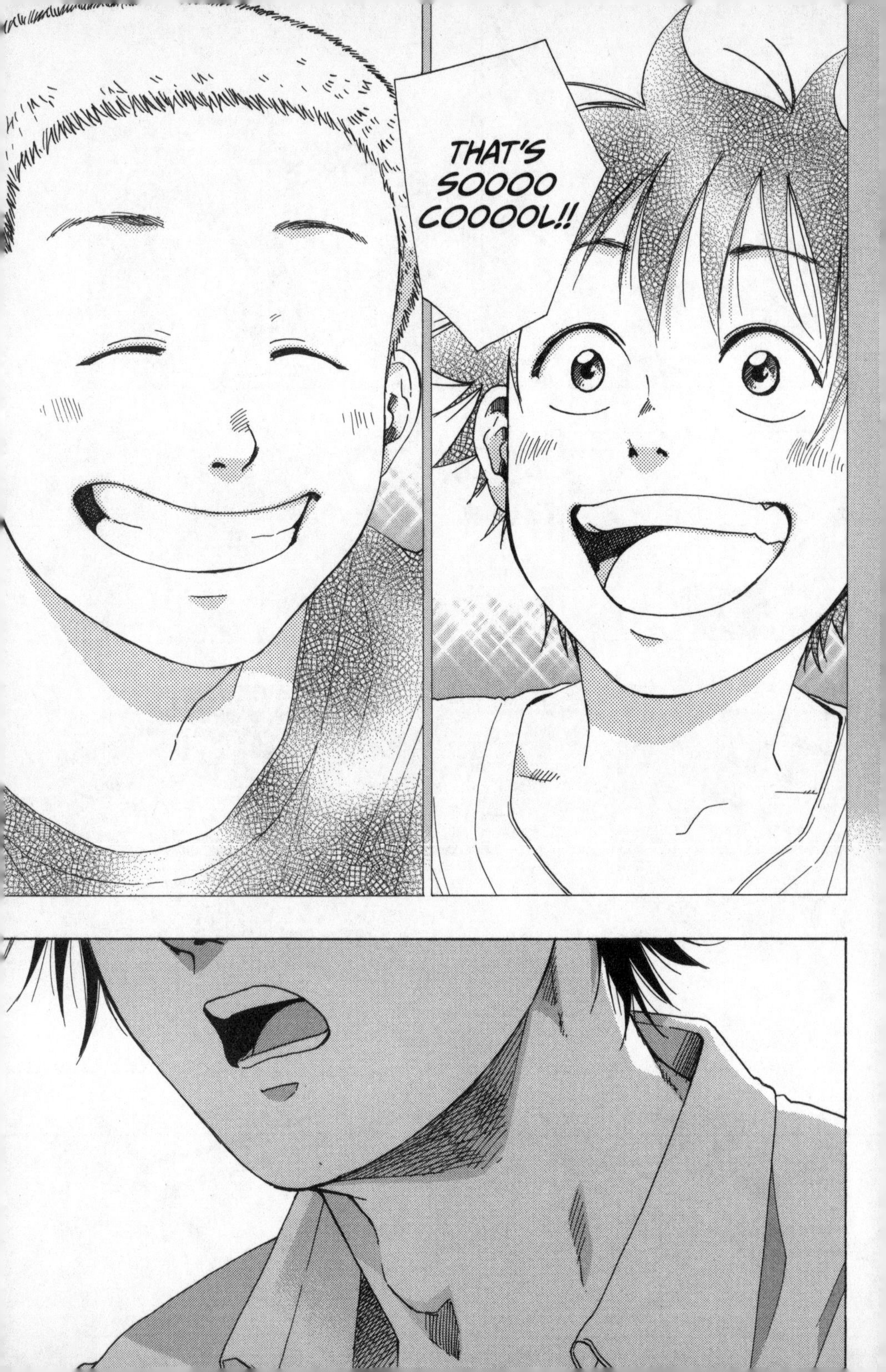
THAT'S SOOOO COOOOL!!

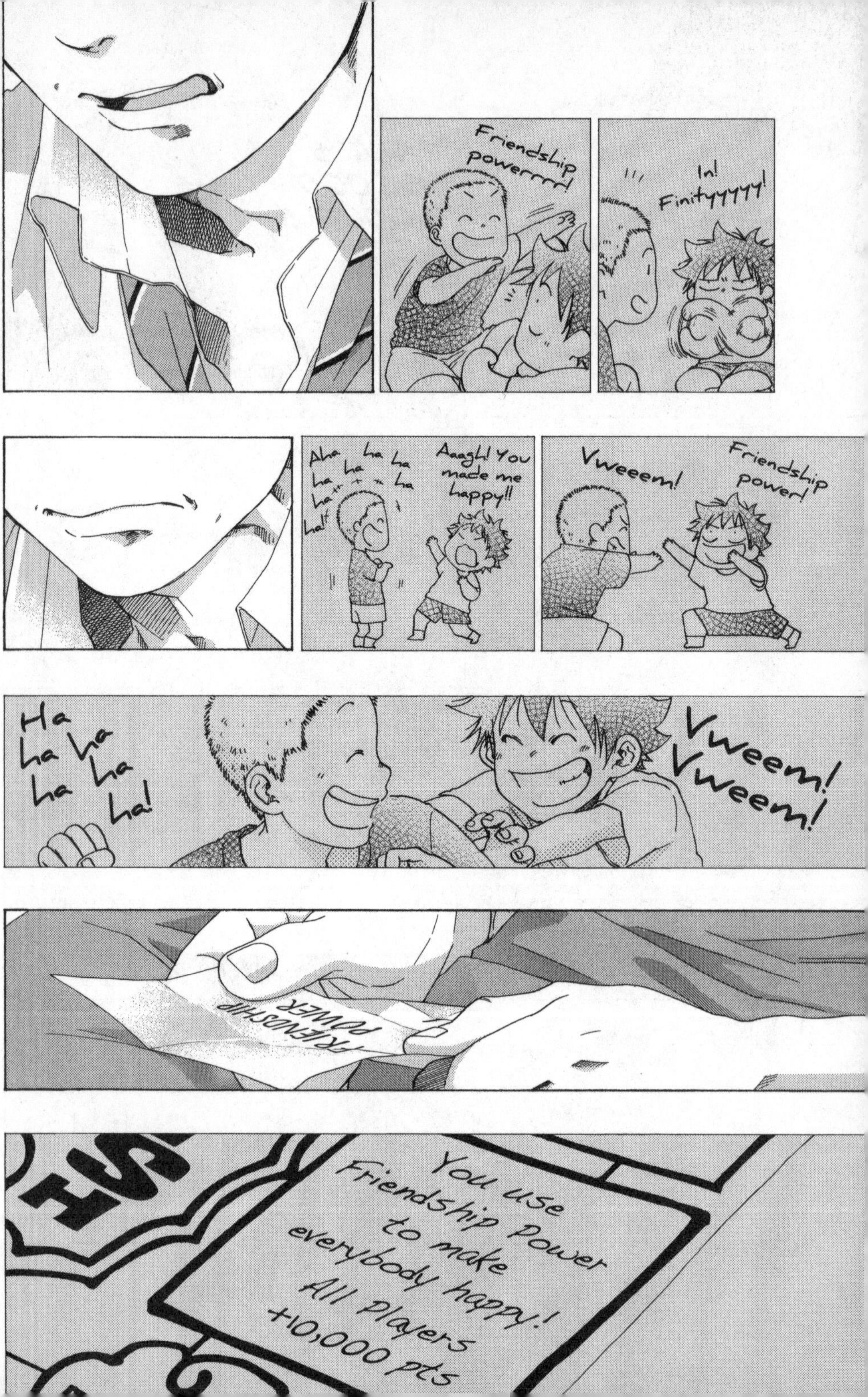
Friendship powerrrrr!
In! Finityyyyy!
Aha ha ha ha ha ha ha ha!
Aaagh! You made me happy!!
Vweeem!
Friendship power!
Ha ha ha ha ha ha!
Vweem! Vweem!
FRIENDSHIP POWER
You use Friendship Power to make everybody happy! All players +10,000 pts

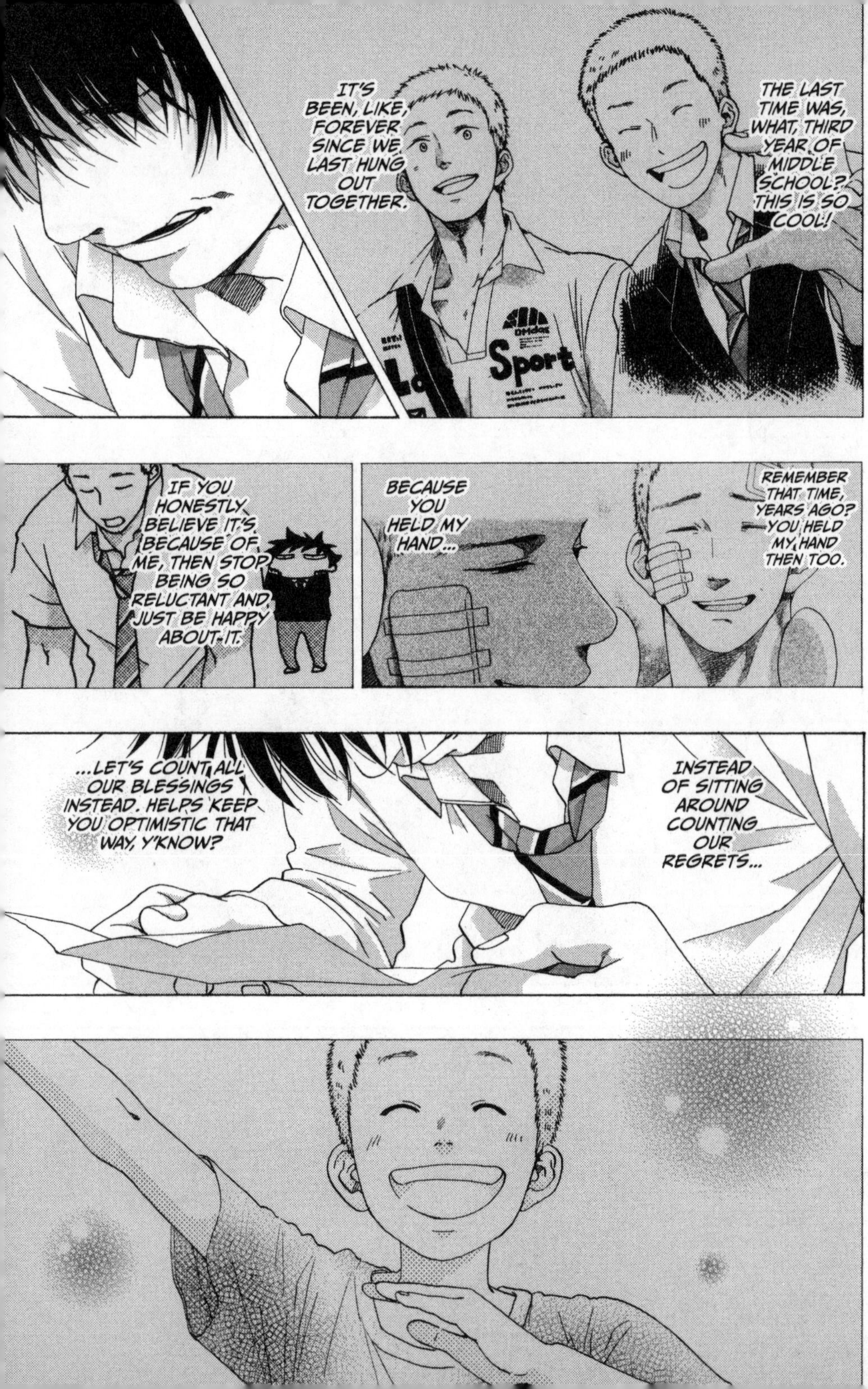
THE LAST TIME WAS, WHAT, THIRD YEAR OF MIDDLE SCHOOL? THIS IS SO COOL!
IT'S BEEN, LIKE, FOREVER SINCE WE LAST HUNG OUT TOGETHER.
REMEMBER THAT TIME, YEARS AGO? YOU HELD MY HAND THEN TOO.
BECAUSE YOU HELD MY HAND...
IF YOU HONESTLY BELIEVE IT'S BECAUSE OF ME, THEN STOP BEING SO RELUCTANT AND JUST BE HAPPY ABOUT IT.
INSTEAD OF SITTING AROUND COUNTING OUR REGRETS...
...LET'S COUNT ALL OUR BLESSINGS INSTEAD. HELPS KEEP YOU OPTIMISTIC THAT WAY, Y'KNOW?

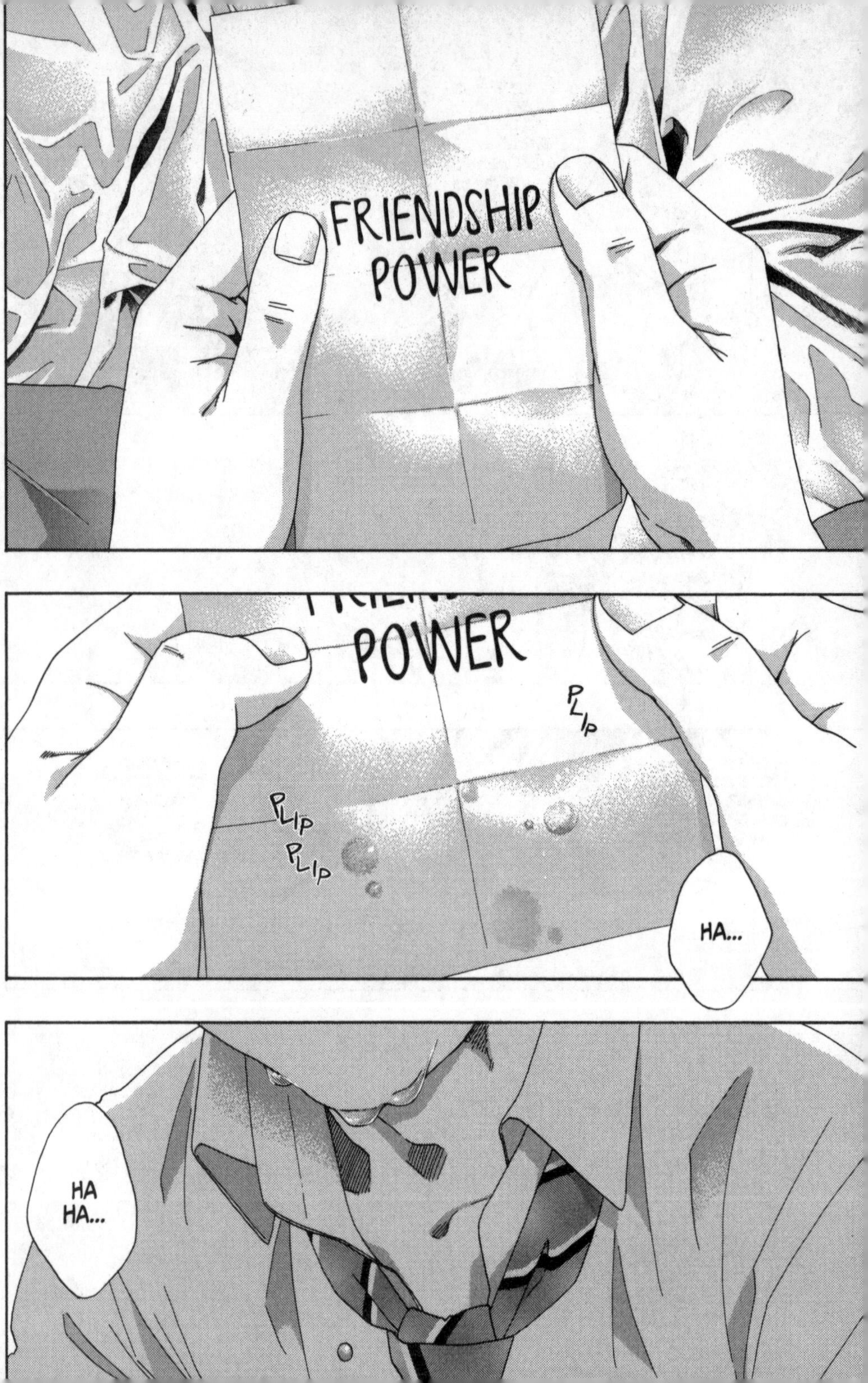
FRIENDSHIP POWER
POWER
PLIP
PLIP
PLIP
HA...
HA HA...

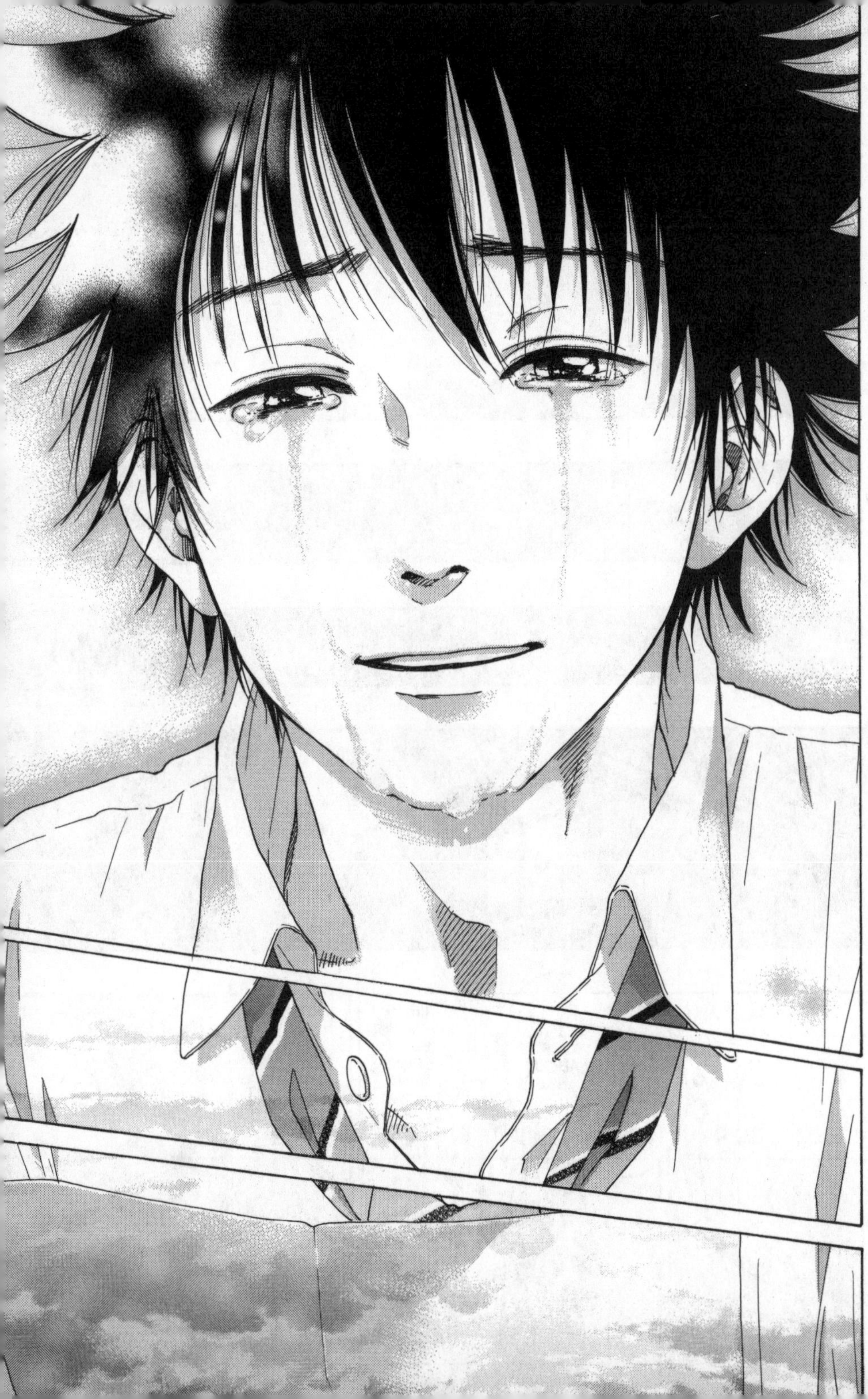

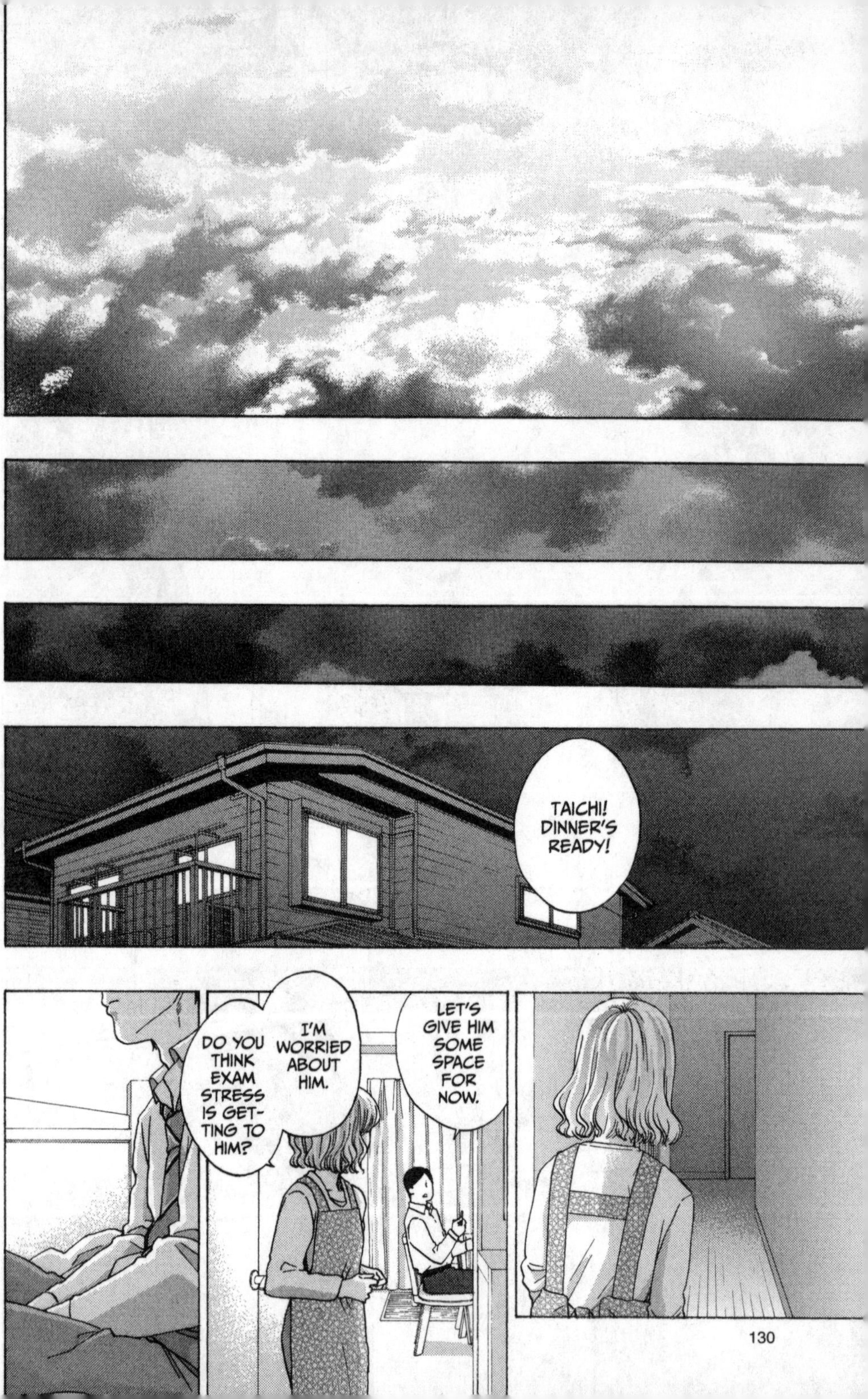
TAICHI! DINNER'S READY!
I'M WORRIED ABOUT HIM.
DO YOU THINK EXAM STRESS IS GET- TING TO HIM?
LET'S GIVE HIM SOME SPACE FOR NOW.

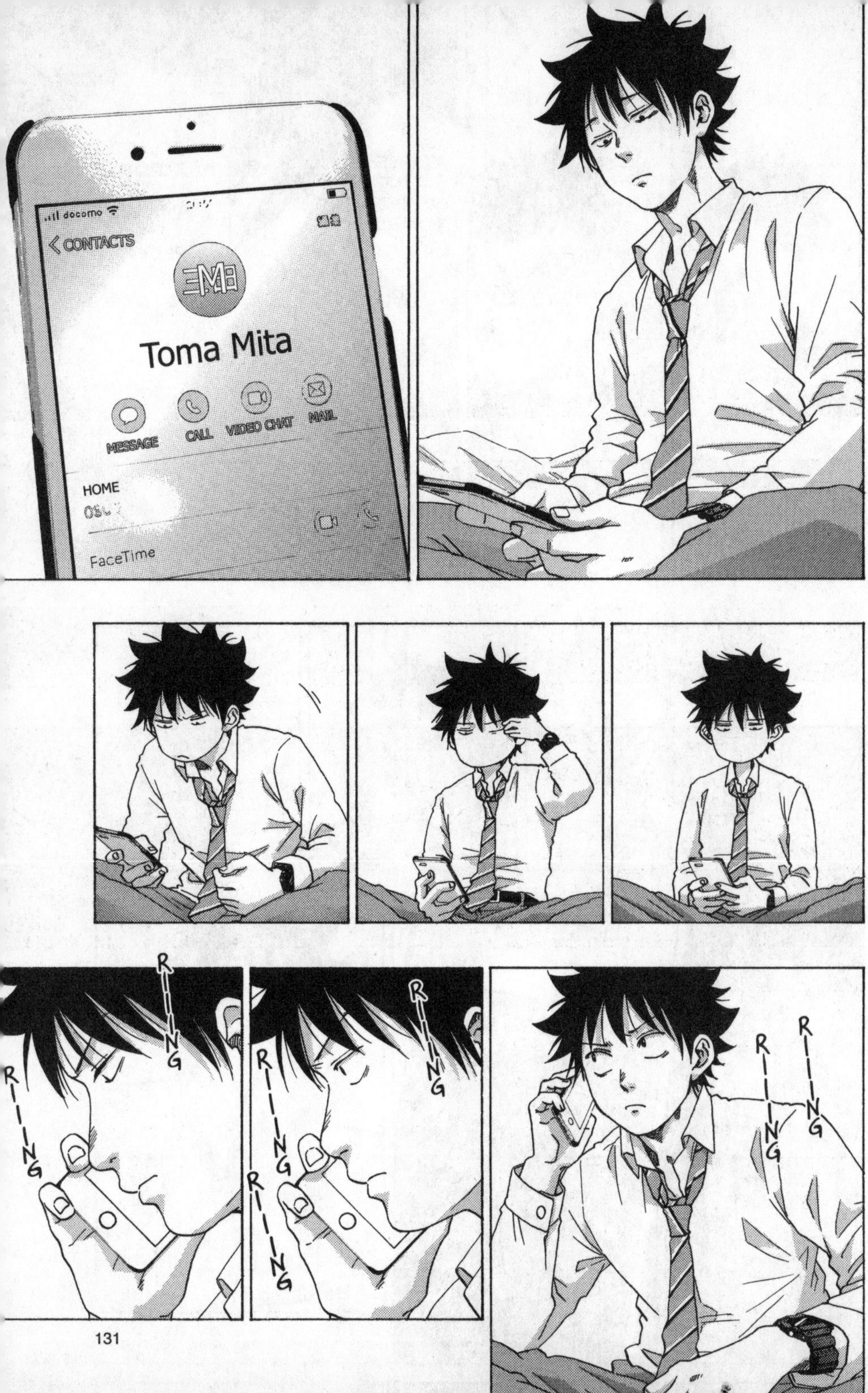
docomo
CONTACTS
Toma Mita
MESSAGE
CALL
VIDEO CHAT
MAIL
HOME
FaceTime
RIIING
RIIING
RIIING
RIIING
RIIING
RIIING

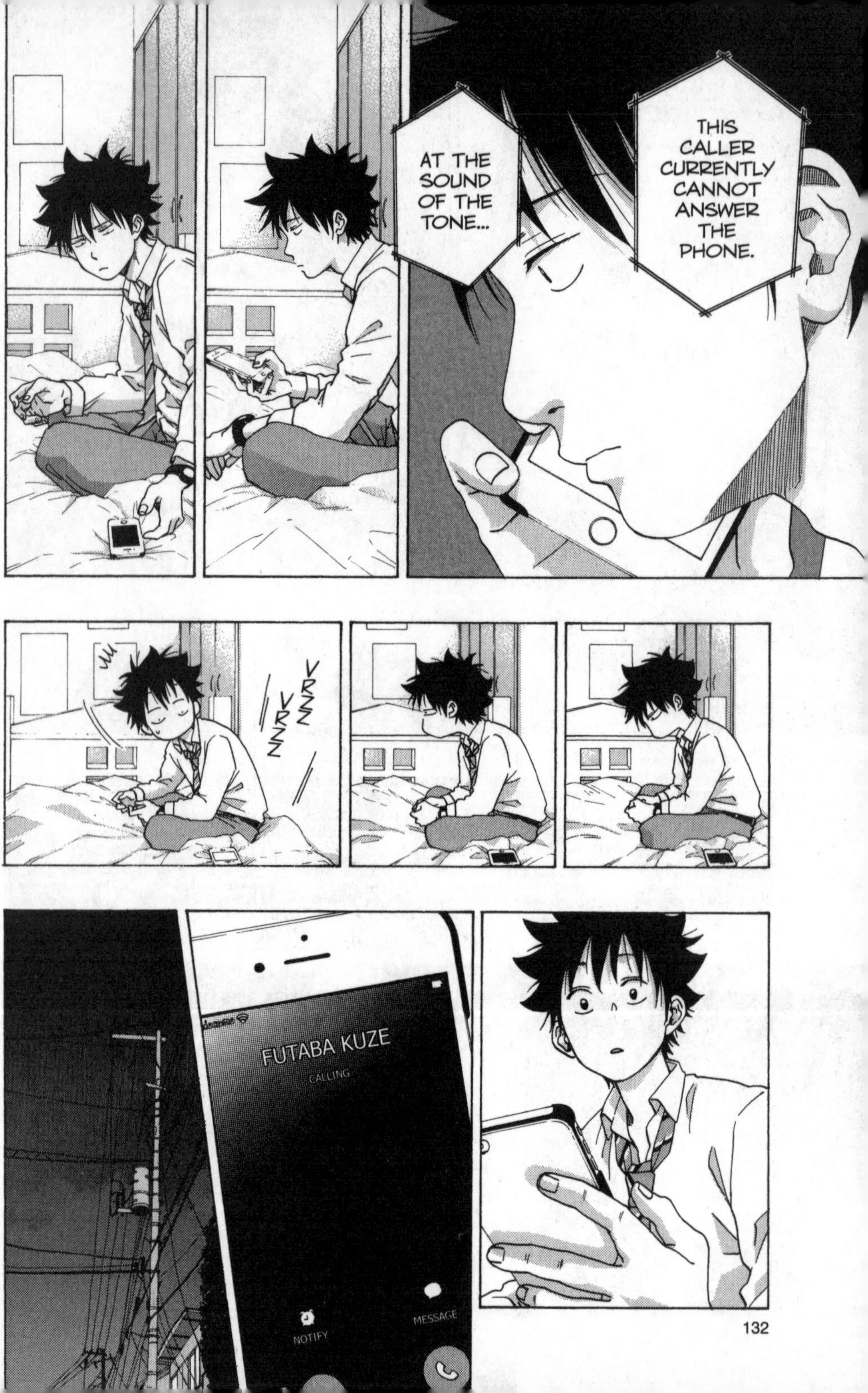
THIS CALLER CURRENTLY CANNOT ANSWER THE PHONE.
AT THE SOUND OF THE TONE...
VRZZ VRZZ
FUTABA KUZE
CALLING
MESSAGE
NOTIFY

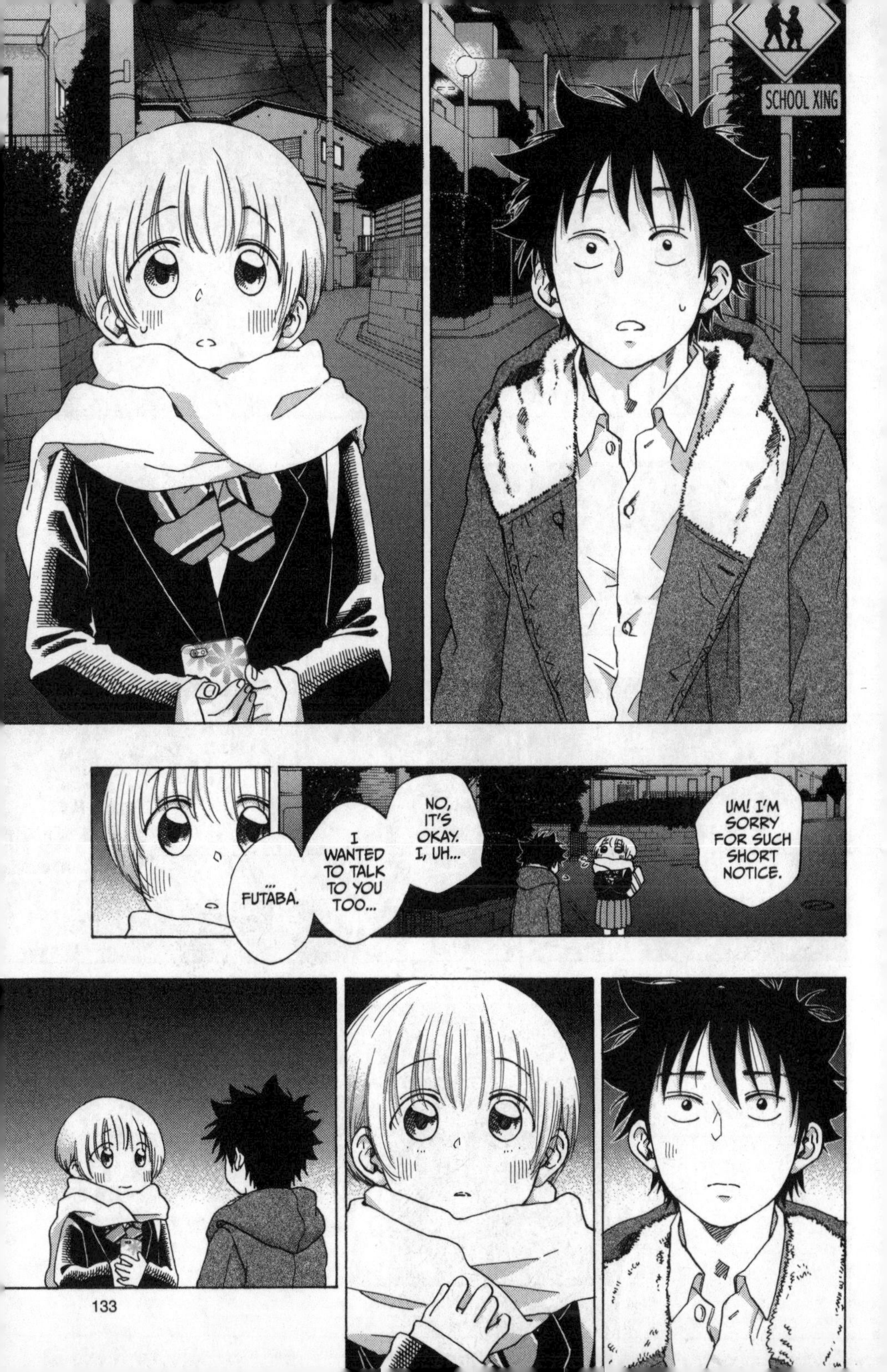
SCHOOL XING
UM! I'M SORRY FOR SUCH SHORT NOTICE.
NO, IT'S OKAY. I, UH...
I WANTED TO TALK TO YOU TOO...
... FUTABA.

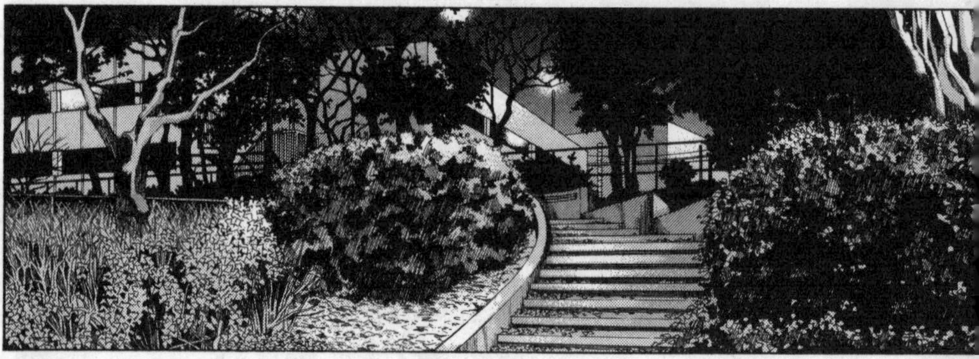
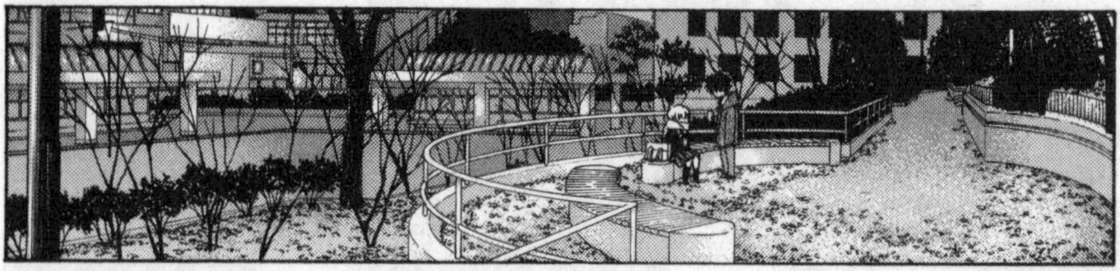
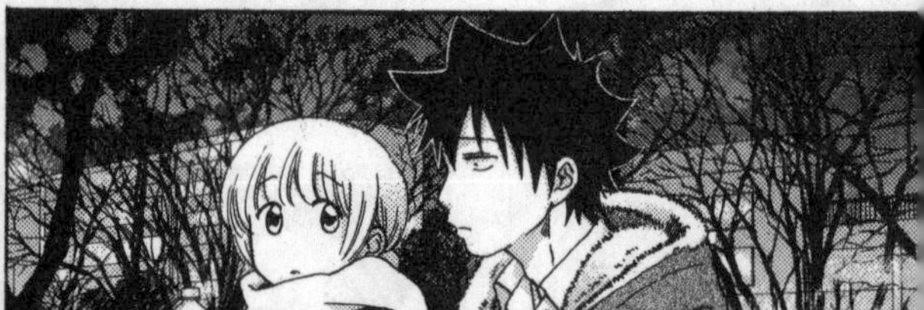
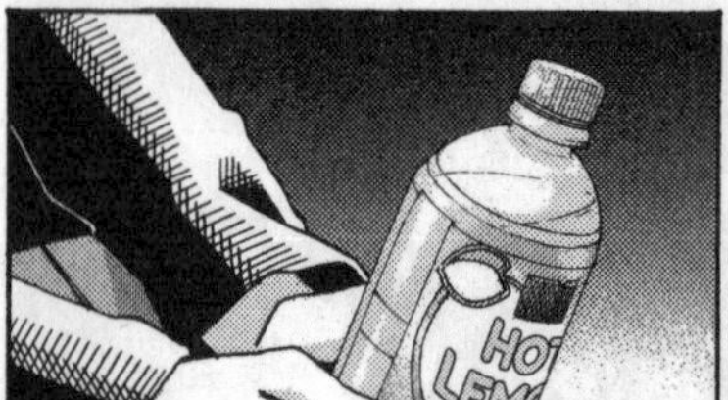
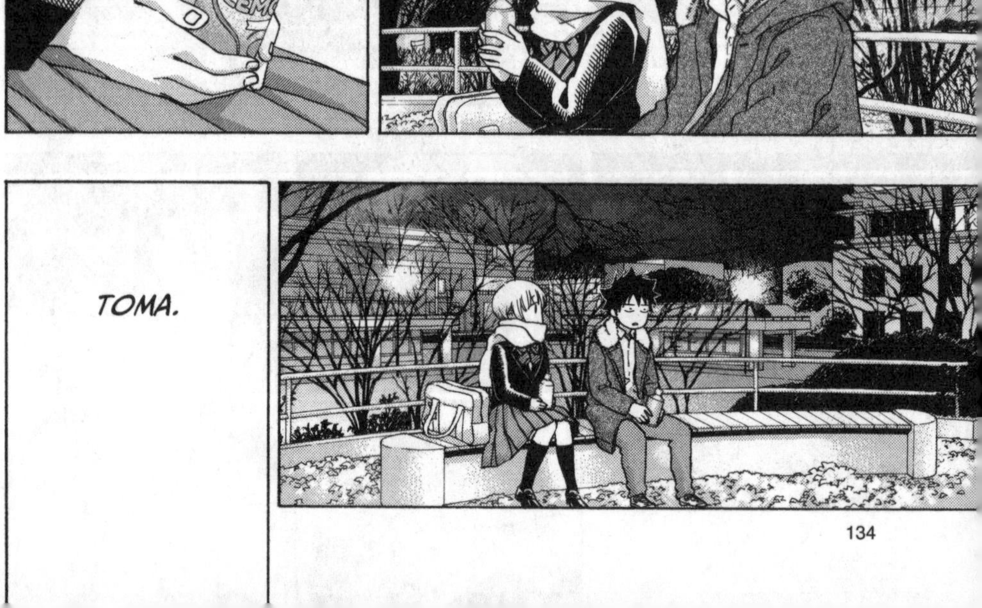

TOMA.

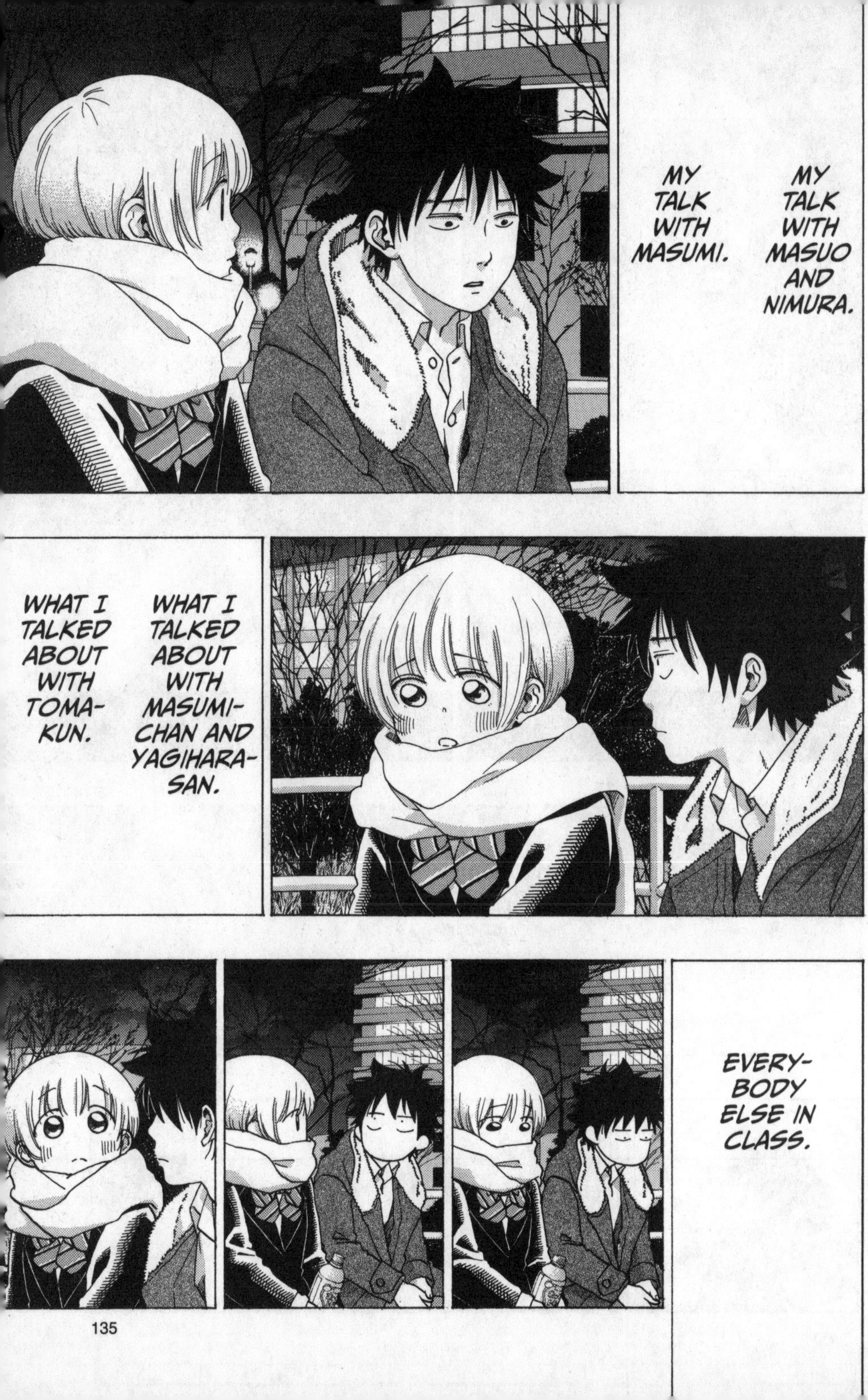
MY TALK WITH MASUO AND NIMURA.
MY TALK WITH MASUMI.
WHAT I TALKED ABOUT WITH MASUMI-CHAN AND YAGIHARA-SAN.
WHAT I TALKED ABOUT WITH TOMA-KUN.
EVERYBODY ELSE IN CLASS.

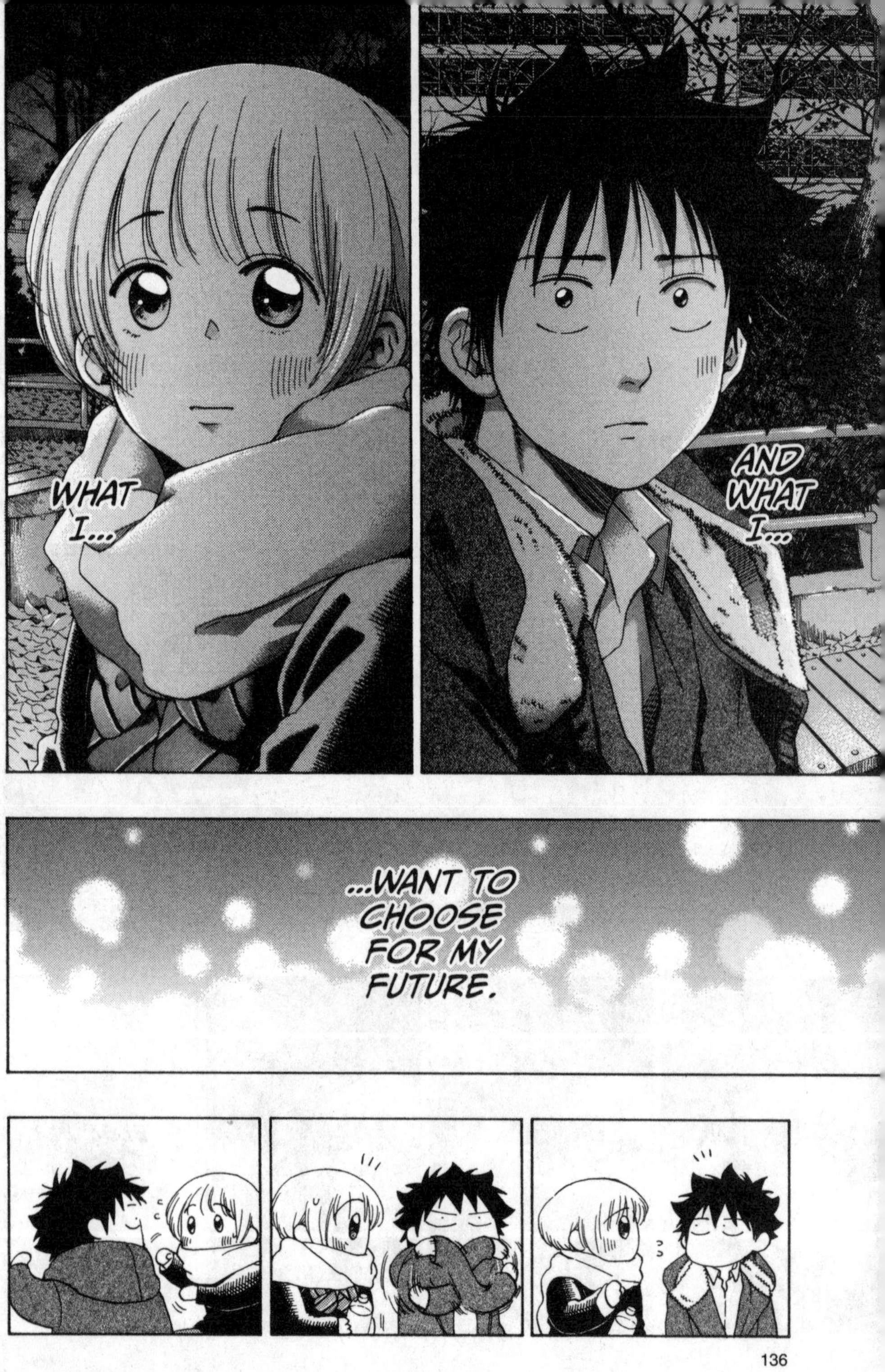
WHAT I...
AND WHAT I...
...WANT TO CHOOSE FOR MY FUTURE.

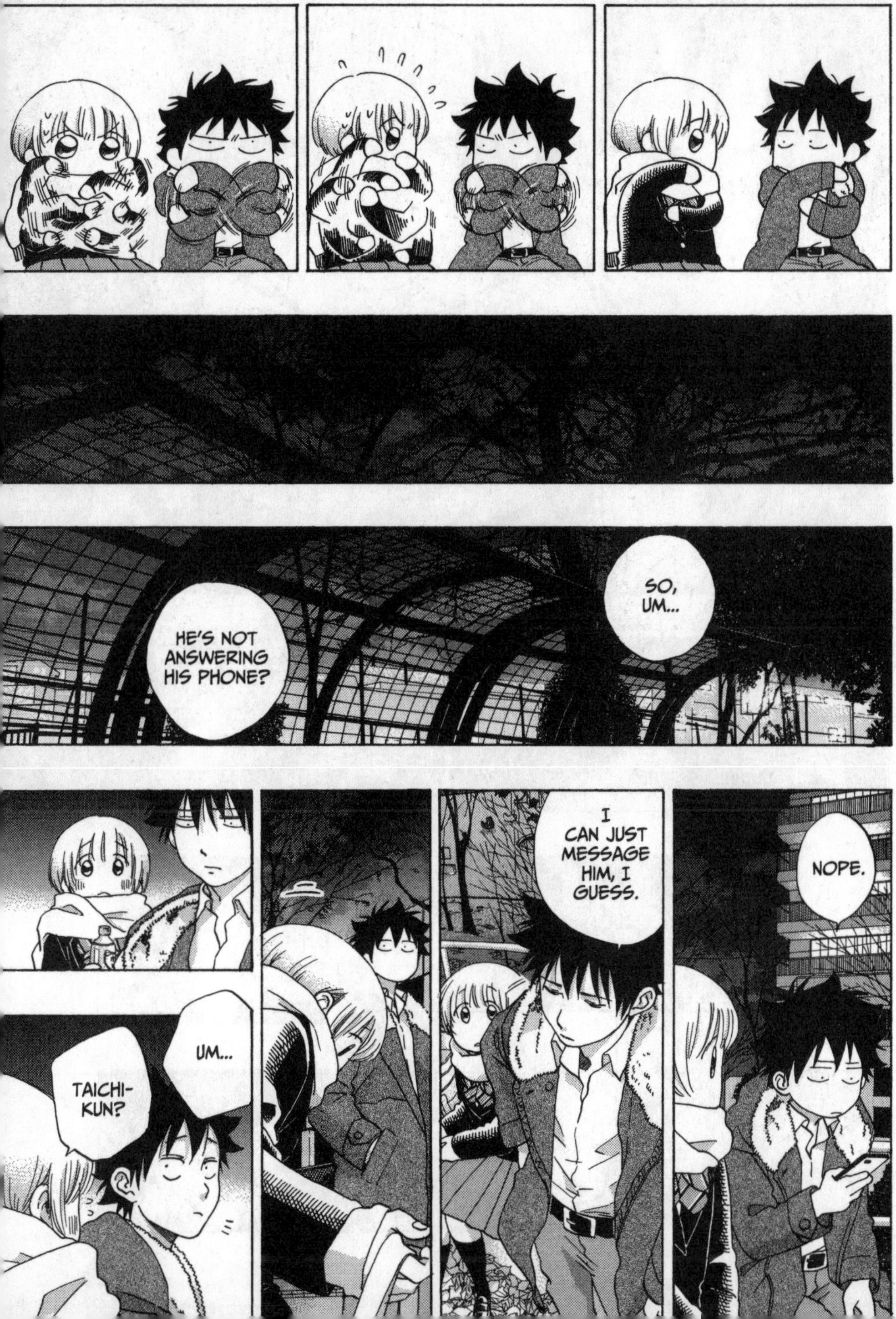
SO, UM...
HE'S NOT ANSWERING HIS PHONE?
NOPE.
I CAN JUST MESSAGE HIM, I GUESS.
UM...
TAICHI-KUN?

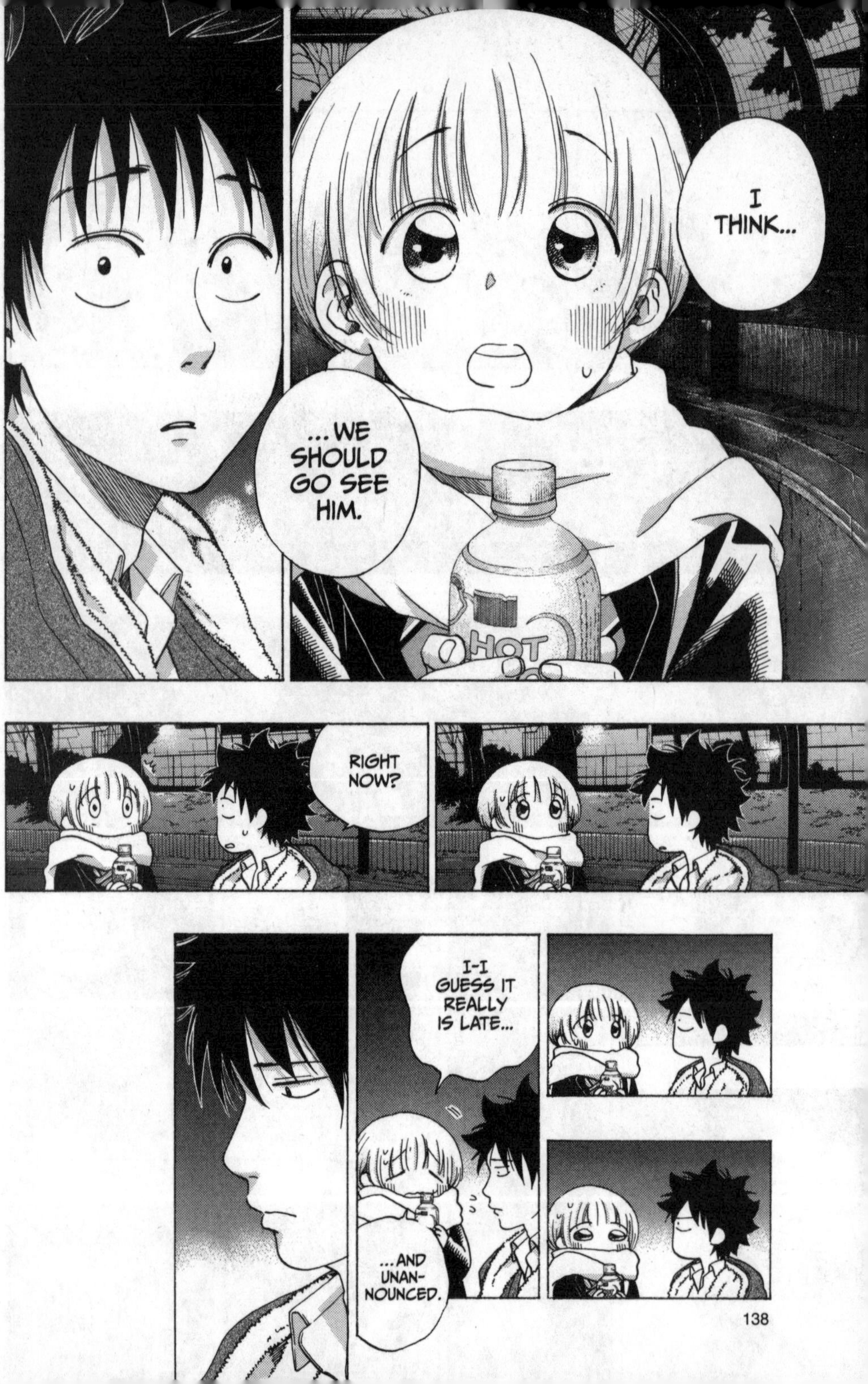
I THINK...
...WE SHOULD GO SEE HIM.
HOT
RIGHT NOW?
I-I GUESS IT REALLY IS LATE...
...AND UNAN-NOUNCED.

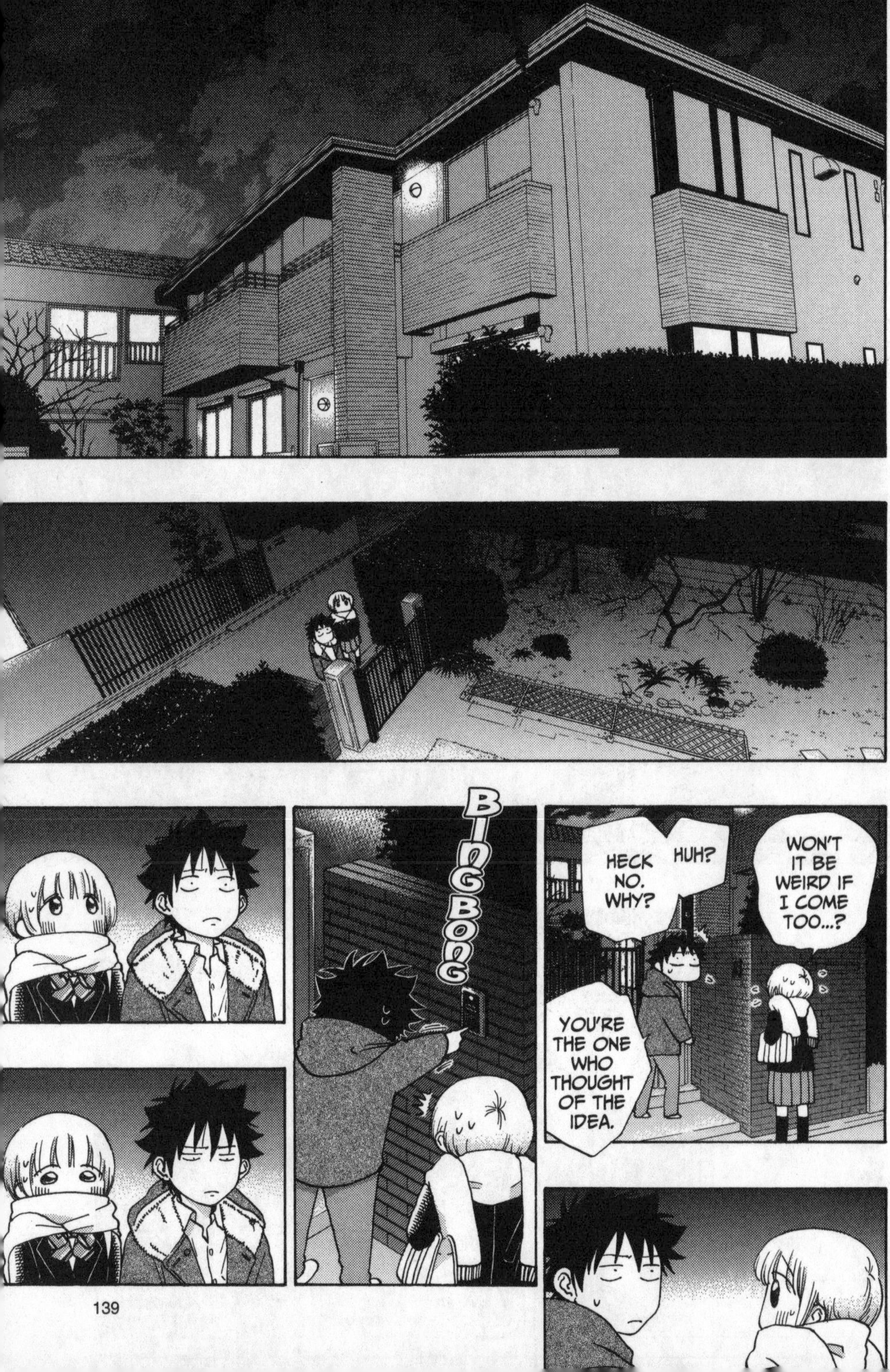
WON'T IT BE WEIRD IF I COME TOO...?
HUH?
HECK NO. WHY?
YOU'RE THE ONE WHO THOUGHT OF THE IDEA.
BINGBONG

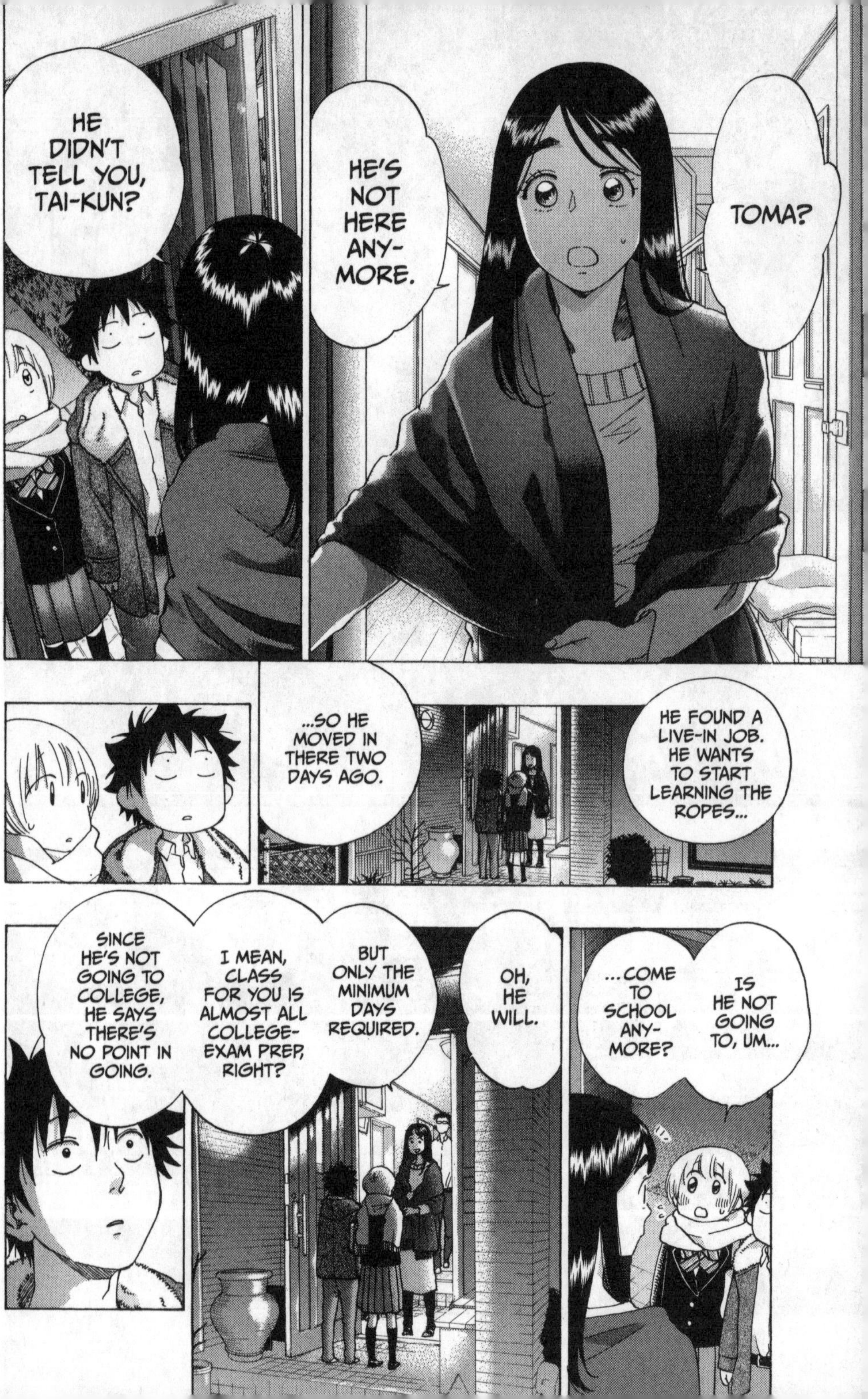
TOMA?
HE'S NOT HERE ANY-MORE.
HE DIDN'T TELL YOU, TAI-KUN?
HE FOUND A LIVE-IN JOB. HE WANTS TO START LEARNING THE ROPES...
...SO HE MOVED IN THERE TWO DAYS AGO.
IS HE NOT GOING TO, UM...
...COME TO SCHOOL ANY-MORE?
OH, HE WILL.
BUT ONLY THE MINIMUM DAYS REQUIRED.
I MEAN, CLASS FOR YOU IS ALMOST ALL COLLEGE-EXAM PREP, RIGHT?
SINCE HE'S NOT GOING TO COLLEGE, HE SAYS THERE'S NO POINT IN GOING.

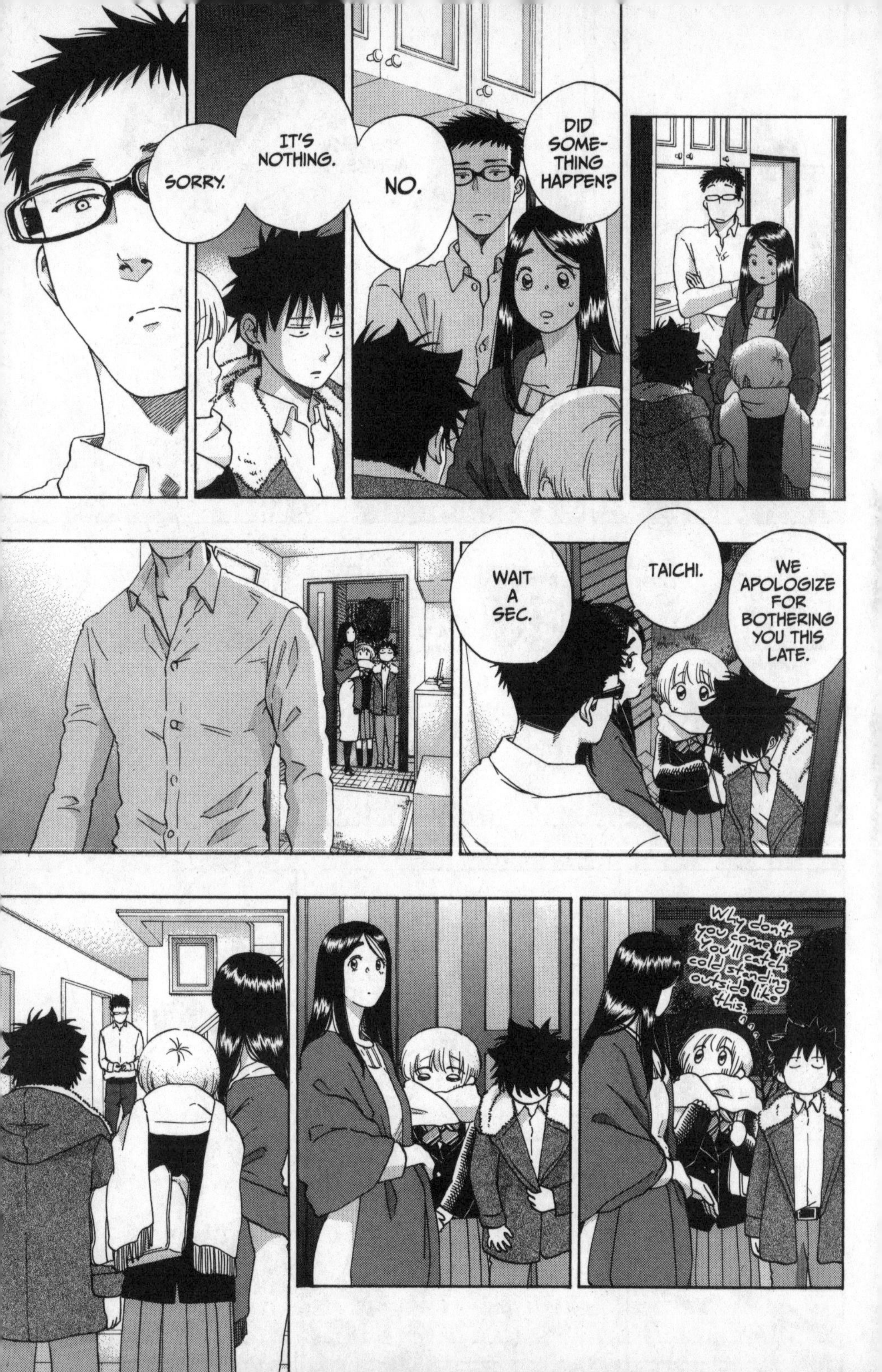
DID SOMETHING HAPPEN?
NO.
IT'S NOTHING.
SORRY.
WE APOLOGIZE FOR BOTHERING YOU THIS LATE.
TAICHI.
WAIT A SEC.
Why don't you come in? You'll catch cold standing outside like this.

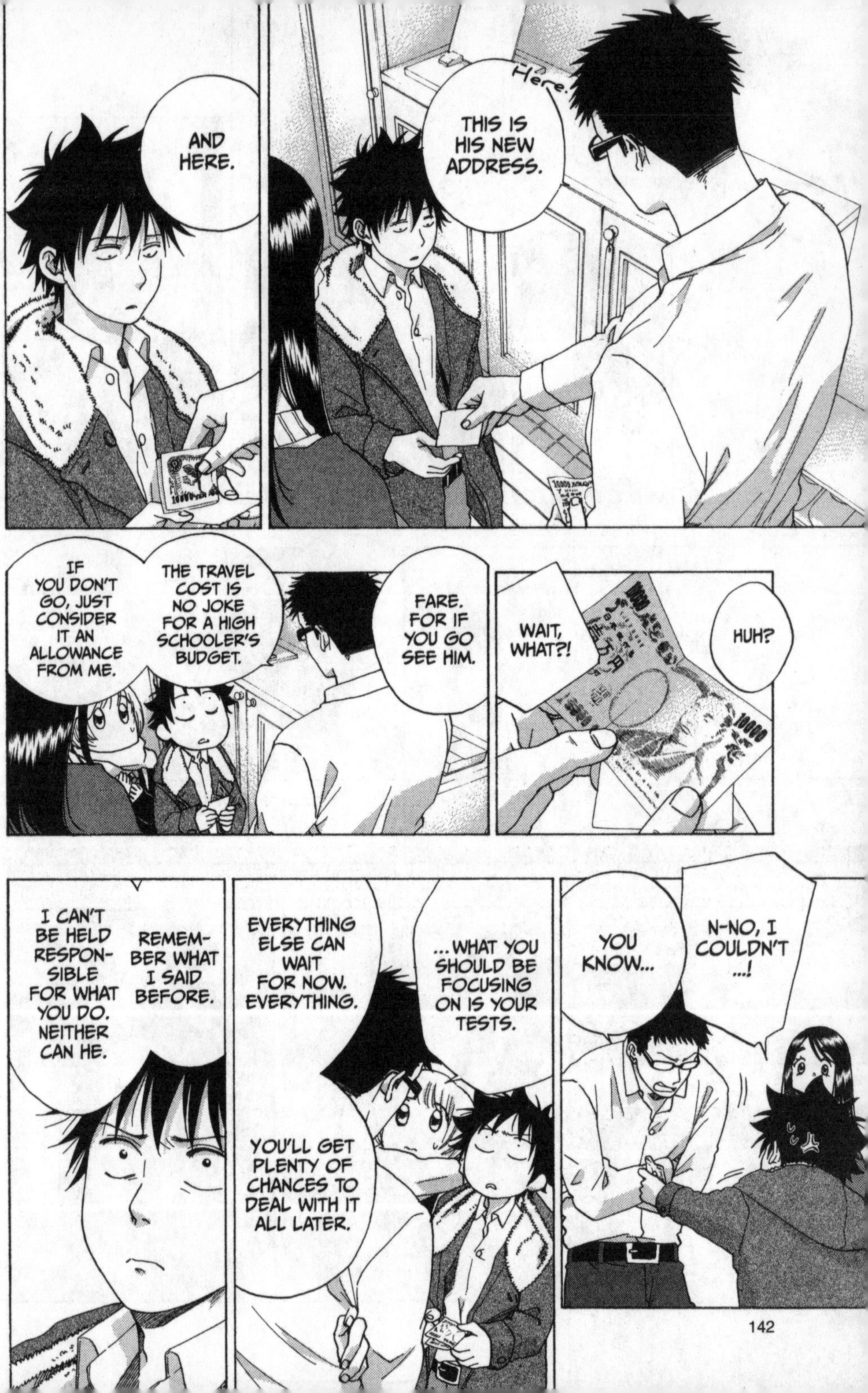
Here.
THIS IS HIS NEW ADDRESS.
AND HERE.
HUH?
WAIT, WHAT?!
FARE. FOR IF YOU GO SEE HIM.
THE TRAVEL COST IS NO JOKE FOR A HIGH SCHOOLER'S BUDGET.
IF YOU DON'T GO, JUST CONSIDER IT AN ALLOWANCE FROM ME.
N-NO, I COULDN'T ...!
YOU KNOW...
...WHAT YOU SHOULD BE FOCUSING ON IS YOUR TESTS.
EVERYTHING ELSE CAN WAIT FOR NOW. EVERYTHING.
YOU'LL GET PLENTY OF CHANCES TO DEAL WITH IT ALL LATER.
REMEM-BER WHAT I SAID BEFORE.
I CAN'T BE HELD RESPON-SIBLE FOR WHAT YOU DO. NEITHER CAN HE.

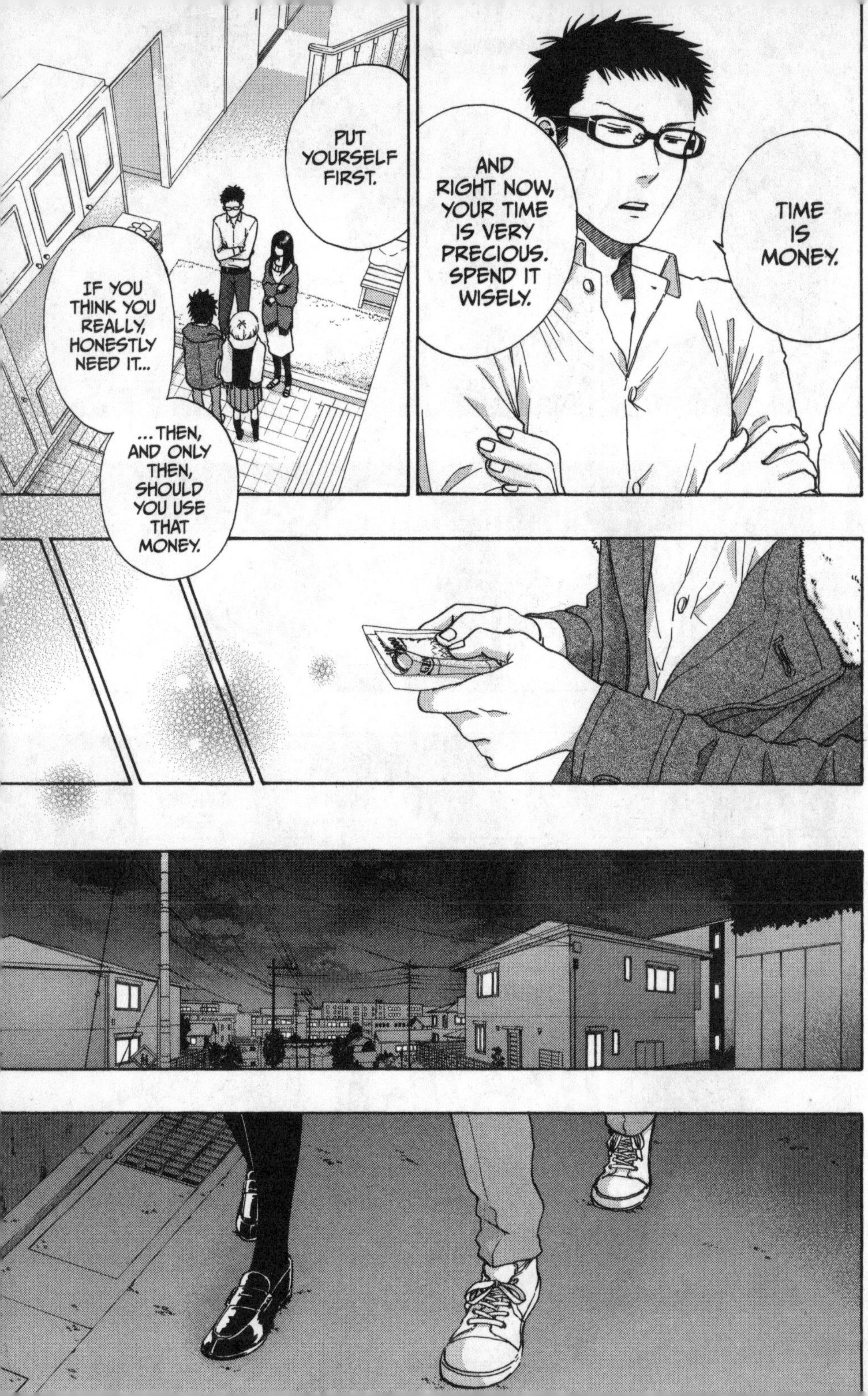
TIME IS MONEY.
AND RIGHT NOW, YOUR TIME IS VERY PRECIOUS. SPEND IT WISELY.
PUT YOURSELF FIRST.
IF YOU THINK YOU REALLY, HONESTLY NEED IT...
...THEN, AND ONLY THEN, SHOULD YOU USE THAT MONEY.

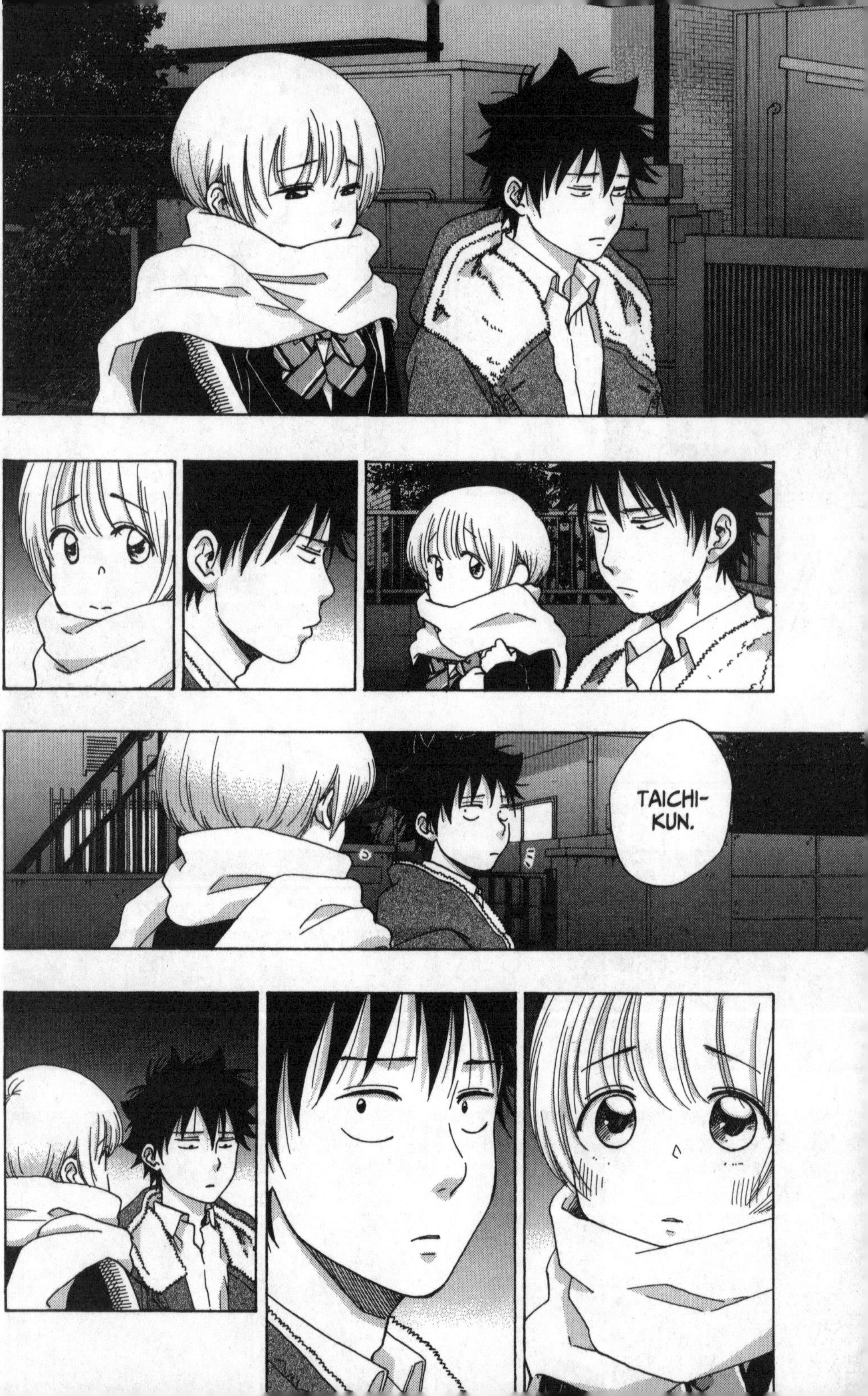
TAICHI-
KUN.

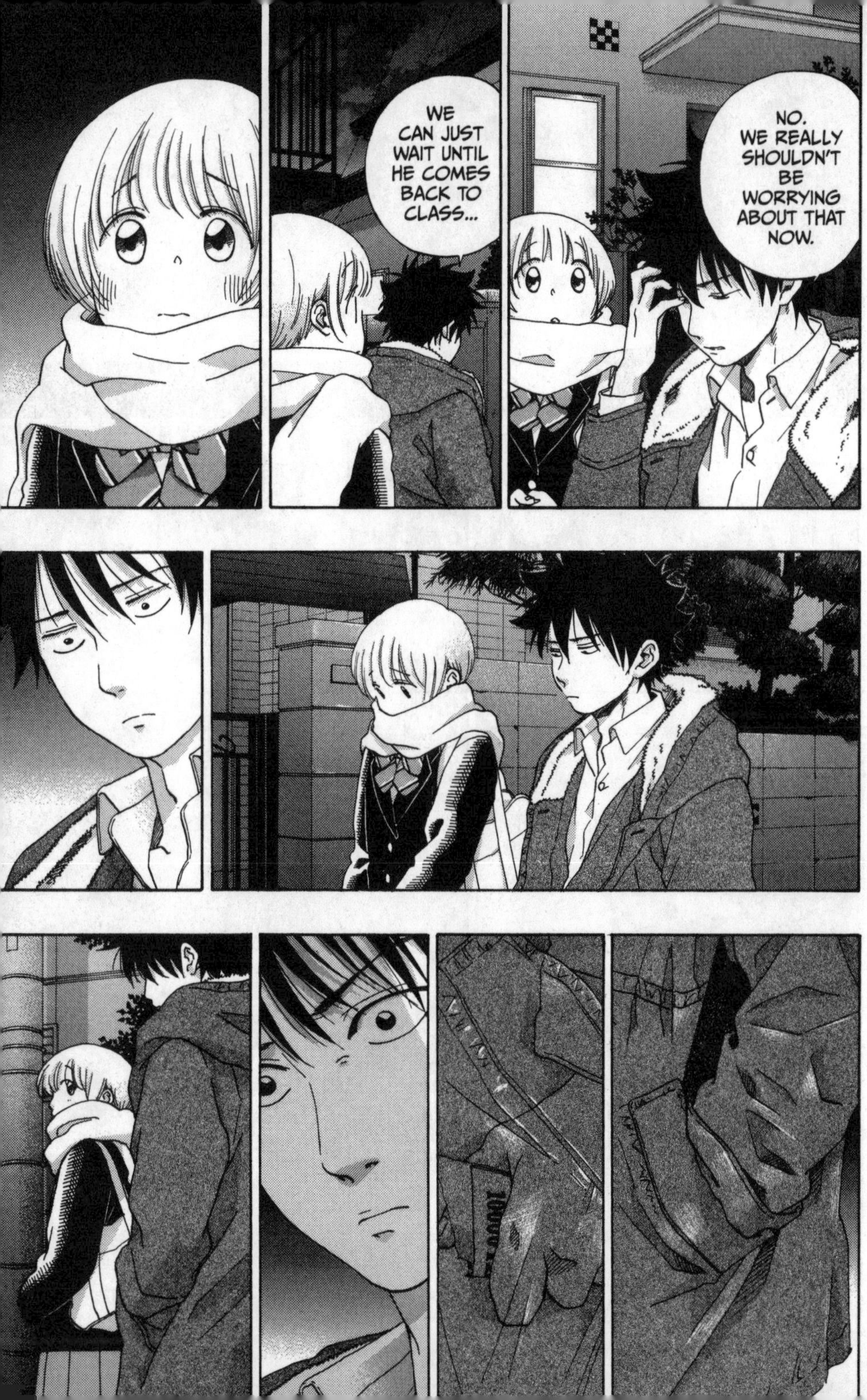
WE CAN JUST WAIT UNTIL HE COMES BACK TO CLASS...
NO. WE REALLY SHOULDN'T BE WORRYING ABOUT THAT NOW.

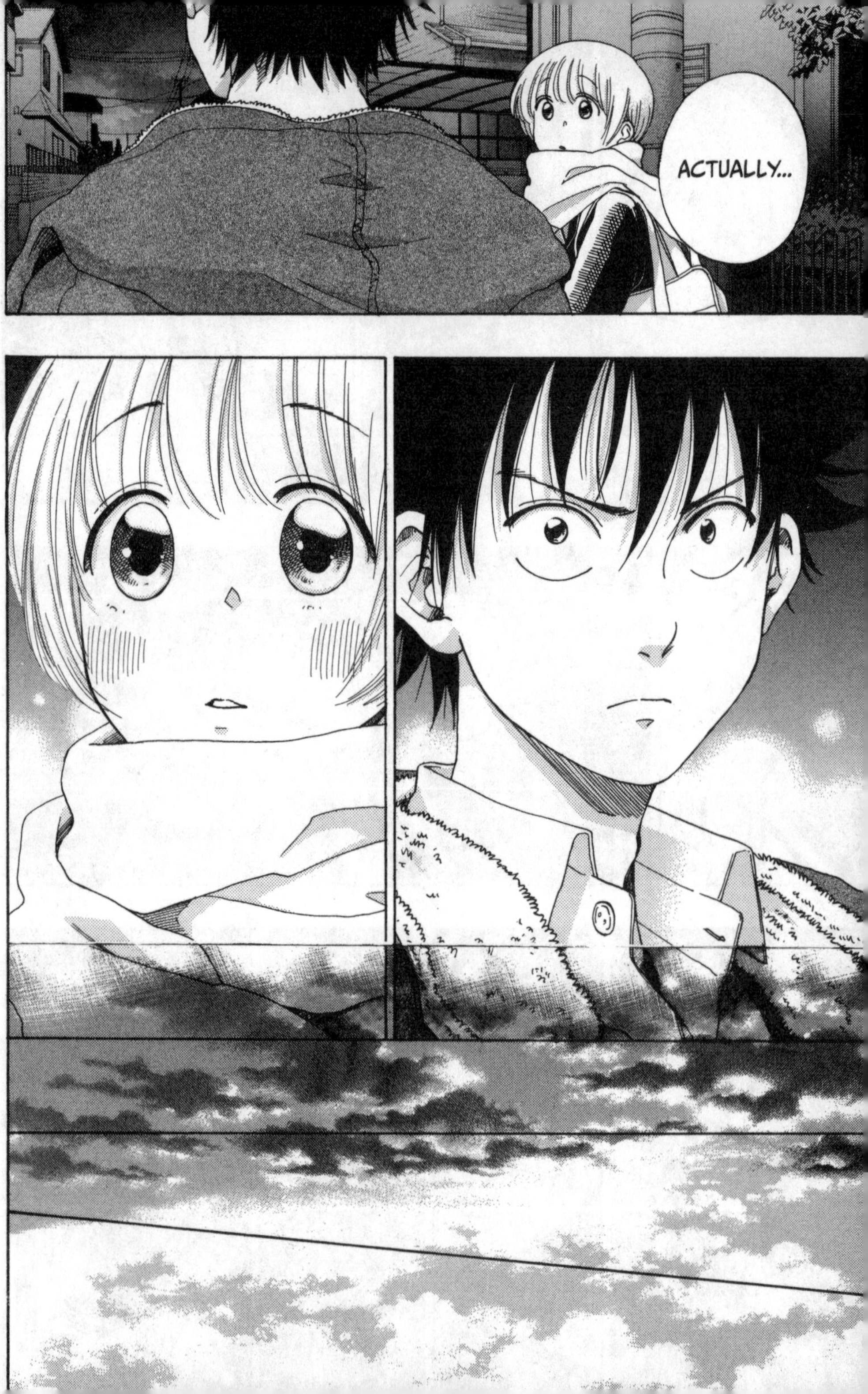
ACTUALLY...

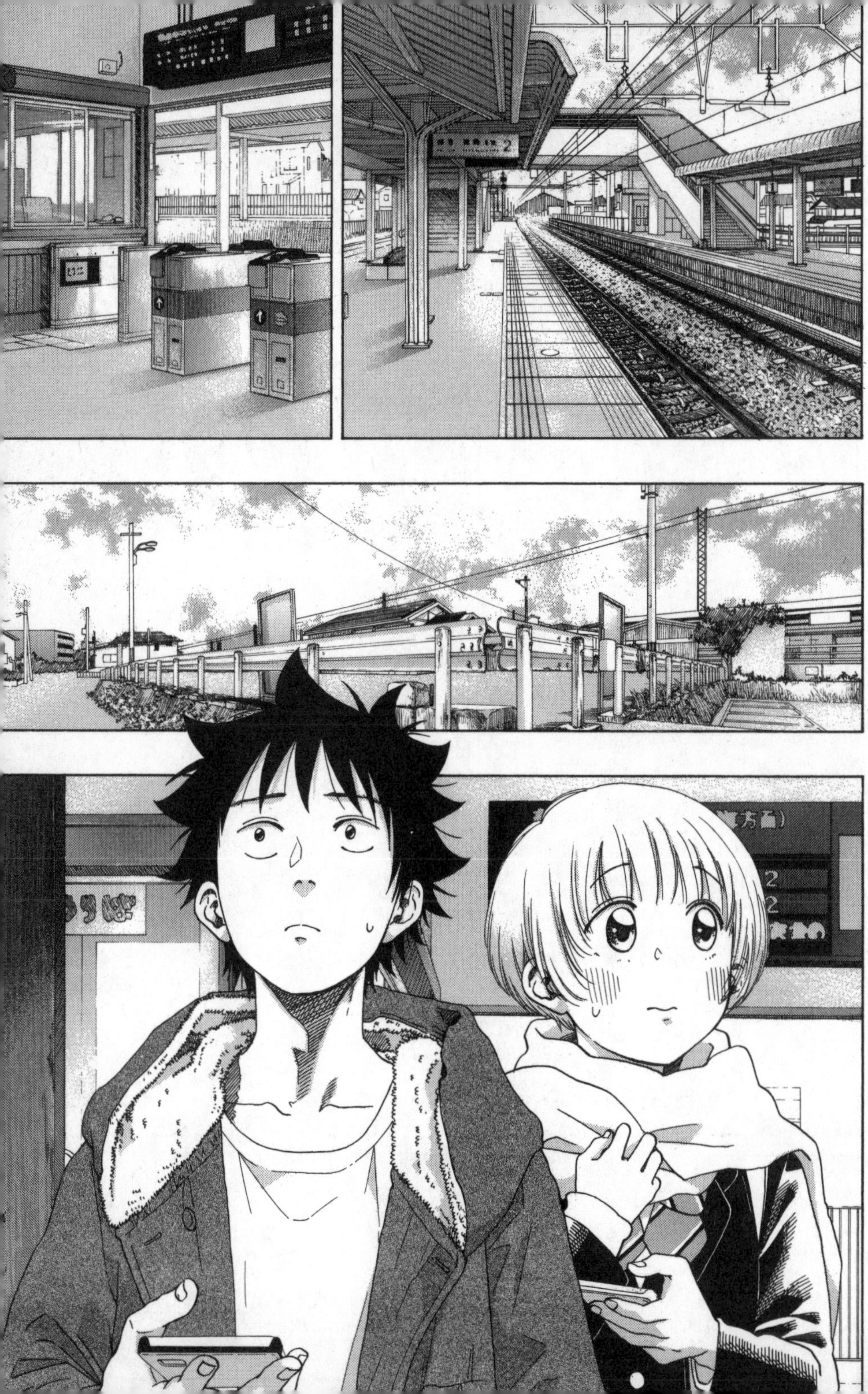

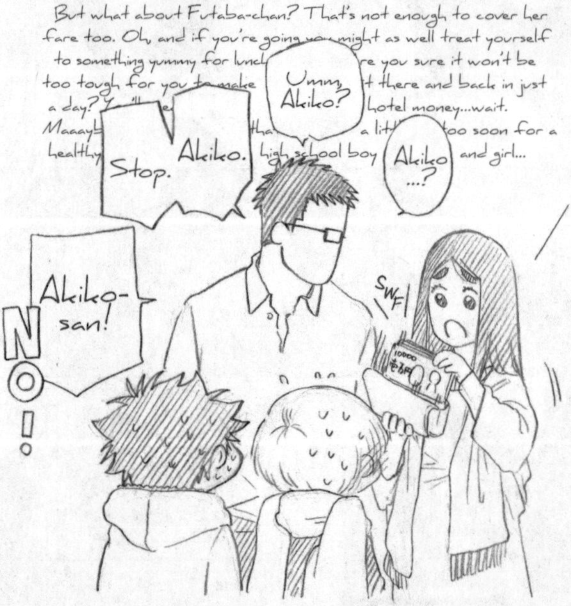
But what about Futaba-chan? That's not enough to cover her fare too. Oh, and if you're going
might as well treat yourself
to something yummy for lunch
re you sure it won't be
too tough for you
t there and back in just
a day?
hotel money...wait.
Maaay
a lit
oo soon for a
healthy
high school boy
and girl...
Akiko ...?
Umm, Akiko?
Akiko.
Stop.
Akiko-san!
SWF
NO!

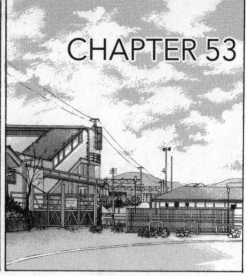

CHAPTER 53

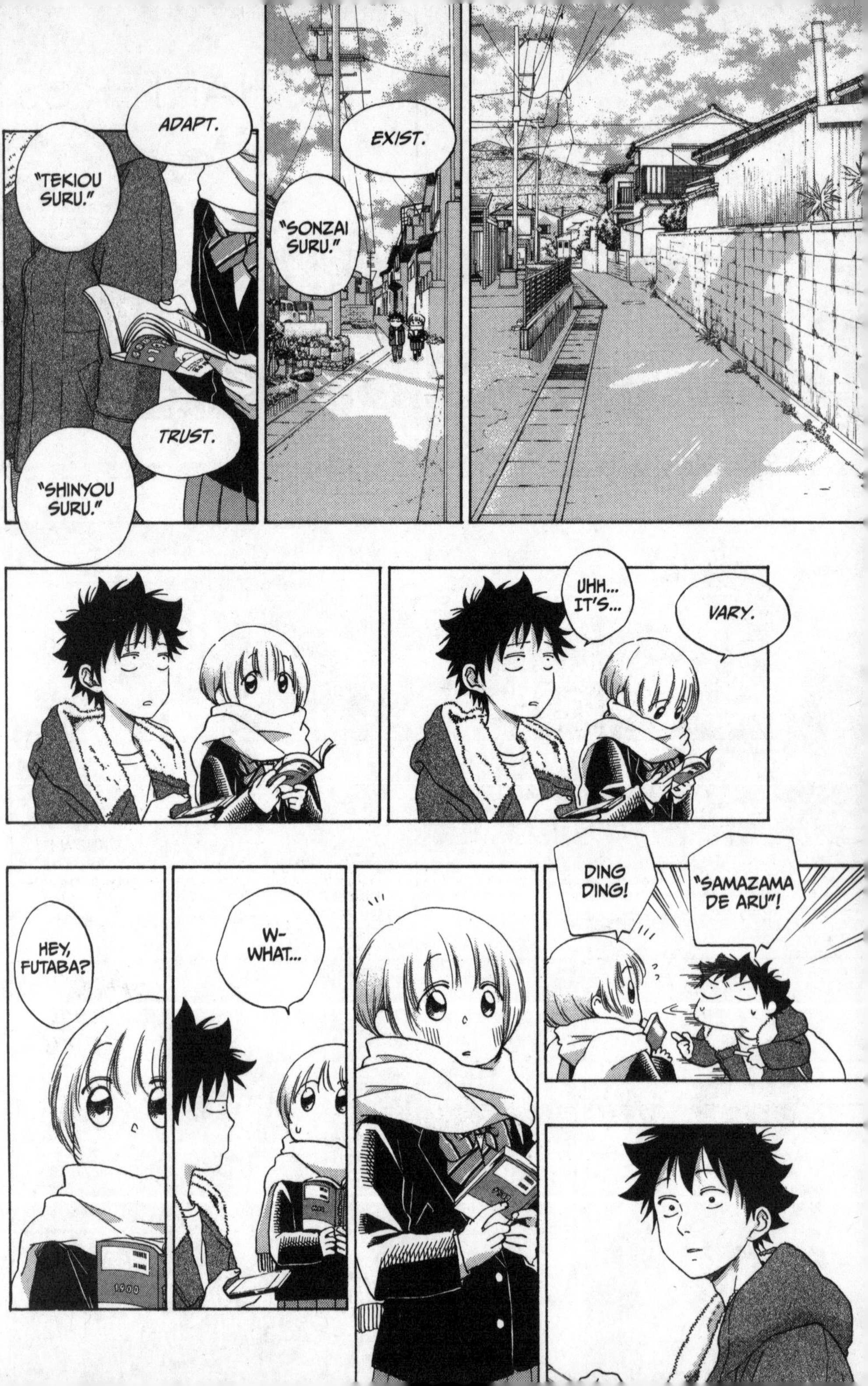
EXIST.
"SONZAI SURU."
ADAPT.
"TEKIOU SURU."
TRUST.
"SHINYOU SURU."
VARY.
UHH... IT'S...
"SAMAZAMA DE ARU"!
DING DING!
W-WHAT...
HEY, FUTABA?

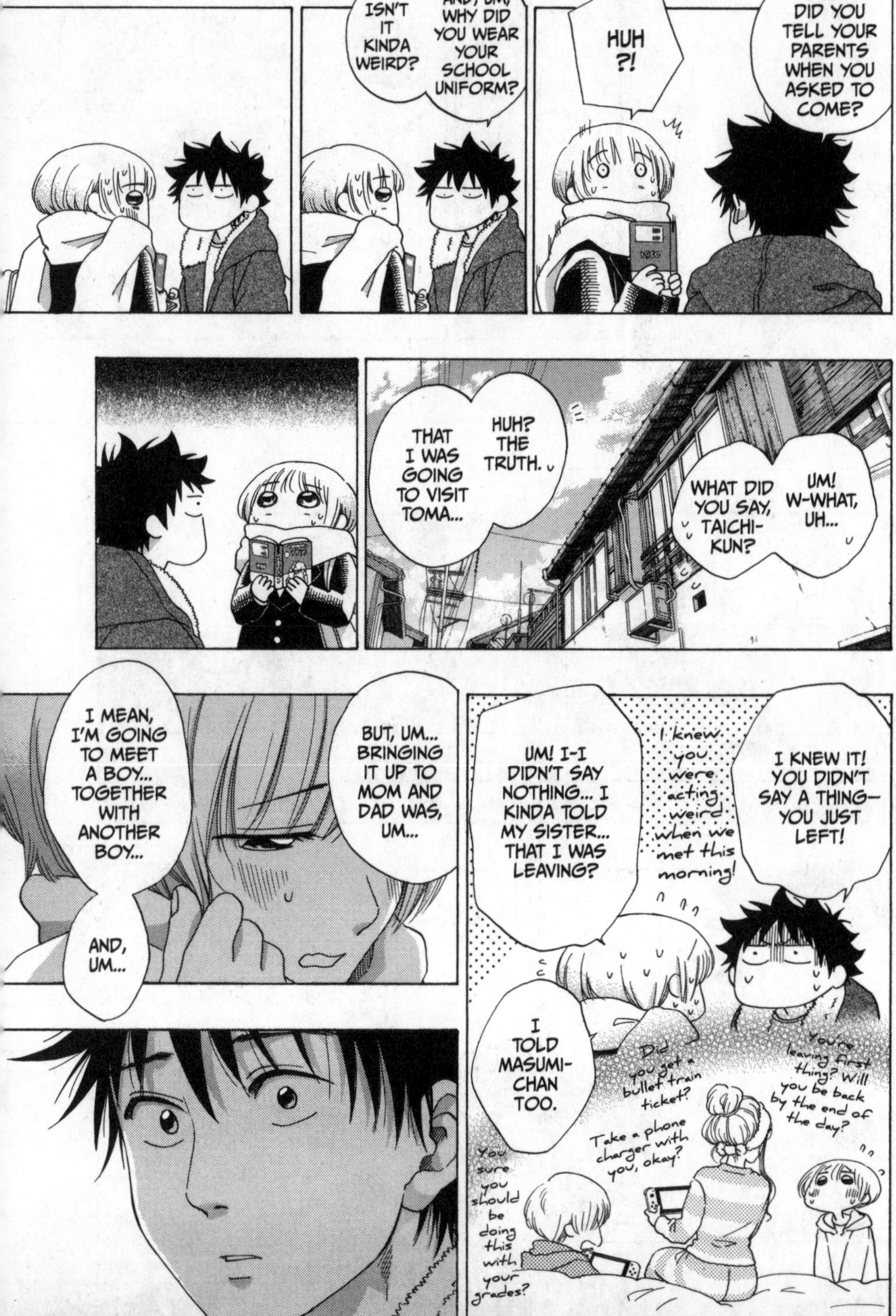
WHAT DID YOU TELL YOUR PARENTS WHEN YOU ASKED TO COME?
HUH ?!
AND, UM, WHY DID YOU WEAR YOUR SCHOOL UNIFORM?
ISN'T IT KINDA WEIRD?
UM! W-WHAT, UH...
WHAT DID YOU SAY, TAICHI-KUN?
HUH? THE TRUTH.
THAT I WAS GOING TO VISIT TOMA...
I KNEW IT! YOU DIDN'T SAY A THING—YOU JUST LEFT!
I knew you were acting weird when we met this morning!
UM! I-I DIDN'T SAY NOTHING... I KINDA TOLD MY SISTER... THAT I WAS LEAVING?
I TOLD MASUMI-CHAN TOO.
You're leaving first thing? Will you be back by the end of the day?
Did you get a bullet train ticket?
Take a phone charger with you, okay?
You sure you should be doing this with your grades?
BUT, UM... BRINGING IT UP TO MOM AND DAD WAS, UM...
I MEAN, I'M GOING TO MEET A BOY... TOGETHER WITH ANOTHER BOY...
AND, UM...

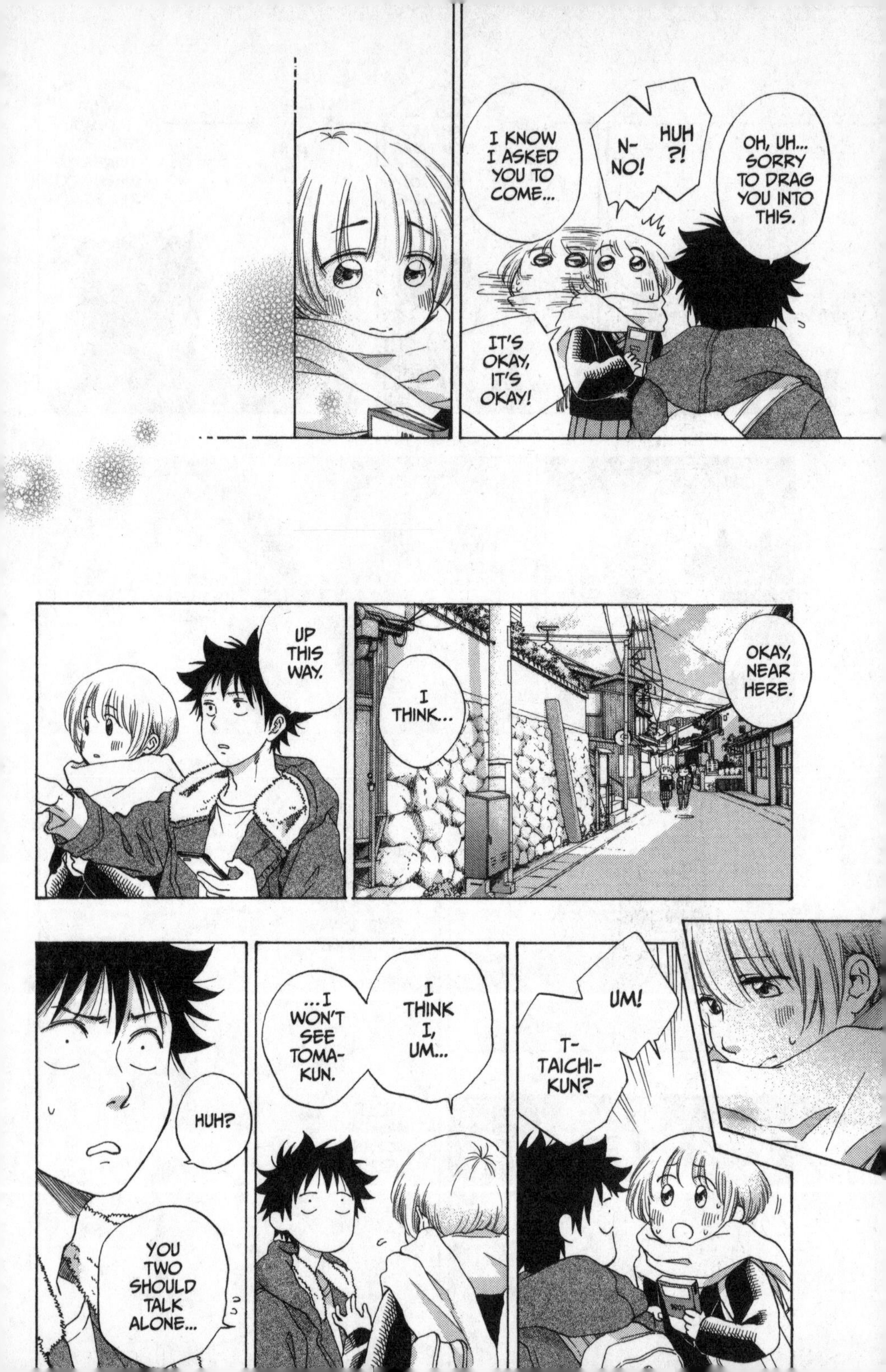
OH, UH... SORRY TO DRAG YOU INTO THIS.
HUH ?!
N-NO!
I KNOW I ASKED YOU TO COME...
IT'S OKAY, IT'S OKAY!
OKAY, NEAR HERE.
I THINK...
UP THIS WAY.
UM!
T-TAICHI-KUN?
I THINK I, UM...
...I WON'T SEE TOMA-KUN.
HUH?
YOU TWO SHOULD TALK ALONE...

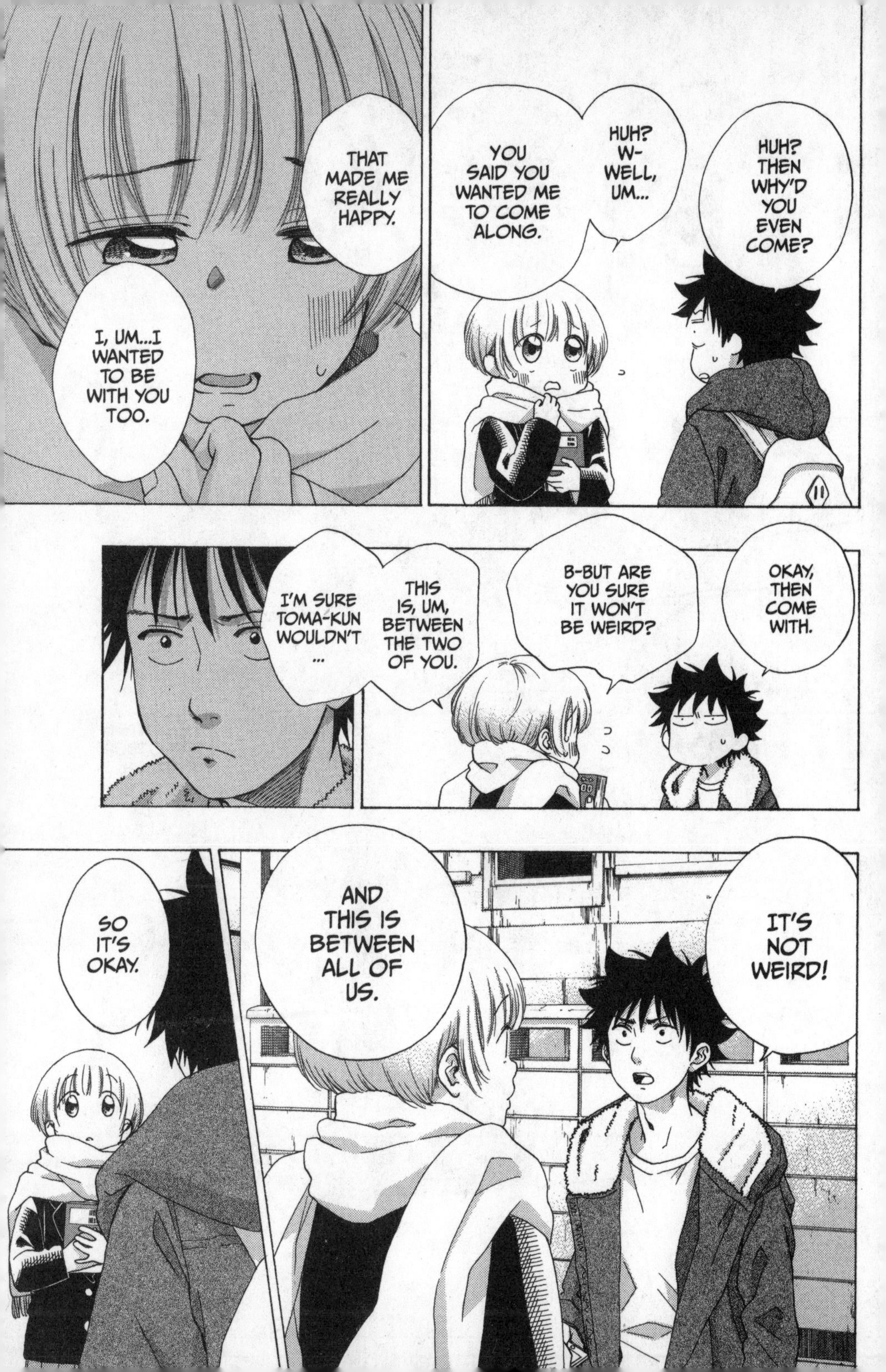
HUH? THEN WHY'D YOU EVEN COME?
HUH? W-WELL, UM...
YOU SAID YOU WANTED ME TO COME ALONG.
THAT MADE ME REALLY HAPPY.
I, UM...I WANTED TO BE WITH YOU TOO.
OKAY, THEN COME WITH.
B-BUT ARE YOU SURE IT WON'T BE WEIRD?
THIS IS, UM, BETWEEN THE TWO OF YOU.
I'M SURE TOMA-KUN WOULDN'T ...
IT'S NOT WEIRD!
AND THIS IS BETWEEN ALL OF US.
SO IT'S OKAY.

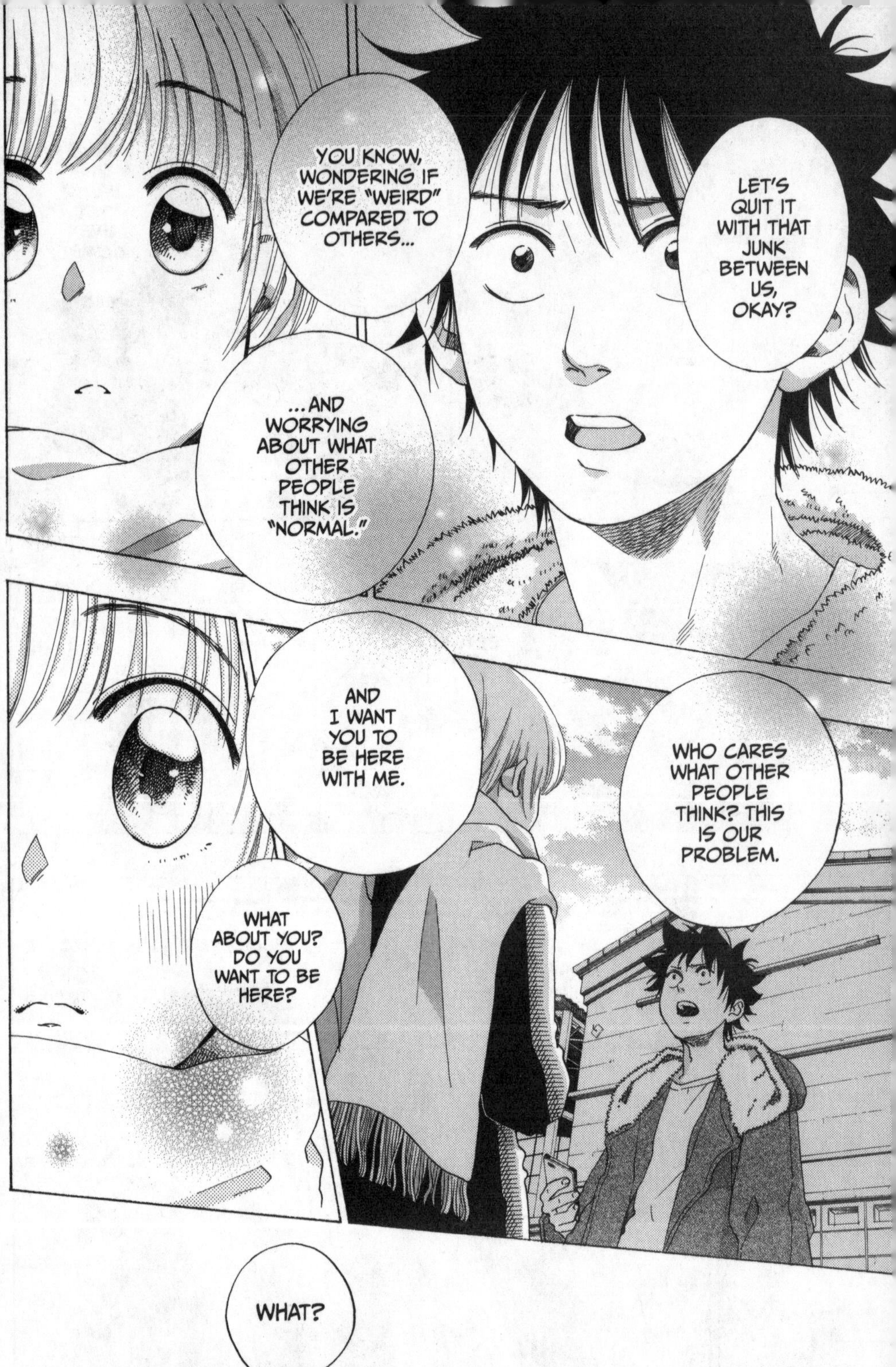
LET'S QUIT IT WITH THAT JUNK BETWEEN US, OKAY?
YOU KNOW, WONDERING IF WE'RE "WEIRD" COMPARED TO OTHERS...
...AND WORRYING ABOUT WHAT OTHER PEOPLE THINK IS "NORMAL."
WHO CARES WHAT OTHER PEOPLE THINK? THIS IS OUR PROBLEM.
AND I WANT YOU TO BE HERE WITH ME.
WHAT ABOUT YOU? DO YOU WANT TO BE HERE?
WHAT?

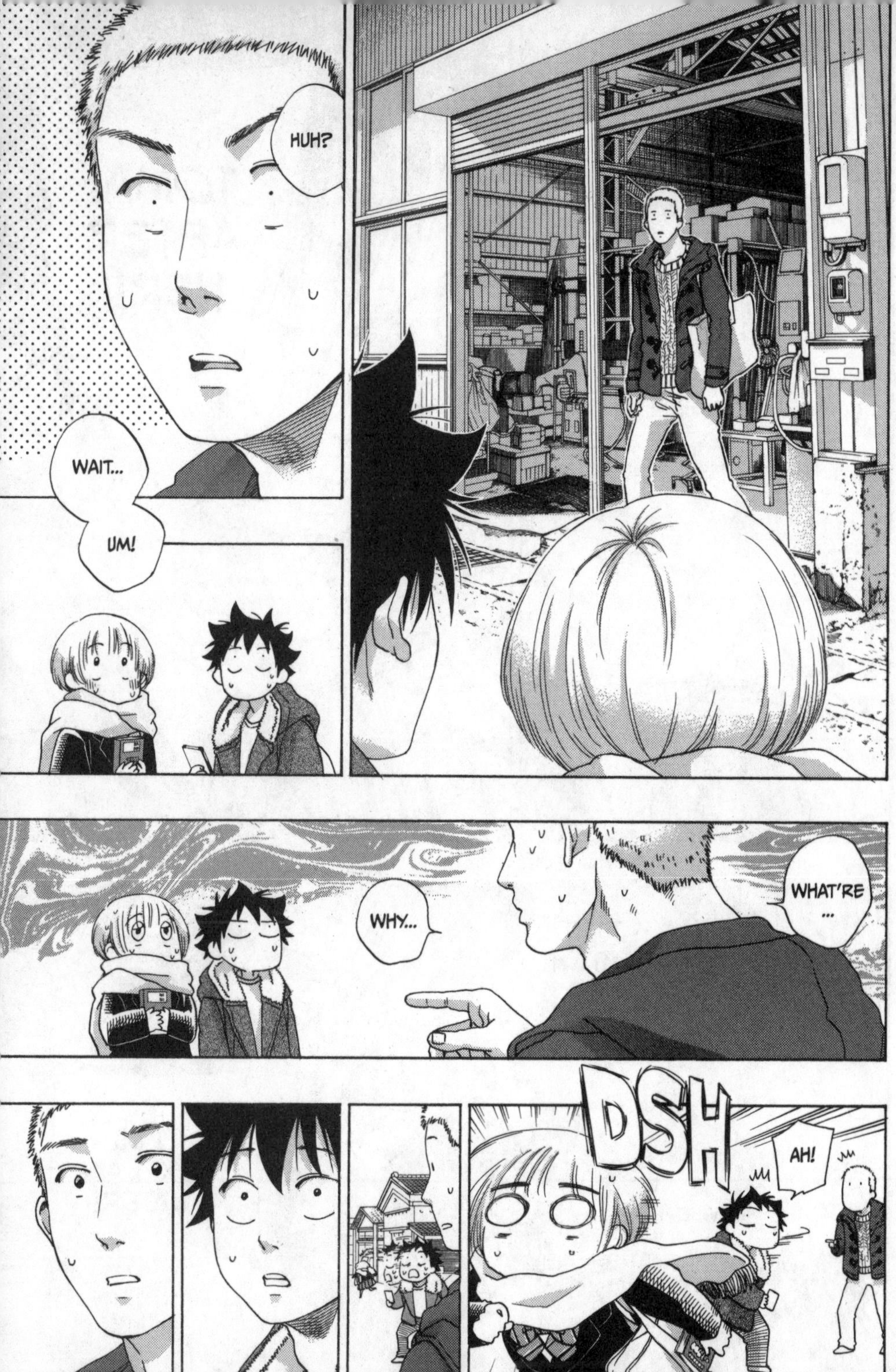
HUH?
WAIT...
UM!
WHAT'RE ...
WHY...
DSH
AH!

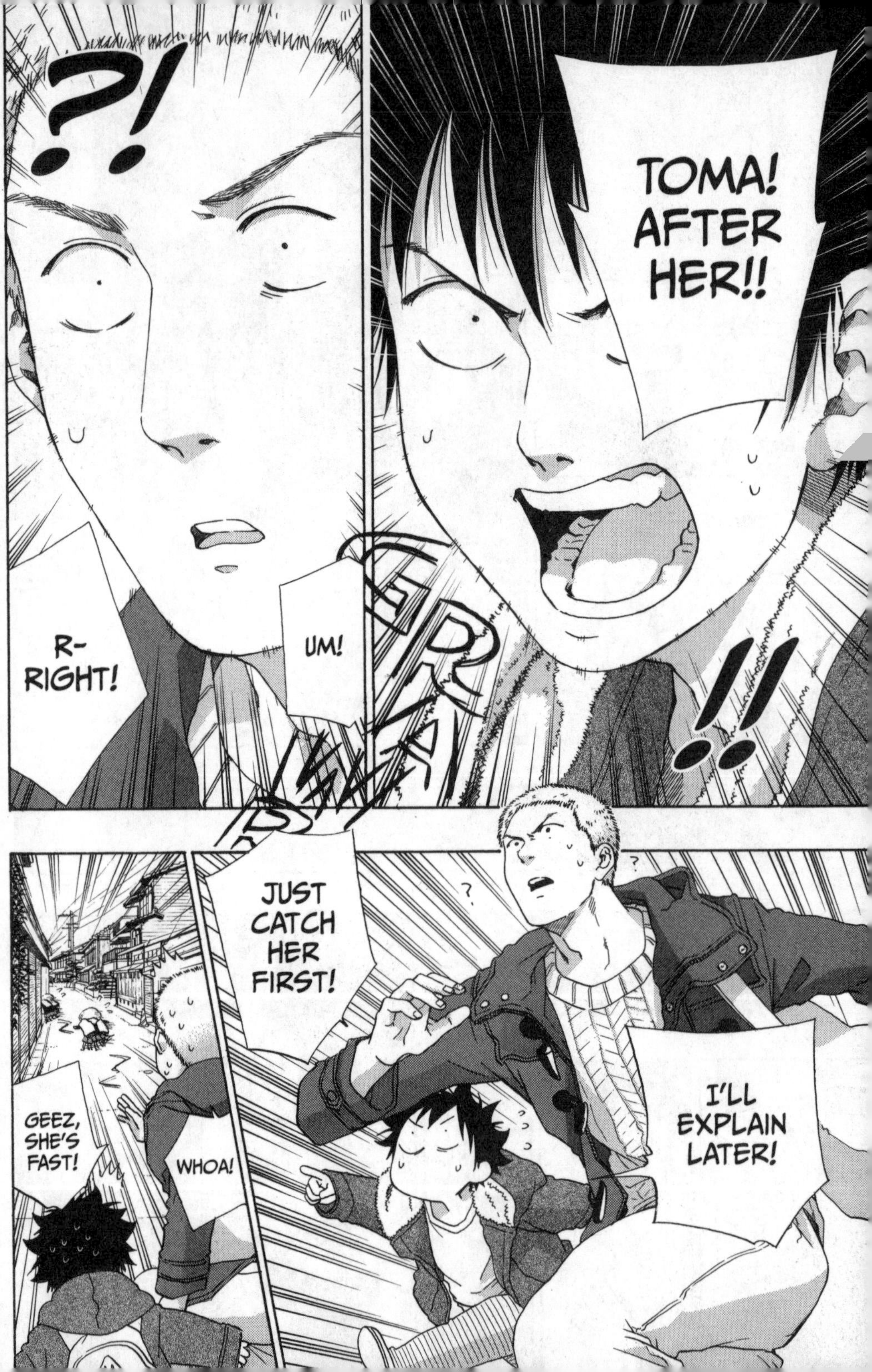
TOMA! AFTER HER!!
!!
?!
UM!
R- RIGHT!
?
?
I'LL EXPLAIN LATER!
JUST CATCH HER FIRST!
WHOA!
GEEZ, SHE'S FAST!

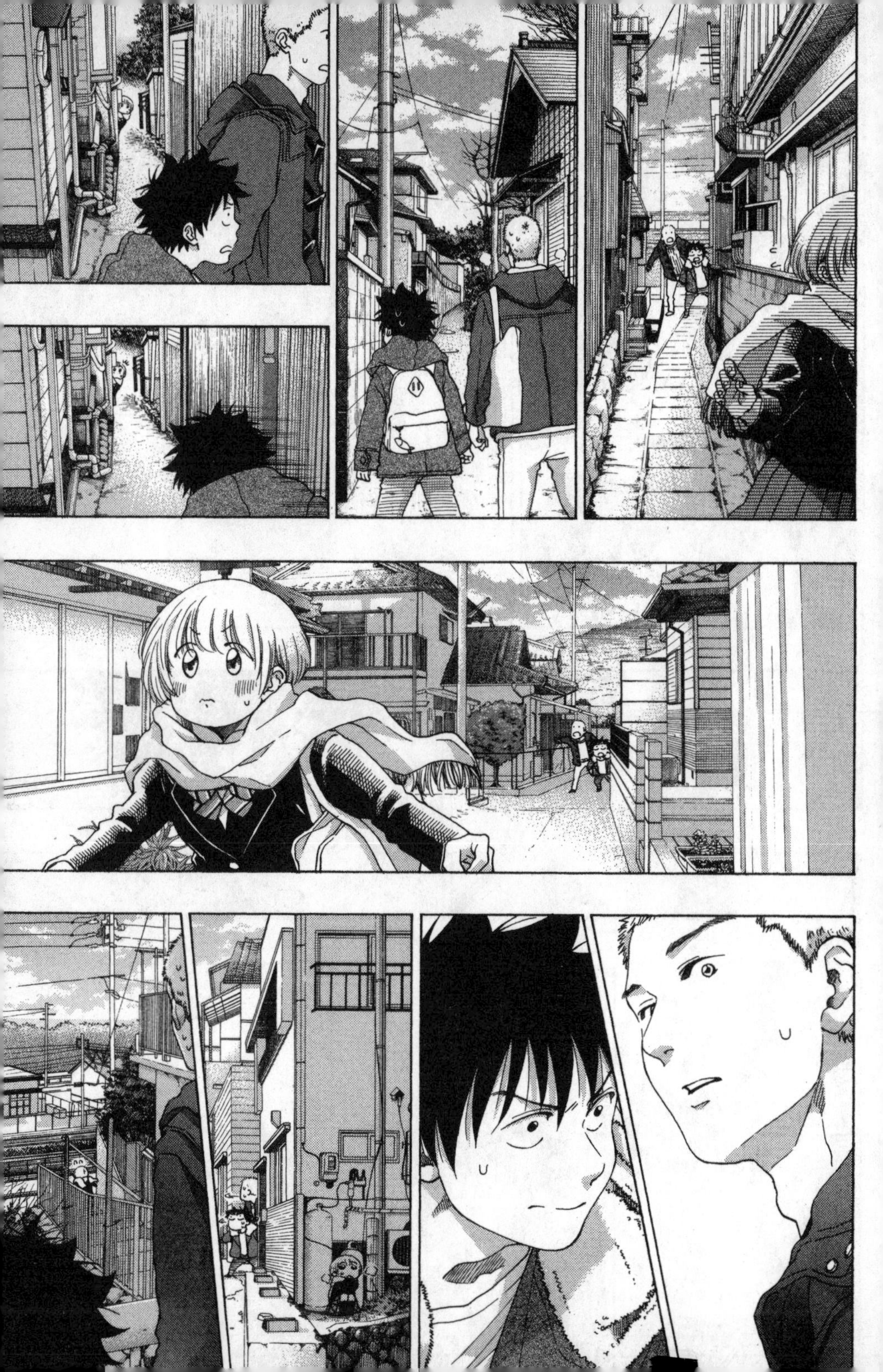

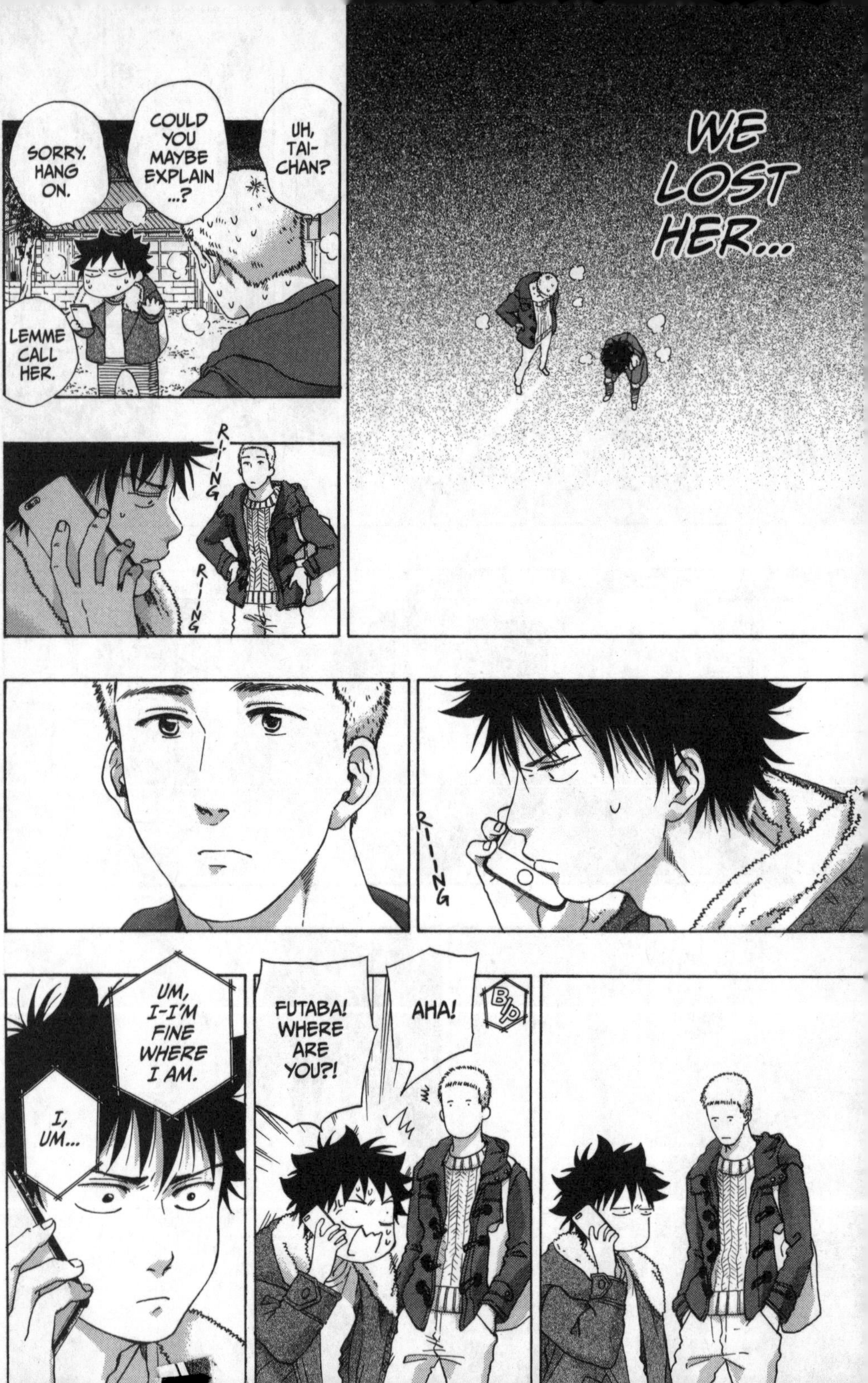
WE LOST HER...
UH, TAI-CHAN?
COULD YOU MAYBE EXPLAIN ...?
SORRY. HANG ON.
LEMME CALL HER.
RIIING
RIIING
RIIIING
BIP
AHA!
FUTABA! WHERE ARE YOU?!
UM, I-I'M FINE WHERE I AM.
I, UM...

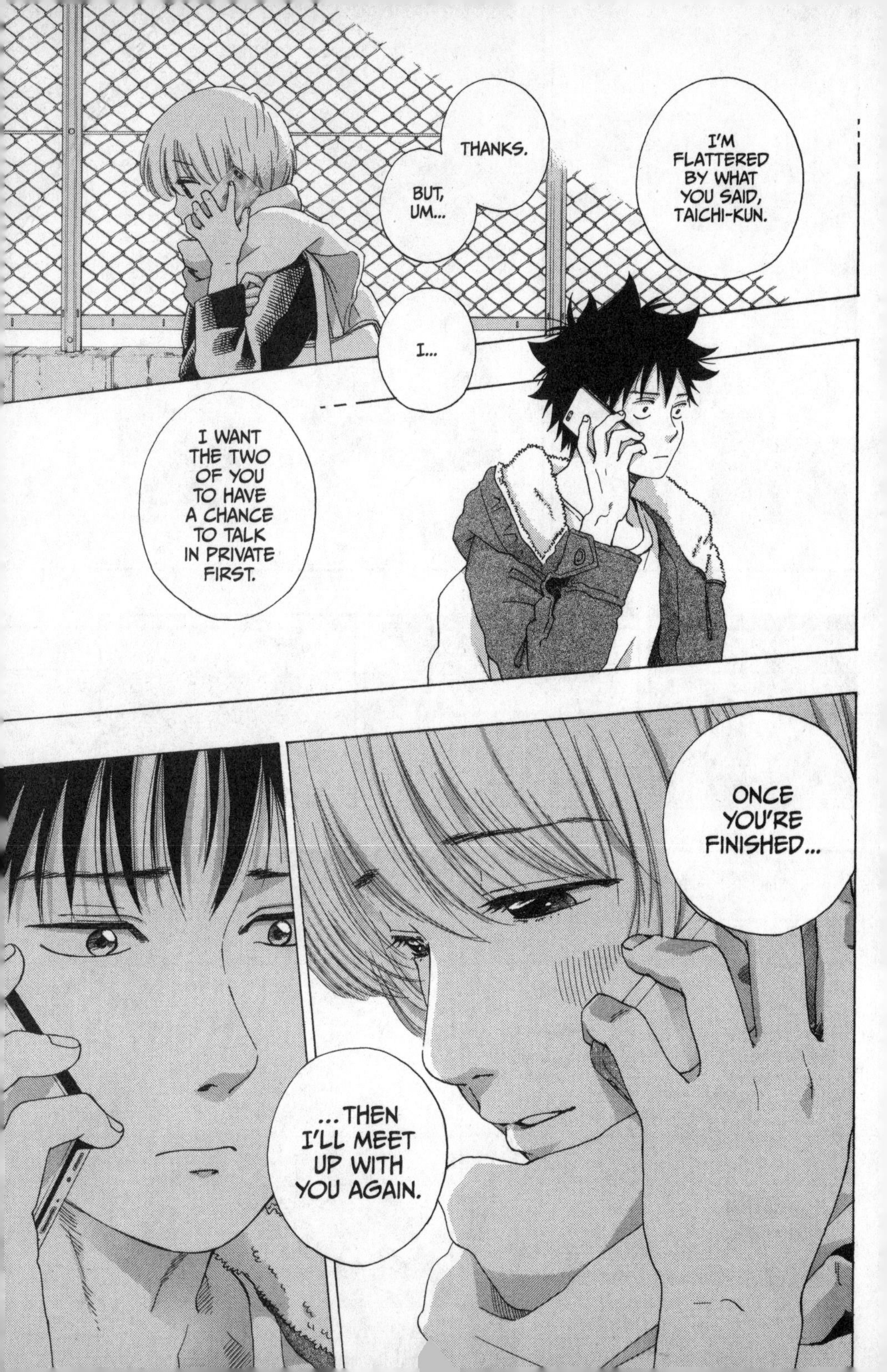
I'M FLATTERED BY WHAT YOU SAID, TAICHI-KUN.
THANKS.
BUT, UM...
I...
I WANT THE TWO OF YOU TO HAVE A CHANCE TO TALK IN PRIVATE FIRST.
ONCE YOU'RE FINISHED...
...THEN I'LL MEET UP WITH YOU AGAIN.

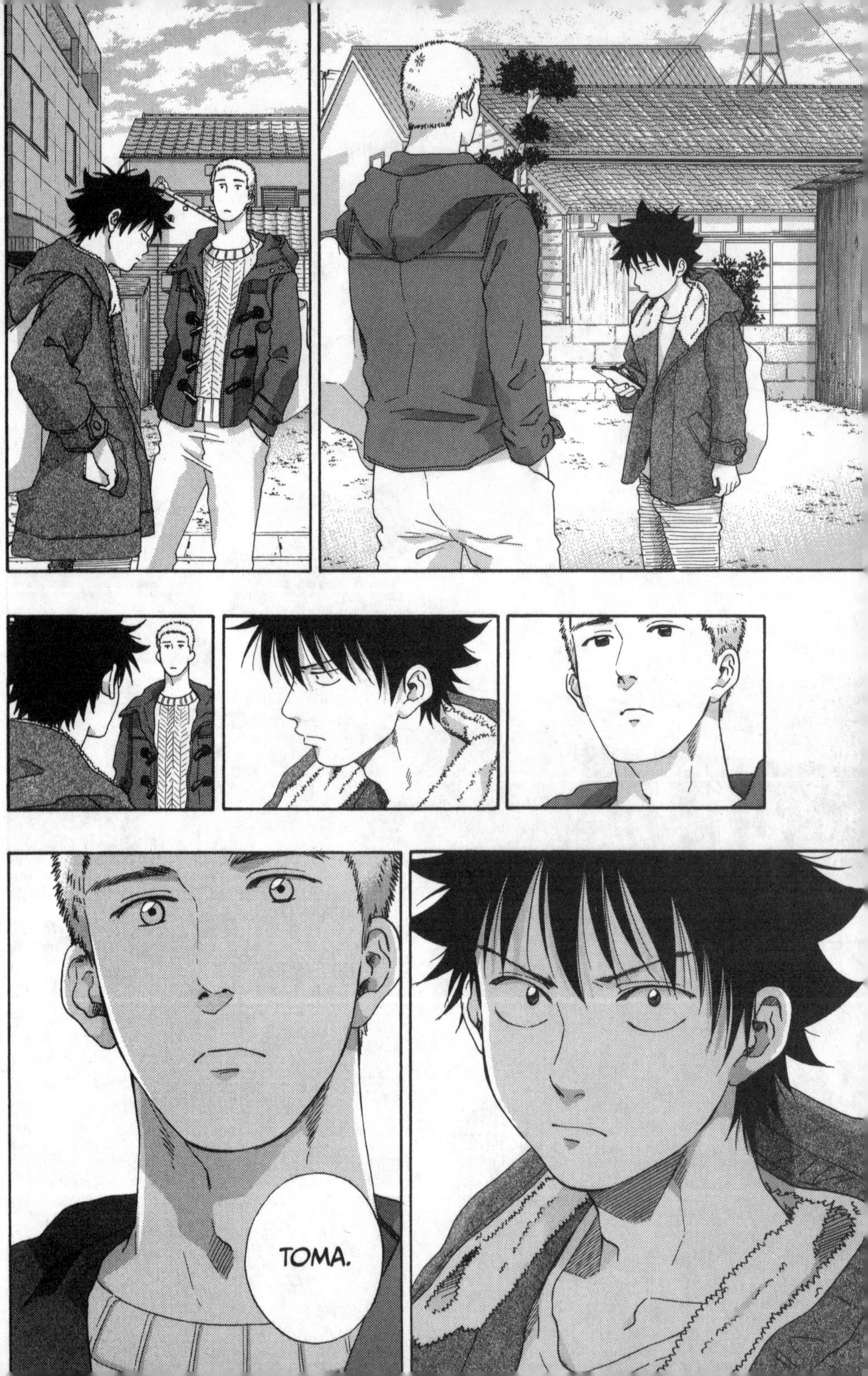
TOMA.

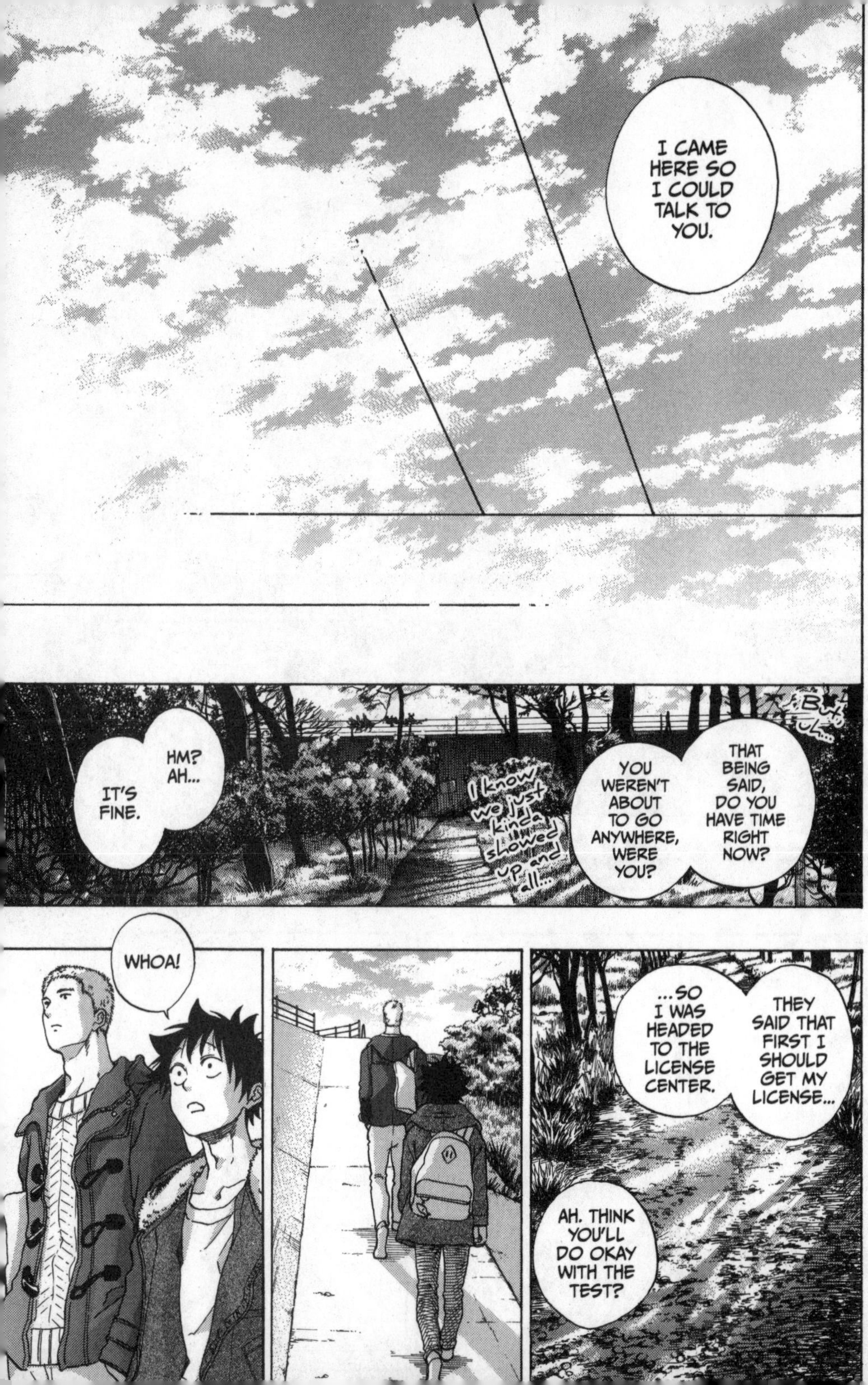
I CAME HERE SO I COULD TALK TO YOU.
THAT BEING SAID, DO YOU HAVE TIME RIGHT NOW?
YOU WEREN'T ABOUT TO GO ANYWHERE, WERE YOU?
I know we just kinda showed up and all...
HM? AH... IT'S FINE.
THEY SAID THAT FIRST I SHOULD GET MY LICENSE...
...SO I WAS HEADED TO THE LICENSE CENTER.
AH. THINK YOU'LL DO OKAY WITH THE TEST?
WHOA!

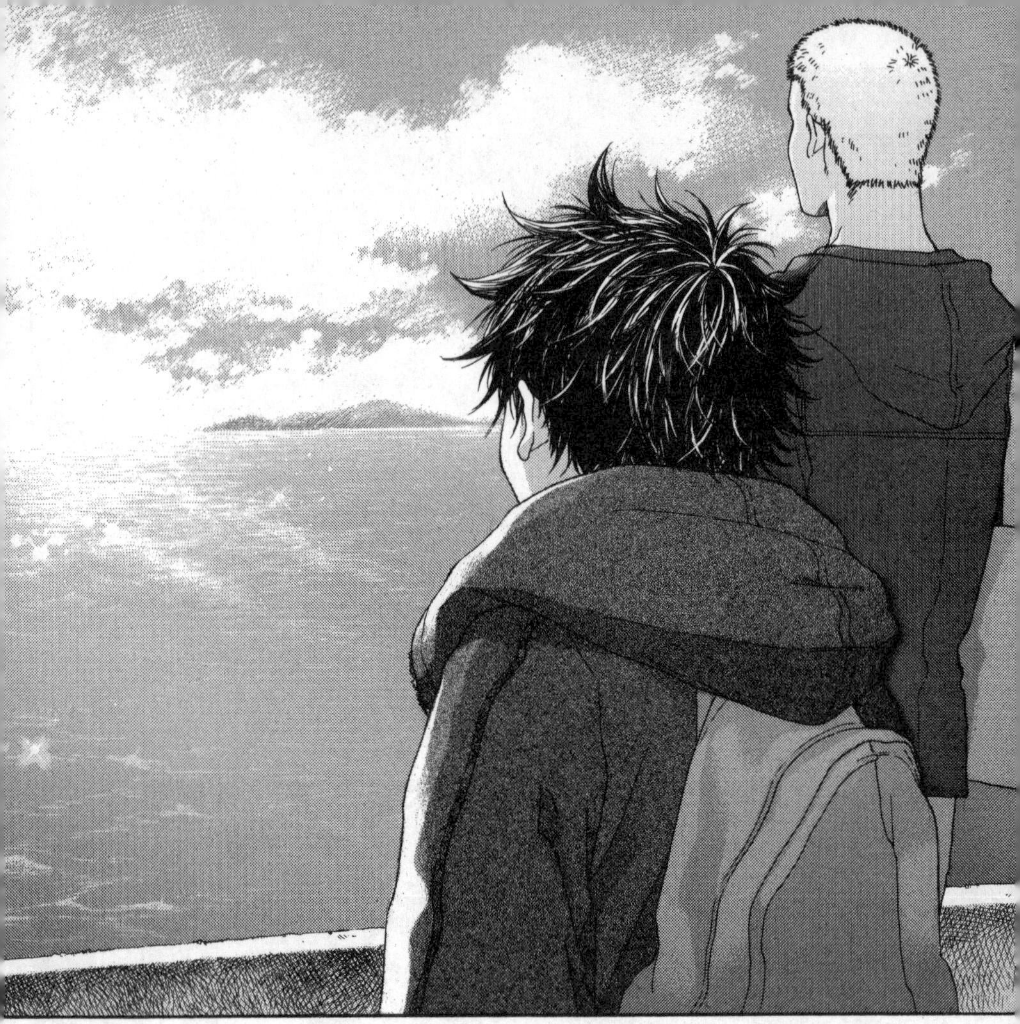
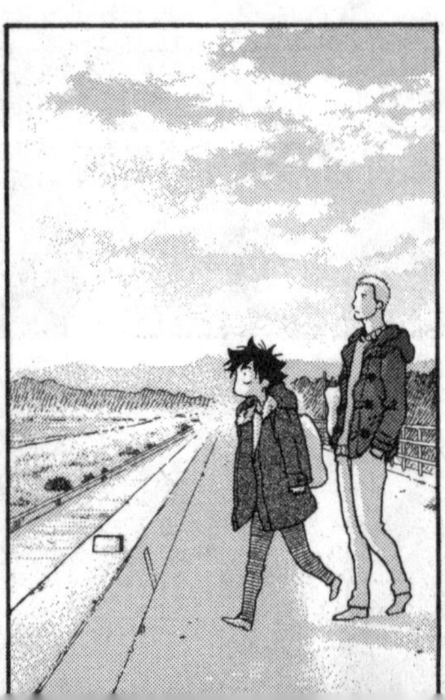
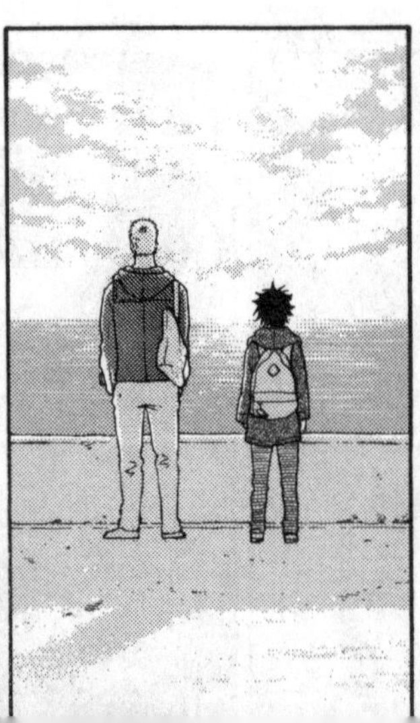
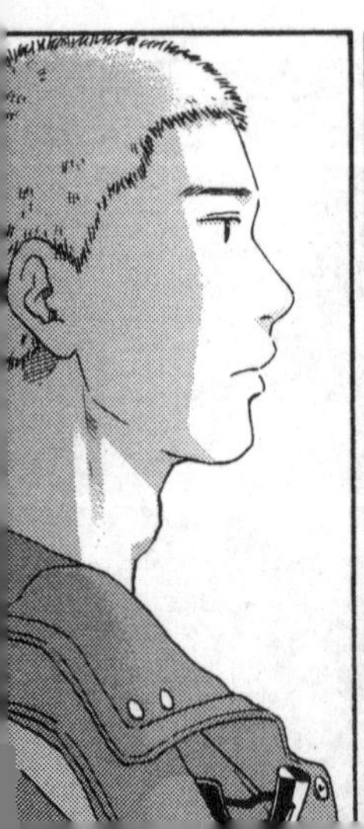

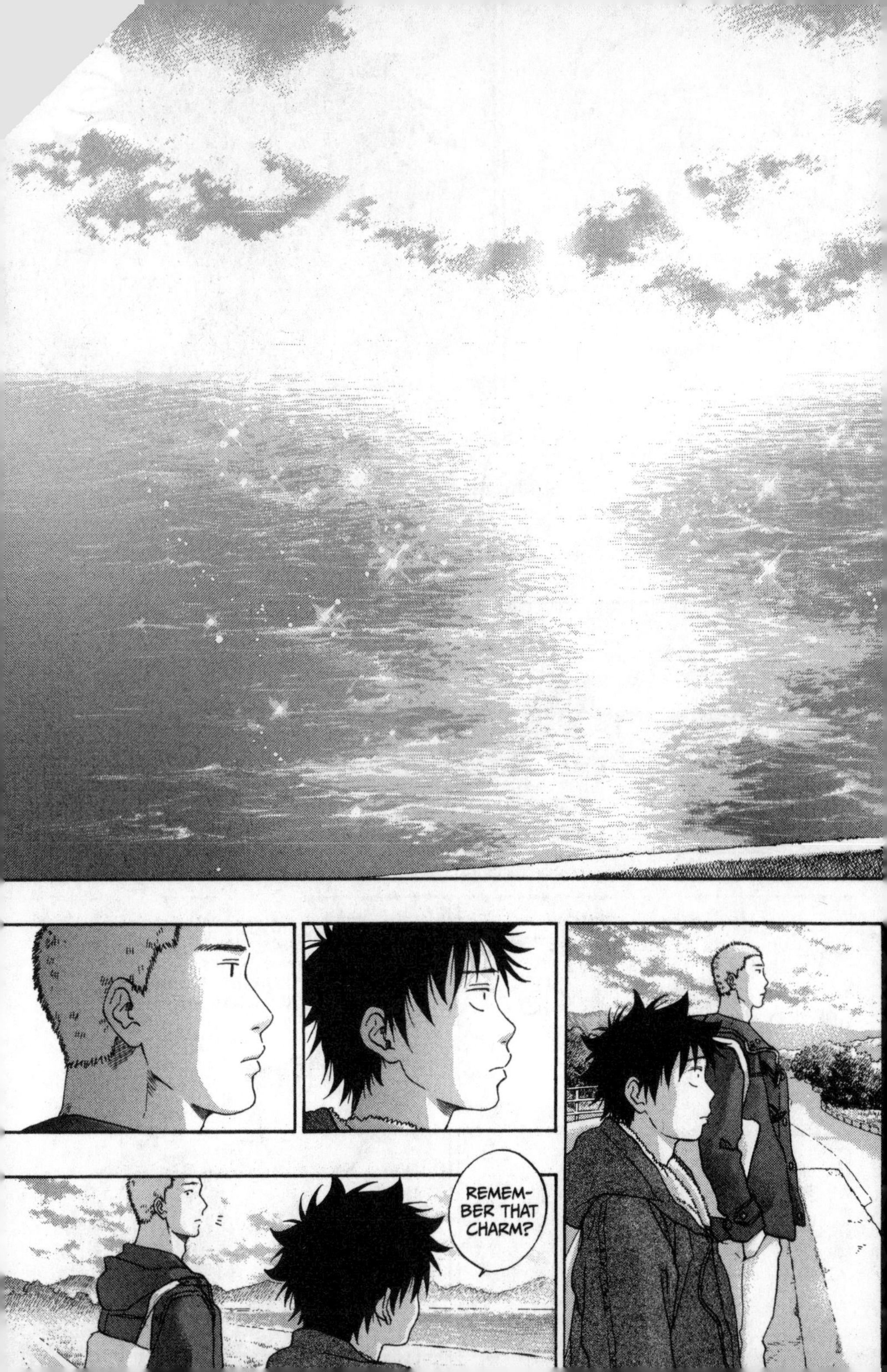
REMEM-
BER THAT
CHARM?

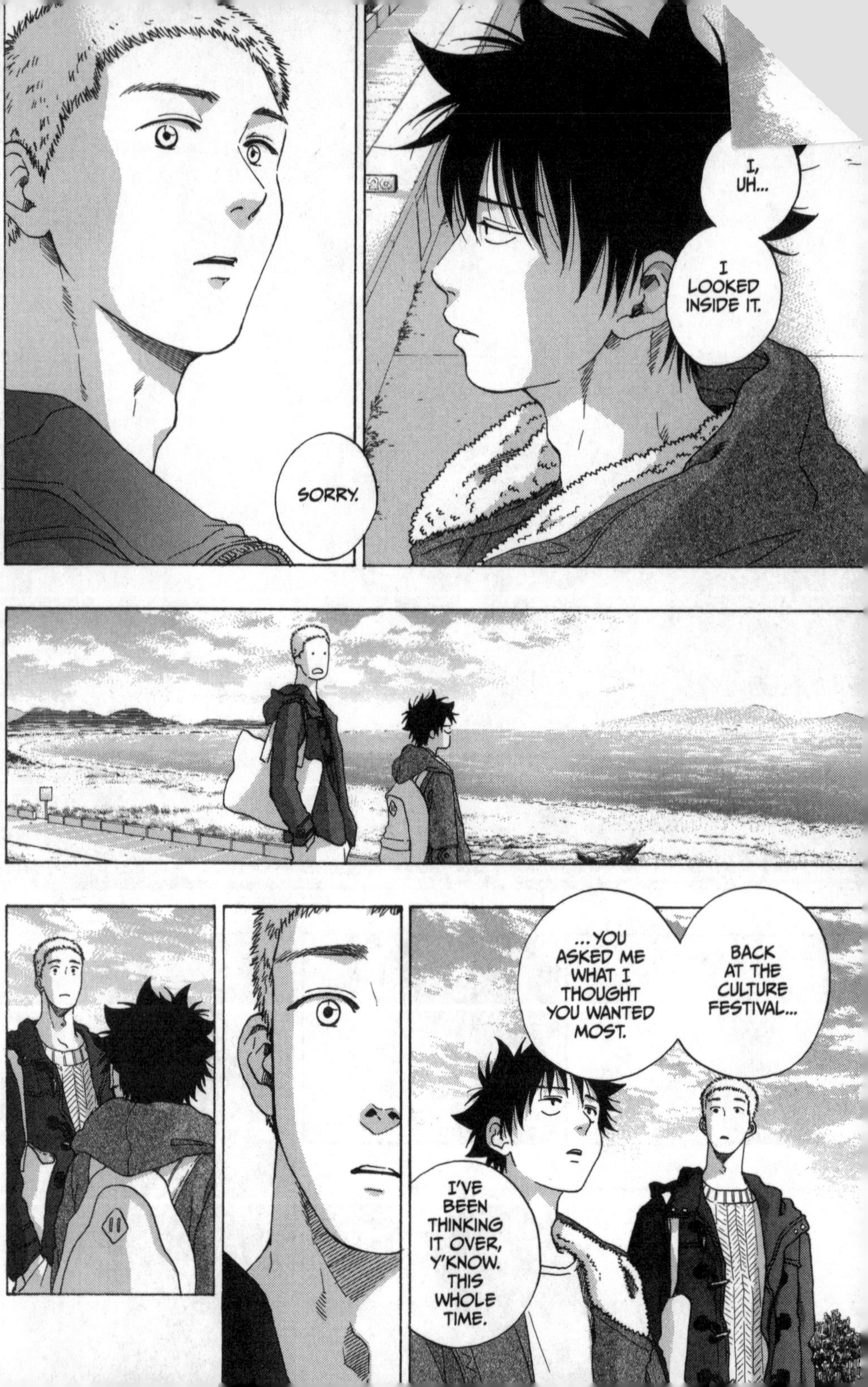
I, UH...
I LOOKED INSIDE IT.
SORRY.
BACK AT THE CULTURE FESTIVAL...
...YOU ASKED ME WHAT I THOUGHT YOU WANTED MOST.
I'VE BEEN THINKING IT OVER, Y'KNOW. THIS WHOLE TIME.

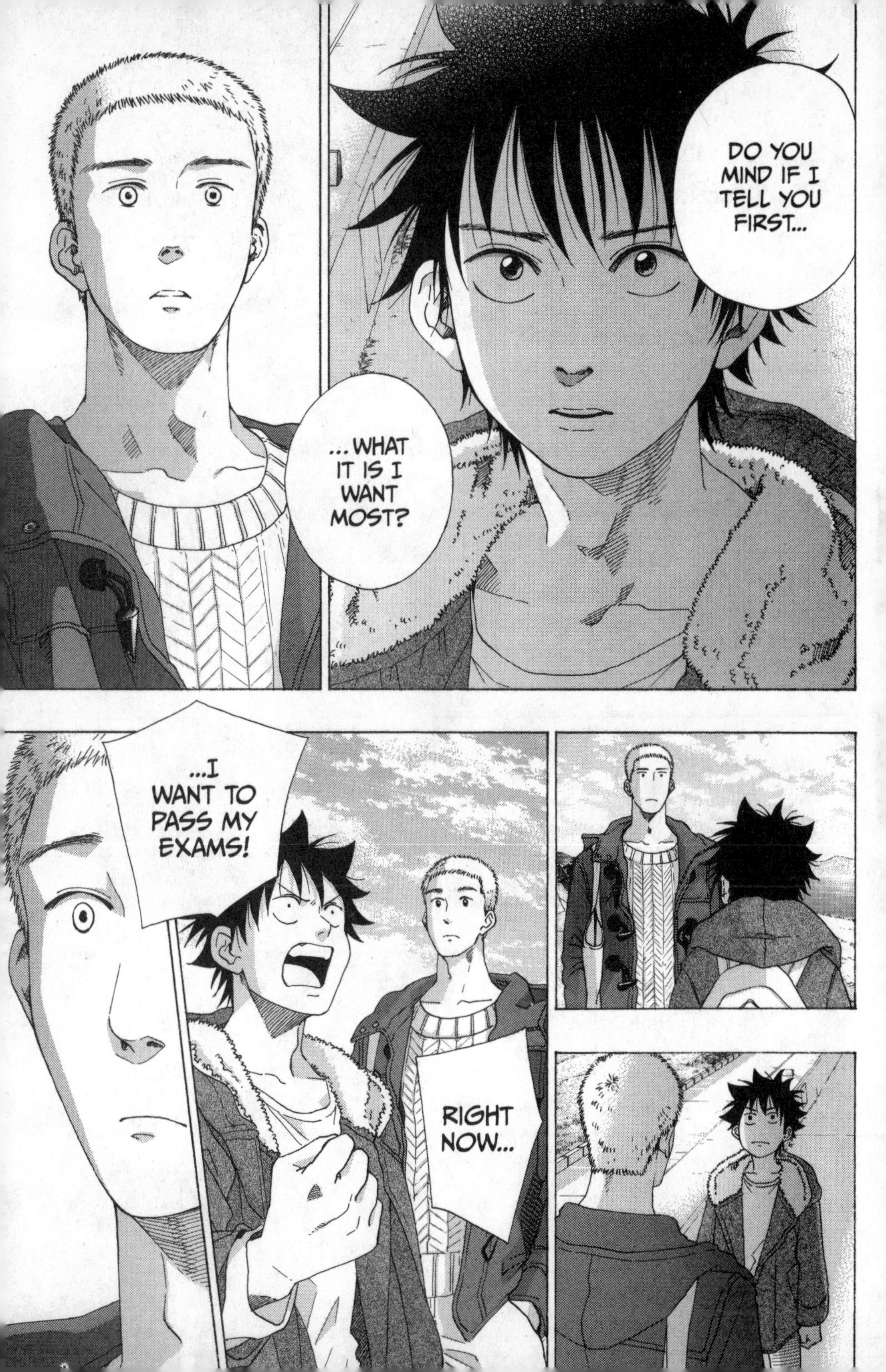
DO YOU MIND IF I TELL YOU FIRST...
...WHAT IT IS I WANT MOST?
...I WANT TO PASS MY EXAMS!
RIGHT NOW...

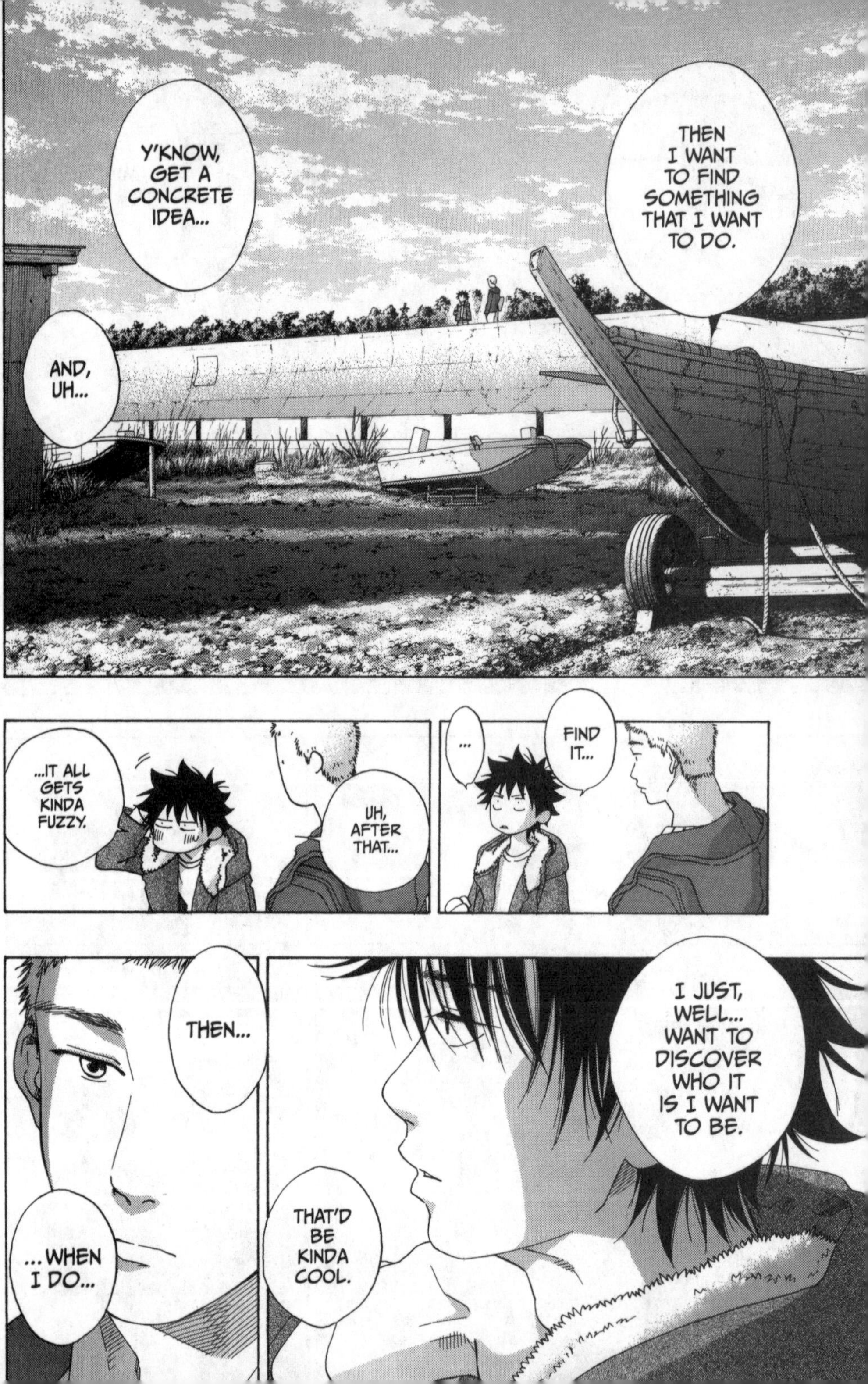
THEN I WANT TO FIND SOMETHING THAT I WANT TO DO.
Y'KNOW, GET A CONCRETE IDEA...
AND, UH...
FIND IT...
...
UH, AFTER THAT...
...IT ALL GETS KINDA FUZZY.
I JUST, WELL... WANT TO DISCOVER WHO IT IS I WANT TO BE.
THAT'D BE KINDA COOL.
THEN...
...WHEN I DO...

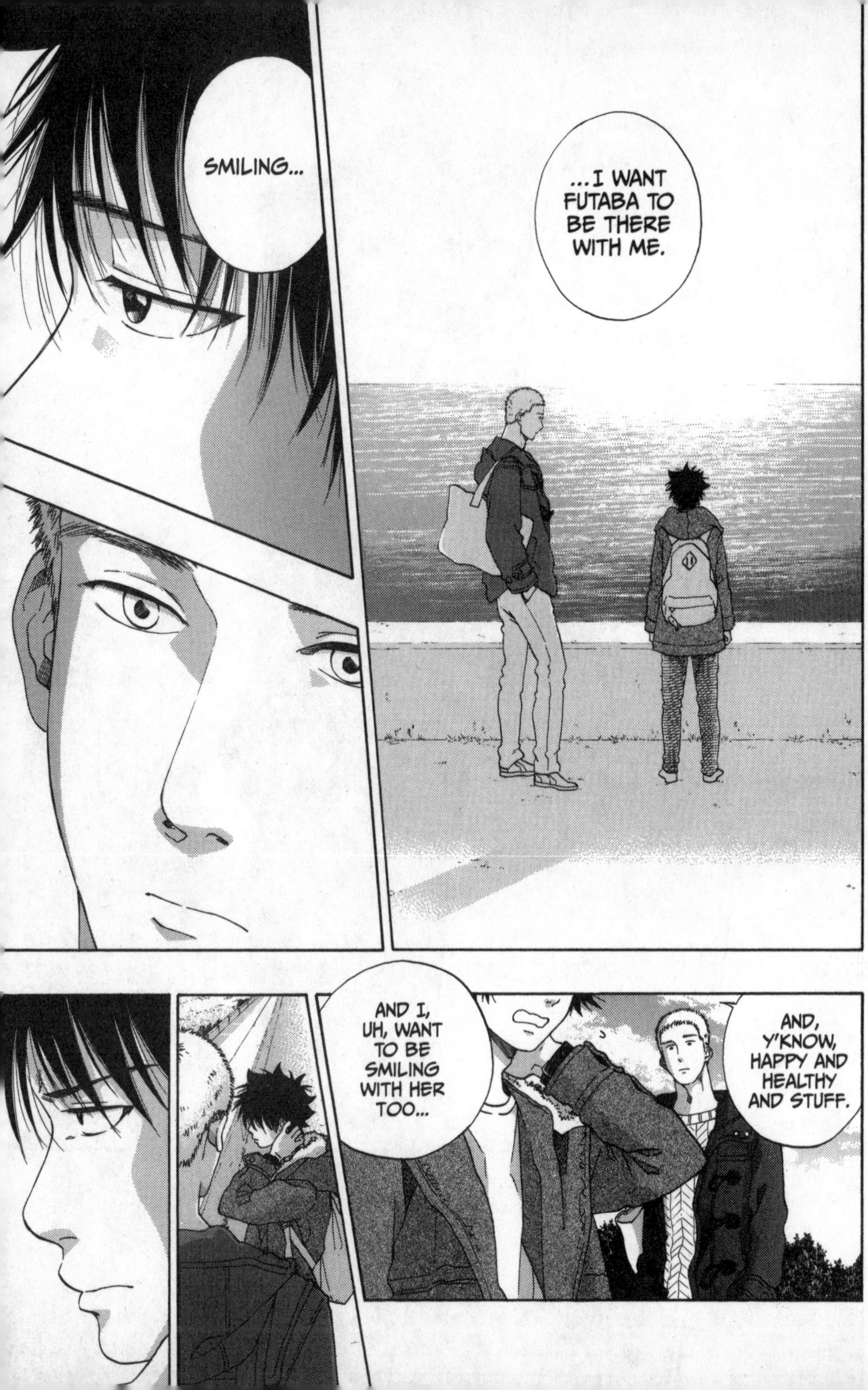
...I WANT FUTABA TO BE THERE WITH ME.
SMILING...
AND, Y'KNOW, HAPPY AND HEALTHY AND STUFF.
AND I, UH, WANT TO BE SMILING WITH HER TOO...

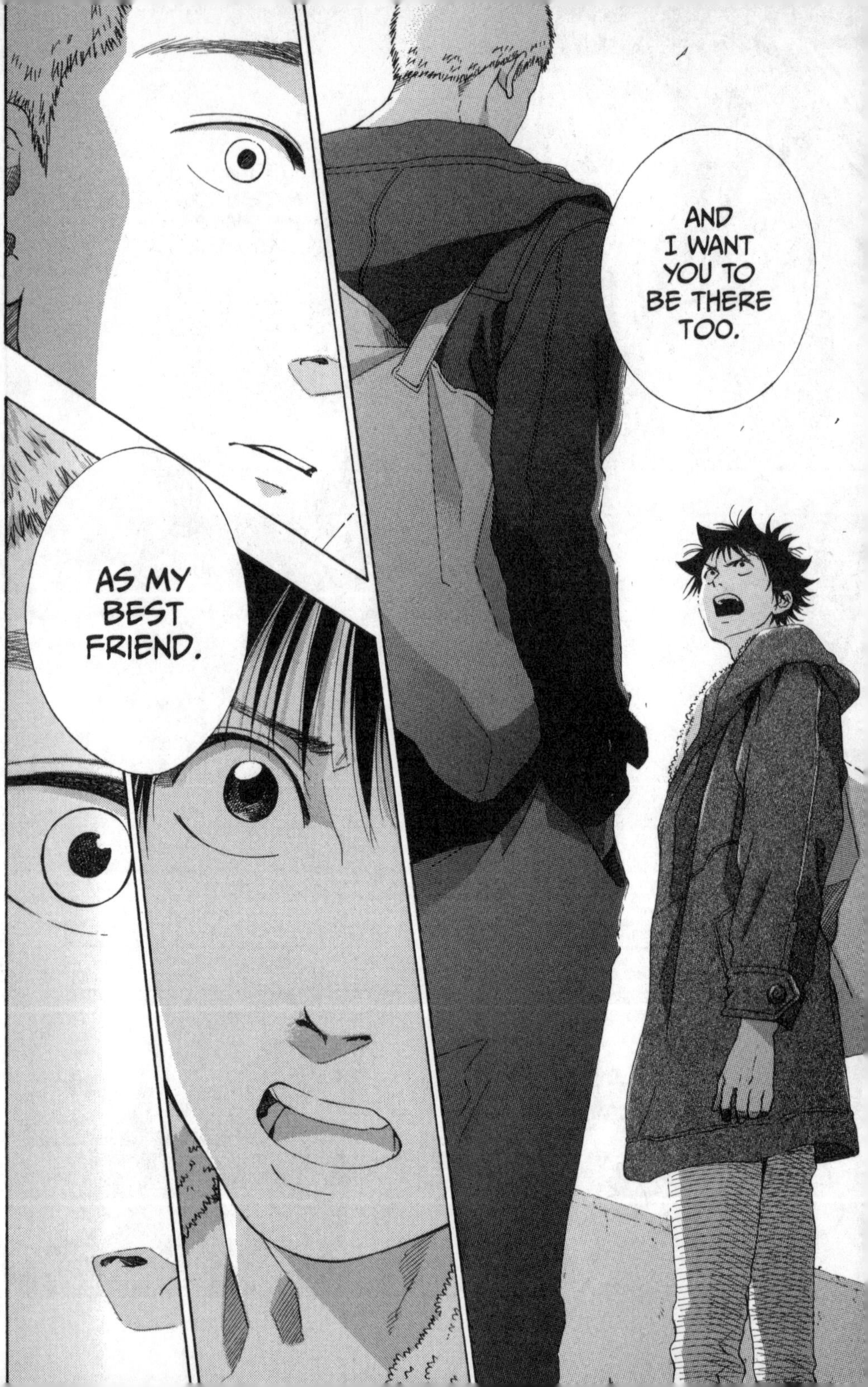
AND I WANT YOU TO BE THERE TOO.
AS MY BEST FRIEND.

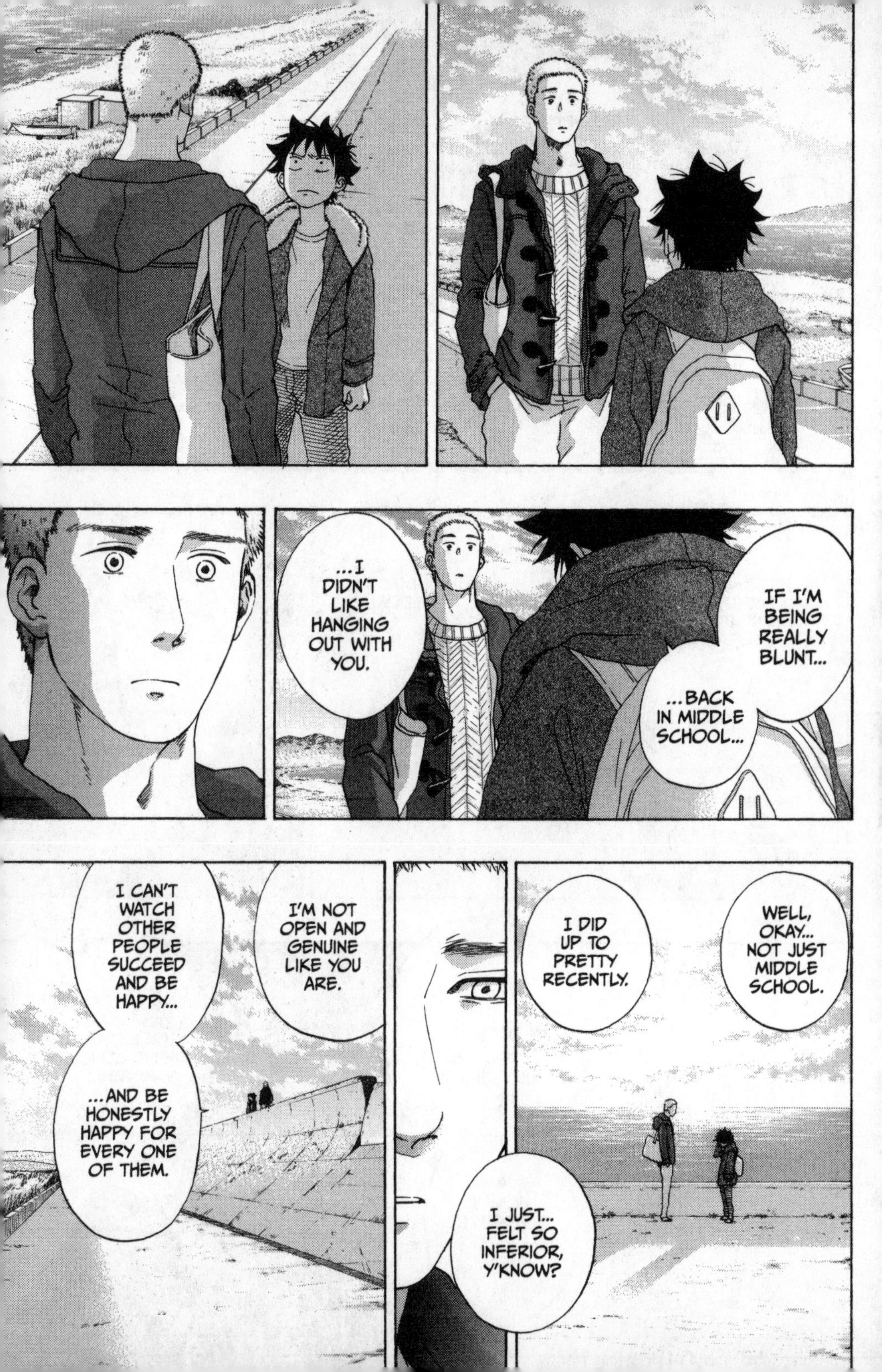
IF I'M BEING REALLY BLUNT...
...BACK IN MIDDLE SCHOOL...
...I DIDN'T LIKE HANGING OUT WITH YOU.
WELL, OKAY... NOT JUST MIDDLE SCHOOL.
I DID UP TO PRETTY RECENTLY.
I JUST... FELT SO INFERIOR, Y'KNOW?
I'M NOT OPEN AND GENUINE LIKE YOU ARE.
I CAN'T WATCH OTHER PEOPLE SUCCEED AND BE HAPPY...
...AND BE HONESTLY HAPPY FOR EVERY ONE OF THEM.

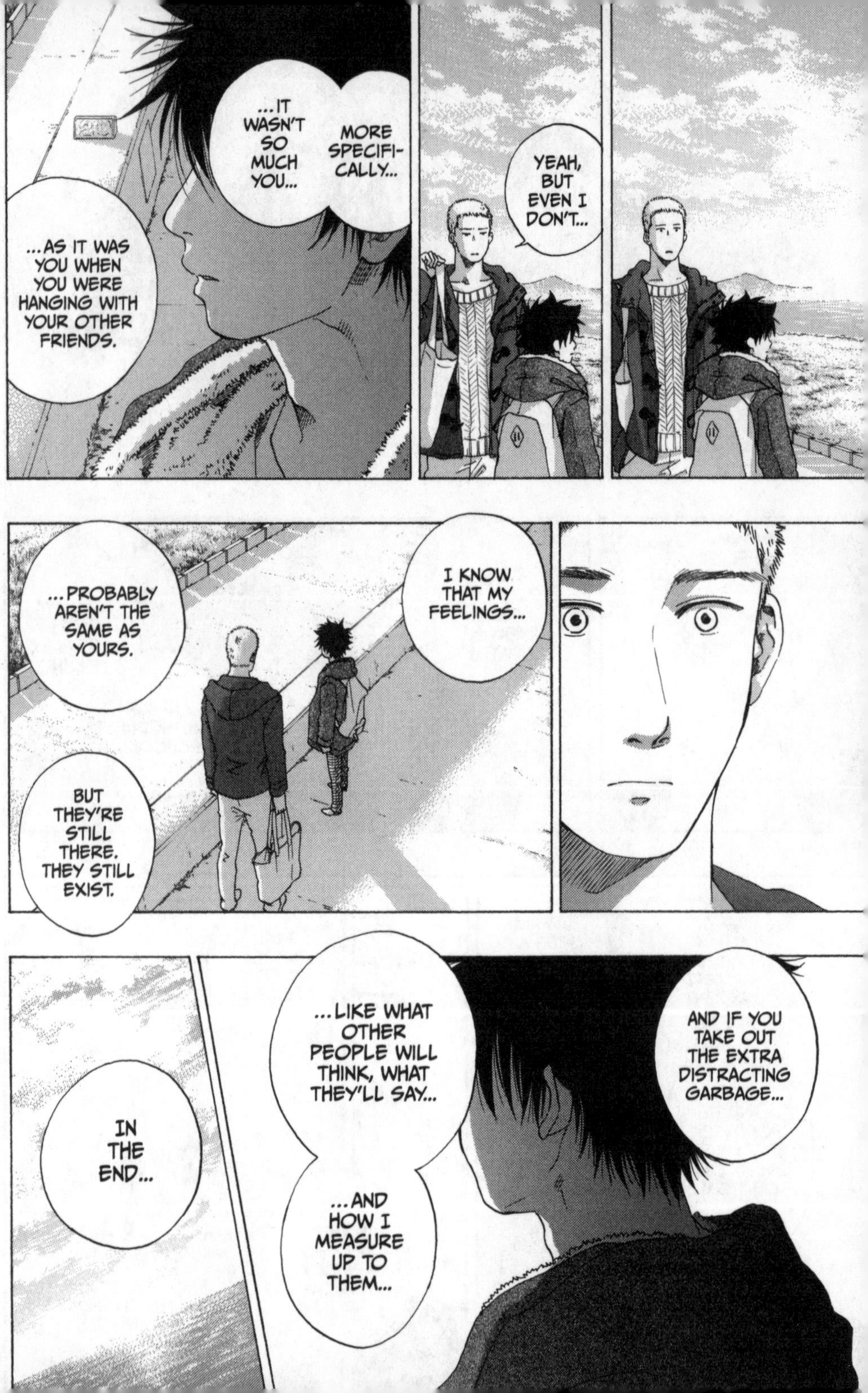
YEAH, BUT EVEN I DON'T...
MORE SPECIFICALLY...
...IT WASN'T SO MUCH YOU...
...AS IT WAS YOU WHEN YOU WERE HANGING WITH YOUR OTHER FRIENDS.
I KNOW THAT MY FEELINGS...
...PROBABLY AREN'T THE SAME AS YOURS.
BUT THEY'RE STILL THERE. THEY STILL EXIST.
AND IF YOU TAKE OUT THE EXTRA DISTRACTING GARBAGE...
...LIKE WHAT OTHER PEOPLE WILL THINK, WHAT THEY'LL SAY...
...AND HOW I MEASURE UP TO THEM...
IN THE END...

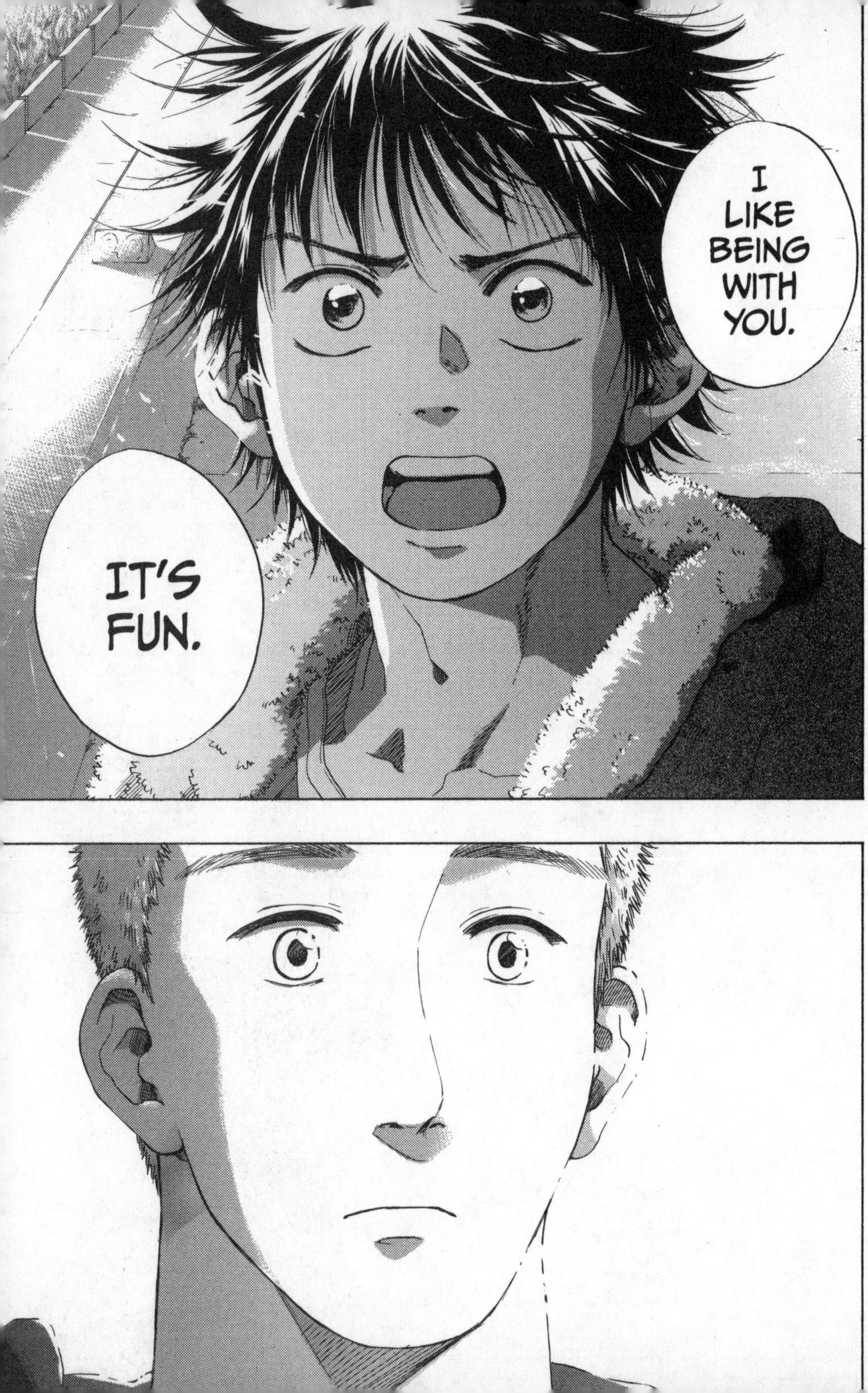
I LIKE BEING WITH YOU.
IT'S FUN.

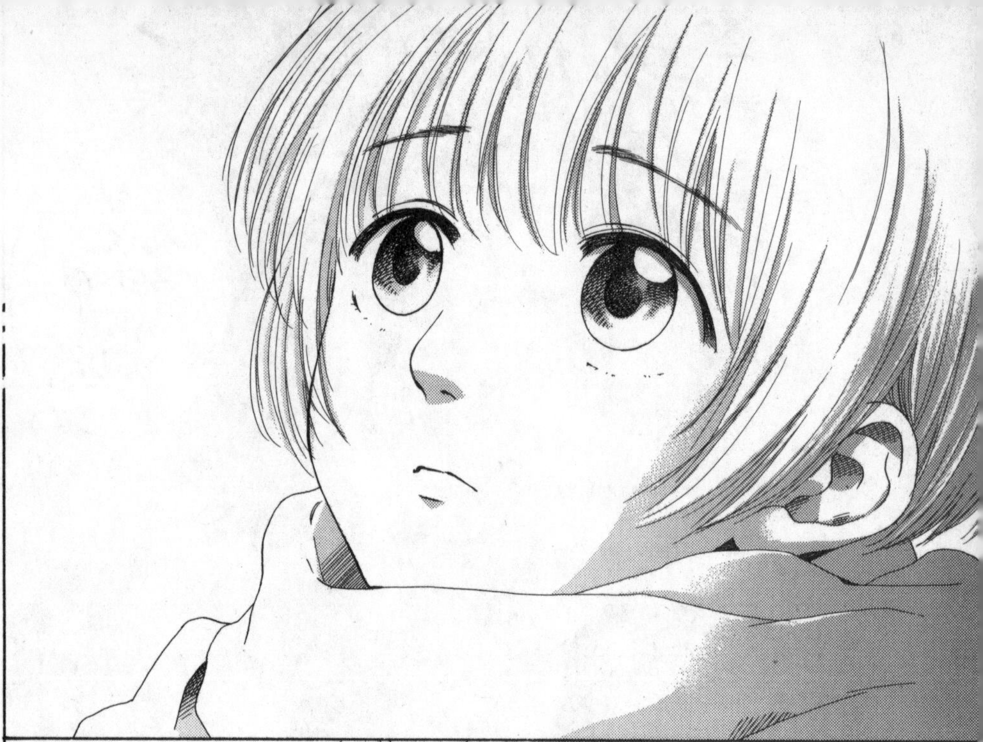

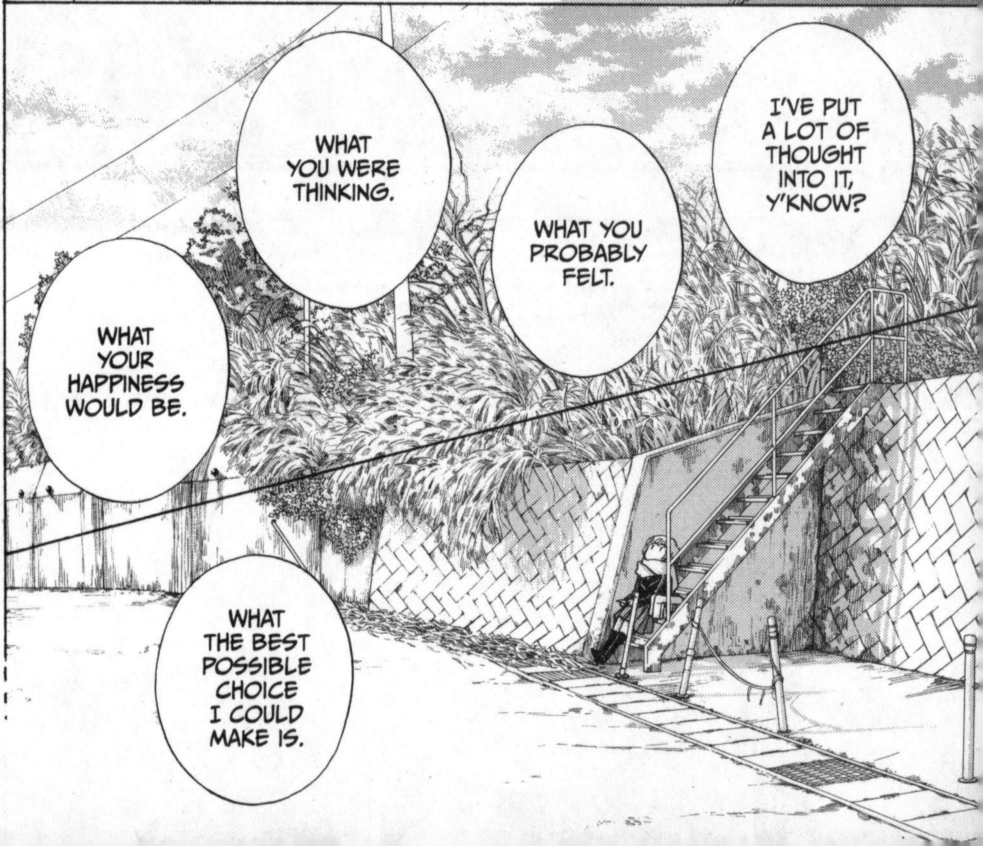
I'VE PUT A LOT OF THOUGHT INTO IT, Y'KNOW?
WHAT YOU PROBABLY FELT.
WHAT YOU WERE THINKING.
WHAT YOUR HAPPINESS WOULD BE.
WHAT THE BEST POSSIBLE CHOICE I COULD MAKE IS.

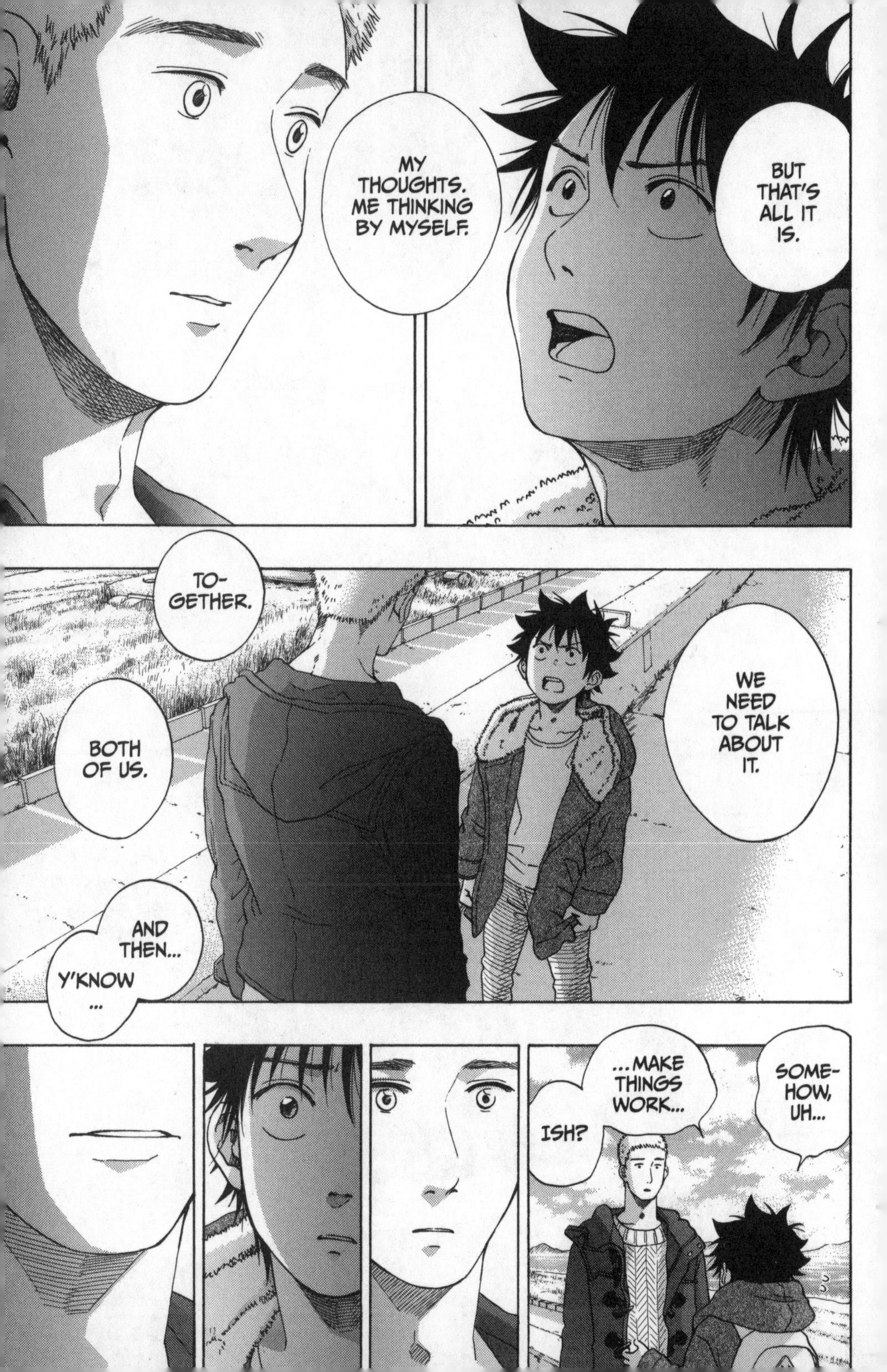
BUT THAT'S ALL IT IS.
MY THOUGHTS. ME THINKING BY MYSELF.
WE NEED TO TALK ABOUT IT.
TO-GETHER.
BOTH OF US.
AND THEN...
Y'KNOW ...
SOME-HOW, UH...
...MAKE THINGS WORK...
ISH?

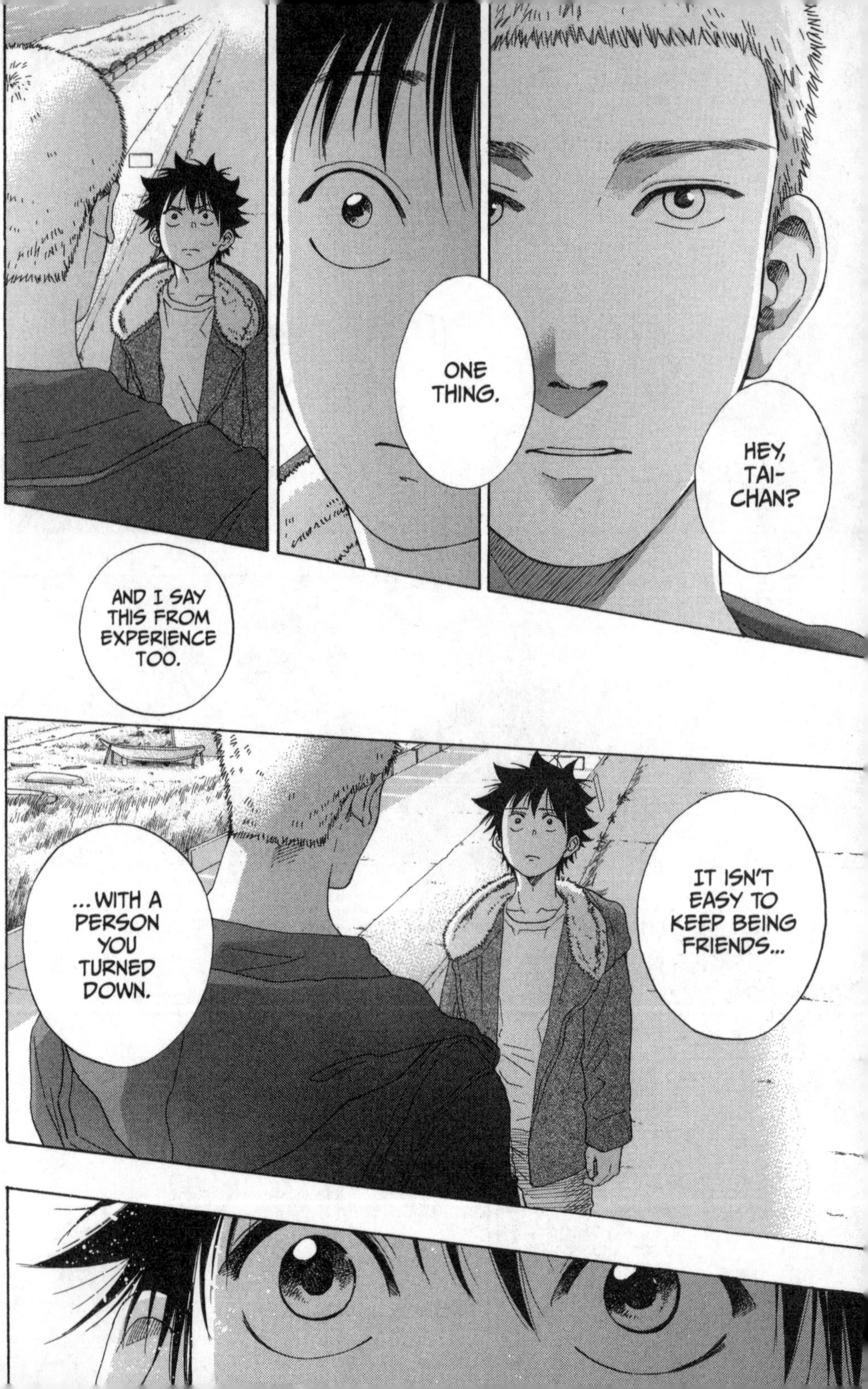
HEY, TAI-CHAN?
ONE THING.
AND I SAY THIS FROM EXPERIENCE TOO.
IT ISN'T EASY TO KEEP BEING FRIENDS...
...WITH A PERSON YOU TURNED DOWN.

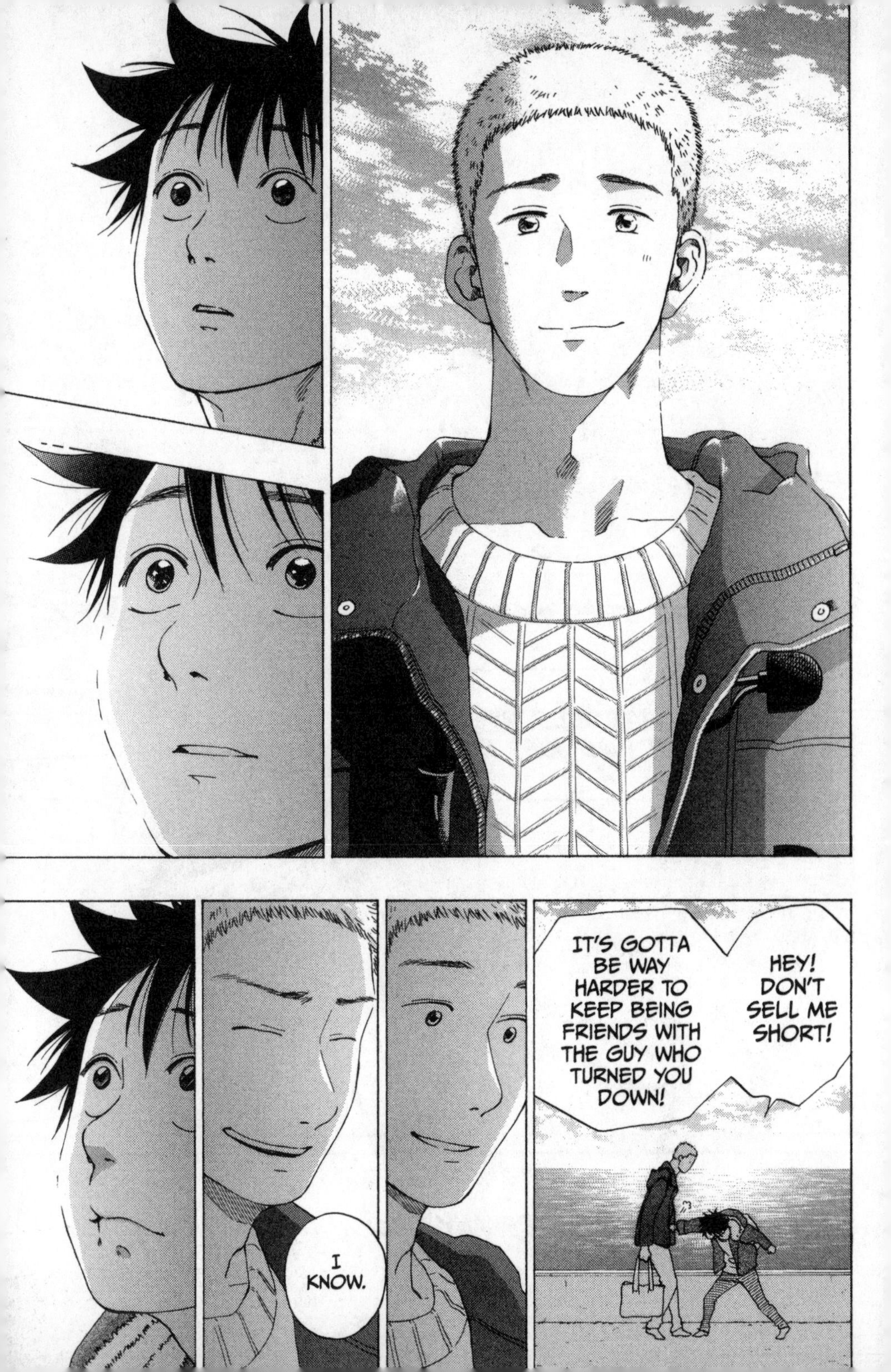
HEY! DON'T SELL ME SHORT!
IT'S GOTTA BE WAY HARDER TO KEEP BEING FRIENDS WITH THE GUY WHO TURNED YOU DOWN!
I KNOW.

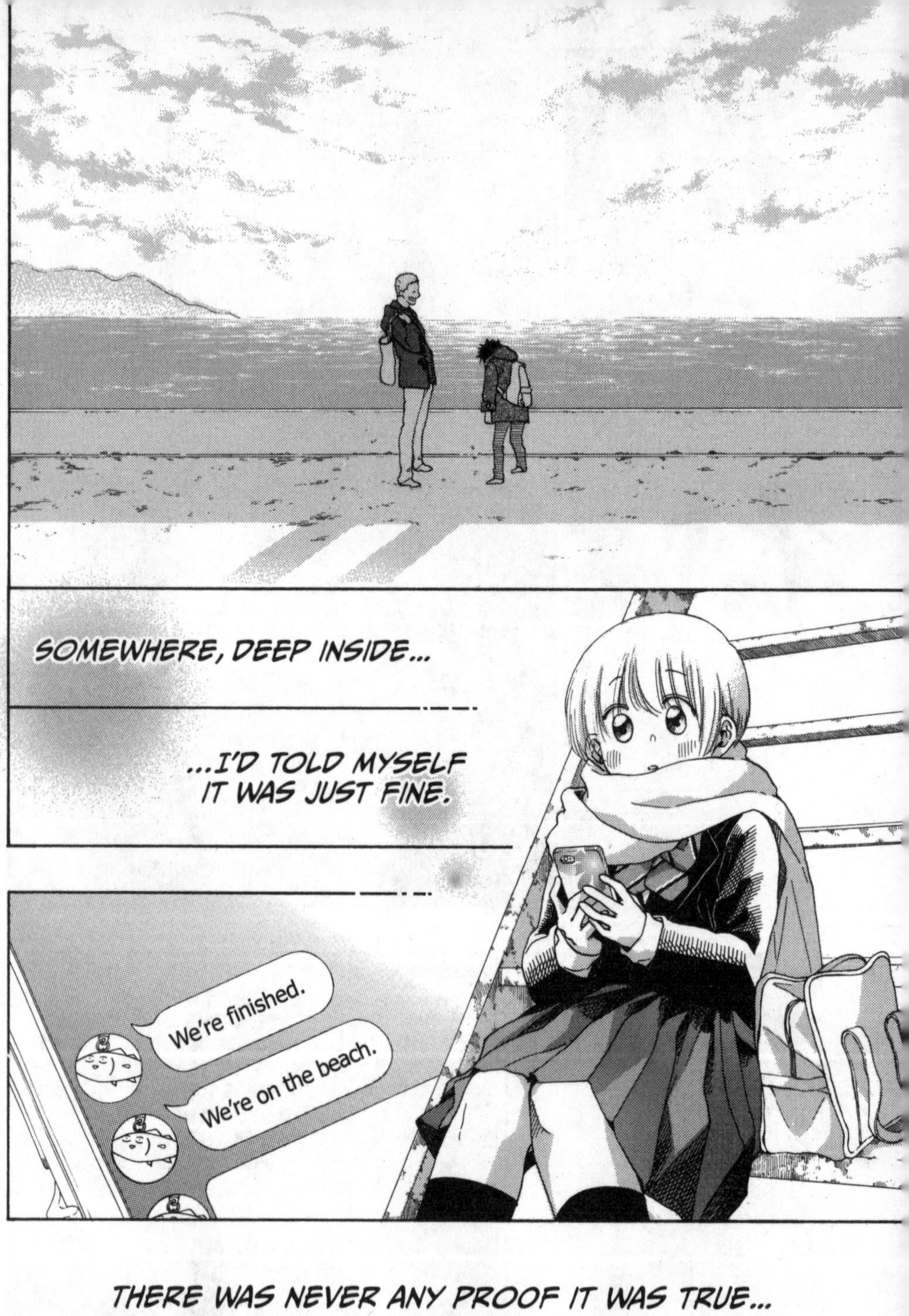
SOMEWHERE, DEEP INSIDE...
...I'D TOLD MYSELF IT WAS JUST FINE.
We're finished.
We're on the beach.

THERE WAS NEVER ANY PROOF IT WAS TRUE...

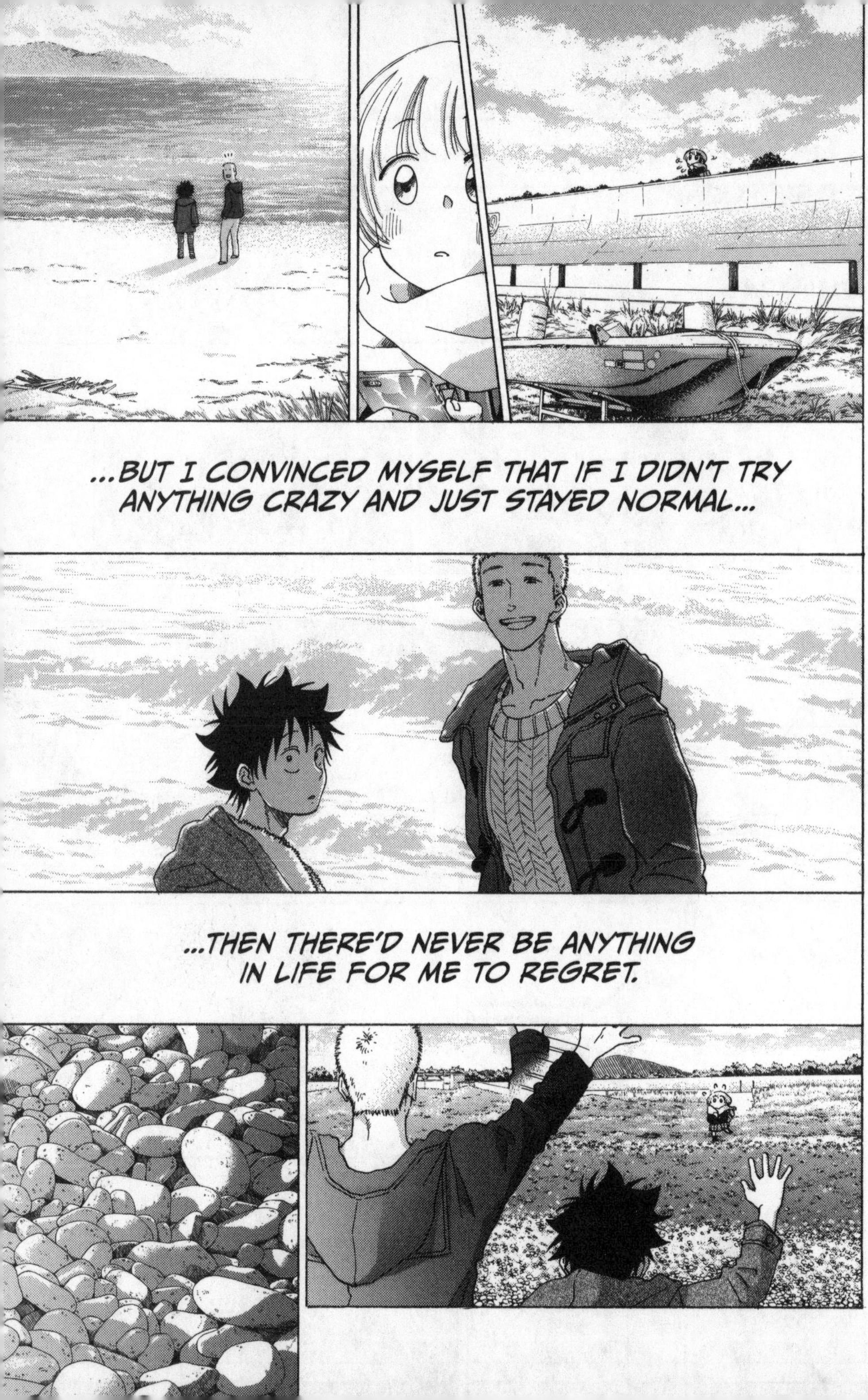
...BUT I CONVINCED MYSELF THAT IF I DIDN'T TRY ANYTHING CRAZY AND JUST STAYED NORMAL...
...THEN THERE'D NEVER BE ANYTHING IN LIFE FOR ME TO REGRET.

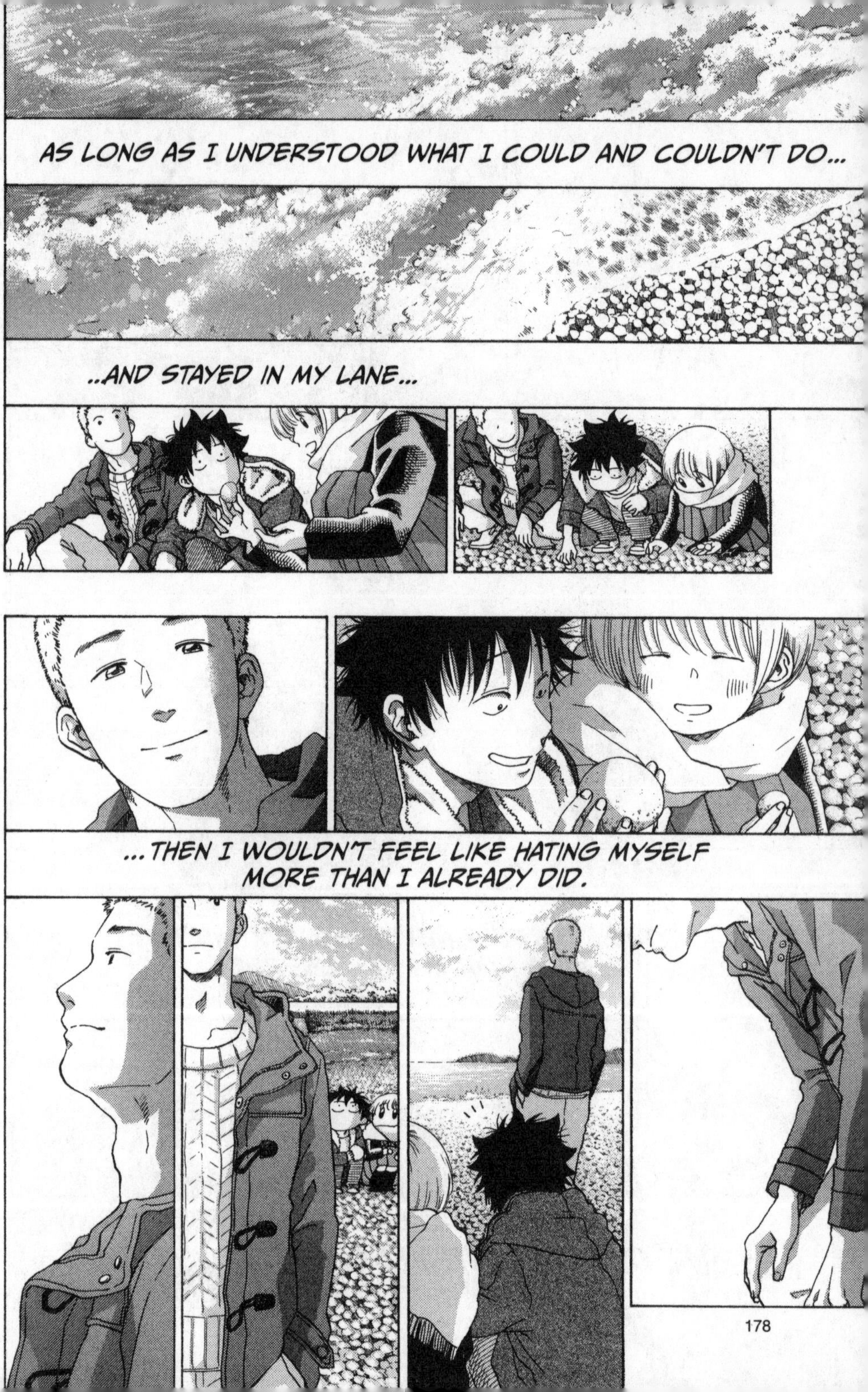
AS LONG AS I UNDERSTOOD WHAT I COULD AND COULDN'T DO...
...AND STAYED IN MY LANE...
...THEN I WOULDN'T FEEL LIKE HATING MYSELF MORE THAN I ALREADY DID.

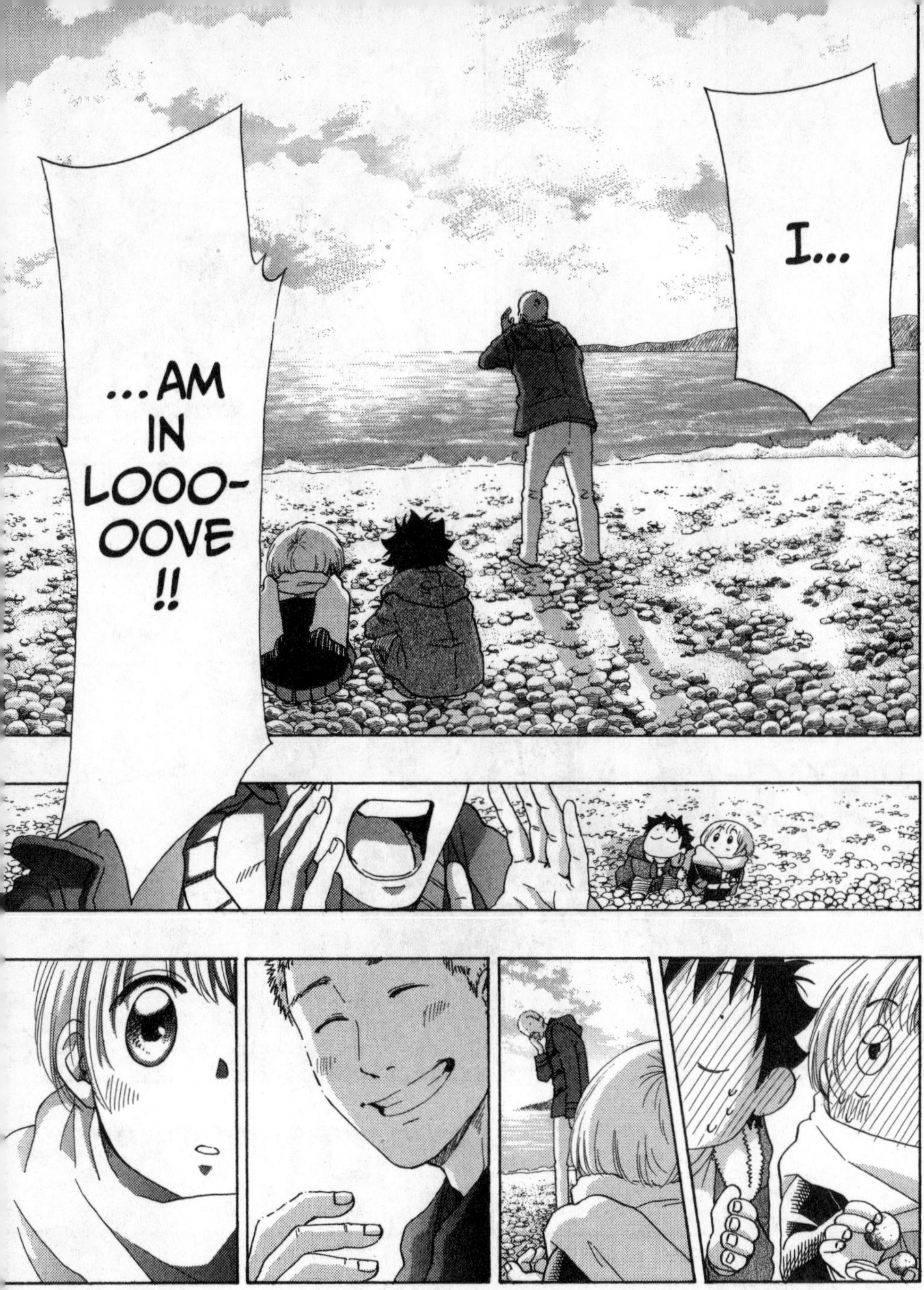
I...
...AM IN LOOO-OOVE!!

BUT THEN YOU CAME ALONG.

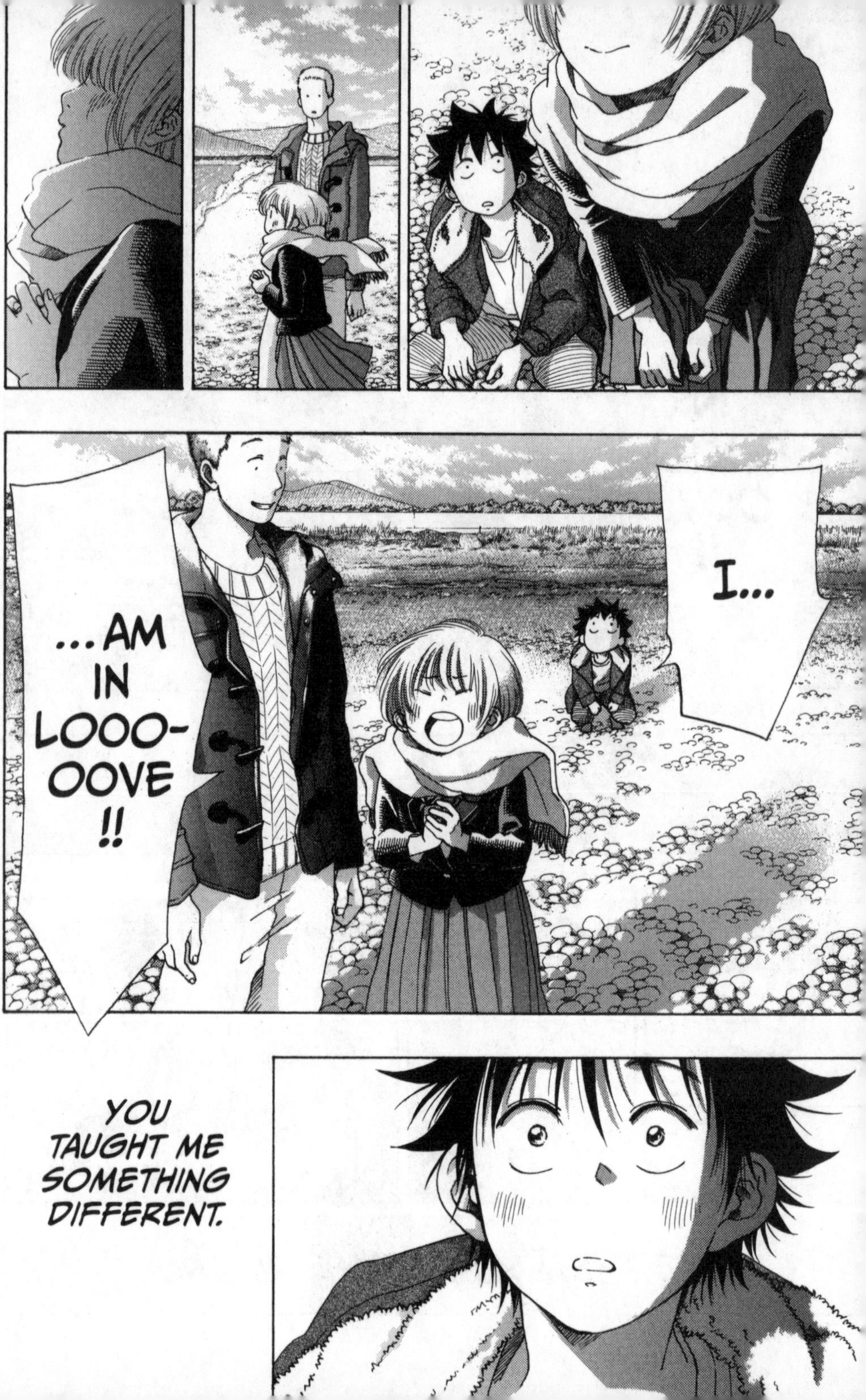
I...
...AM IN LOOOO-OOVE!!
YOU TAUGHT ME SOMETHING DIFFERENT.

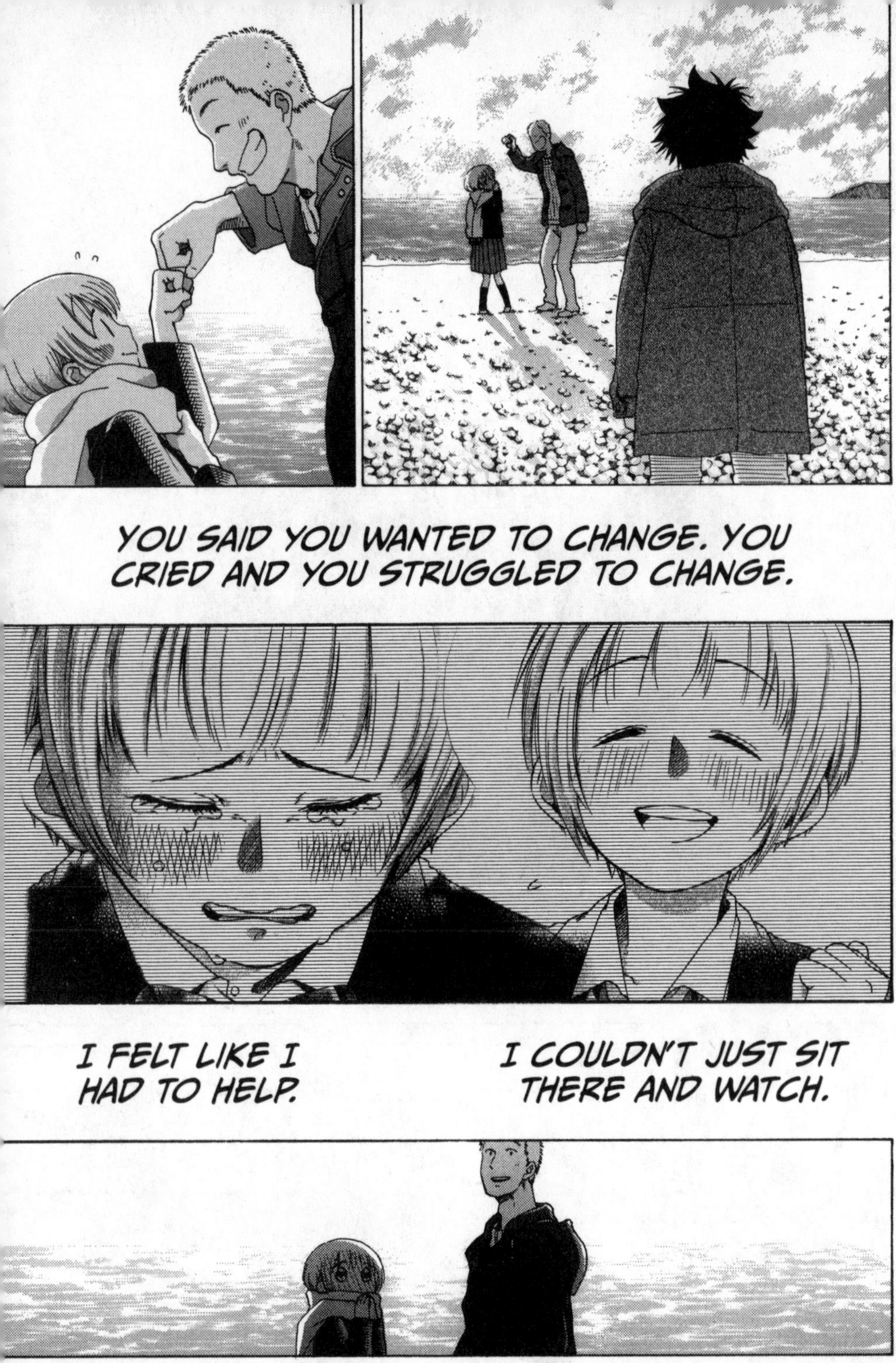
YOU SAID YOU WANTED TO CHANGE. YOU CRIED AND YOU STRUGGLED TO CHANGE.
I FELT LIKE I HAD TO HELP.
I COULDN'T JUST SIT THERE AND WATCH.

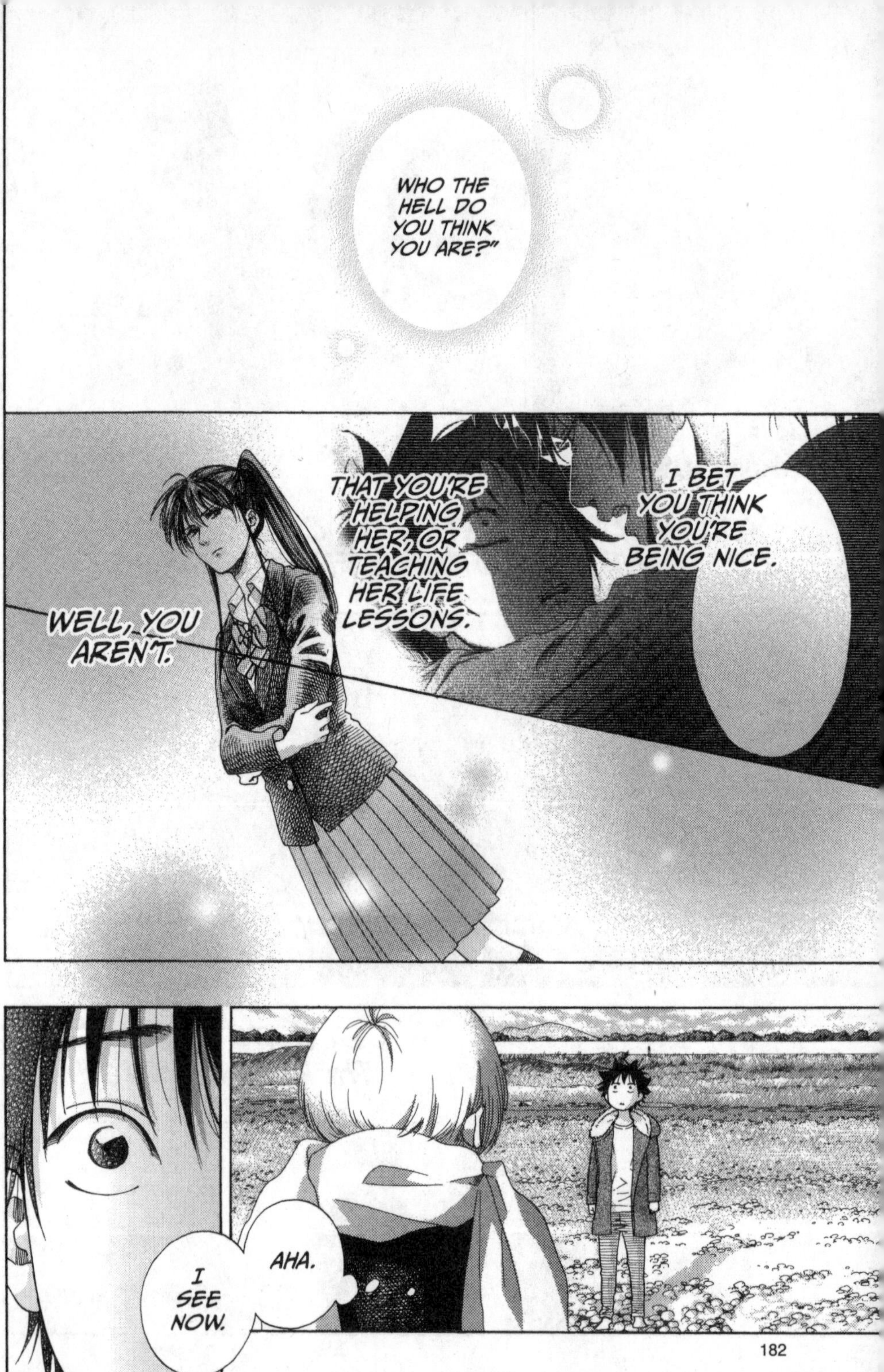
WHO THE HELL DO YOU THINK YOU ARE?"
I BET YOU THINK YOU'RE BEING NICE.
THAT YOU'RE HELPING HER, OR TEACHING HER LIFE LESSONS.
WELL, YOU AREN'T.
AHA.
I SEE NOW.

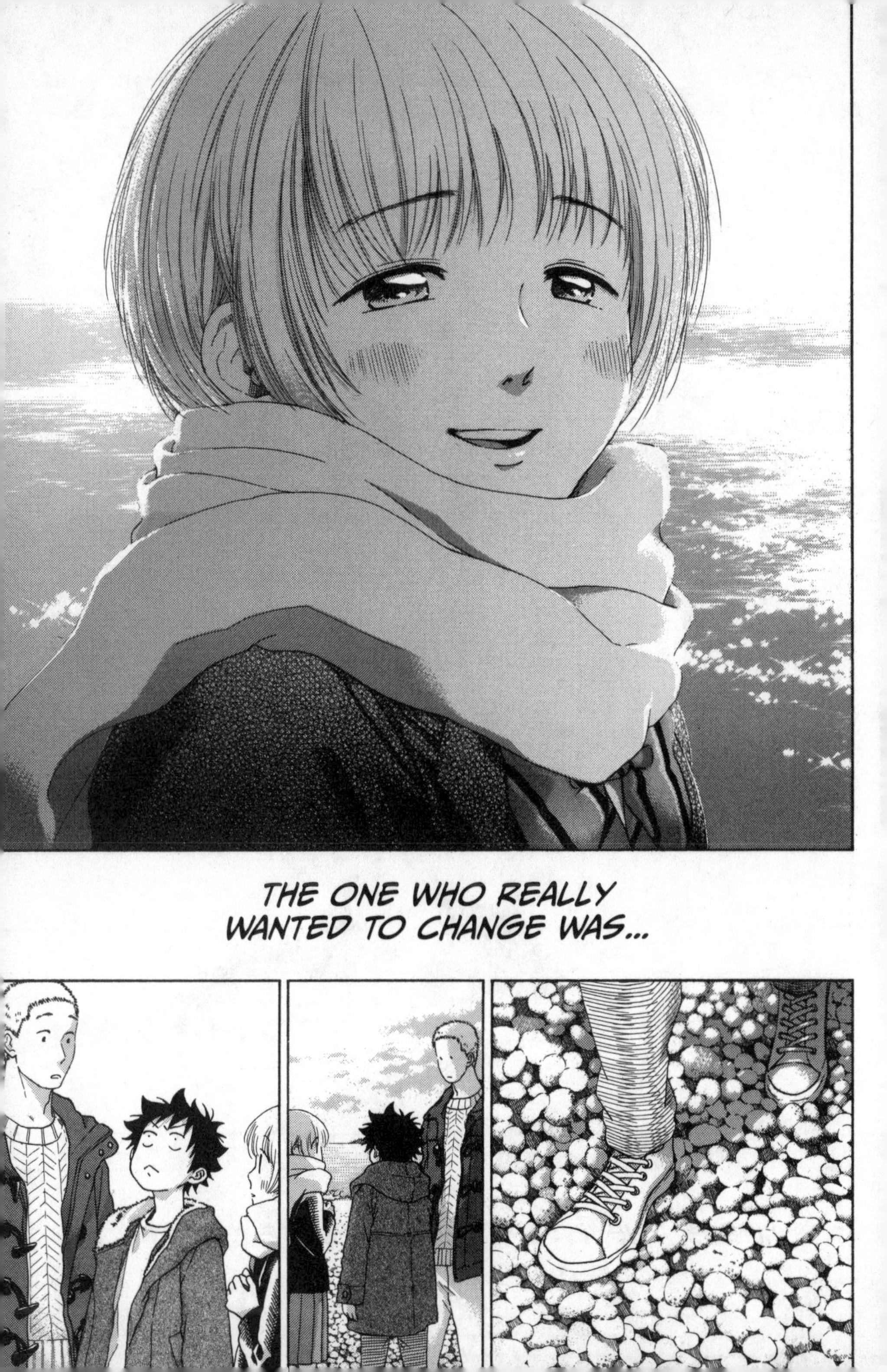
THE ONE WHO REALLY WANTED TO CHANGE WAS...

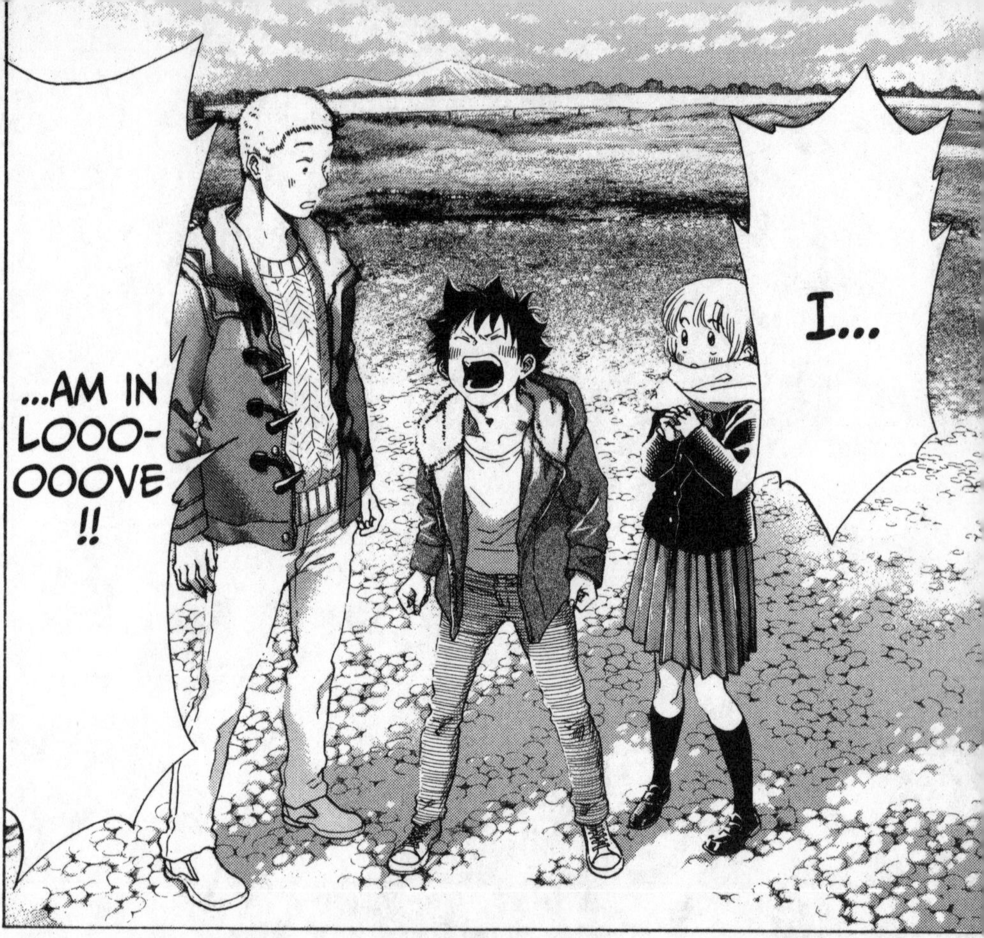
I...
...AM IN LOOO-OOOVE !!
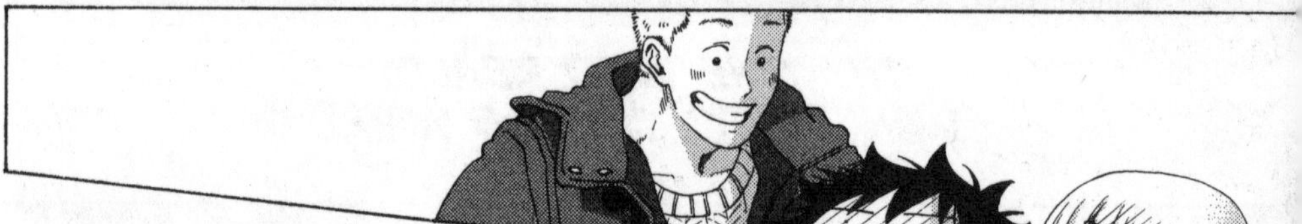
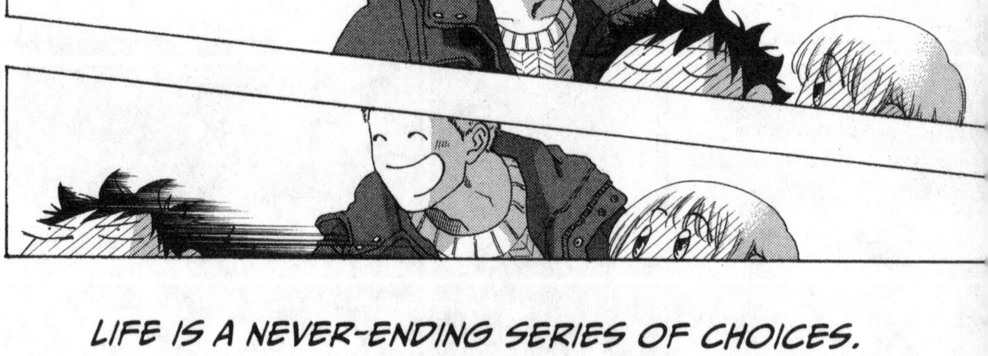

LIFE IS A NEVER-ENDING SERIES OF CHOICES.

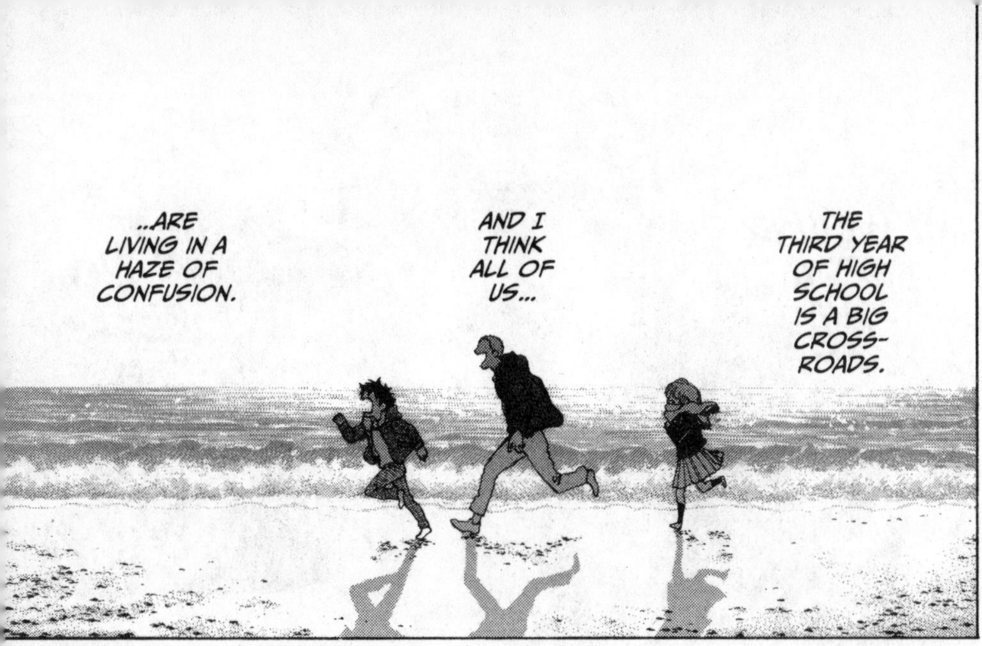
THE THIRD YEAR OF HIGH SCHOOL IS A BIG CROSS-ROADS.
AND I THINK ALL OF US...
...ARE LIVING IN A HAZE OF CONFUSION.

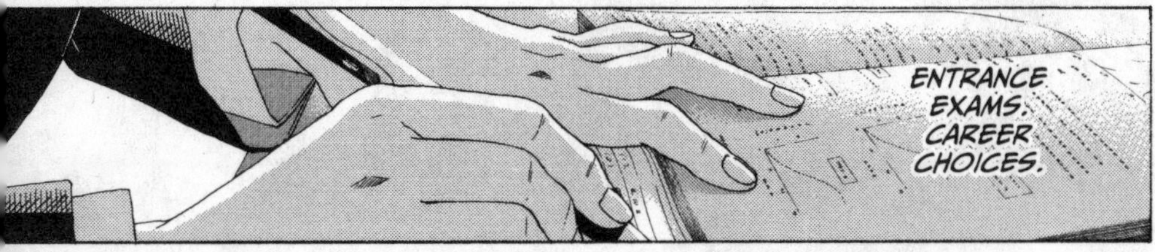
ENTRANCE EXAMS. CAREER CHOICES.

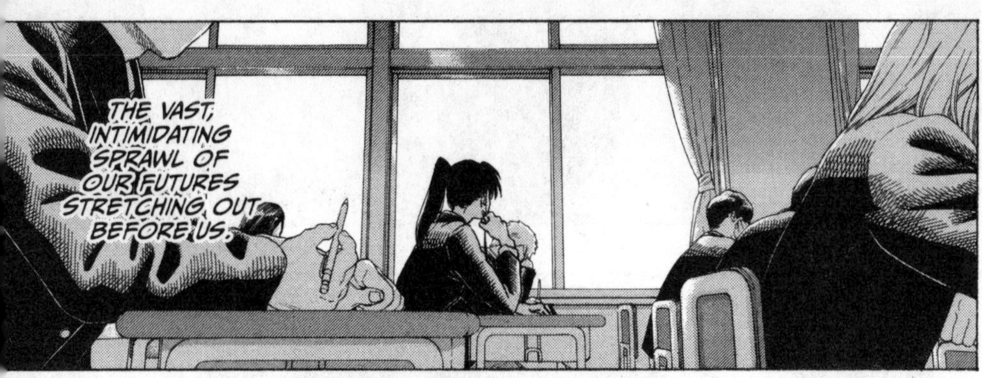
THE VAST, INTIMIDATING SPRAWL OF OUR FUTURES STRETCHING OUT BEFORE US.

IT'S A STUPIDLY BUSY TIME.

IT'S A STUPIDLY COMPLICATED TIME.

YET, IT WAS THEN...

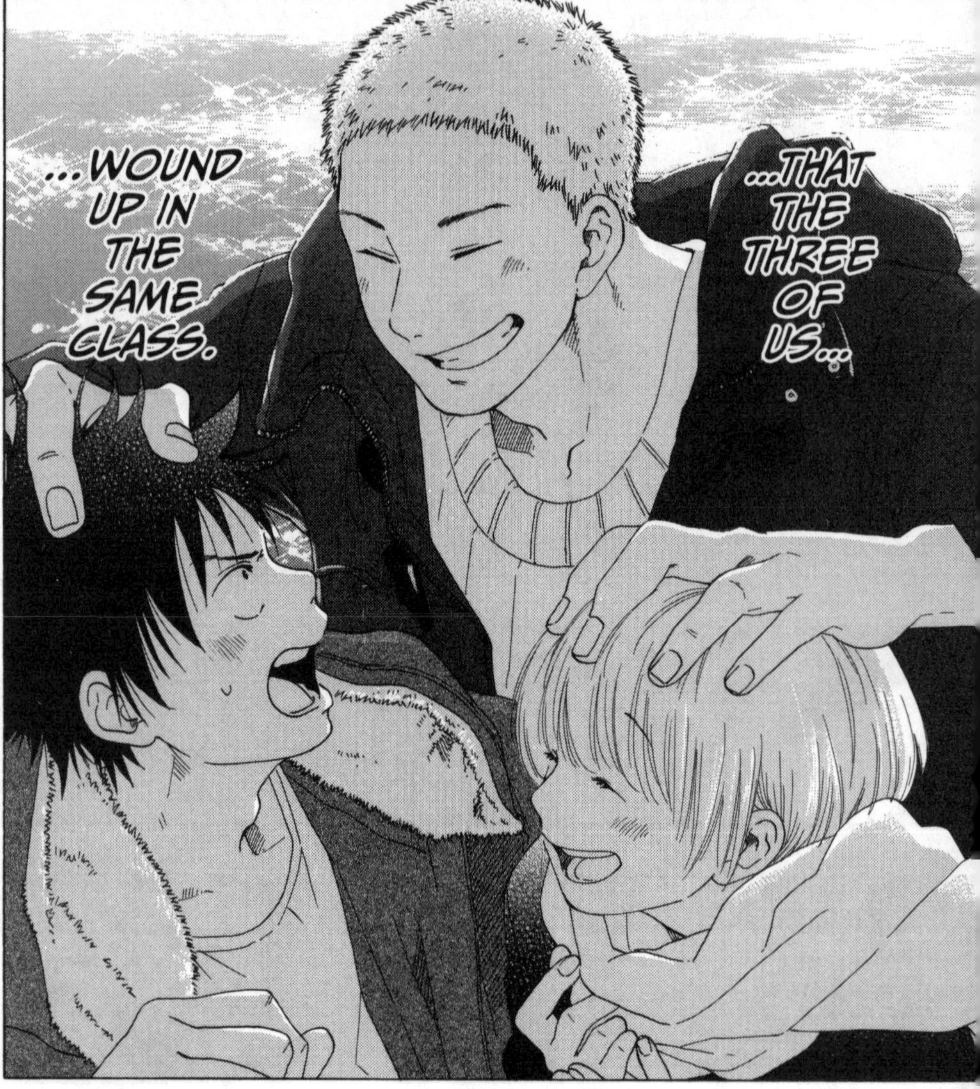
...THAT THE THREE OF US...
...WOUND UP IN THE SAME CLASS.

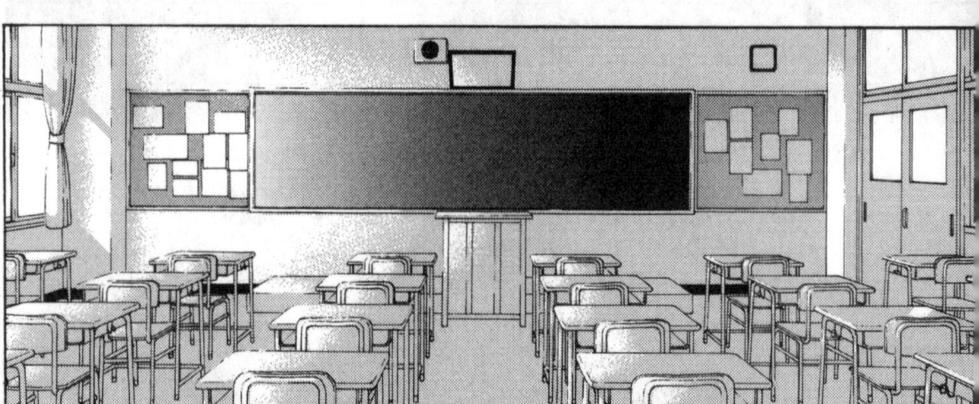

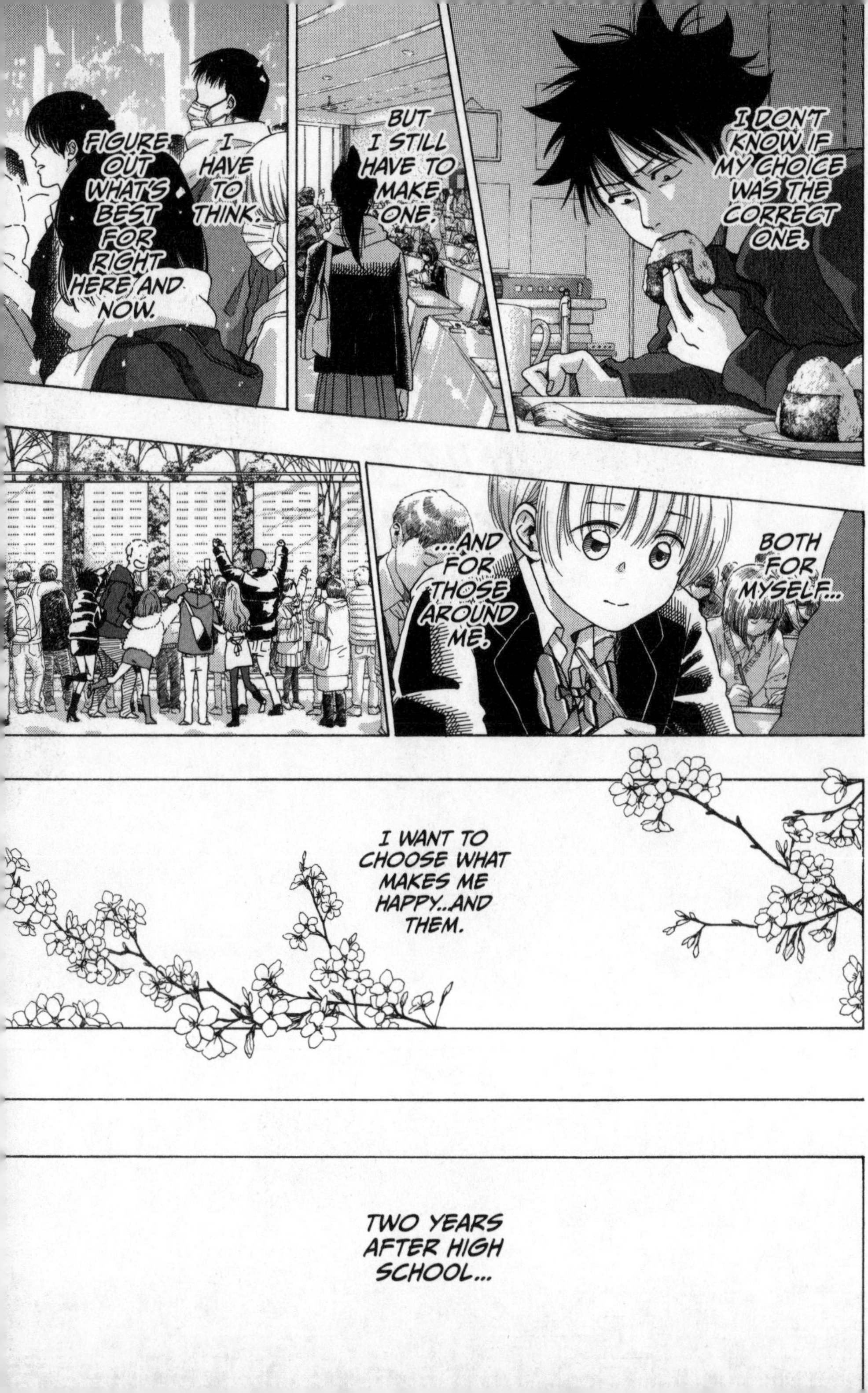
I DON'T KNOW IF MY CHOICE WAS THE CORRECT ONE.
BUT I STILL HAVE TO MAKE ONE.
I HAVE TO THINK.
FIGURE OUT WHAT'S BEST FOR RIGHT HERE AND NOW.
BOTH FOR MYSELF...
...AND FOR THOSE AROUND ME.
I WANT TO CHOOSE WHAT MAKES ME HAPPY..AND THEM.
TWO YEARS AFTER HIGH SCHOOL...

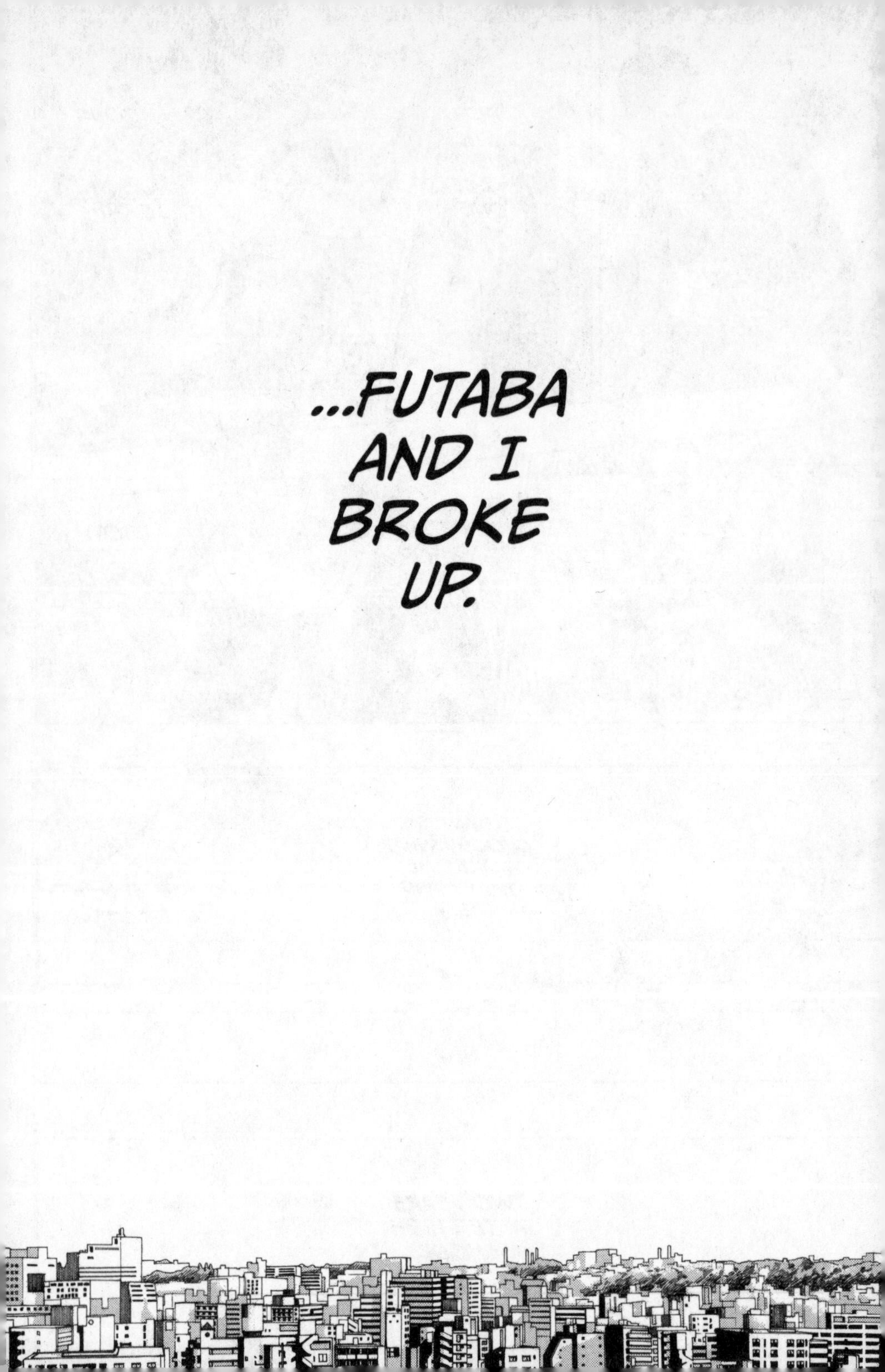
...FUTABA AND I BROKE UP.

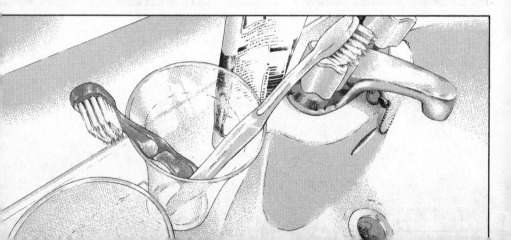

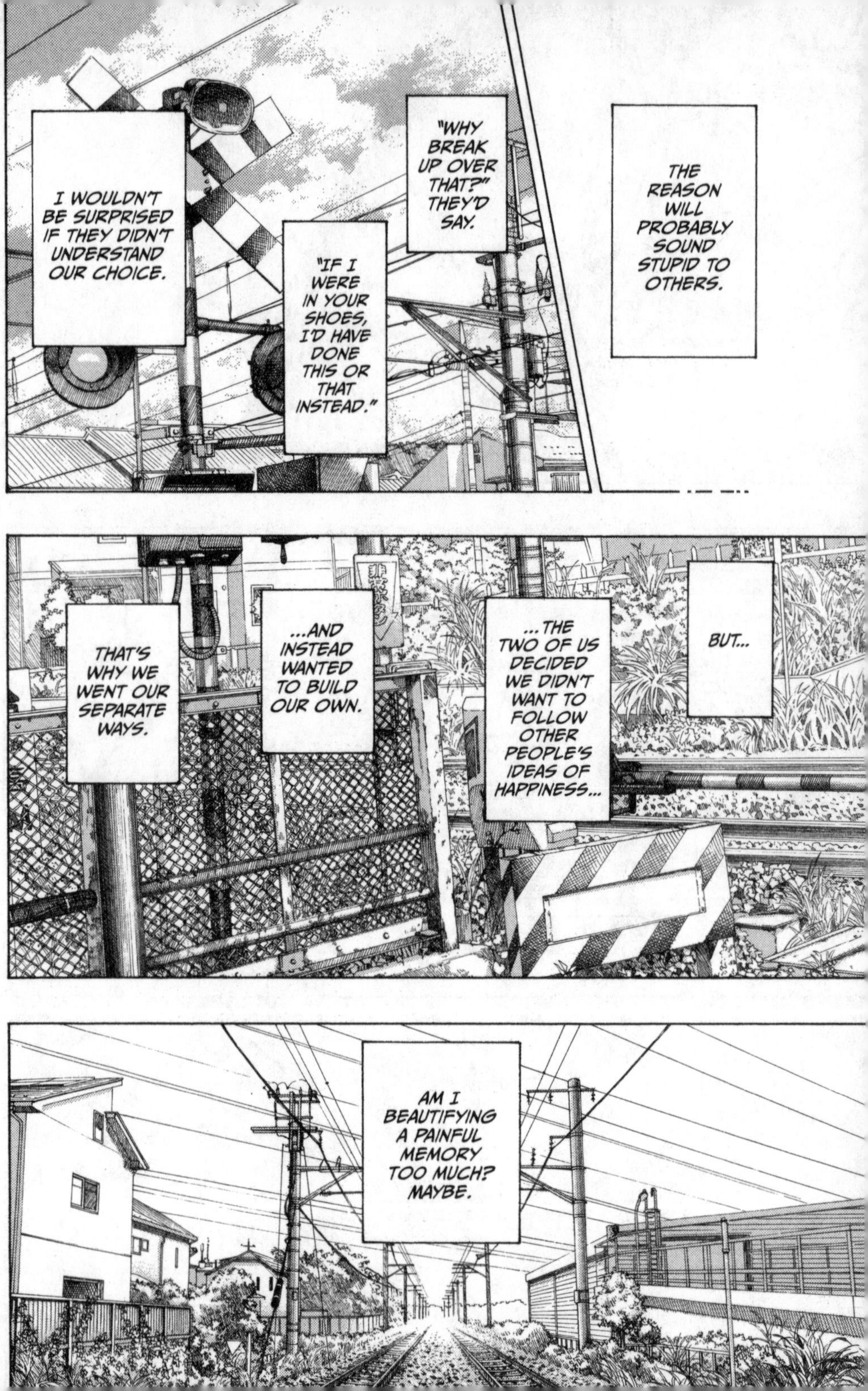
THE REASON WILL PROBABLY SOUND STUPID TO OTHERS.
"WHY BREAK UP OVER THAT?" THEY'D SAY.
"IF I WERE IN YOUR SHOES, I'D HAVE DONE THIS OR THAT INSTEAD."
I WOULDN'T BE SURPRISED IF THEY DIDN'T UNDERSTAND OUR CHOICE.
BUT...
...THE TWO OF US DECIDED WE DIDN'T WANT TO FOLLOW OTHER PEOPLE'S IDEAS OF HAPPINESS...
...AND INSTEAD WANTED TO BUILD OUR OWN.
THAT'S WHY WE WENT OUR SEPARATE WAYS.
AM I BEAUTIFYING A PAINFUL MEMORY TOO MUCH? MAYBE.

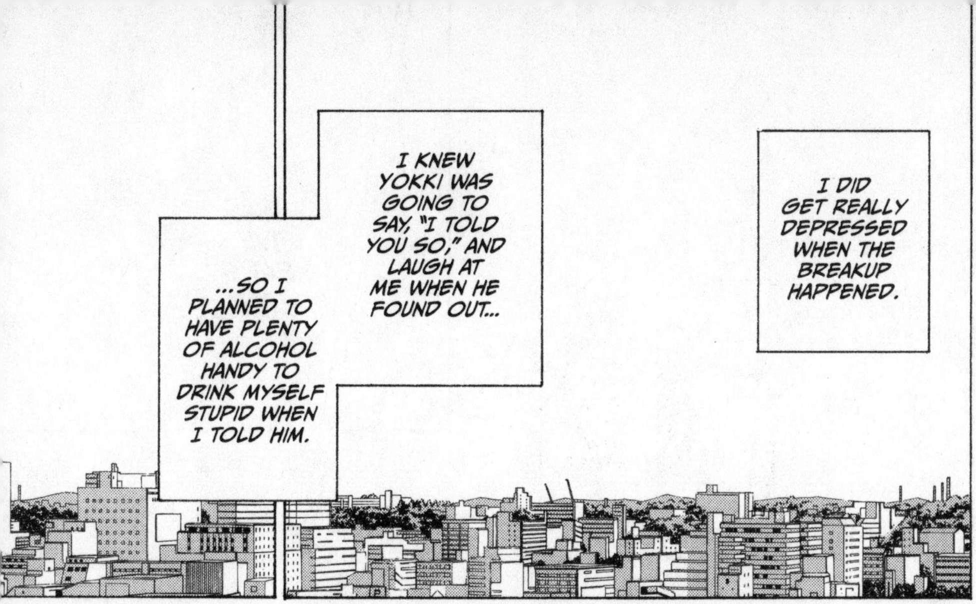
I DID GET REALLY DEPRESSED WHEN THE BREAKUP HAPPENED.
I KNEW YOKKI WAS GOING TO SAY, "I TOLD YOU SO," AND LAUGH AT ME WHEN HE FOUND OUT...
...SO I PLANNED TO HAVE PLENTY OF ALCOHOL HANDY TO DRINK MYSELF STUPID WHEN I TOLD HIM.
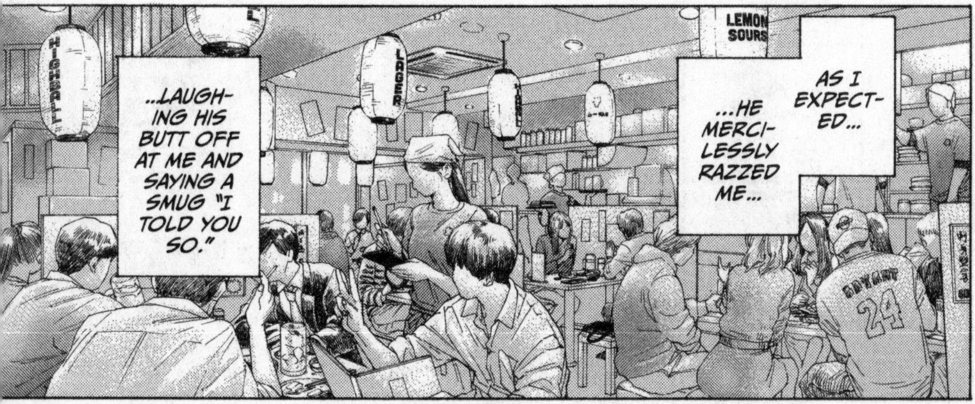
LEMON SOURS
AS I EXPECTED...
...HE MERCILESSLY RAZZED ME...
LAGER
HIGHBALL
...LAUGHING HIS BUTT OFF AT ME AND SAYING A SMUG "I TOLD YOU SO."
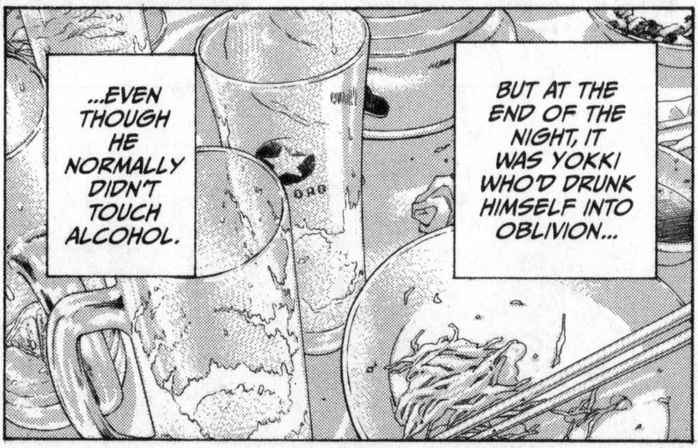
BUT AT THE END OF THE NIGHT, IT WAS YOKKI WHO'D DRUNK HIMSELF INTO OBLIVION...
...EVEN THOUGH HE NORMALLY DIDN'T TOUCH ALCOHOL.

THE NEXT TIME I SAW FUTABA...

...WAS FIVE YEARS LATER.

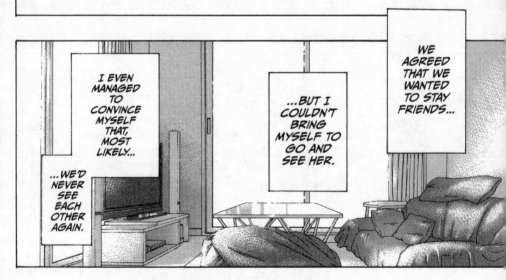

WE AGREED THAT WE WANTED TO STAY FRIENDS...

...BUT I COULDN'T BRING MYSELF TO GO AND SEE HER.

I EVEN MANAGED TO CONVINCE MYSELF THAT, MOST LIKELY...

...WE'D NEVER SEE EACH OTHER AGAIN.

BUT TOMA HAD KEPT IN TOUCH WITH BOTH FUTABA AND MASUMI.

ONE DAY, OUT OF NOWHERE...

...HE INVITED ALL OF US TO COME HANG OUT TOGETHER AGAIN.

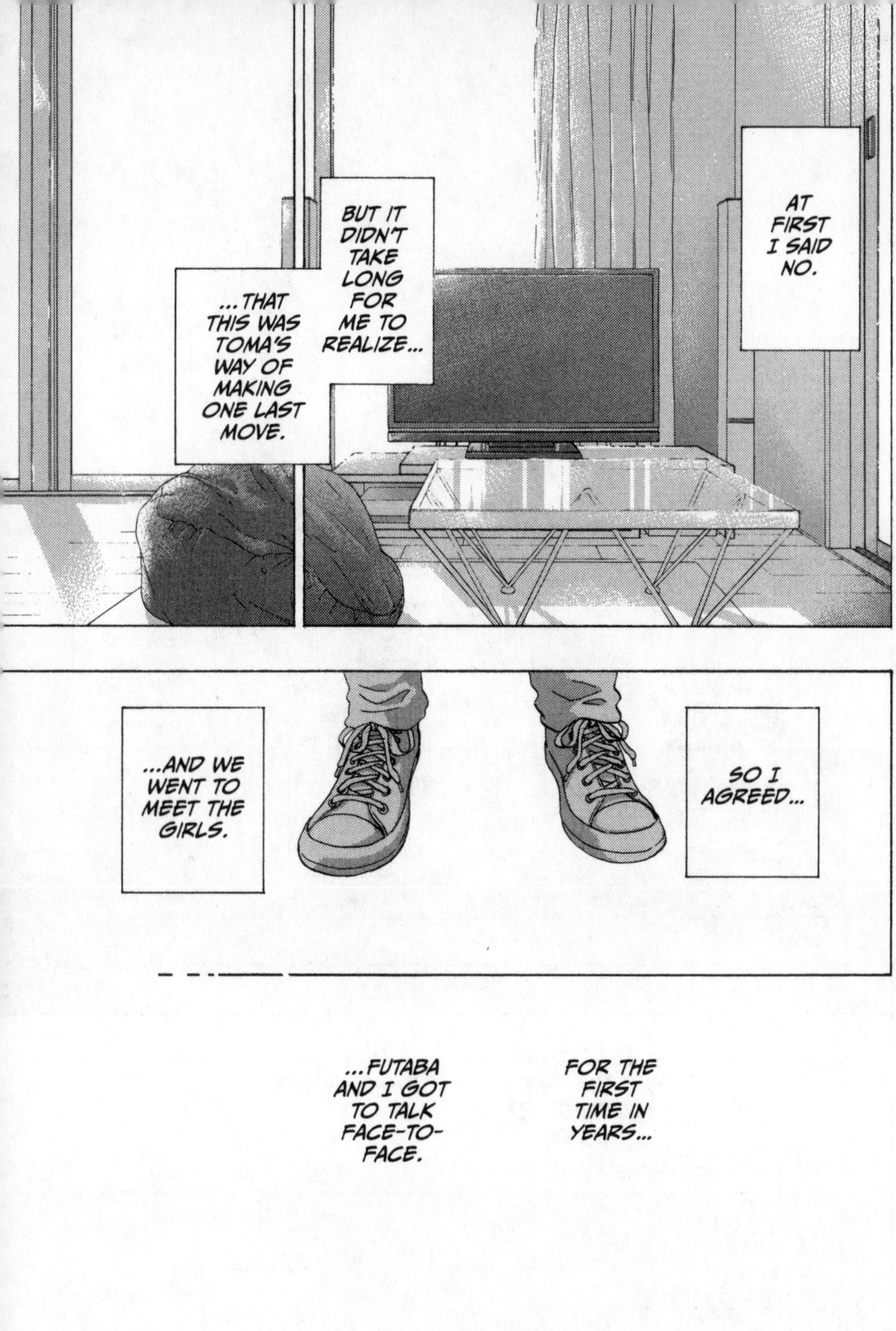
AT FIRST I SAID NO.
BUT IT DIDN'T TAKE LONG FOR ME TO REALIZE...
...THAT THIS WAS TOMA'S WAY OF MAKING ONE LAST MOVE.
SO I AGREED...
...AND WE WENT TO MEET THE GIRLS.
FOR THE FIRST TIME IN YEARS...
...FUTABA AND I GOT TO TALK FACE-TO-FACE.

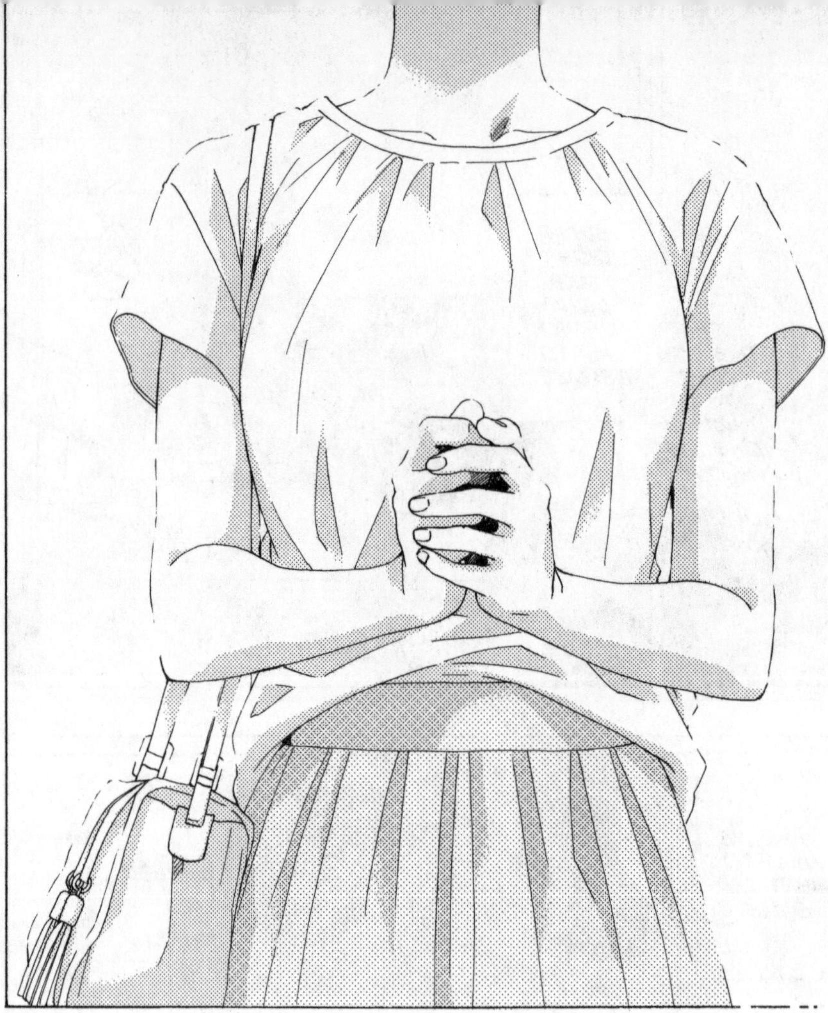

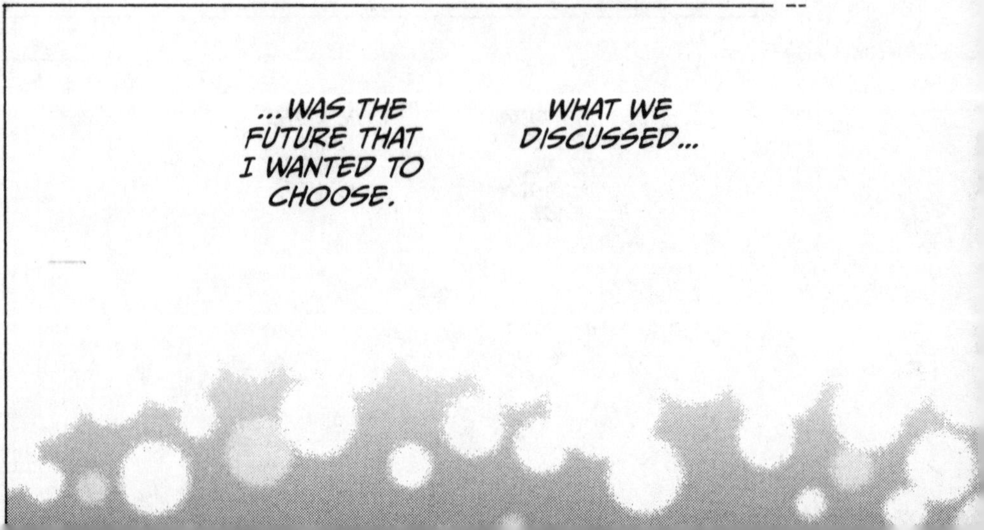
WHAT WE DISCUSSED...
...WAS THE FUTURE THAT I WANTED TO CHOOSE.

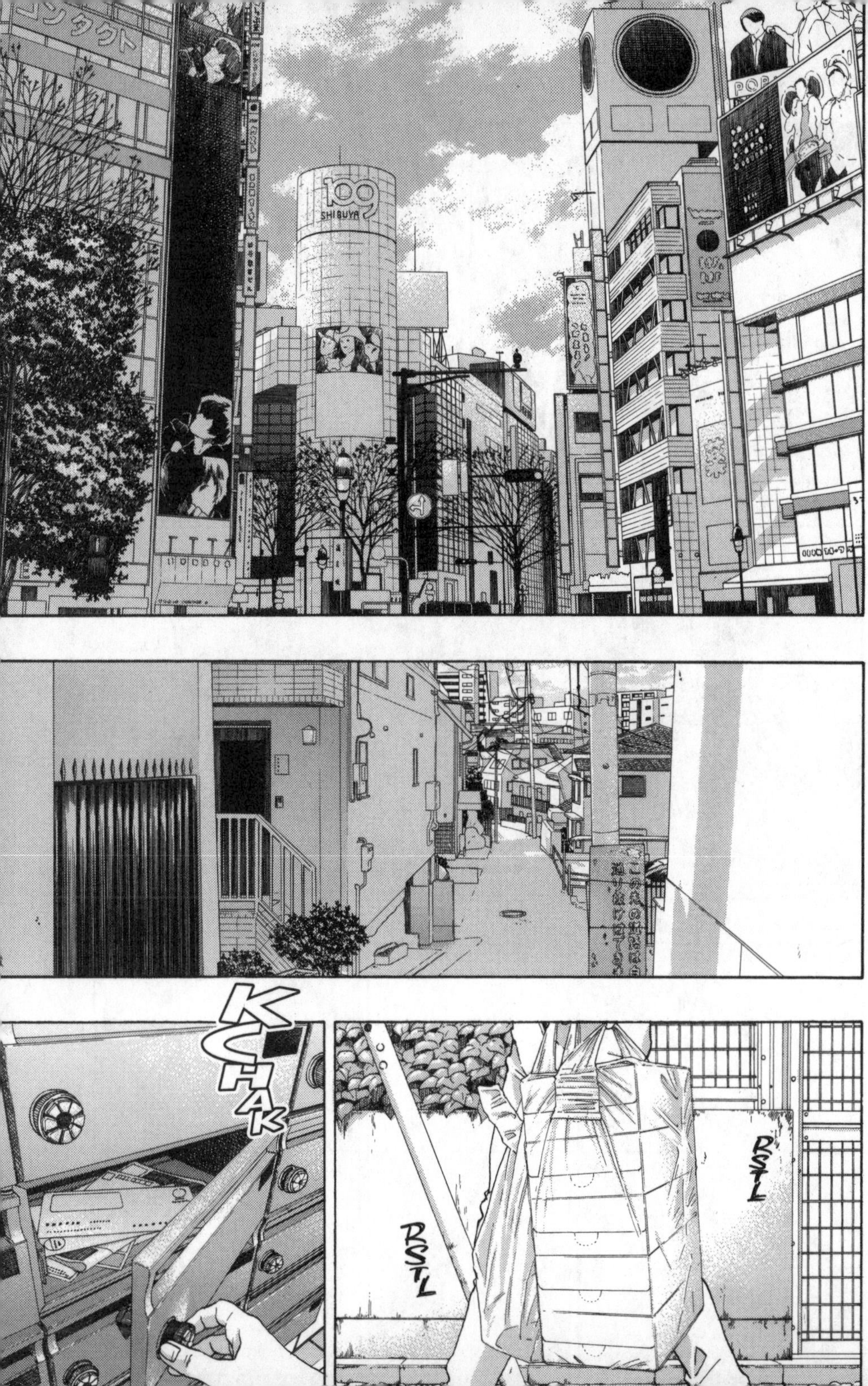
コンタクト
109
SHIBUYA
RSTL
RSTL
KCHAK

TUMP
TUMP
TUMP

RATLKLK

KREE

RATATL

I'M HOOOME.

HELLO?

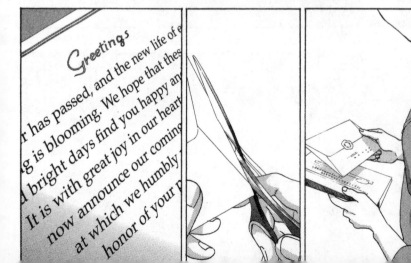

Greetings

...r has passed, and the new life of...
...g is blooming. We hope that thes...
...d bright days find you happy an...
...It is with great joy in our heart...
now announce our coming...
at which we humbly...
honor of your p...

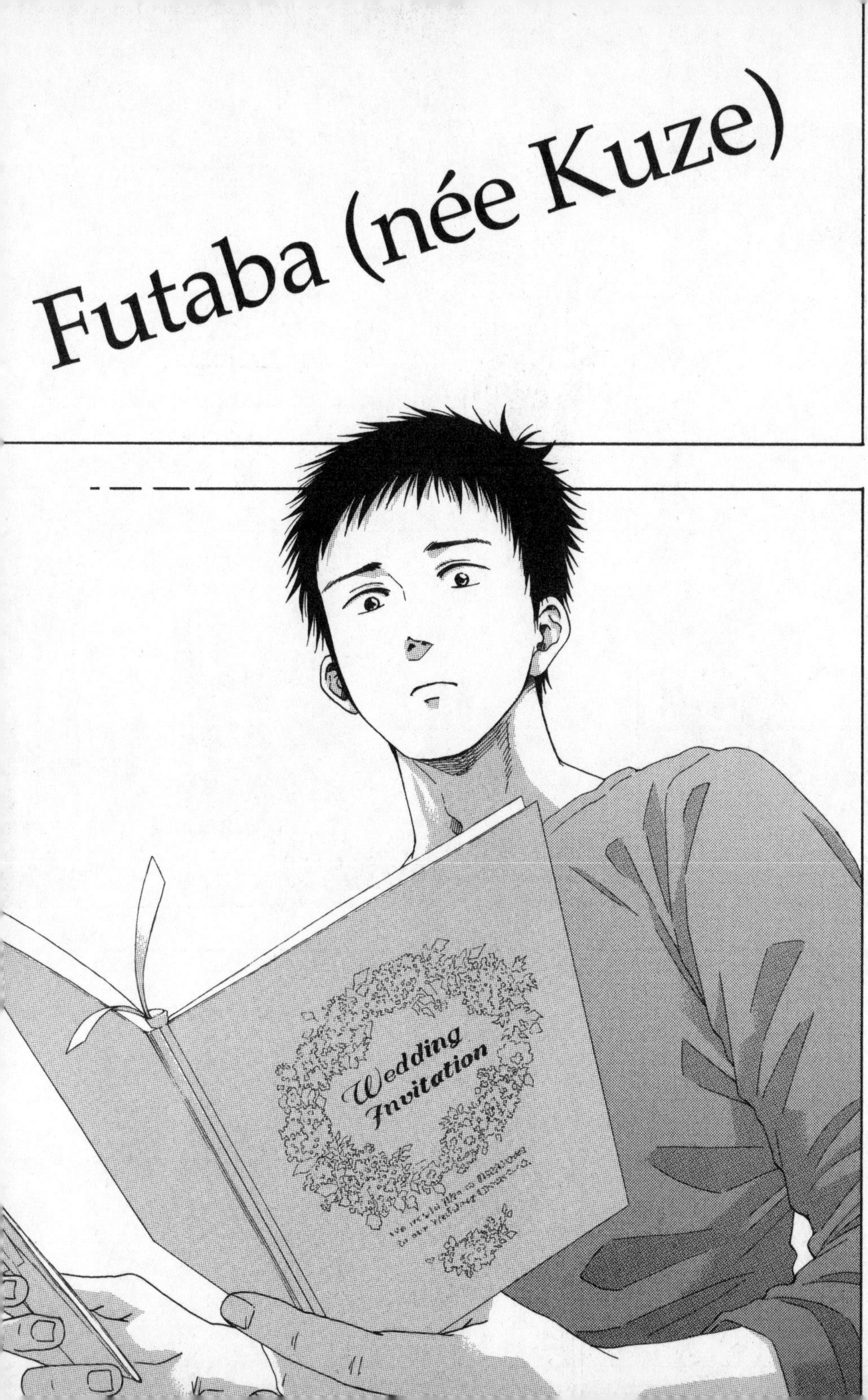
Futaba (née Kuze)
Wedding Invitation

FINAL CHAPTER

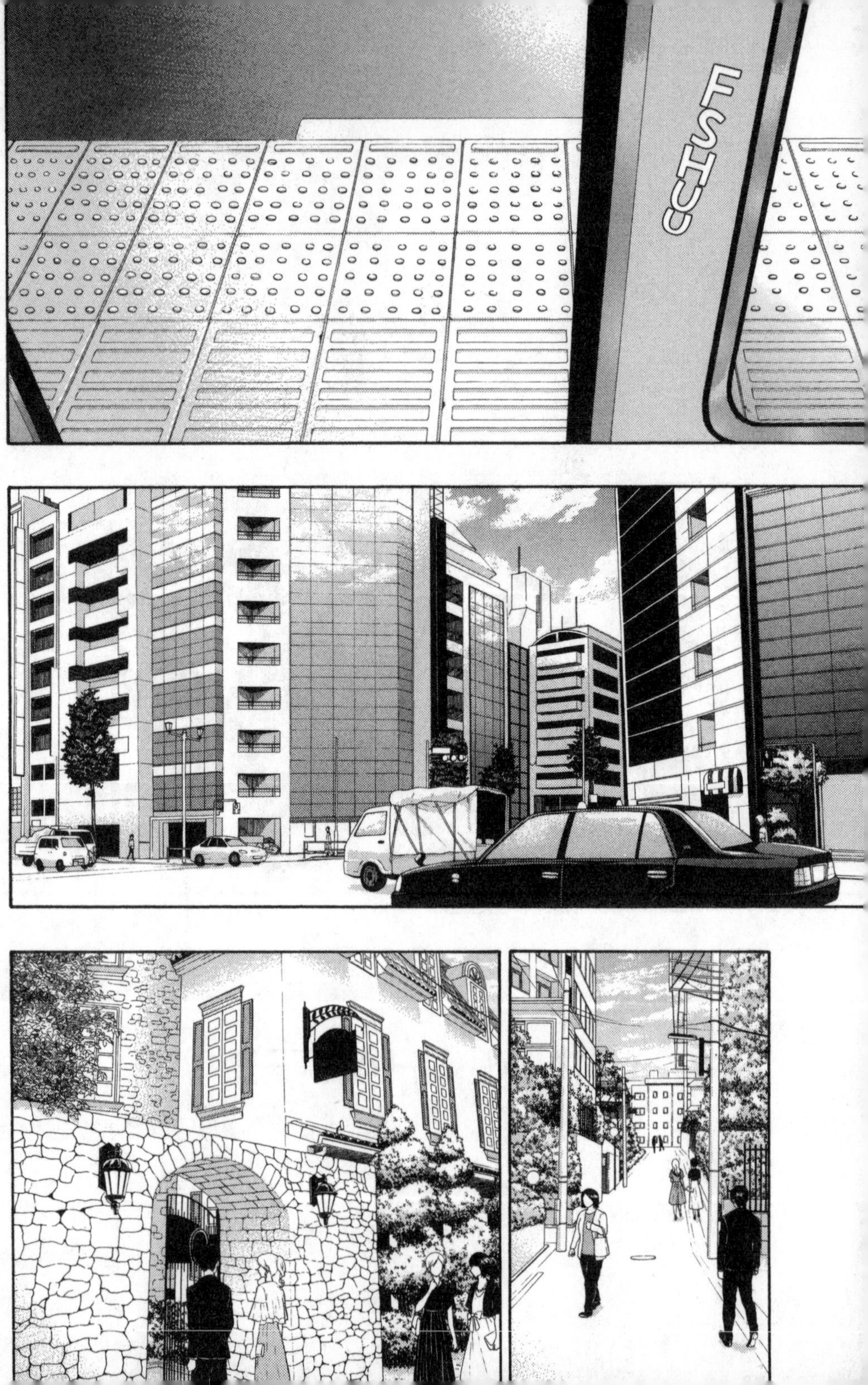
FSHU

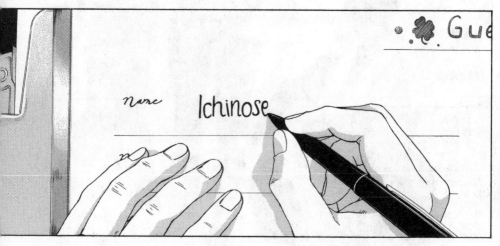

Name Ichinose

AHA.

I
SEE
HIM.

OVER
HERE.

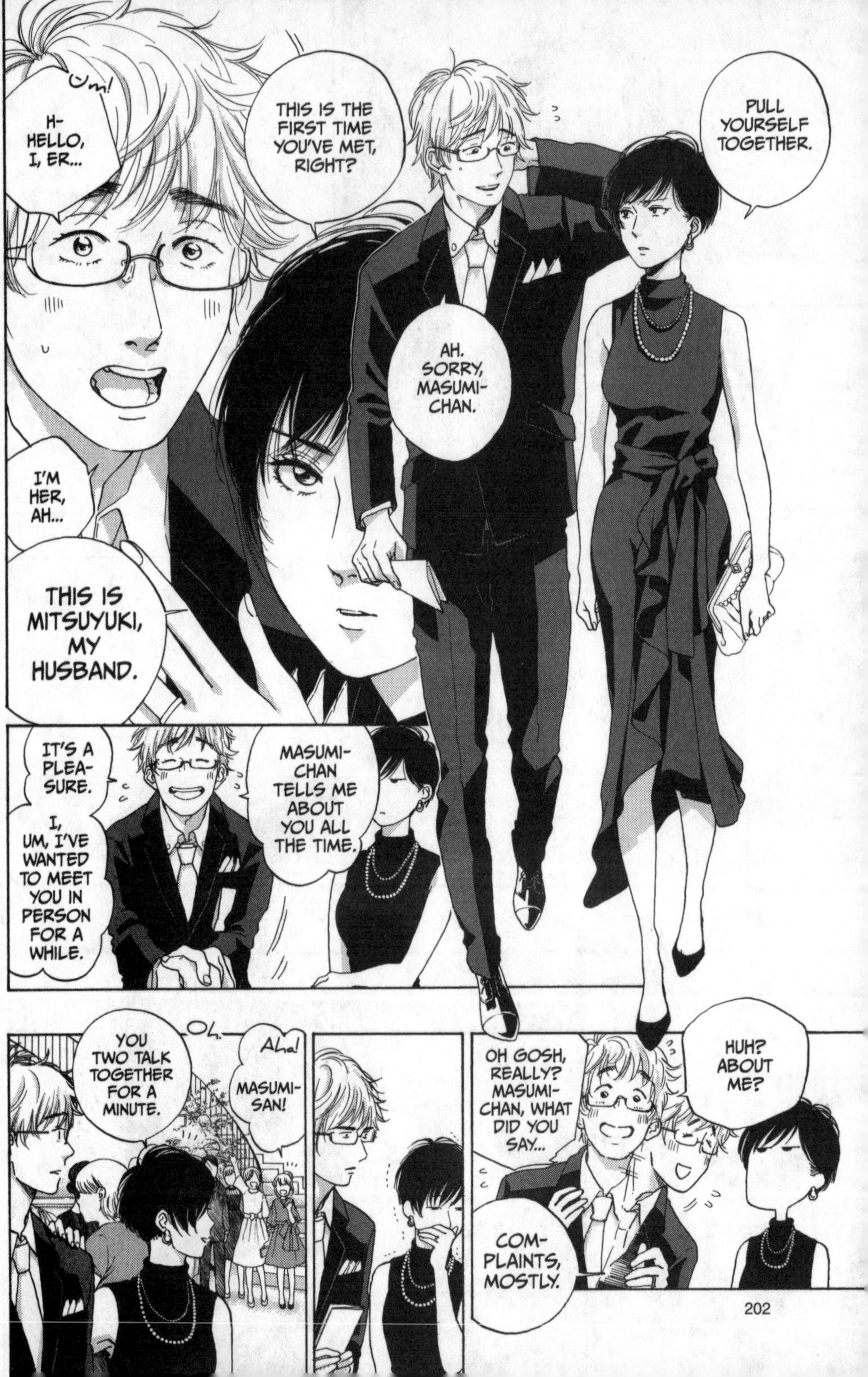
PULL YOURSELF TOGETHER.
AH. SORRY, MASUMI-CHAN.
THIS IS THE FIRST TIME YOU'VE MET, RIGHT?
THIS IS MITSUYUKI, MY HUSBAND.
Um!
H-HELLO, I, ER...
I'M HER, AH...
MASUMI-CHAN TELLS ME ABOUT YOU ALL THE TIME.
IT'S A PLEA-SURE.
I, UM, I'VE WANTED TO MEET YOU IN PERSON FOR A WHILE.
OH GOSH, REALLY? MASUMI-CHAN, WHAT DID YOU SAY...
COM-PLAINTS, MOSTLY.
HUH? ABOUT ME?
Ah!
MASUMI-SAN!
Oh.
YOU TWO TALK TOGETHER FOR A MINUTE.

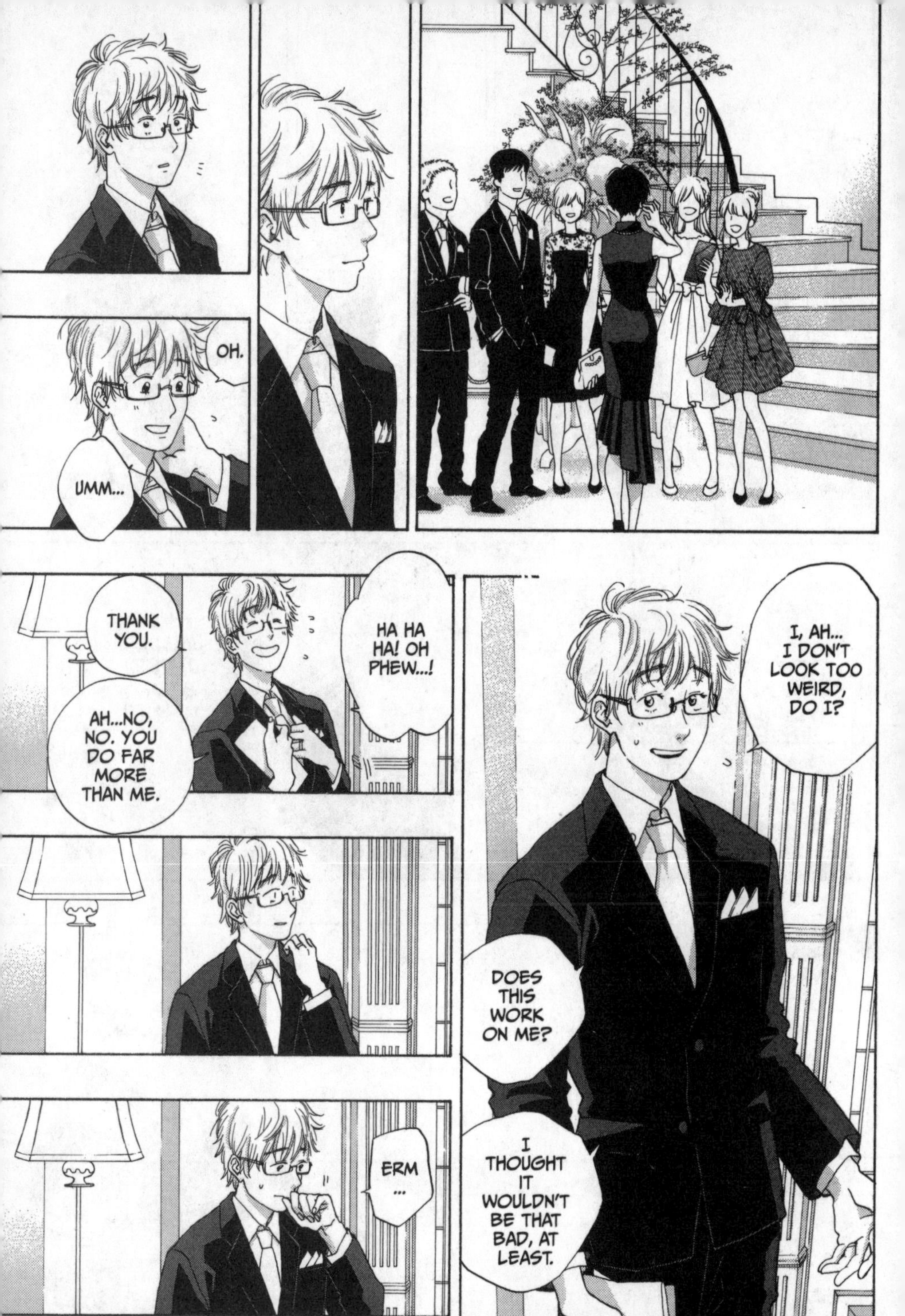
OH.
UMM...
I, AH... I DON'T LOOK TOO WEIRD, DO I?
DOES THIS WORK ON ME?
I THOUGHT IT WOULDN'T BE THAT BAD, AT LEAST.
HA HA HA! OH PHEW...!
THANK YOU.
AH...NO, NO. YOU DO FAR MORE THAN ME.
ERM ...

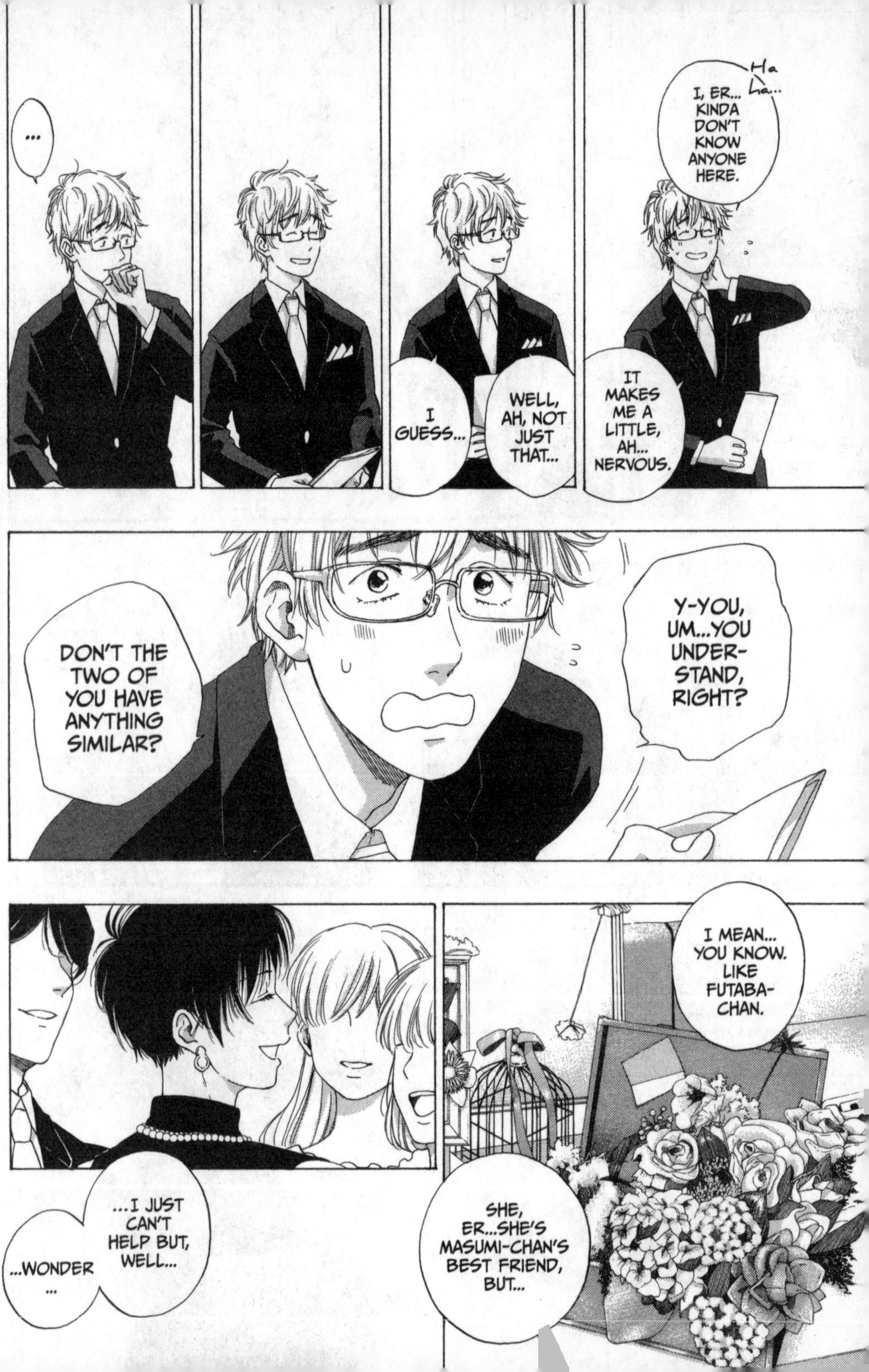
Ha Ha...
I, ER... KINDA DON'T KNOW ANYONE HERE.
IT MAKES ME A LITTLE, AH... NERVOUS.
WELL, AH, NOT JUST THAT...
I GUESS...
...
Y-YOU, UM...YOU UNDER-STAND, RIGHT?
DON'T THE TWO OF YOU HAVE ANYTHING SIMILAR?
I MEAN... YOU KNOW. LIKE FUTABA-CHAN.
SHE, ER...SHE'S MASUMI-CHAN'S BEST FRIEND, BUT...
...I JUST CAN'T HELP BUT, WELL...
...WONDER ...

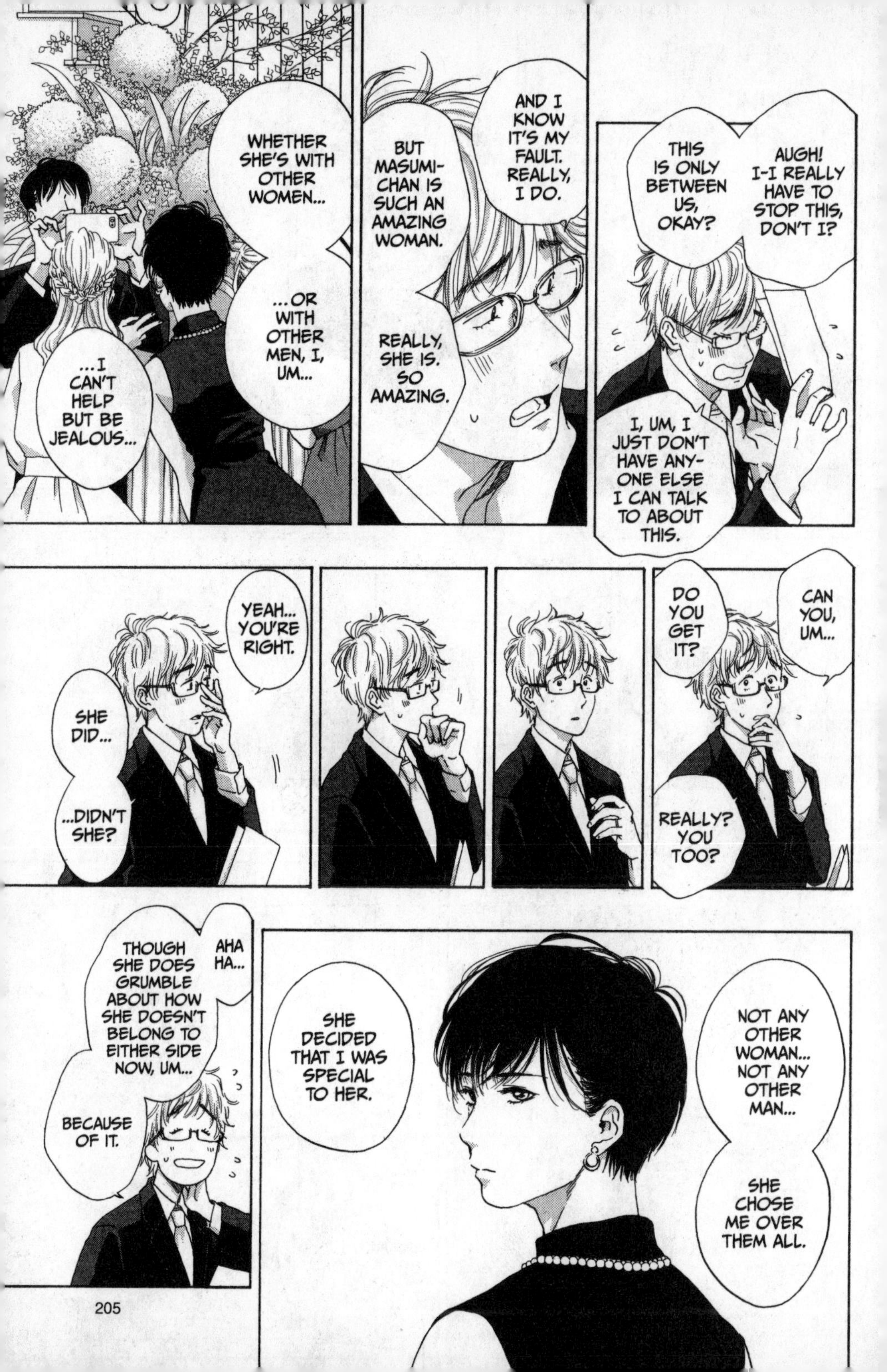
AUGH! I-I REALLY HAVE TO STOP THIS, DON'T I?
THIS IS ONLY BETWEEN US, OKAY?
I, UM, I JUST DON'T HAVE ANY-ONE ELSE I CAN TALK TO ABOUT THIS.
AND I KNOW IT'S MY FAULT. REALLY, I DO.
BUT MASUMI-CHAN IS SUCH AN AMAZING WOMAN.
REALLY, SHE IS. SO AMAZING.
WHETHER SHE'S WITH OTHER WOMEN...
...OR WITH OTHER MEN, I, UM...
...I CAN'T HELP BUT BE JEALOUS...
CAN YOU, UM...
DO YOU GET IT?
REALLY? YOU TOO?
YEAH... YOU'RE RIGHT.
SHE DID...
...DIDN'T SHE?
NOT ANY OTHER WOMAN... NOT ANY OTHER MAN...
SHE CHOSE ME OVER THEM ALL.
SHE DECIDED THAT I WAS SPECIAL TO HER.
AHA HA...
THOUGH SHE DOES GRUMBLE ABOUT HOW SHE DOESN'T BELONG TO EITHER SIDE NOW, UM...
BECAUSE OF IT.

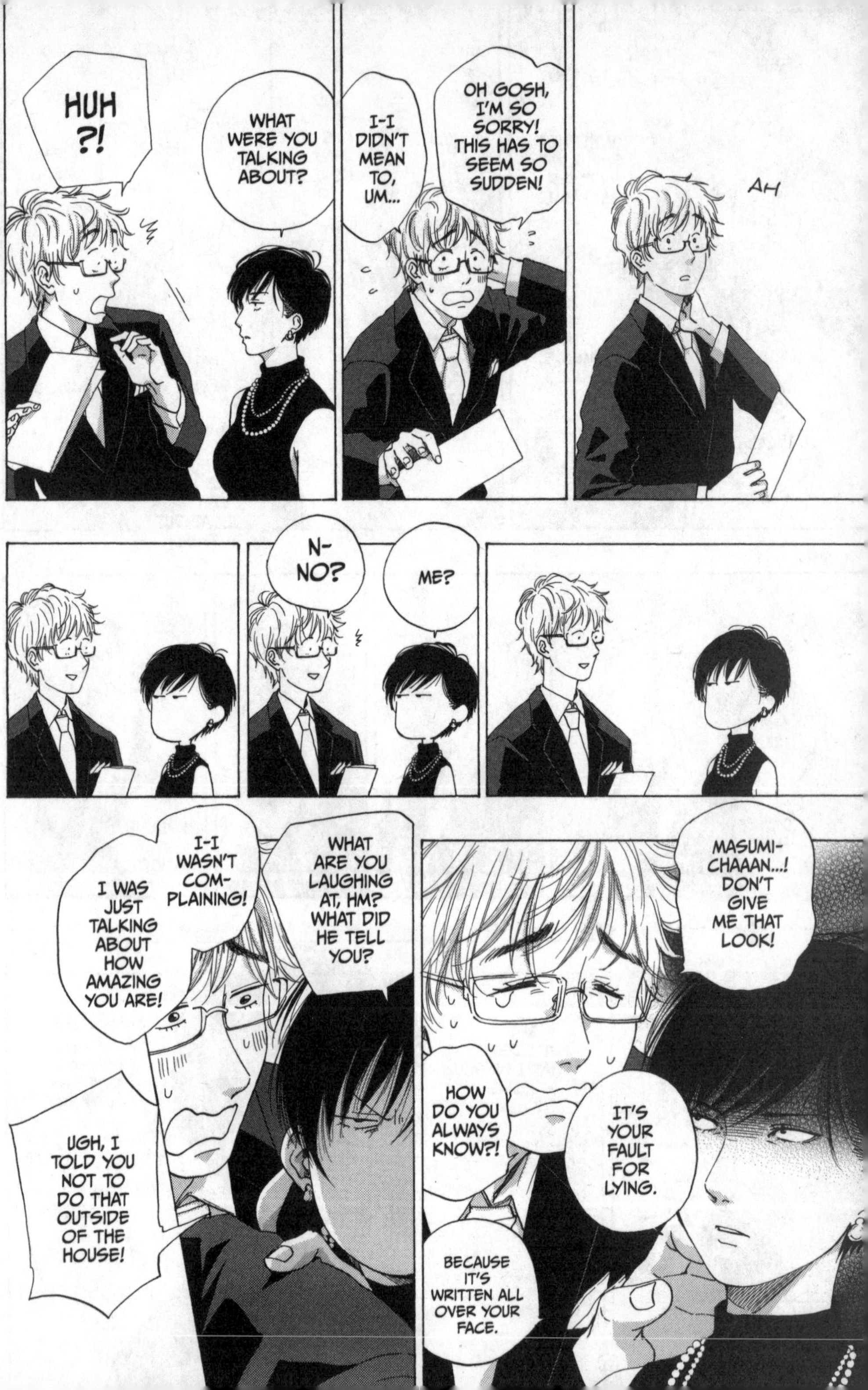
HUH ?!
WHAT WERE YOU TALKING ABOUT?
I-I DIDN'T MEAN TO, UM...
OH GOSH, I'M SO SORRY! THIS HAS TO SEEM SO SUDDEN!
AH
N-NO?
ME?
WHAT ARE YOU LAUGHING AT, HM? WHAT DID HE TELL YOU?
I-I WASN'T COM-PLAINING!
I WAS JUST TALKING ABOUT HOW AMAZING YOU ARE!
UGH, I TOLD YOU NOT TO DO THAT OUTSIDE OF THE HOUSE!
MASUMI-CHAAAN...! DON'T GIVE ME THAT LOOK!
HOW DO YOU ALWAYS KNOW?!
IT'S YOUR FAULT FOR LYING.
BECAUSE IT'S WRITTEN ALL OVER YOUR FACE.

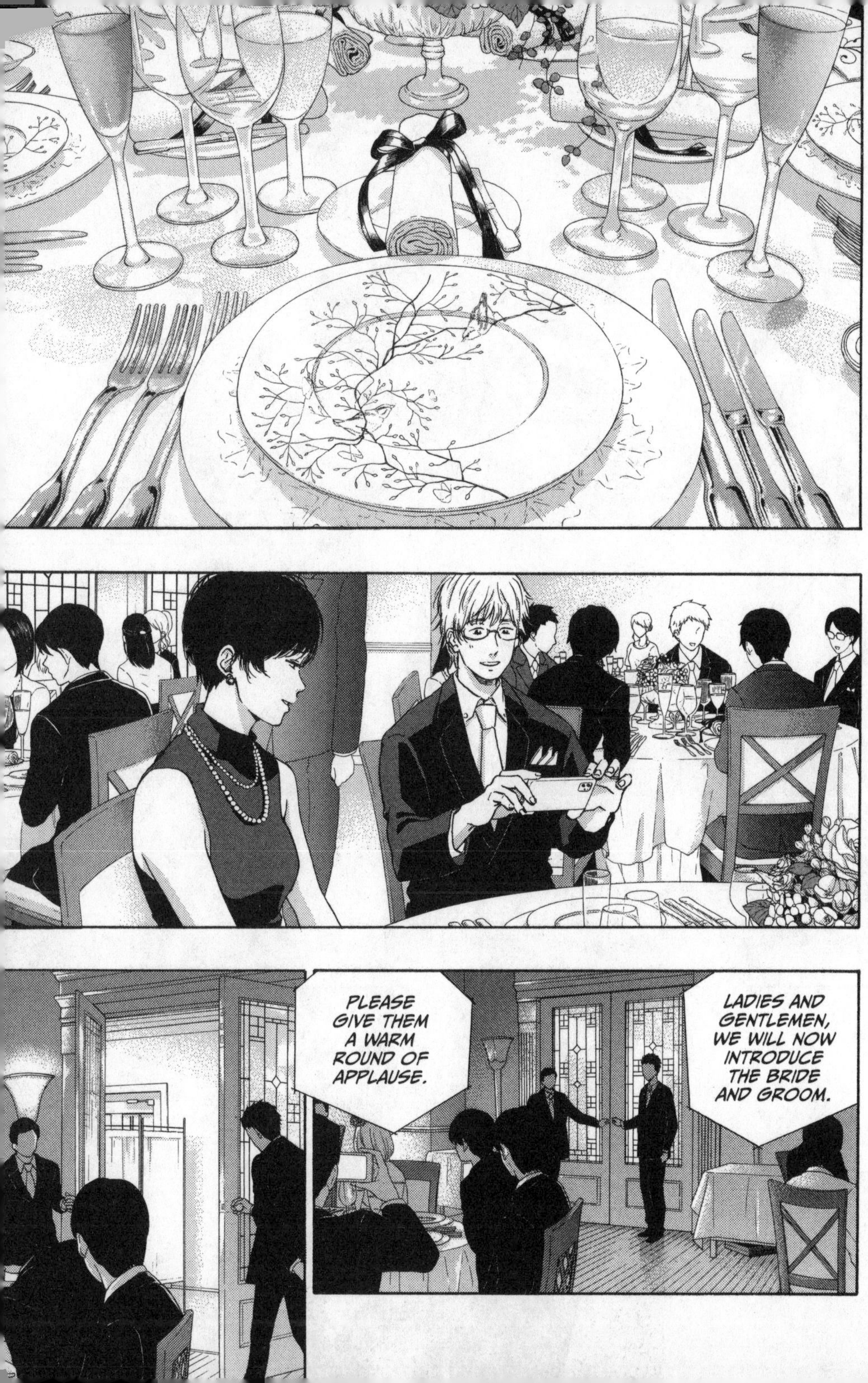
LADIES AND GENTLEMEN, WE WILL NOW INTRODUCE THE BRIDE AND GROOM.
PLEASE GIVE THEM A WARM ROUND OF APPLAUSE.

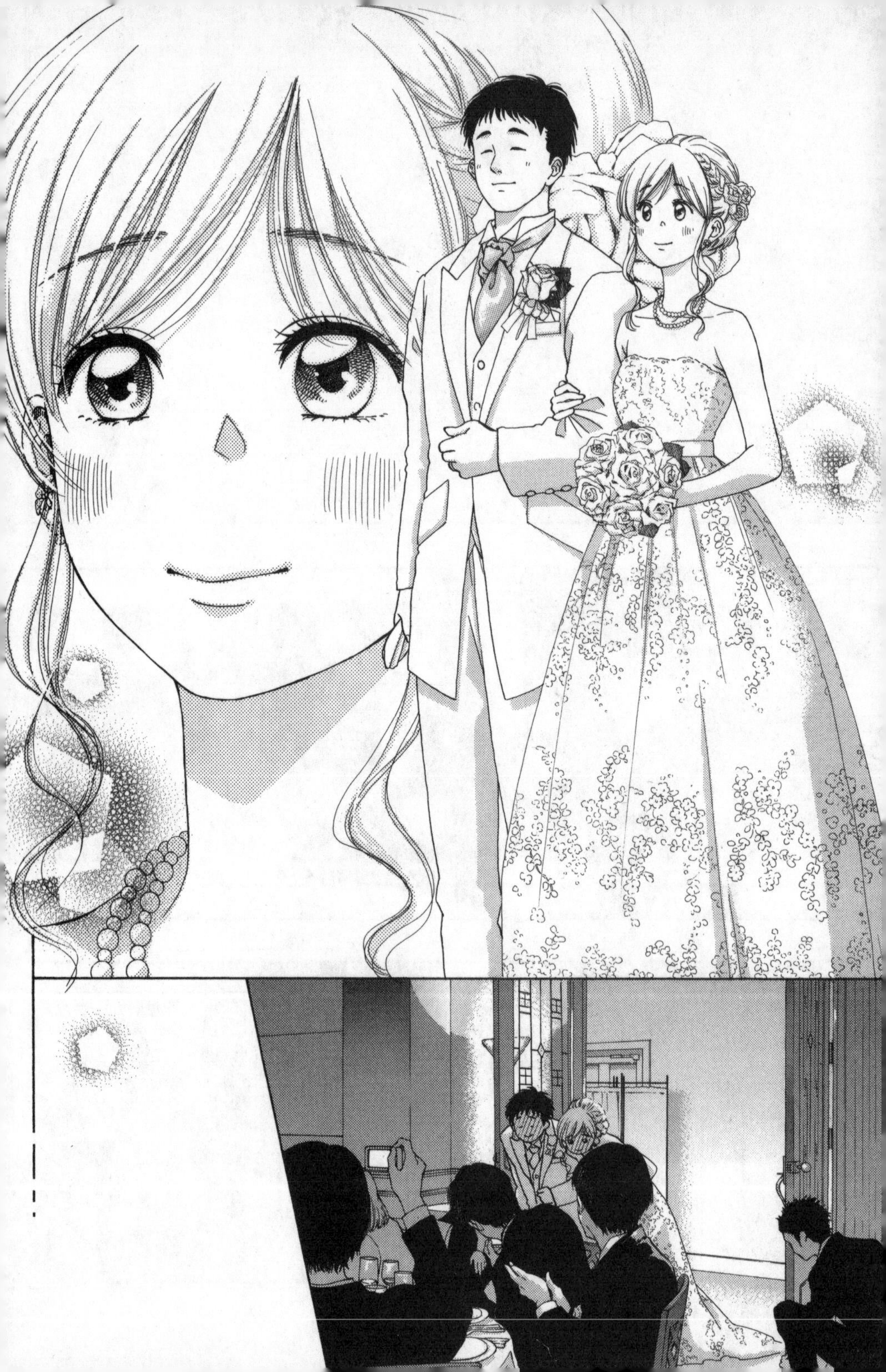

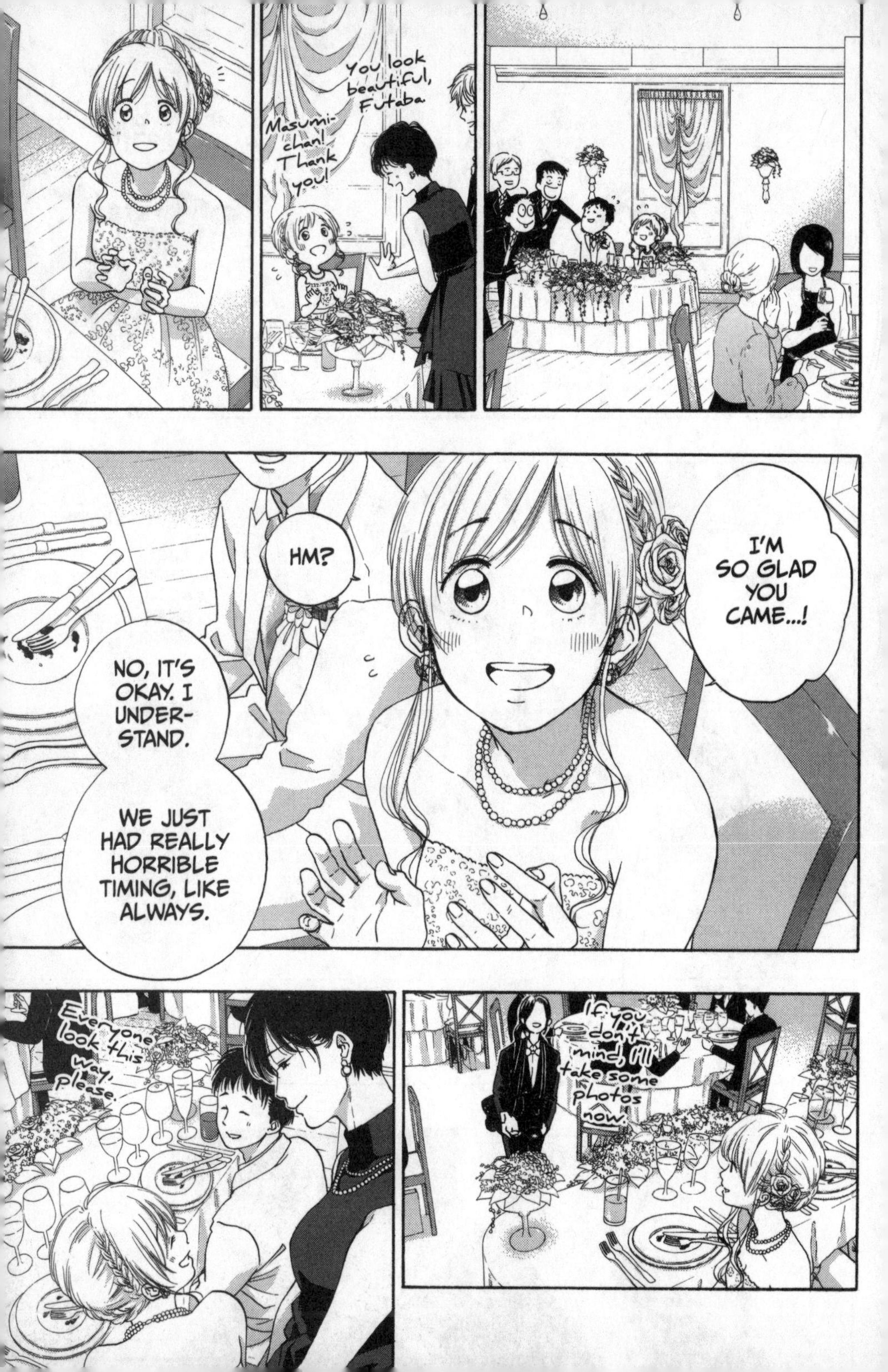
You look beautiful, Futaba.
Masumi-chan! Thank you!
I'M SO GLAD YOU CAME...!
HM?
NO, IT'S OKAY. I UNDERSTAND.
WE JUST HAD REALLY HORRIBLE TIMING, LIKE ALWAYS.
If you don't mind, I'll take some photos now.
Everyone look this way, please.

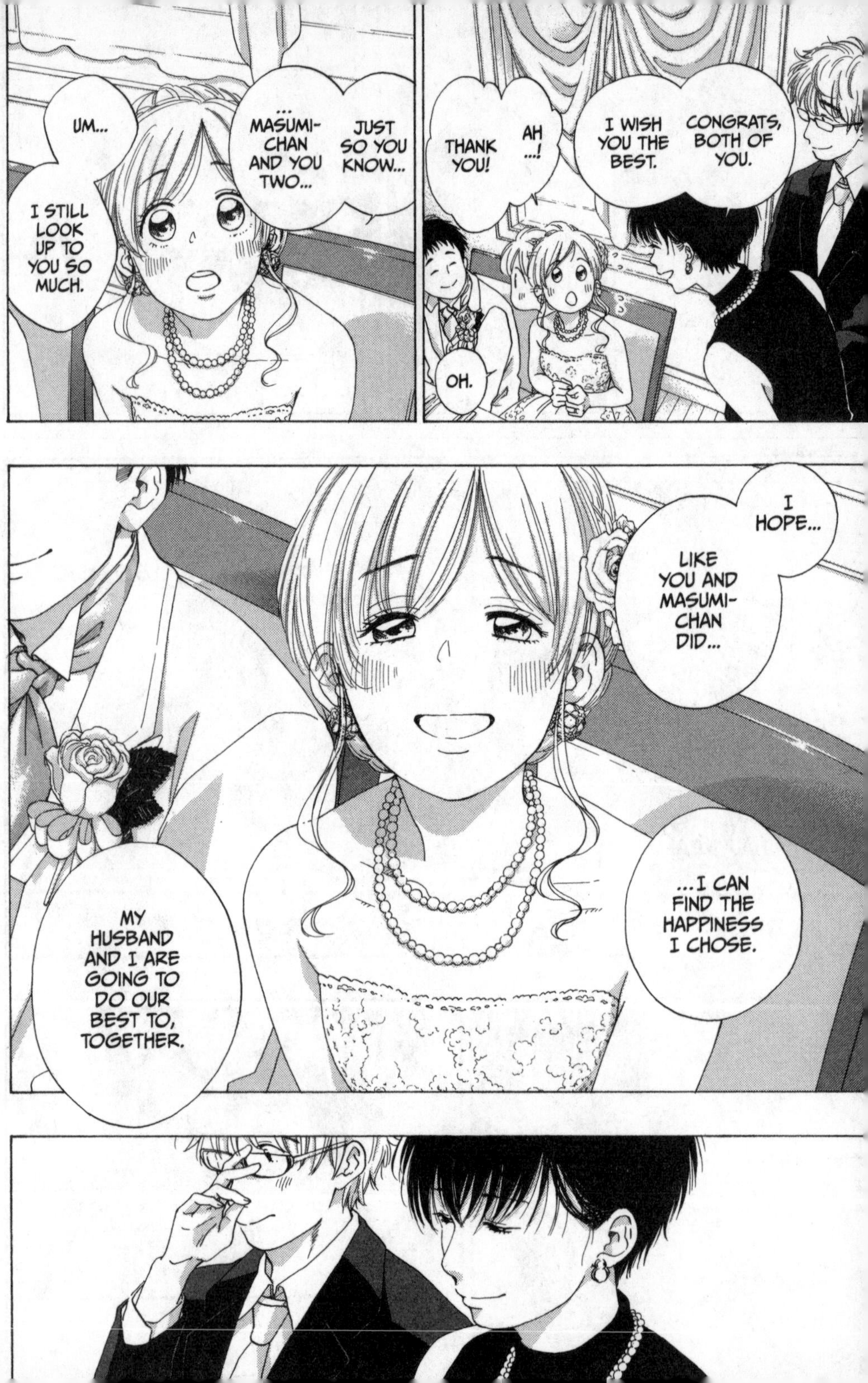
CONGRATS, BOTH OF YOU.
I WISH YOU THE BEST.
AH ...!
THANK YOU!
OH.
JUST SO YOU KNOW...
... MASUMI-CHAN AND YOU TWO...
UM...
I STILL LOOK UP TO YOU SO MUCH.
I HOPE...
LIKE YOU AND MASUMI-CHAN DID...
...I CAN FIND THE HAPPINESS I CHOSE.
MY HUSBAND AND I ARE GOING TO DO OUR BEST TO, TOGETHER.

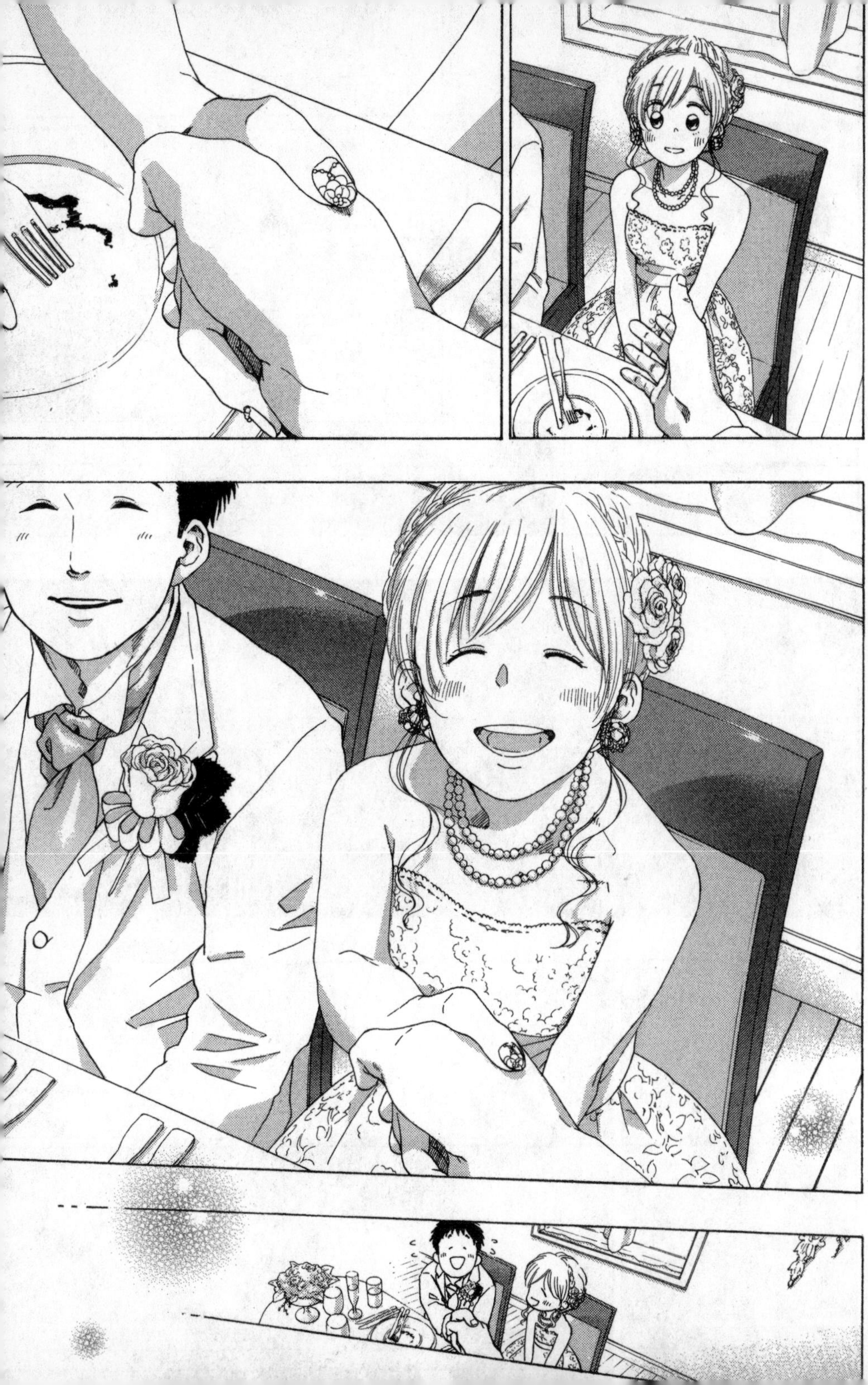

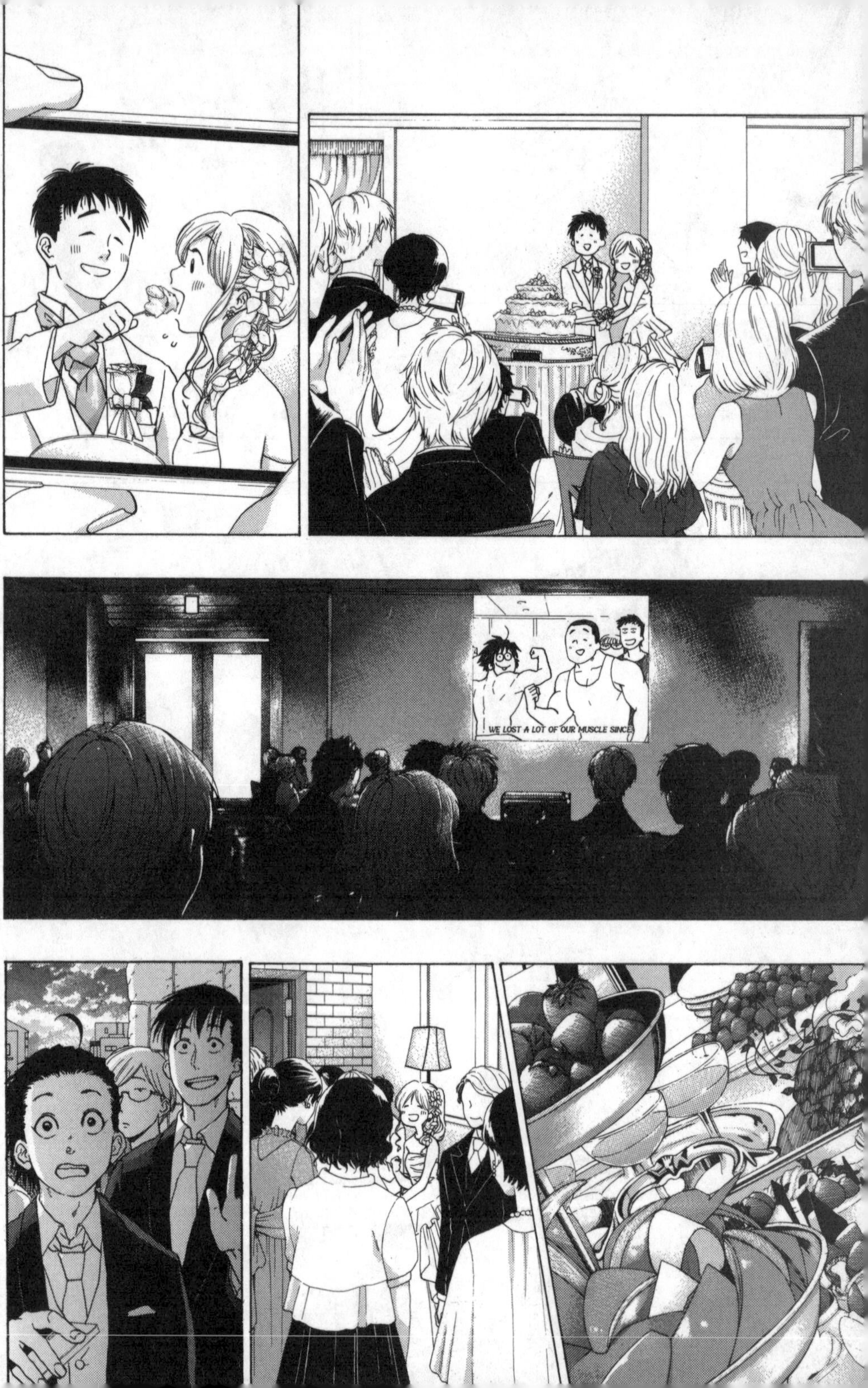
WE LOST A LOT OF OUR MUSCLE SINCE.

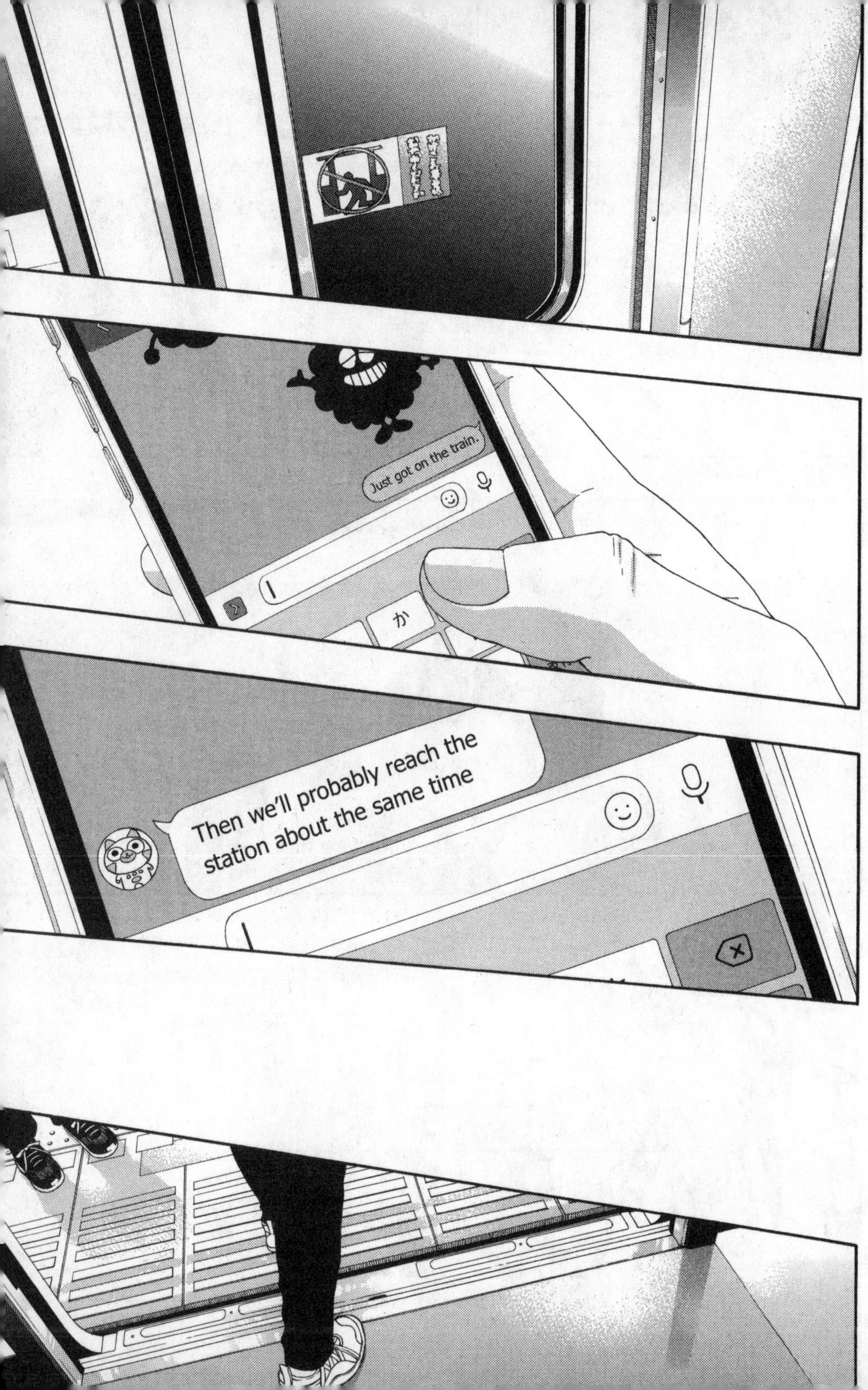
Just got on the train.
か
Then we'll probably reach the station about the same time

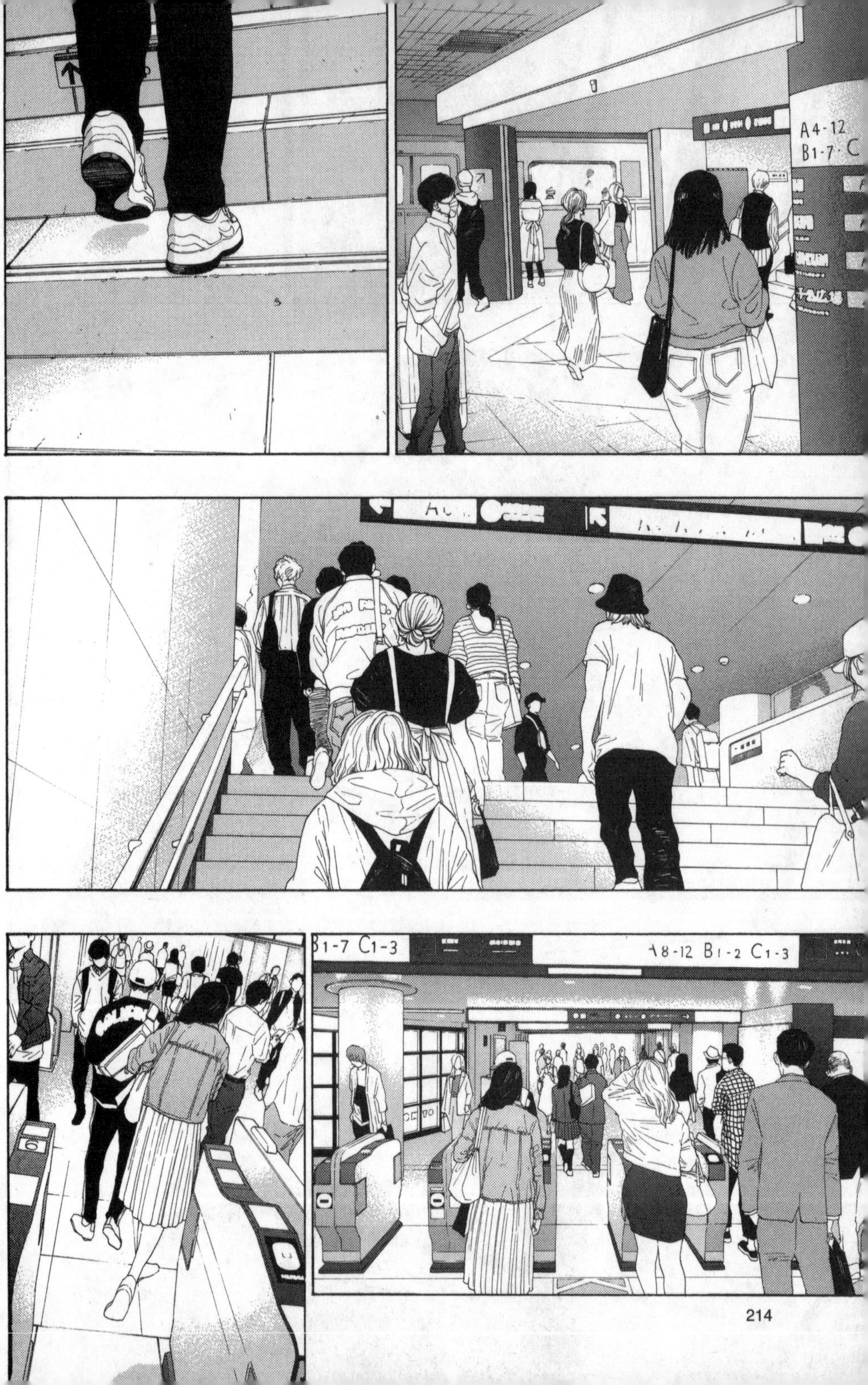
A4-12
B1-7·C
B1-7 C1-3
8-12 B1-2 C1-3

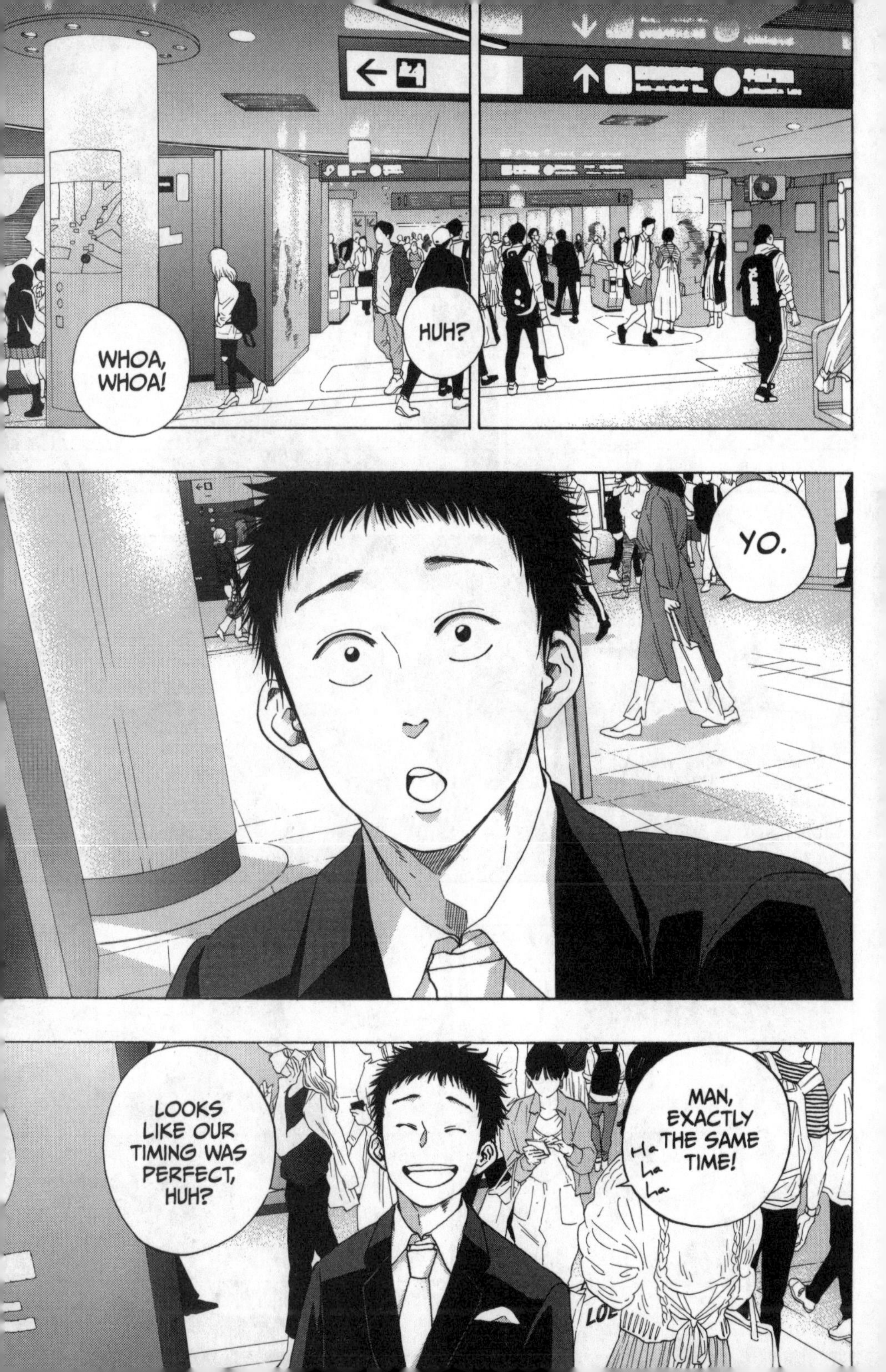
HUH?
WHOA, WHOA!
YO.
MAN, EXACTLY THE SAME TIME!
Ha Ha Ha
LOOKS LIKE OUR TIMING WAS PERFECT, HUH?
LOL

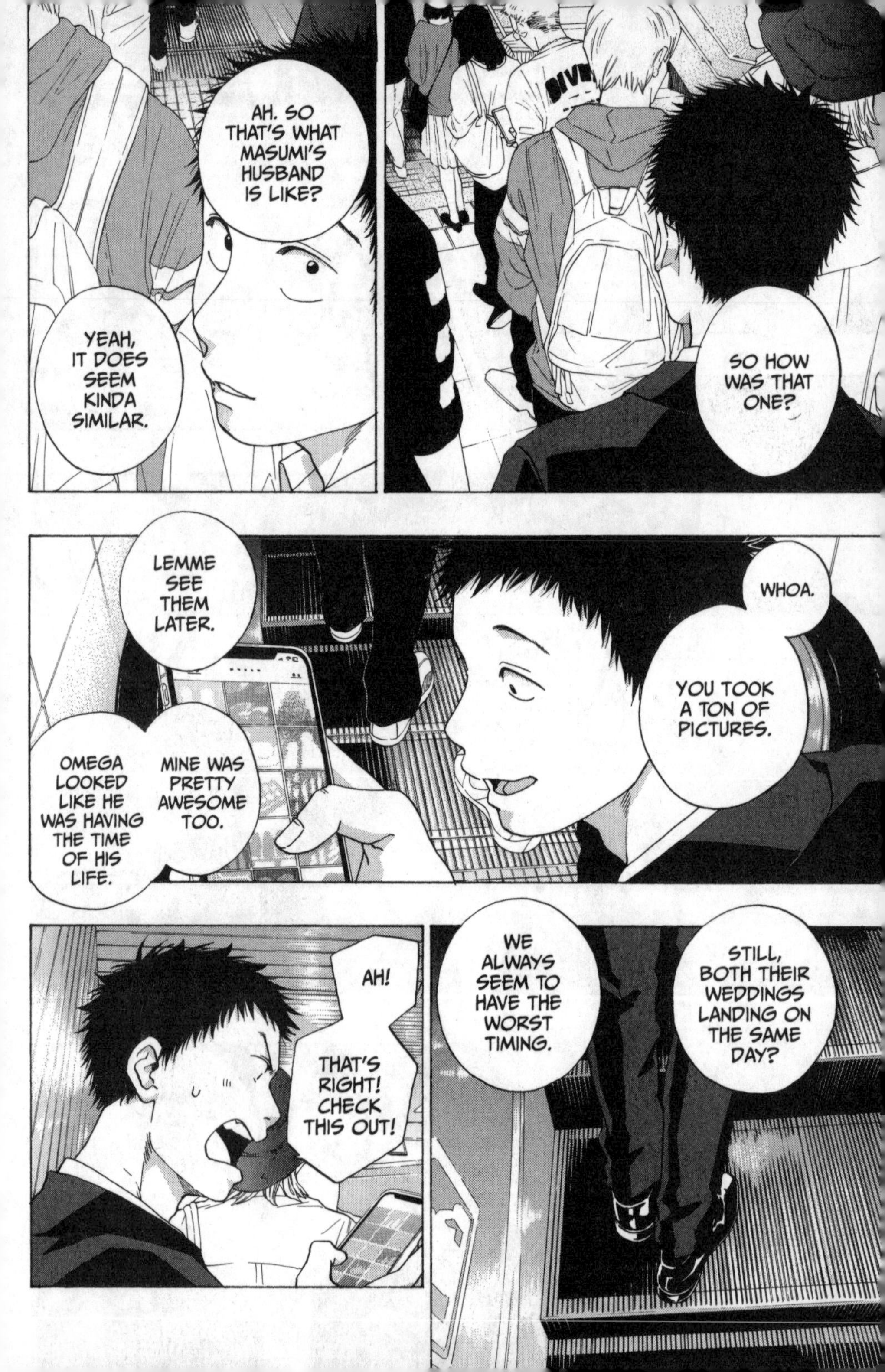
SO HOW WAS THAT ONE?
AH. SO THAT'S WHAT MASUMI'S HUSBAND IS LIKE?
YEAH, IT DOES SEEM KINDA SIMILAR.
WHOA.
YOU TOOK A TON OF PICTURES.
LEMME SEE THEM LATER.
MINE WAS PRETTY AWESOME TOO.
OMEGA LOOKED LIKE HE WAS HAVING THE TIME OF HIS LIFE.
STILL, BOTH THEIR WEDDINGS LANDING ON THE SAME DAY?
WE ALWAYS SEEM TO HAVE THE WORST TIMING.
AH!
THAT'S RIGHT! CHECK THIS OUT!

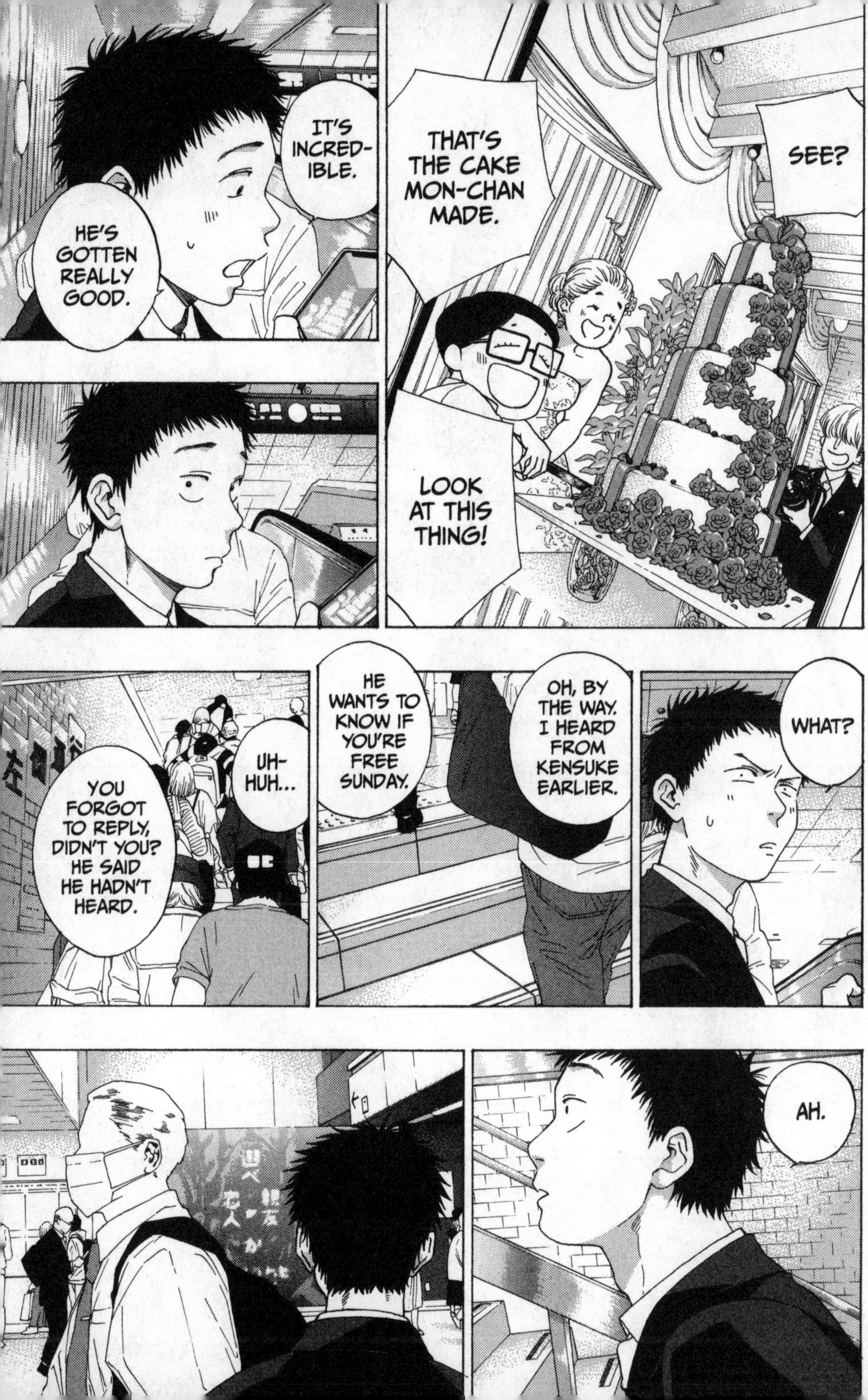
SEE?
THAT'S THE CAKE MON-CHAN MADE.
LOOK AT THIS THING!
IT'S INCRED-IBLE.
HE'S GOTTEN REALLY GOOD.
WHAT?
OH, BY THE WAY. I HEARD FROM KENSUKE EARLIER.
HE WANTS TO KNOW IF YOU'RE FREE SUNDAY.
UH-HUH...
YOU FORGOT TO REPLY, DIDN'T YOU? HE SAID HE HADN'T HEARD.
AH.

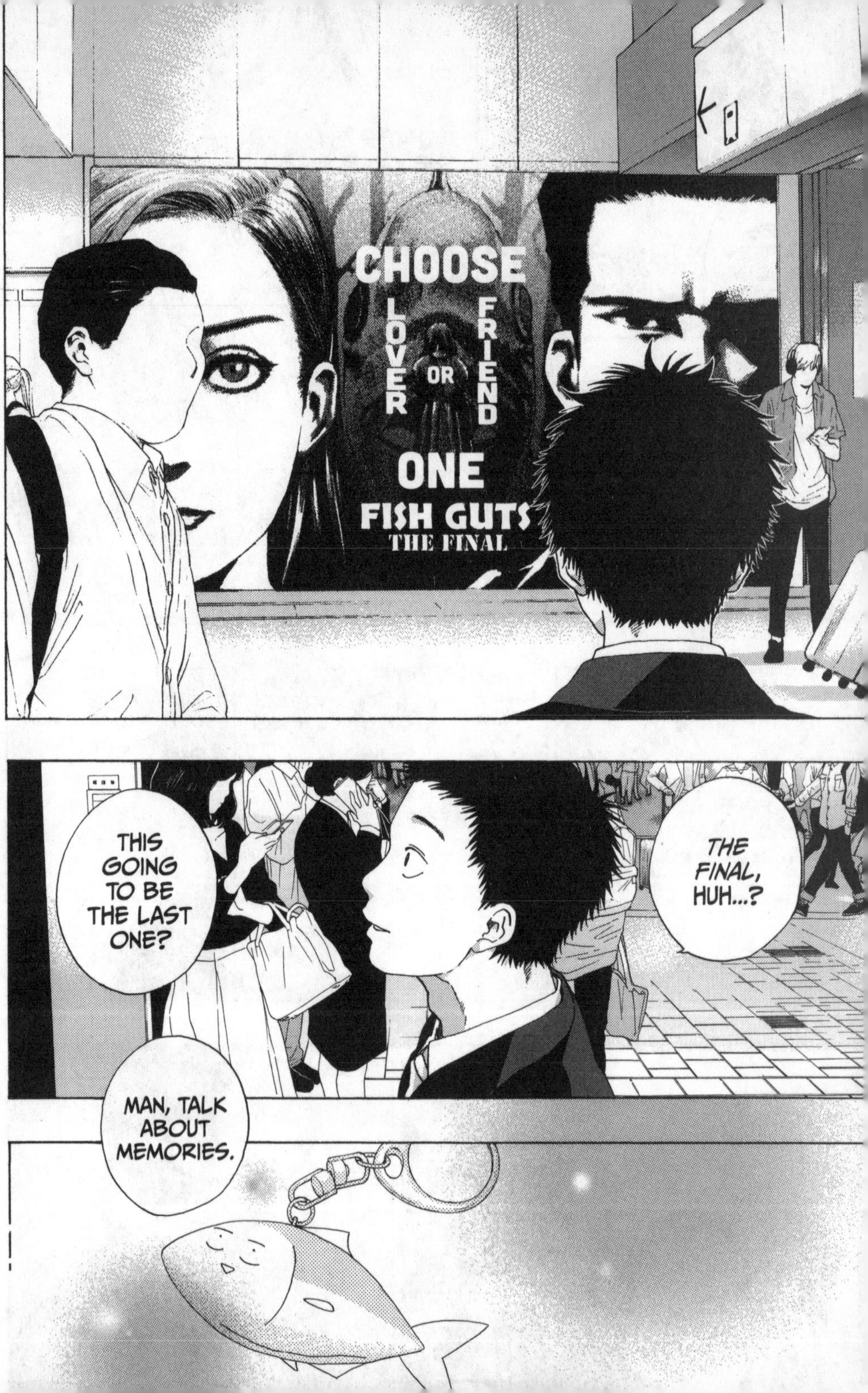
CHOOSE
LOVER
OR
FRIEND
ONE
FISH GUTS
THE FINAL
THE FINAL, HUH...?
THIS GOING TO BE THE LAST ONE?
MAN, TALK ABOUT MEMORIES.

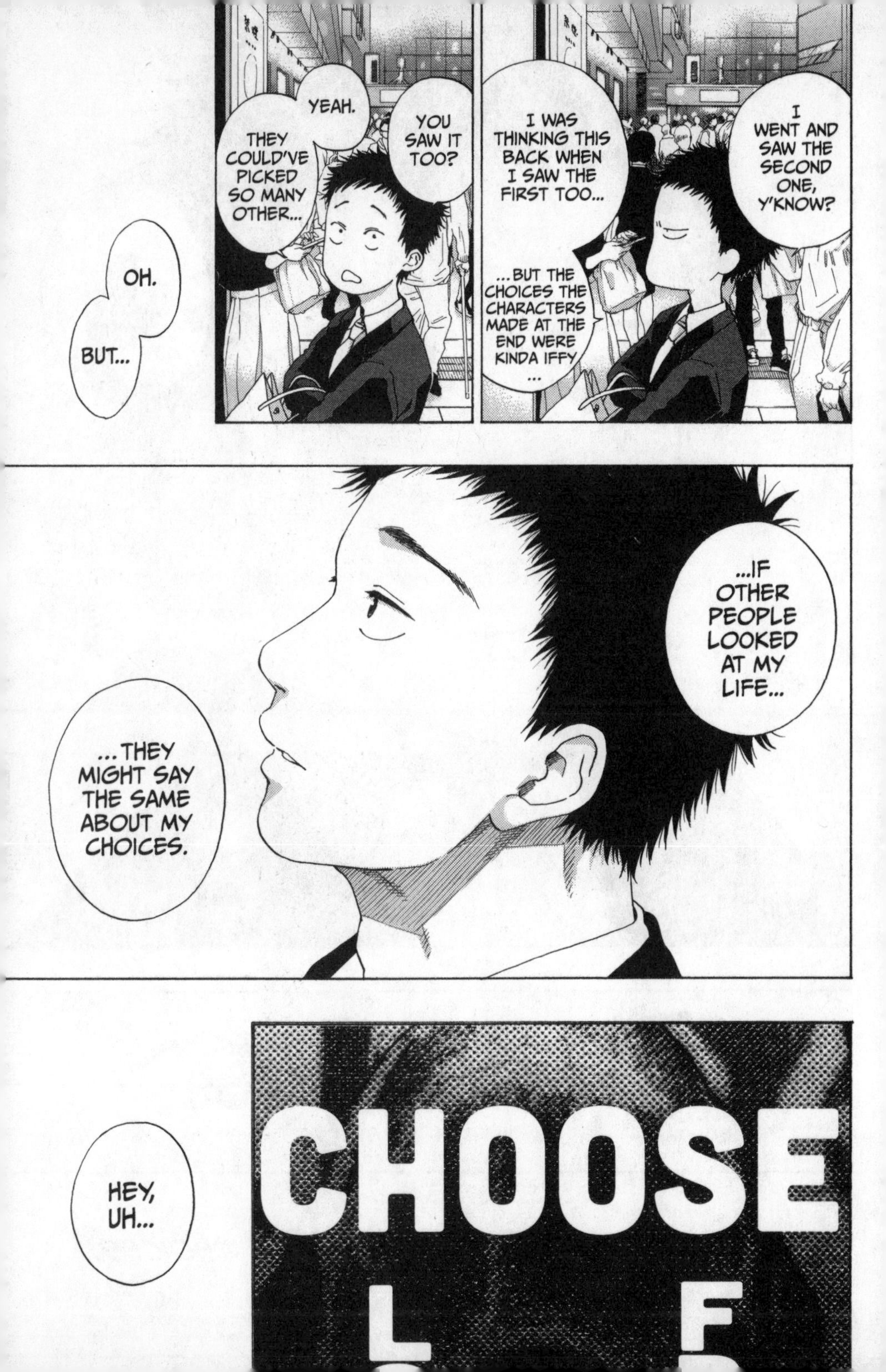
I WENT AND SAW THE SECOND ONE, Y'KNOW?
I WAS THINKING THIS BACK WHEN I SAW THE FIRST TOO...
...BUT THE CHOICES THE CHARACTERS MADE AT THE END WERE KINDA IFFY...
YOU SAW IT TOO?
YEAH.
THEY COULD'VE PICKED SO MANY OTHER...
OH.
BUT...
...IF OTHER PEOPLE LOOKED AT MY LIFE...
...THEY MIGHT SAY THE SAME ABOUT MY CHOICES.
CHOOSE
HEY, UH...

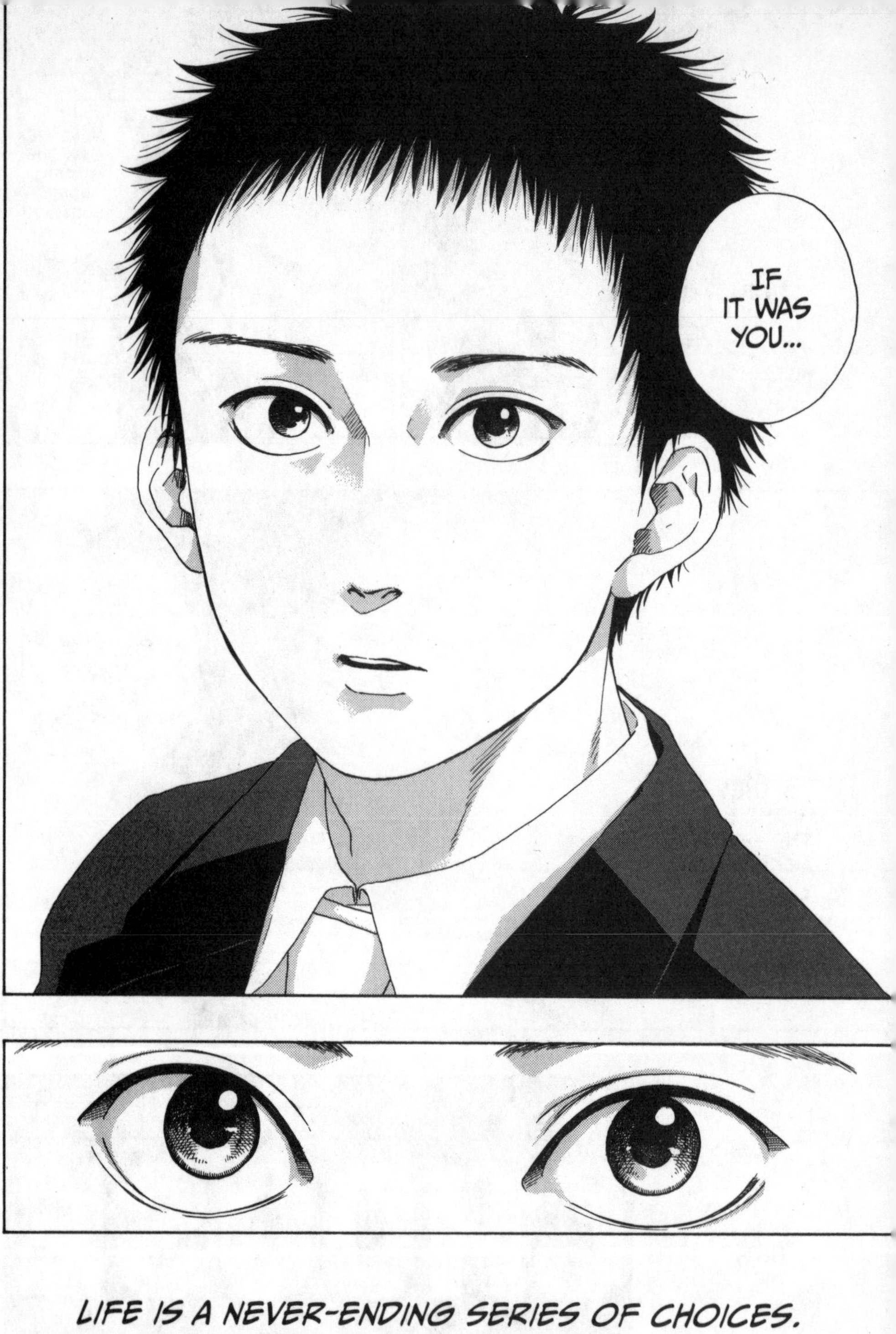
IF IT WAS YOU...

LIFE IS A NEVER-ENDING SERIES OF CHOICES.

EVEN WHEN YOU TRY TO MAKE THE BEST CHOICE YOU CAN...

YOU MIGHT HURT SOMEONE.

YOU MIGHT HURT YOURSELF.

YOU MIGHT WIND UP REGRETTING THE WHOLE THING.

CONVERSELY...

...ONE CHOICE MIGHT GO SO WELL...

...AND YOU MIGHT FIND HAPPINESS SO PRECIOUS TO YOU...

...THAT YOU FEAR MAKING THE NEXT CHOICE THAT FACES YOU.

HA HA!

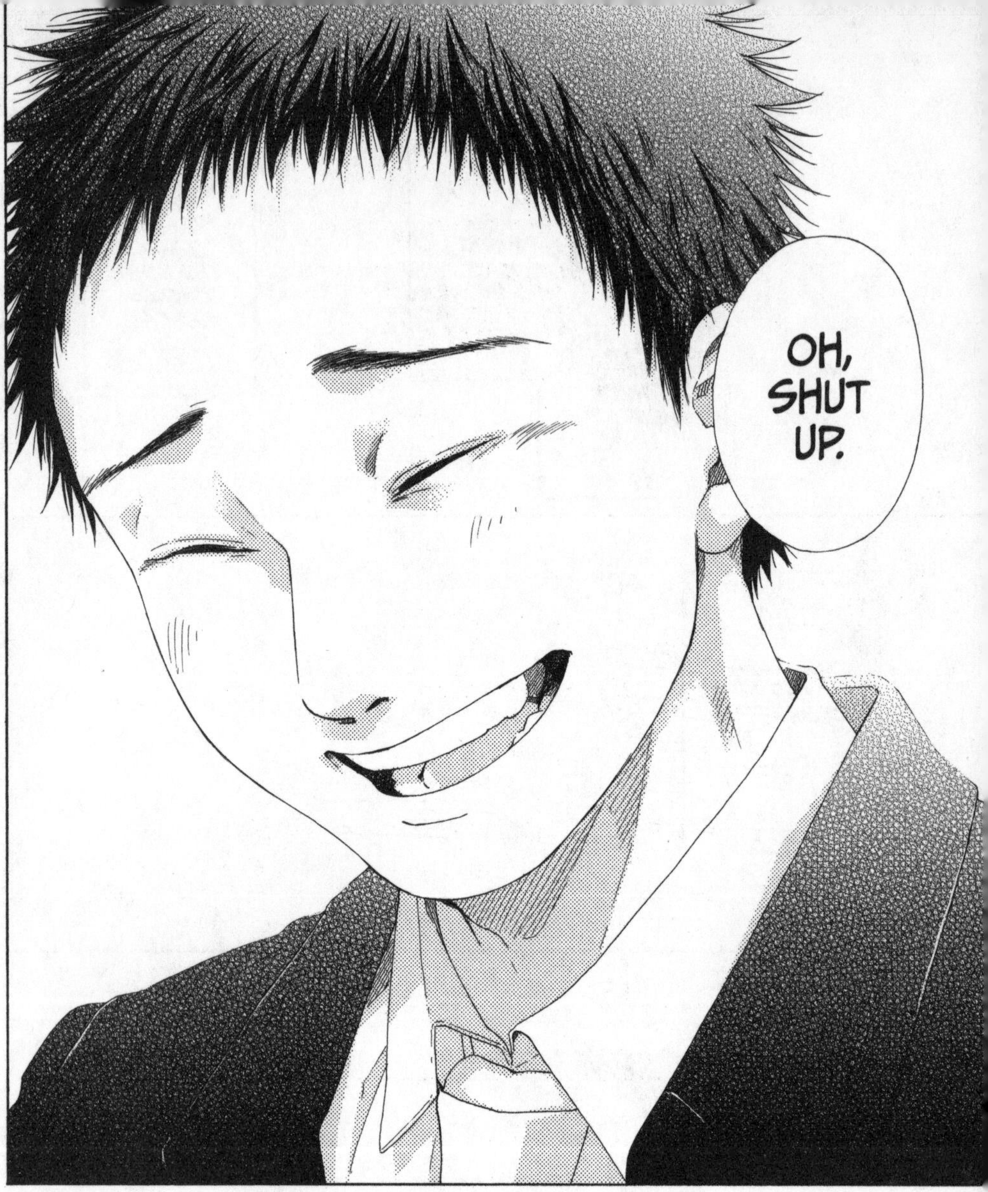
OH, SHUT UP.

AND YET, WE HAVE NO CHOICE...

...BUT TO KEEP CHOOSING, OVER AND OVER.

IF SO,
THEN I
HOPE THAT,
AT LEAST...

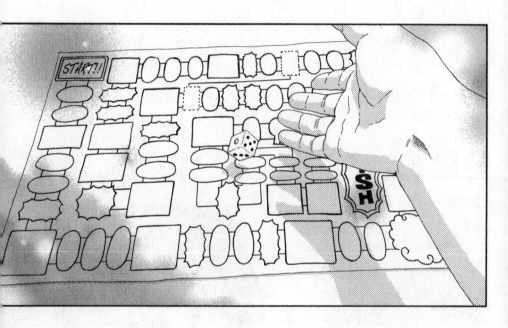

...THE
FUTURE
YOUR
CHOICES
LEAD YOU
TO IS...

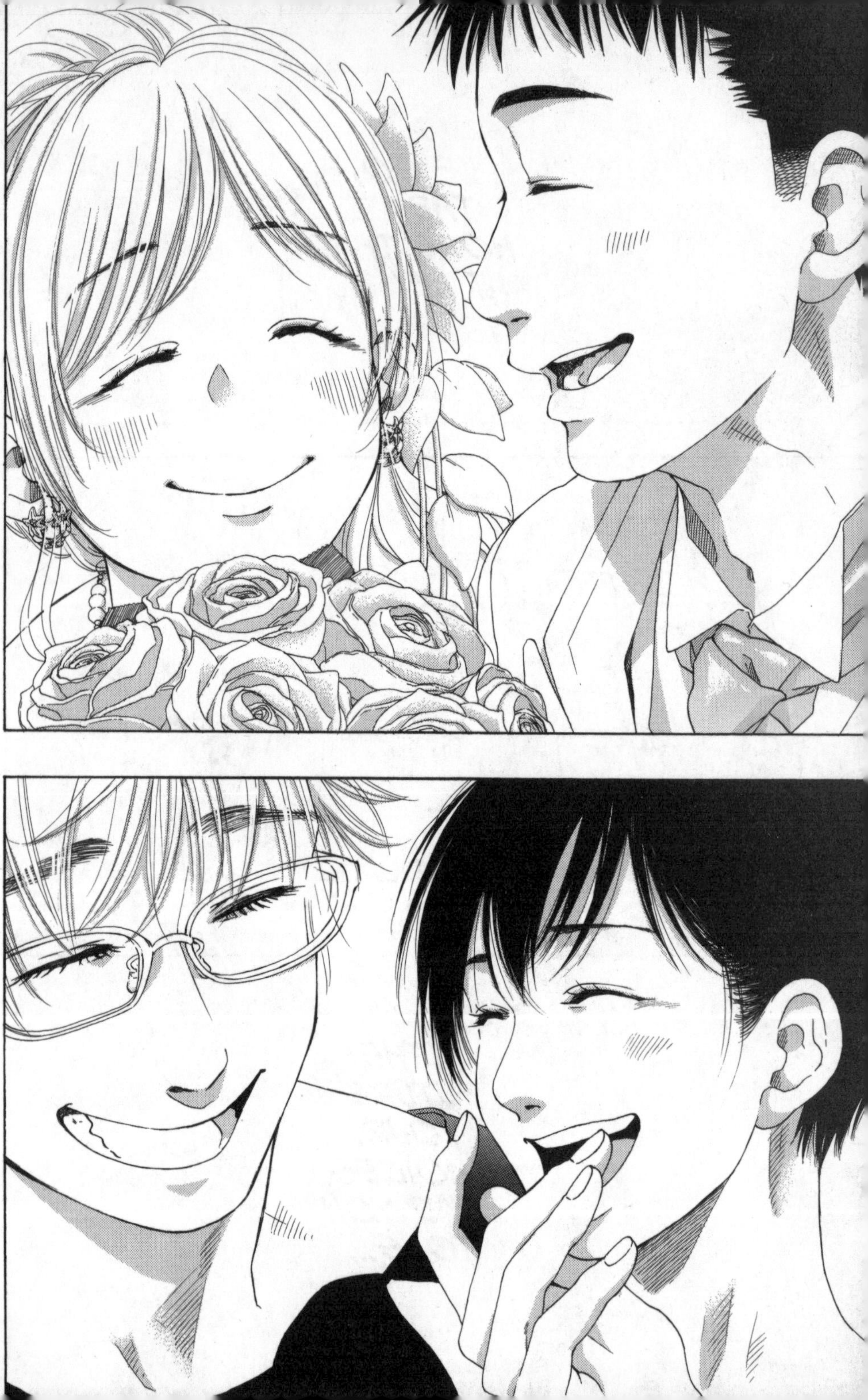

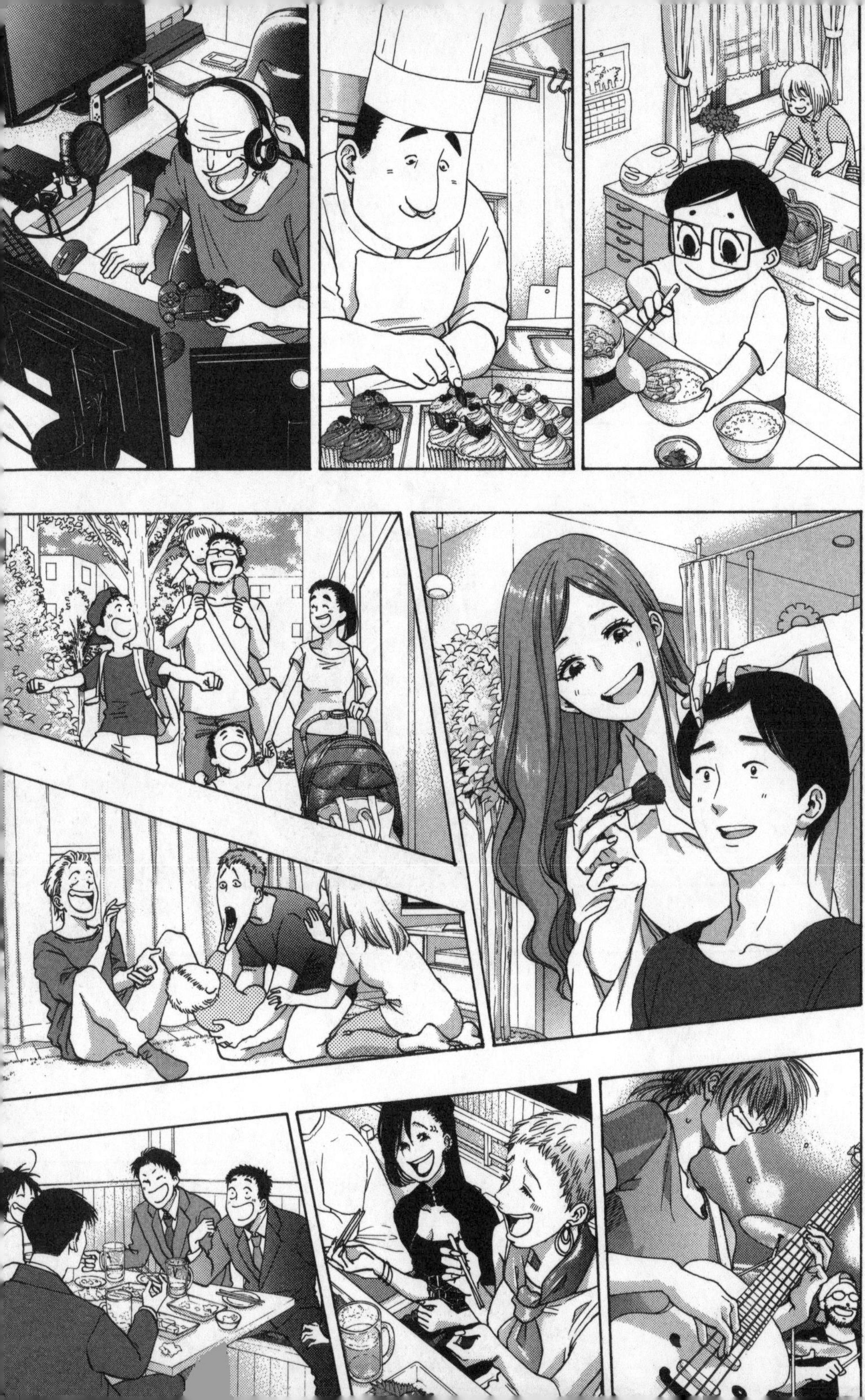

GEEZ, WHAT A BIG BAG.

WHAT KIND OF PARTY FAVORS DID YOU GET?

OH YEAH... AND WHAT DO WE STILL HAVE IN THE FRIDGE?

AH WELL.

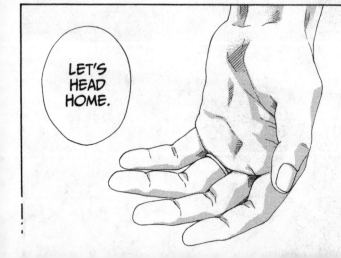

LET'S HEAD HOME.

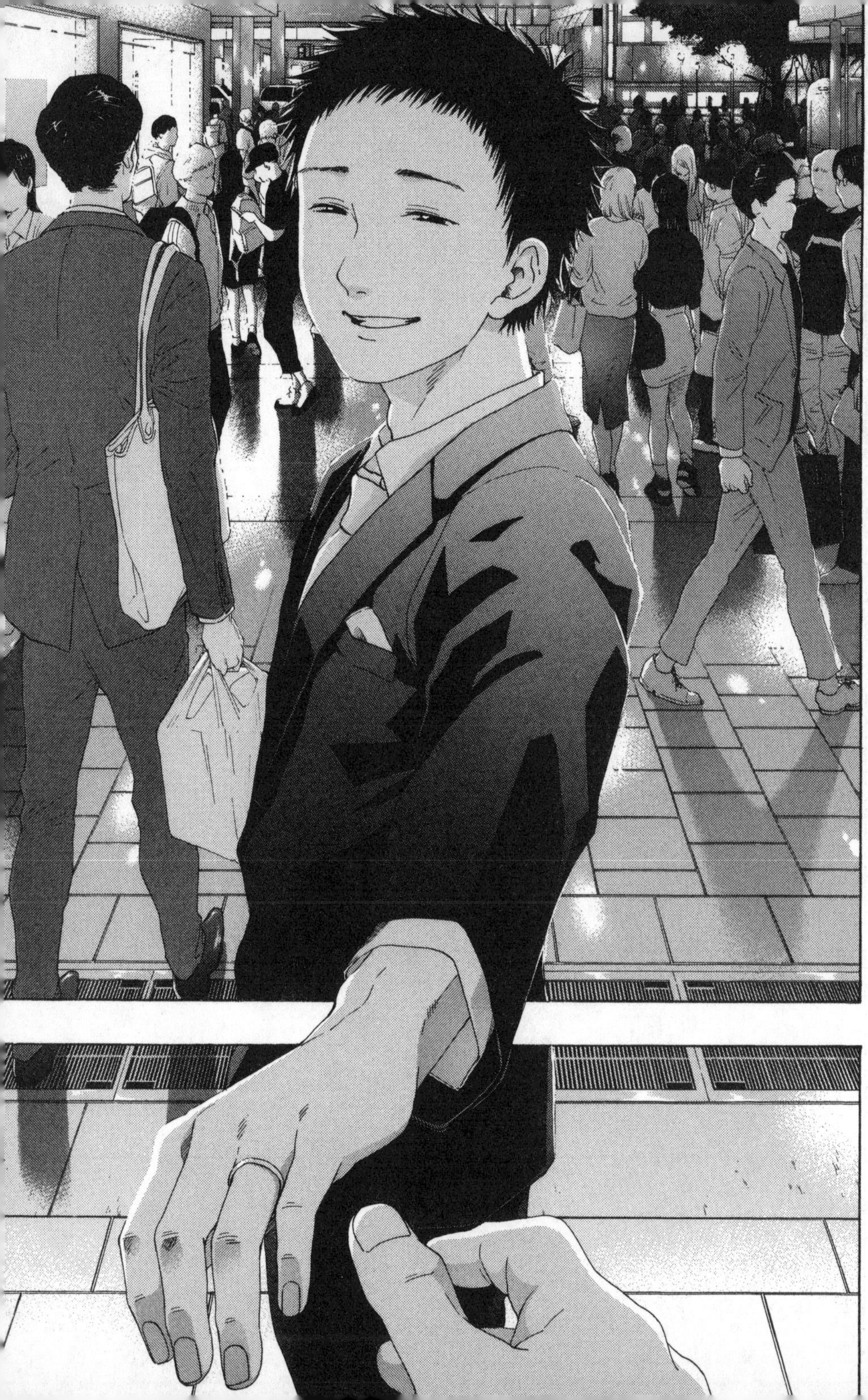

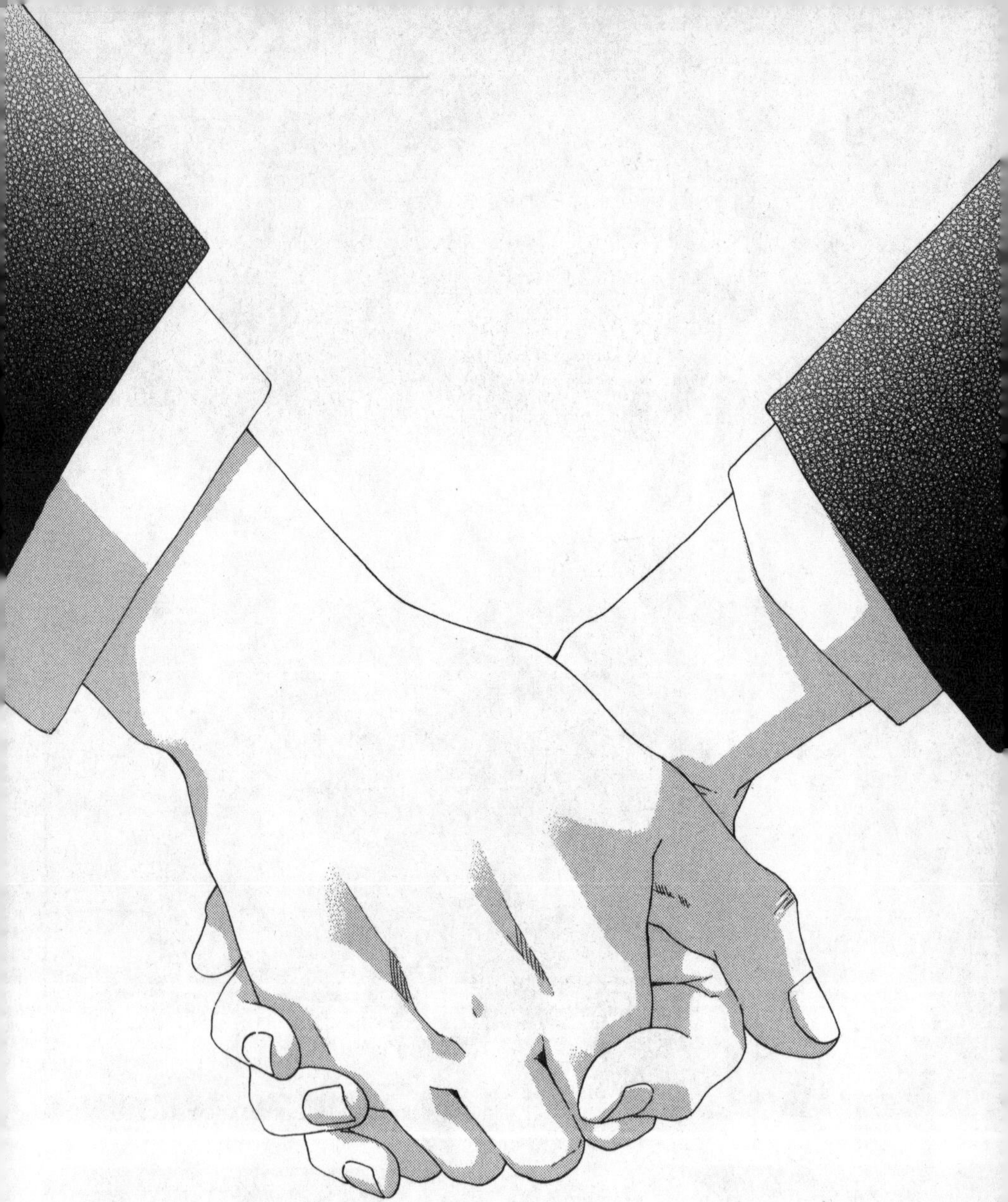

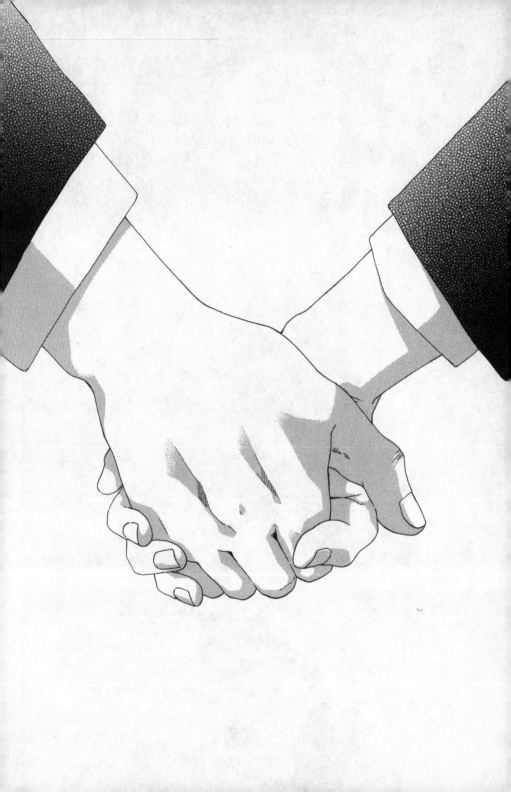

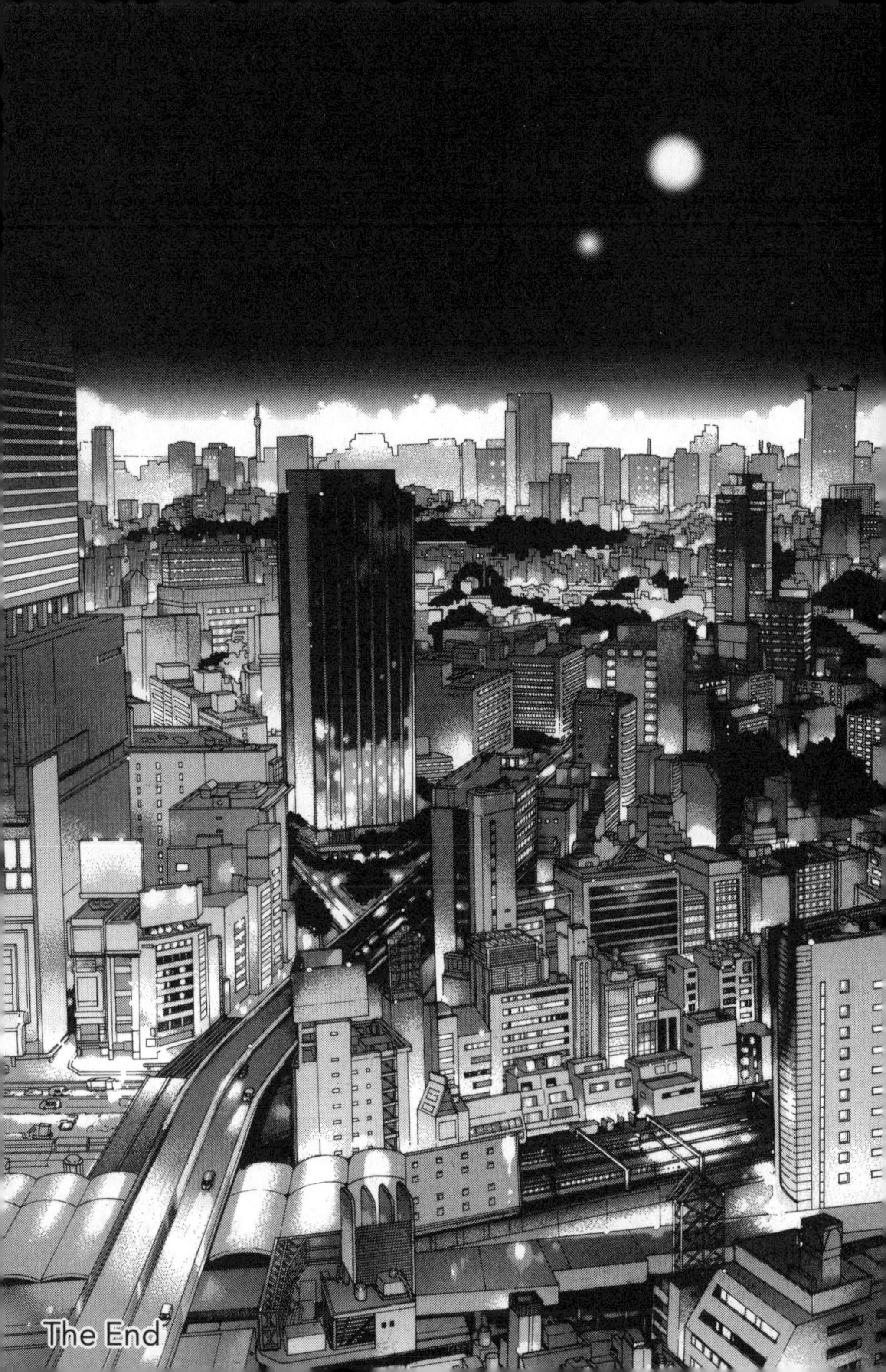
The End

Blue Flag

Blue Flag Original Design Collection

Original
Character
Design
Sketches

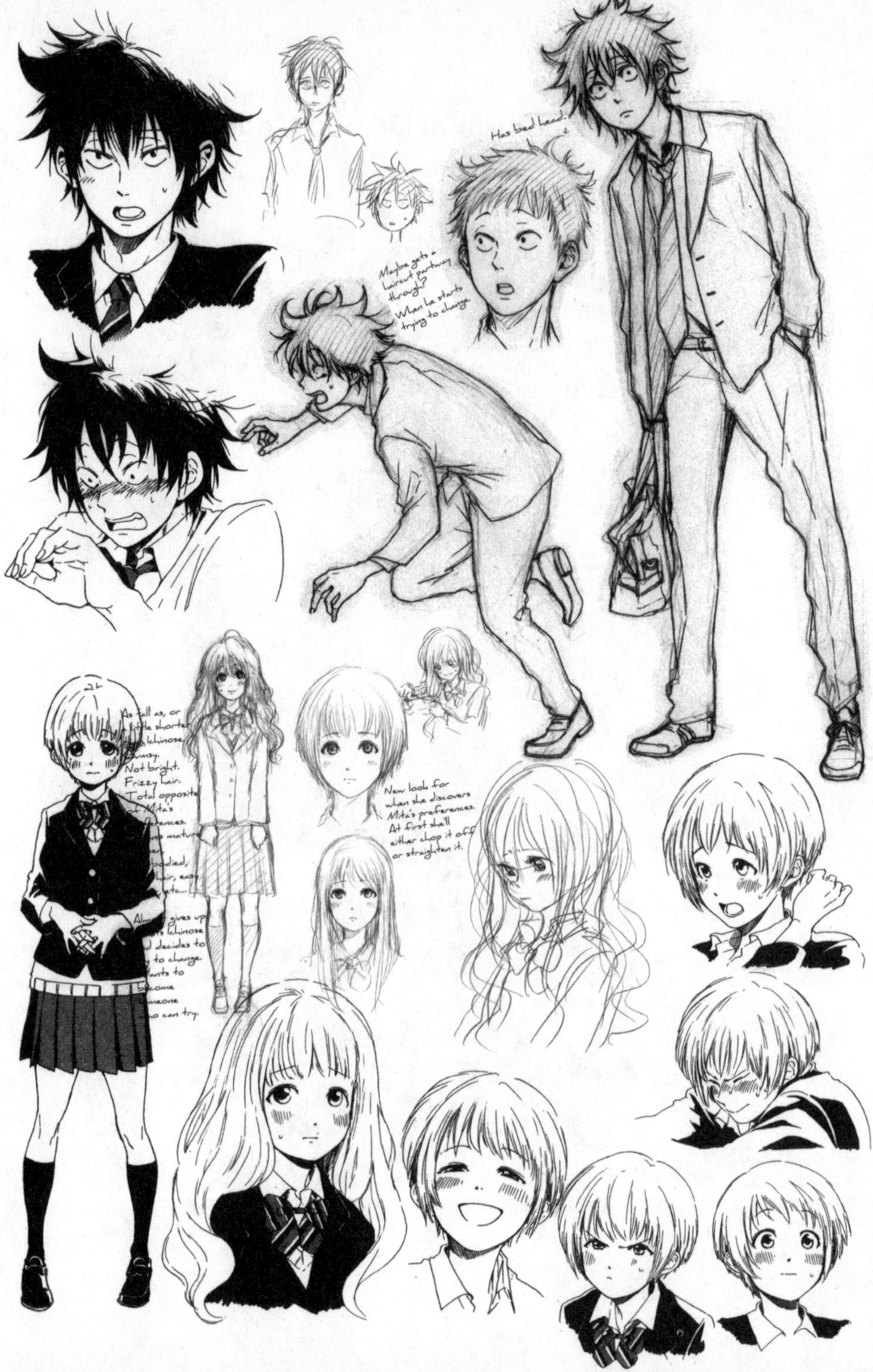
Has bed head.
Maybe gets a haircut partway through? When he starts trying to change.
New look for when she discovers Mita's preferences. At first she'll either chop it off or straighten it.
As tall as, or
little shorter
Ichinose.
umsy.
Not bright.
Frizzy hair.
Total opposite
of Mita's
ferences.
mature
bodied,
hair, easy
etc...
gives up
Ichinose
decides to
to change.
ants to
become
meone
can try.

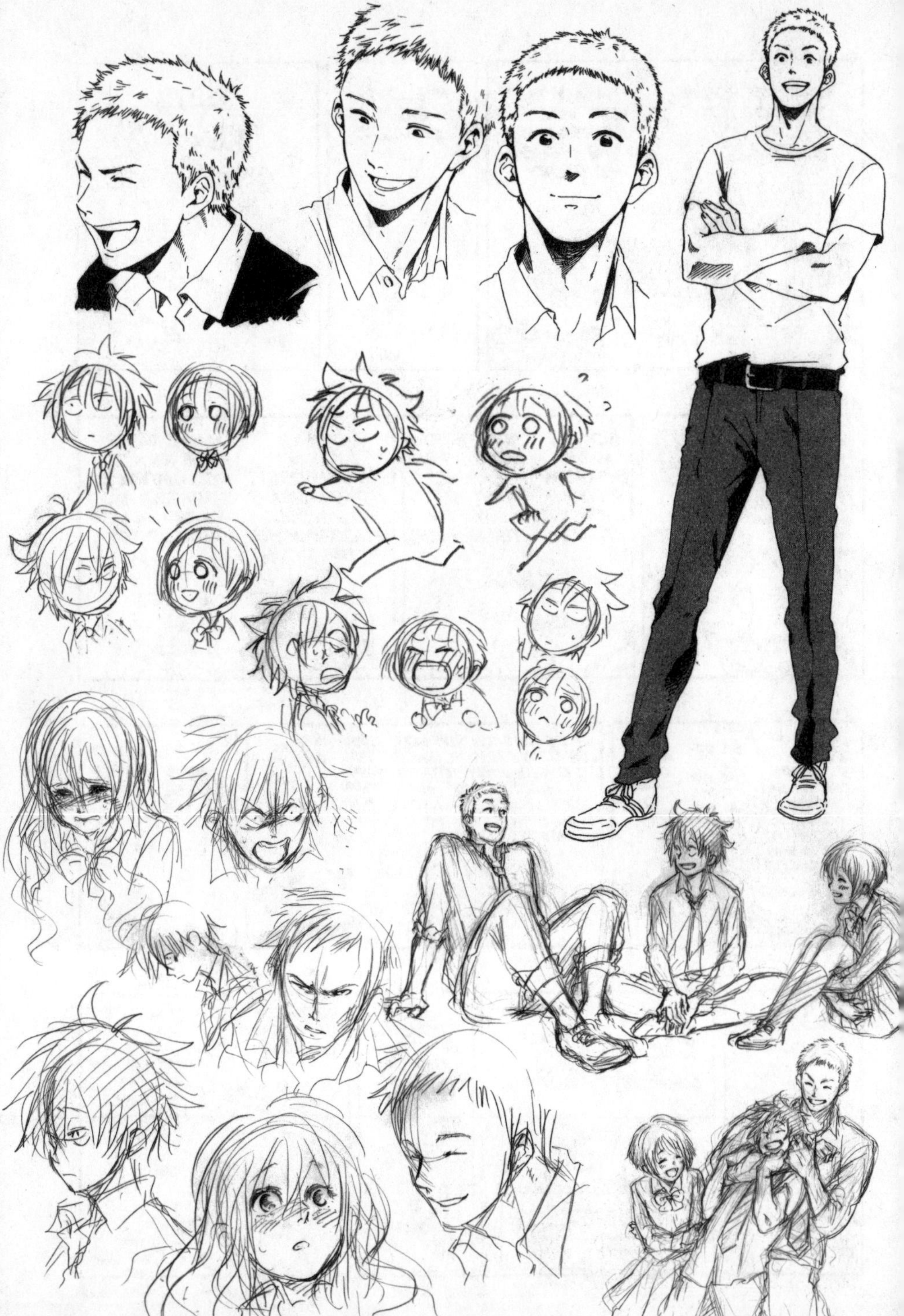

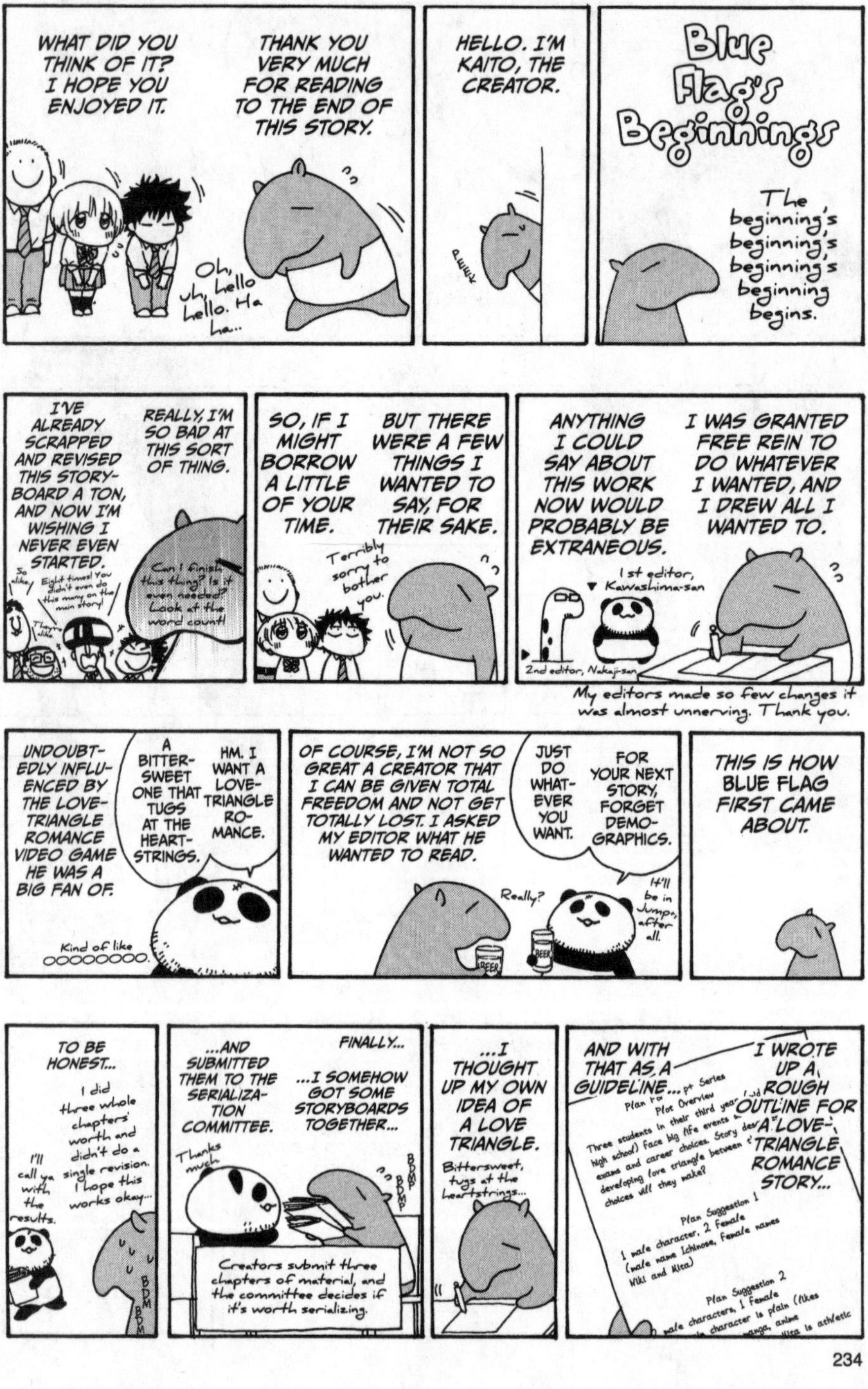

Blue Flag's Beginnings
The beginning's beginning's beginning's beginning begins.
HELLO. I'M KAITO, THE CREATOR.
PEEK
THANK YOU VERY MUCH FOR READING TO THE END OF THIS STORY.
WHAT DID YOU THINK OF IT? I HOPE YOU ENJOYED IT.
Oh, uh, hello hello. Ha ha...
I WAS GRANTED FREE REIN TO DO WHATEVER I WANTED, AND I DREW ALL I WANTED TO.
ANYTHING I COULD SAY ABOUT THIS WORK NOW WOULD PROBABLY BE EXTRANEOUS.
1st editor, Kawashima-san
2nd editor, Nakaji-san
My editors made so few changes it was almost unnerving. Thank you.
BUT THERE WERE A FEW THINGS I WANTED TO SAY, FOR THEIR SAKE.
SO, IF I MIGHT BORROW A LITTLE OF YOUR TIME.
Terribly sorry to bother you.
REALLY, I'M SO BAD AT THIS SORT OF THING.
I'VE ALREADY SCRAPPED AND REVISED THIS STORYBOARD A TON, AND NOW I'M WISHING I NEVER EVEN STARTED.
Can I finish this thing? Is it even needed? Look at the word count!
Eight times! You didn't even do this many on the main story!
So alike.
They're alike.
THIS IS HOW BLUE FLAG FIRST CAME ABOUT.
FOR YOUR NEXT STORY, FORGET DEMOGRAPHICS.
JUST DO WHATEVER YOU WANT.
OF COURSE, I'M NOT SO GREAT A CREATOR THAT I CAN BE GIVEN TOTAL FREEDOM AND NOT GET TOTALLY LOST. I ASKED MY EDITOR WHAT HE WANTED TO READ.
It'll be in Jump, after all.
Really?
BEER
BEER
HM. I WANT A LOVE-TRIANGLE ROMANCE.
A BITTERSWEET ONE THAT TUGS AT THE HEARTSTRINGS.
UNDOUBTEDLY INFLUENCED BY THE LOVE-TRIANGLE ROMANCE VIDEO GAME HE WAS A BIG FAN OF.
Kind of like OOOOOOOO.
I WROTE UP A ROUGH OUTLINE FOR A LOVE-TRIANGLE ROMANCE STORY...
AND WITH THAT AS A GUIDELINE...
Plot Overview
Plan Suggestion 1
1 male character, 2 female
(male name Ichinose, female names
Niki and Mita)
Plan Suggestion 2
...I THOUGHT UP MY OWN IDEA OF A LOVE TRIANGLE.
Bittersweet, tugs at the heartstrings...
FINALLY...
...I SOMEHOW GOT SOME STORYBOARDS TOGETHER...
...AND SUBMITTED THEM TO THE SERIALIZATION COMMITTEE.
Thanks much
BDMP BDMP
Creators submit three chapters of material, and the committee decides if it's worth serializing.
TO BE HONEST...
I did three whole chapters' worth and didn't do a single revision. I hope this works okay...
I'll call ya with the results.
BDM BDM

AT THIS POINT IN THE PROCESS...
...I DIDN'T INTEND TO REVEAL WHO IT WAS TOMA LIKED.
Huh?!
I wanted to try writing it so that it looked like he liked different people to different readers.
A frighteningly plain and annoying wrinkle nobody who reads Jump would want
SEE, I THOUGHT OF A BIG...
THEME
...AROUND WHICH THE BLUE FLAG STORY WOULD REVOLVE.
Well, duh. Most stories have themes.
THE ROMANCE WAS DEFINITELY GOING TO BE A PART OF THE THEME, BUT THE IMPORTANT PART TO ME WAS "CHARACTERS STRUGGLING WITH THEIR VALUES." I FELT I COULD WRITE THAT STORY WITHOUT NECESSARILY SPELLING OUT WHO WAS IN LOVE WITH WHOM.
In the end, that theme didn't change. I was able to write all I wanted on it.
BUT WHEN THE RESULTS FROM THE SERIAL-IZATION COMMITTEE CAME IN...
THEY SAID IT'S OKAY IF YOU MAKE TOMA'S LOVE INTEREST THE MAIN CHARACTER (TAICHI).
PHONE
Huh...? Umm...
PHONE
I TOLD MY EDITOR THAT, THOUGH I HADN'T INTENDED TO REVEAL TOMA'S LOVE INTEREST, IT WAS ALWAYS GOING TO BE TAICHI ANYWAY.
Um, he technically already is...
I knew it was a frighteningly plain and annoying wrinkle nobody who reads Jump would want, so I was just going to sneak it in there...
PHONE
OKAY, THEN JUST REVISE IT SO IT'S CLEARER FROM THE BEGINNING THAT TOMA'S IN LOVE WITH TAICHI, AND THAT SHOULD BE GOOD.
Umm...
I'll give it a try, I guess...
...
Is that really the important part?
LONG STORY SHORT...
...I RESUBMITTED THE STORYBOARDS MOSTLY UNTOUCHED...
AND THOSE BECAME THE FIRST THREE CHAPTERS.
Hmm... Is it not too blatant?! I hope it's okay...
It's not unnatural, is it? Toe the line... Carefully toe the line...
The parts I changed were the number of panels from Toma's viewpoint in chapter 1 and the sweat drops in chapter 3.
THAT WAS RIGHT ABOUT THE TIME THE ACRONYM LGBT WAS STARTING TO GET POPULAR ACROSS THE WORLD.
I'M EMBARRASSED TO ADMIT THAT I DIDN'T PAY ATTENTION TO THE NEWS WHILE I WAS WORKING, SO I GOT LEFT BEHIND ON THIS. IT WAS ONLY AFTER I GOT THE REVISIONS BACK THAT I NOTICED DIVERSITY HAD BECOME A BIG TOPIC OF DISCUSSION.
Aha! Those revisions.
Could this be why?
Oh
AND YES, FROM THE BEGINNING...
...DIVERSITY HAD KINDA BEEN A PART OF THE THEME OF THIS WORK.
THEME
ROMANCE
GENDER
HOMOSEXUAL
HETEROSEXUAL
The pieces that make up the theme

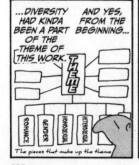

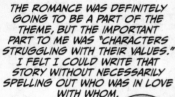

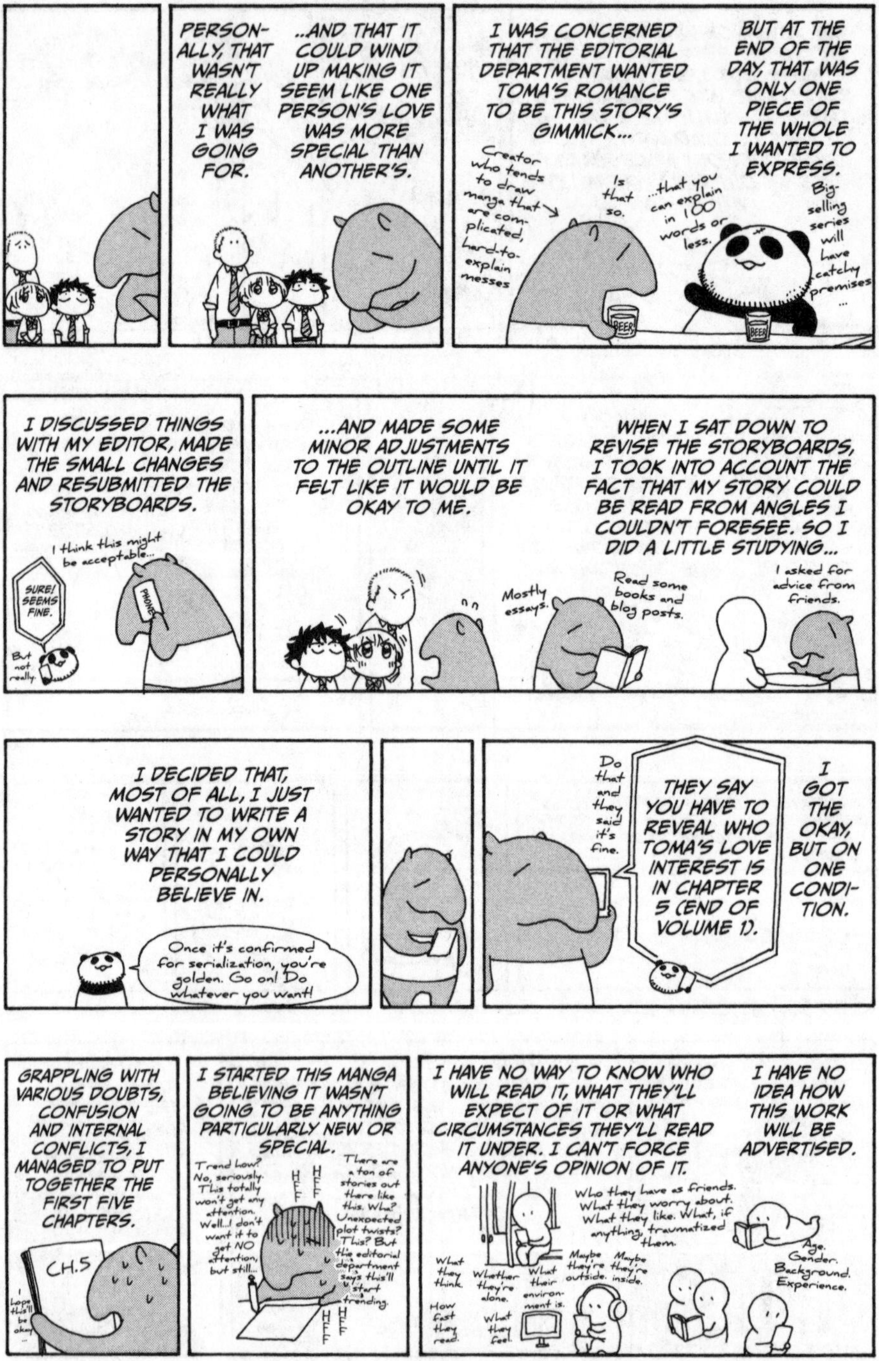

BUT AT THE END OF THE DAY, THAT WAS ONLY ONE PIECE OF THE WHOLE I WANTED TO EXPRESS.
I WAS CONCERNED THAT THE EDITORIAL DEPARTMENT WANTED TOMA'S ROMANCE TO BE THIS STORY'S GIMMICK...
Big-selling series will have catchy premises...
...that you can explain in 100 words or less.
Is that so.
Creator who tends to draw manga that are complicated, hard-to-explain messes
BEER
BEER
...AND THAT IT COULD WIND UP MAKING IT SEEM LIKE ONE PERSON'S LOVE WAS MORE SPECIAL THAN ANOTHER'S.
PERSONALLY, THAT WASN'T REALLY WHAT I WAS GOING FOR.
WHEN I SAT DOWN TO REVISE THE STORYBOARDS, I TOOK INTO ACCOUNT THE FACT THAT MY STORY COULD BE READ FROM ANGLES I COULDN'T FORESEE. SO I DID A LITTLE STUDYING...
I asked for advice from friends.
Read some books and blog posts.
Mostly essays.
...AND MADE SOME MINOR ADJUSTMENTS TO THE OUTLINE UNTIL IT FELT LIKE IT WOULD BE OKAY TO ME.
I DISCUSSED THINGS WITH MY EDITOR, MADE THE SMALL CHANGES AND RESUBMITTED THE STORYBOARDS.
I think this might be acceptable...
PHONE
SURE! SEEMS FINE.
But not really.
I GOT THE OKAY, BUT ON ONE CONDITION.
THEY SAY YOU HAVE TO REVEAL WHO TOMA'S LOVE INTEREST IS IN CHAPTER 5 (END OF VOLUME 1).
Do that and they said it's fine.
I DECIDED THAT, MOST OF ALL, I JUST WANTED TO WRITE A STORY IN MY OWN WAY THAT I COULD PERSONALLY BELIEVE IN.
Once it's confirmed for serialization, you're golden. Go on! Do whatever you want!
I HAVE NO IDEA HOW THIS WORK WILL BE ADVERTISED.
I HAVE NO WAY TO KNOW WHO WILL READ IT, WHAT THEY'LL EXPECT OF IT OR WHAT CIRCUMSTANCES THEY'LL READ IT UNDER. I CAN'T FORCE ANYONE'S OPINION OF IT.
Age. Gender. Background. Experience.
Who they have as friends. What they worry about. What they like. What, if anything, traumatized them.
Maybe they're inside.
Maybe they're outside.
What their environment is.
Whether they're alone.
What they think.
What they feel.
How fast they read.
I STARTED THIS MANGA BELIEVING IT WASN'T GOING TO BE ANYTHING PARTICULARLY NEW OR SPECIAL.
There are a ton of stories out there like this. Wha? Unexpected plot twists? This? But the editorial department says this'll start trending.
Trend how? No, seriously. This totally won't get any attention. Well...I don't want it to get NO attention, but still...
HFF HFF
HFF HFF
GRAPPLING WITH VARIOUS DOUBTS, CONFUSION AND INTERNAL CONFLICTS, I MANAGED TO PUT TOGETHER THE FIRST FIVE CHAPTERS.
CH.5
I hope this'll be okay...

I honestly have absolutely no idea how my manga are advertised. I see it at the same time readers do—when the volume finally goes on sale. Some ads I never see at all. →

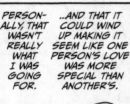

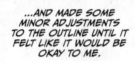

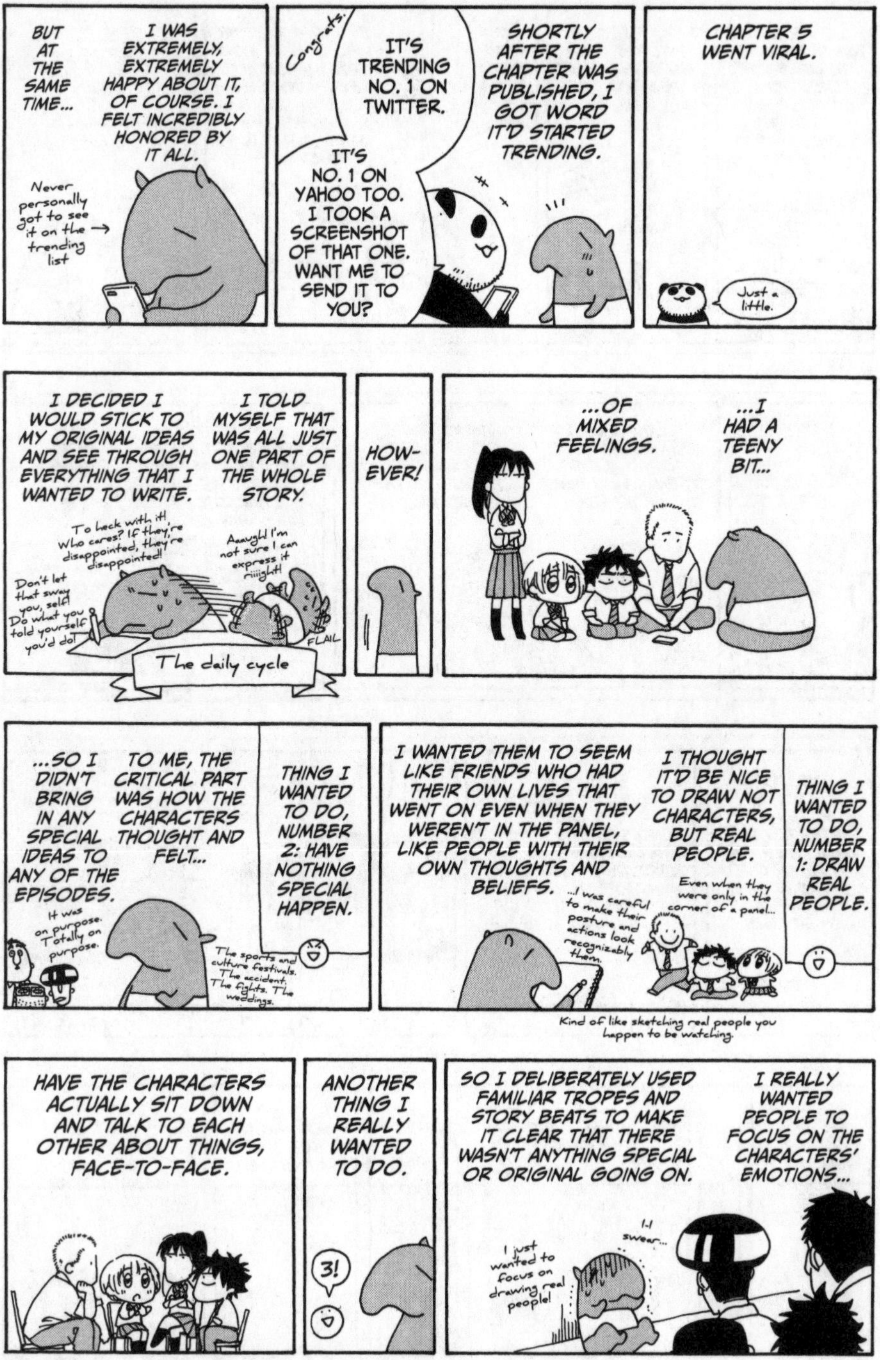
CHAPTER 5 WENT VIRAL.
Just a little.
SHORTLY AFTER THE CHAPTER WAS PUBLISHED, I GOT WORD IT'D STARTED TRENDING.
IT'S TRENDING NO. 1 ON TWITTER.
Congrats.
IT'S NO. 1 ON YAHOO TOO. I TOOK A SCREENSHOT OF THAT ONE. WANT ME TO SEND IT TO YOU?
I WAS EXTREMELY, EXTREMELY HAPPY ABOUT IT, OF COURSE. I FELT INCREDIBLY HONORED BY IT ALL.
BUT AT THE SAME TIME...
Never personally got to see it on the trending list →
...I HAD A TEENY BIT...
...OF MIXED FEELINGS.
HOW-EVER!
I TOLD MYSELF THAT WAS ALL JUST ONE PART OF THE WHOLE STORY.
I DECIDED I WOULD STICK TO MY ORIGINAL IDEAS AND SEE THROUGH EVERYTHING THAT I WANTED TO WRITE.
Aaaugh! I'm not sure I can express it riiiight!
To heck with it! Who cares? If they're disappointed, they're disappointed!
Don't let that sway you, self! Do what you told yourself you'd do!
FLAIL
The daily cycle
THING I WANTED TO DO, NUMBER 1: DRAW REAL PEOPLE.
I THOUGHT IT'D BE NICE TO DRAW NOT CHARACTERS, BUT REAL PEOPLE.
I WANTED THEM TO SEEM LIKE FRIENDS WHO HAD THEIR OWN LIVES THAT WENT ON EVEN WHEN THEY WEREN'T IN THE PANEL, LIKE PEOPLE WITH THEIR OWN THOUGHTS AND BELIEFS.
Even when they were only in the corner of a panel...
...I was careful to make their posture and actions look recognizably them.
Kind of like sketching real people you happen to be watching.
THING I WANTED TO DO, NUMBER 2: HAVE NOTHING SPECIAL HAPPEN.
TO ME, THE CRITICAL PART WAS HOW THE CHARACTERS THOUGHT AND FELT...
...SO I DIDN'T BRING IN ANY SPECIAL IDEAS TO ANY OF THE EPISODES.
The sports and culture festivals. The accident. The fights. The weddings.
It was on purpose. Totally on purpose.
I REALLY WANTED PEOPLE TO FOCUS ON THE CHARACTERS' EMOTIONS...
SO I DELIBERATELY USED FAMILIAR TROPES AND STORY BEATS TO MAKE IT CLEAR THAT THERE WASN'T ANYTHING SPECIAL OR ORIGINAL GOING ON.
I-I swear...
I just wanted to focus on drawing real people!
ANOTHER THING I REALLY WANTED TO DO.
3!
HAVE THE CHARACTERS ACTUALLY SIT DOWN AND TALK TO EACH OTHER ABOUT THINGS, FACE-TO-FACE.

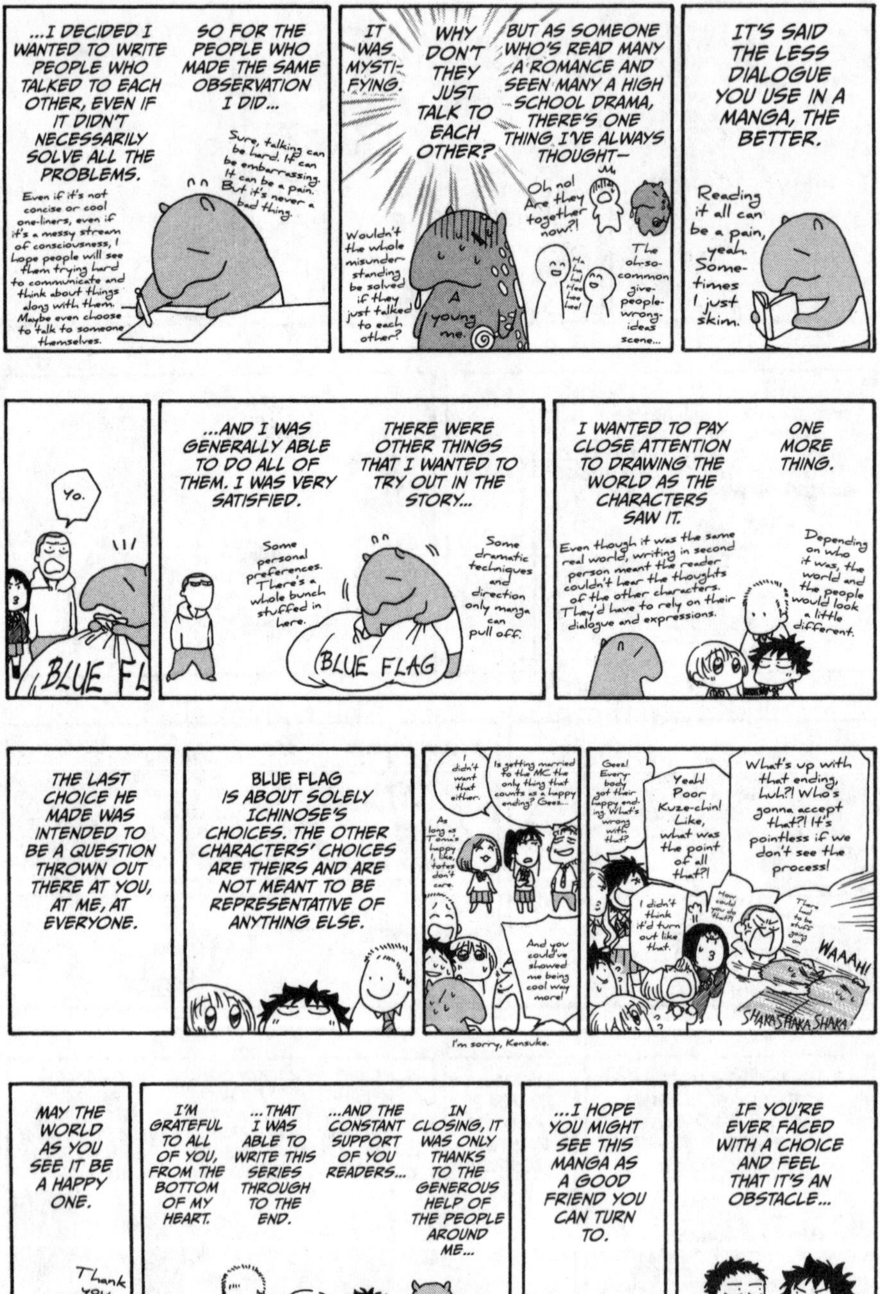
IT'S SAID THE LESS DIALOGUE YOU USE IN A MANGA, THE BETTER.
Reading it all can be a pain, yeah. Sometimes I just skim.
BUT AS SOMEONE WHO'S READ MANY A ROMANCE AND SEEN MANY A HIGH SCHOOL DRAMA, THERE'S ONE THING I'VE ALWAYS THOUGHT—
WHY DON'T THEY JUST TALK TO EACH OTHER?
IT WAS MYSTIFYING.
Oh no! Are they together now?!
Ha ha ha! Hee hee hee!
The oh-so-common give-people-wrong-ideas scene...
Wouldn't the whole misunderstanding be solved if they just talked to each other?
A young me.
SO FOR THE PEOPLE WHO MADE THE SAME OBSERVATION I DID...
Sure, talking can be hard. It can be embarrassing. It can be a pain. But it's never a bad thing.
...I DECIDED I WANTED TO WRITE PEOPLE WHO TALKED TO EACH OTHER, EVEN IF IT DIDN'T NECESSARILY SOLVE ALL THE PROBLEMS.
Even if it's not concise or cool one-liners, even if it's a messy stream of consciousness, I hope people will see them trying hard to communicate and think about things along with them. Maybe even choose to talk to someone themselves.
ONE MORE THING.
I WANTED TO PAY CLOSE ATTENTION TO DRAWING THE WORLD AS THE CHARACTERS SAW IT.
Depending on who it was, the world and the people would look a little different.
Even though it was the same real world, writing in second person meant the reader couldn't hear the thoughts of the other characters. They'd have to rely on their dialogue and expressions.
THERE WERE OTHER THINGS THAT I WANTED TO TRY OUT IN THE STORY...
Some dramatic techniques and direction only manga can pull off.
Some personal preferences. There's a whole bunch stuffed in here.
BLUE FLAG
...AND I WAS GENERALLY ABLE TO DO ALL OF THEM. I WAS VERY SATISFIED.
Yo.
BLUE FL
What's up with that ending, huh?! Who's gonna accept that?! It's pointless if we don't see the process!
Yeah! Poor Kuze-chin! Like, what was the point of all that?!
Geez! Everybody got their happy ending. What's wrong with that?
How could you do that?!
There had to be stuff going on!
I didn't think it'd turn out like that.
WAAAH!
SHAKA SHAKA SHAKA
Is getting married to the MC the only thing that counts as a happy ending? Geez...
I didn't want that either.
As long as Toma's happy I, like, totes don't care.
And you could've showed me being cool way more!
I'm sorry, Kensuke.
BLUE FLAG IS ABOUT SOLELY ICHINOSE'S CHOICES. THE OTHER CHARACTERS' CHOICES ARE THEIRS AND ARE NOT MEANT TO BE REPRESENTATIVE OF ANYTHING ELSE.
THE LAST CHOICE HE MADE WAS INTENDED TO BE A QUESTION THROWN OUT THERE AT YOU, AT ME, AT EVERYONE.
IF YOU'RE EVER FACED WITH A CHOICE AND FEEL THAT IT'S AN OBSTACLE...
...I HOPE YOU MIGHT SEE THIS MANGA AS A GOOD FRIEND YOU CAN TURN TO.
BLUE FLAG
IN CLOSING, IT WAS ONLY THANKS TO THE GENEROUS HELP OF THE PEOPLE AROUND ME...
...AND THE CONSTANT SUPPORT OF YOU READERS...
...THAT I WAS ABLE TO WRITE THIS SERIES THROUGH TO THE END.
I'M GRATEFUL TO ALL OF YOU, FROM THE BOTTOM OF MY HEART.
MAY THE WORLD AS YOU SEE IT BE A HAPPY ONE.
Thank you.

\<ASSISTANTS\>

Guu
Ishida Man
Yu Miki
Nitori
Nakamaru Nakagawa

Yoi Kaneko
Kakazu Kazu
Makoto Hakari
Suzu

Hide Kamei   Minami   Suzuki   Erupi
Nagao Okada   Kawamoto   Yuto Saezu

\<COOPERATION\>
Iori

\<EDITORS\>
Naoki Kawashima   Seijiro Nakaji

\<VOLUME EDITING\>
Yumi Koshimura

\<VOLUME DESIGN\>
Misa Iwai

\<MANGA\>
KAITO

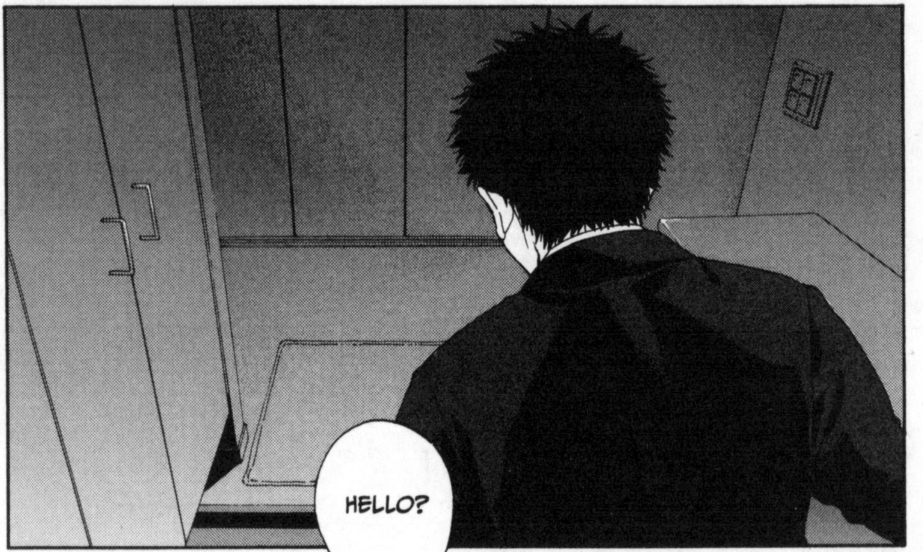
HELLO?

Bonus Story

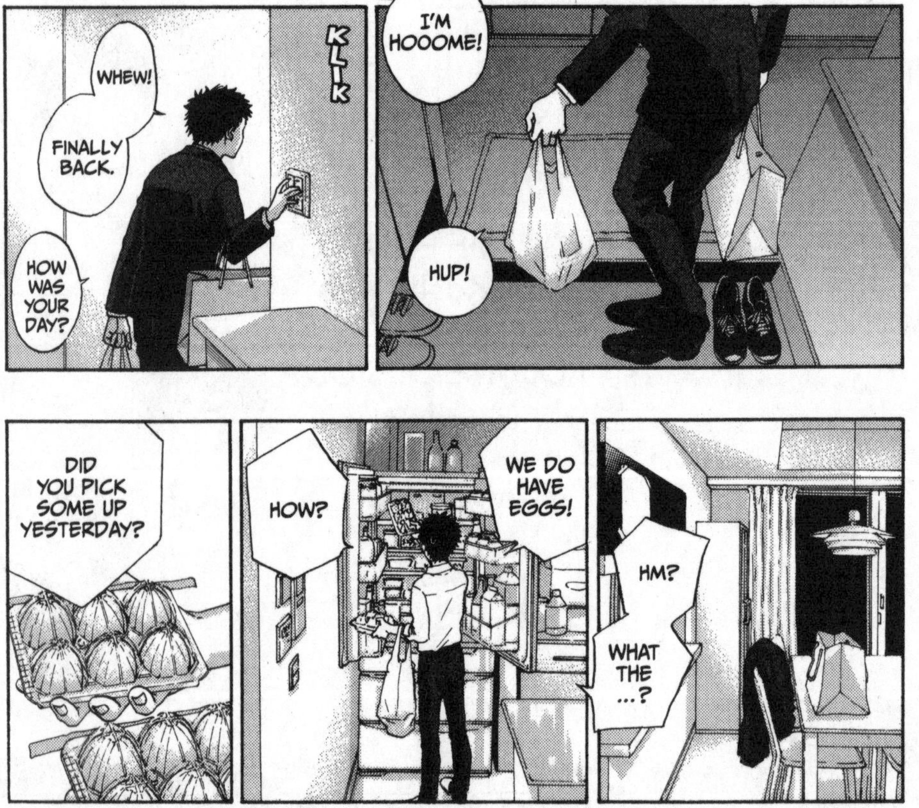
I'M HOOOME!
HUP!
KLIK
WHEW!
FINALLY BACK.
HOW WAS YOUR DAY?
HM?
WHAT THE ...?
WE DO HAVE EGGS!
HOW?
DID YOU PICK SOME UP YESTERDAY?

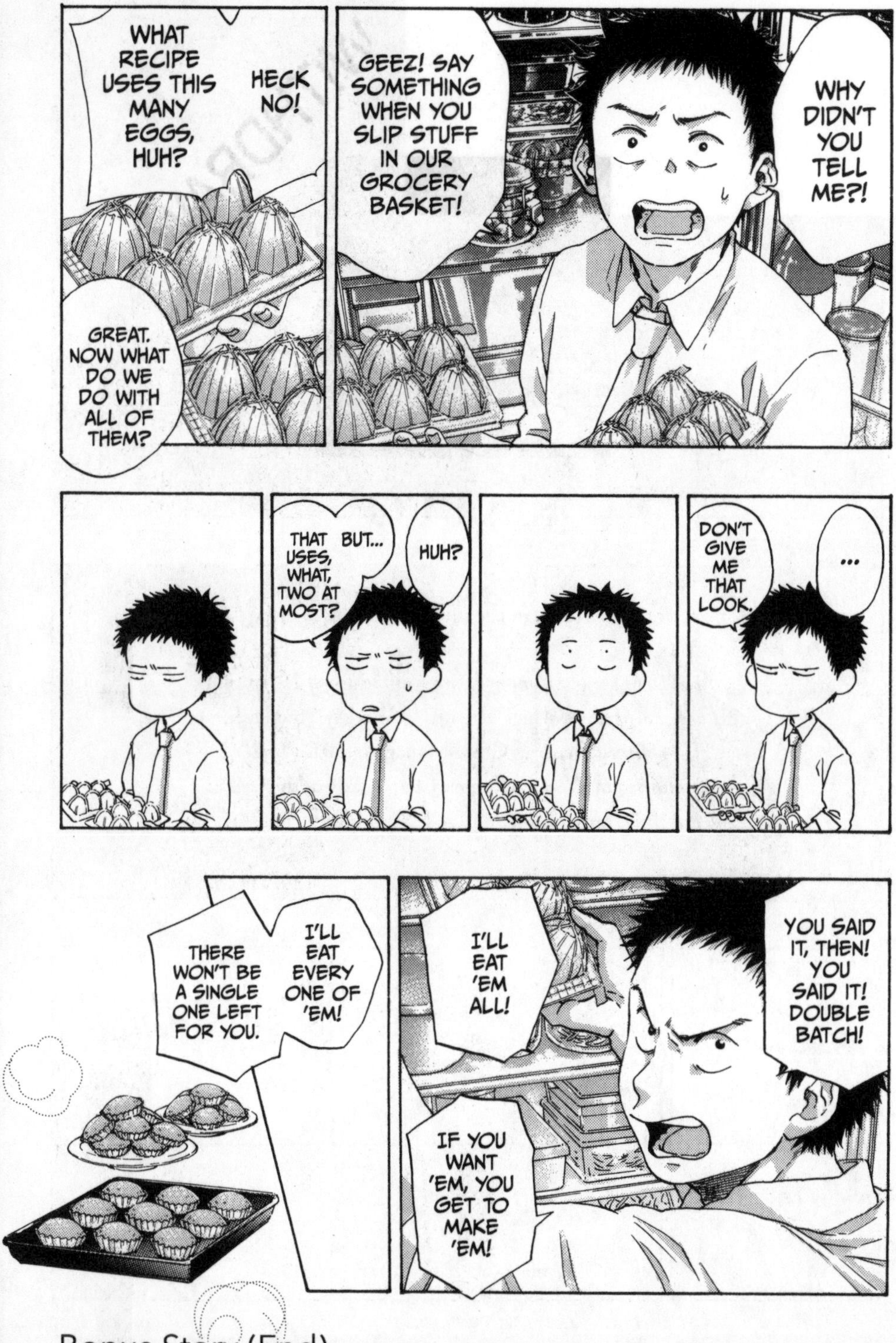
WHY DIDN'T YOU TELL ME?!
GEEZ! SAY SOMETHING WHEN YOU SLIP STUFF IN OUR GROCERY BASKET!
WHAT RECIPE USES THIS MANY EGGS, HUH? HECK NO!
GREAT. NOW WHAT DO WE DO WITH ALL OF THEM?
...
DON'T GIVE ME THAT LOOK.
HUH?
BUT... THAT USES, WHAT, TWO AT MOST?
YOU SAID IT, THEN! YOU SAID IT! DOUBLE BATCH!
I'LL EAT 'EM ALL!
IF YOU WANT 'EM, YOU GET TO MAKE 'EM!
I'LL EAT EVERY ONE OF 'EM!
THERE WON'T BE A SINGLE ONE LEFT FOR YOU.

Bonus Story (End)

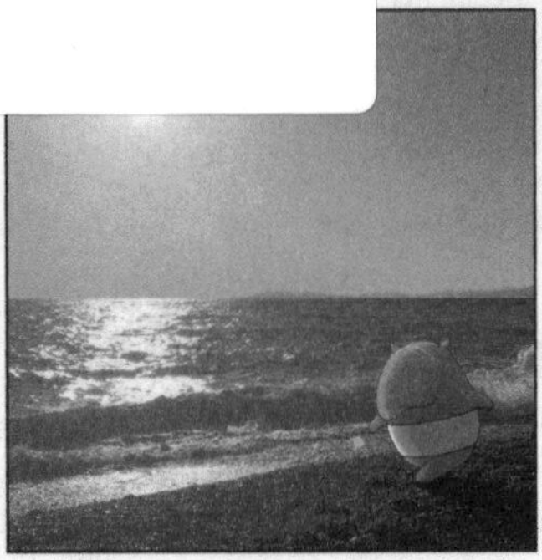

KAITO

Until next time, in the future our choices bring.

KAITO began his manga career at the age of 20, when his one-shot "Happy Magi" debuted in Weekly Shonen Jump. *He published the series* Cross Manage *in 2012. In 2015, he returned to* Weekly Shonen Jump *with* Buddy Strike. *KAITO started work on* Blue Flag *in* Jump+ *in 2017.*

BLUE FLAG

VOL. 8

VIZ SIGNATURE EDITION

story and art by
KAITO

Translation / Adrienne Beck
Lettering / Annaliese "Ace" Christman
Design / Jimmy Presler
Editor / Rae First

AO NO FLAG © 2017 by KAITO
All rights reserved.
First published in Japan in 2017 by SHUEISHA Inc., Tokyo.
English translation rights arranged by SHUEISHA Inc.

Printed in Canada

Published by VIZ Media, LLC
P.O. Box 77010
San Francisco, CA 94107

10 9 8 7 6 5 4 3 2 1
First printing, June 2021

PARENTAL ADVISORY
BLUE FLAG is rated T+ for Older Teen
and is recommended for ages 16 and
up for mature themes.

viz.com   vizsignature.com

Blue Flag reads from right to left,
starting in the upper-right corner. Japanese is read
from right to left, meaning that action, sound
effects and word-balloon order are completely
reversed from English order.

YOU'RE
READING THE
WRONG WAY...